P9-EJI-410

CORK ERICKSON
5834 N.DETROIT AVENUE
PORTLAND, OR 97217
285-6257 or 667-1515

# Commentary on
# Luke

OTHER BOOKS BY RAY SUMMERS

*Essentials of New Testament Greek*
*Worthy Is the Lamb*
*The Life Beyond*
*Ephesians: Pattern for Christian Living*
*Secret Sayings of the Living Jesus*

Jesus, the Universal Savior

# Commentary on
# Luke

## Ray Summers

WORD BOOKS, Publisher

Waco, Texas

First Printing—January 1973
Second Printing—March 1974
Third Printing—January 1975
Fourth Printing—April 1975

COMMENTARY ON LUKE

Copyright © 1972 by Word Incorporated, Waco, Texas 76703. All rights reserved. No part of this book may be reproduced in any form, except for brief quotations in reviews, without the written permission of the publisher.

Library of Congress catalog card number: 72-84172
Printed in the United States of America

Scripture quotations, unless otherwise noted, are from the Revised Standard Version of the Bible, copyright 1946, 1952 by the Division of Christian Education of the National Council of the Churches of Christ in the United States of America, and are used by permission.

# CONTENTS

# INTRODUCTION

In accredited, documented history the oldest collection of books now making up the New Testament is that of Marcion, dating from around A.D. 140–150. Marcion's collection included the Gospel of Luke. From that date, when the Christians could begin to speak realistically of their having a canon of Christian writings, i.e., an approved list of "Scriptures," the place of the Gospel of Luke has been secure and practically unchallenged.

Many other books of our New Testament are clearly quoted by Christian writers before Marcion's time. Numerous fragments of the Gospels and Epistles are quoted in the writings of Christian leaders from about A.D. 90–150. Clement of Rome (writing about A.D. 90–100) gives ample evidence of acquaintance with the Gospels and many of the Epistles. Ignatius, who was martyred some time between A.D. 107 and 117, knew all four of the Gospels, preferring Matthew and John, and the Epistles of Paul. Polycarp wrote his famous letter to the Philippians just after the martyrdom of Ignatius. His letter is saturated with references to the books which later came to make up the New Testament. The Didache (Teaching of the Apostles) probably existed in its present form as early as A.D. 120; it contains more than twenty references to New Testament books touching a majority of those books.

These New Testament books were also known and used by outright opponents of the Christians and by men who thought of themselves as Christian but were branded as heretics by the Christians. About A.D. 90–100, a Jew named Cerinthus was so formidable an enemy to the Christians that according to a not-too-dependable tradition John the apostle rushed from a public bath when Cerinthus came in because he feared the roof would fall in! By a probably less dependable tradition Cerinthus was later killed by a falling roof. Cerinthus knew and used Matthew and probably other Gospels. His main interest was in the Book of Revelation, and some Christians rejected it as a Christian writing and even attributed its authorship to Cerinthus. Another Jewish heretic, Basilides of Alexandria, around A.D. 130 quoted Matthew, Luke, John, Romans, 1 Corinthians, Ephesians, and Colossians; his writings contained probable allusions to 1 Timothy and 1 Peter. He was the earliest writer to quote the Christian writings in exactly the same way that he quoted the Old Testament.

All of this indicates extensive knowledge of and use of the New Testament books prior to Marcion's first accredited collection. Marcion, too, was regarded as a heretic by many Christians. Polycarp called him "Satan's first-born"! After quarreling with the church leaders both in the east (including his own father who was a bishop) and the west, he founded his own church around A.D. 144, starting a sect which persisted as late as the fifth century.

As one committed to the Gnostic doctrine which identified the God of the Old Testament with the stupid and corrupt Gnostic god of creation, the Demiurge, Marcion rejected everything Jewish. For this reason he chose Luke over Matthew, Mark, and John, and deleted from Luke all sections which he regarded as "Jewish," such as the infancy narratives and the genealogy of Jesus. He was the first man in accredited history to weigh evidences in Christian writings, form value judgments on intrinsic values (according to his own standards, of course), and make an approved list or canon of Christian writings.

Other steps in the accredited history of the development of the Christian canon would follow. Tatian's famous *Diatessaron,* mislabeled as a "harmony of the Gospels," is dated A.D. 170. The collection named Muratorian for the librarian Muratori who discovered it in the Ambrosian Library at Milan in 1740 probably was intact by A.D. 190. The place of the Gospel of Luke was secure in all these, as well as in the collections agreed upon by the different councils climaxing in the Council of Carthage, A.D. 397, which affirmed the consensus of the churches that these twenty-seven books composed the approved list of Christian writings by which other writings and doctrines would be checked. From that date the Christians could speak of a "New Testament" —of which Luke was a part.

## AUTHOR

Who wrote this Gospel? From its earliest appearance among the Christian writings it has been identified with Luke, the traveling companion of the Apostle Paul. This identification appeared at a very early time in the caption of the Greek manuscripts—"according to Luke." As in the case of all the New Testament Gospels, the caption was not a part of the text but was added for the purpose of distinguishing between the four. The identification has hardly been challenged.

There is no claim of authorship in the Gospel. The internal evidences for Luke as the author lie along two lines: the sometimes difficult to define "Pauline influences" reflected in the Gospel, and the very direct link with the writer of the Acts of the Apostles (Luke 1:3–4 and Acts 1:1). The appearance in Acts of large sections in which the pronoun "we" is used has identified the author of Acts with some traveling companion of Paul. The first major section, beginning with Paul's Macedonian call (16:9ff), marks the appearance of Luke as one of those traveling companions. Some interpreters are inclined to identify Luke as the Macedonian man who appeared in Paul's dream-vision calling for Paul to come to the spiritual aid of the Macedonians.

The external evidence for Luke as the author has a very early witness. Irenaeus around A.D. 180–185 named Luke as the author, identified him as a follower of Paul, and stated that this was the gospel preached by Paul. The Muratorian Canon (A.D. 170–190) named Luke as the author and stated that he wrote on the basis of report, in contrast to personal witness. The willingness of the church at that early date to accept a book which did not come from an apostle is witness to the intrinsic value which they found in the book. Objections to Luke as the author relate more to problems in Acts than in the Gospel. An example is the differences in Paul's account of the council in

Jerusalem (Gal. 2:1–10) and the account in Acts 15:1–29. The place for that problem, a greatly exaggerated one, is in a treatment of Acts rather than Luke. The quality of both internal and external witness for Luke is such that the burden of proof must rest upon the one who denies his authorship.

When did Luke become associated with Paul in mission work, and what can we know about him? The Macedonian call passage cited above is the first definite use of the pronoun "we" in such way as to associate Paul and Luke. Some interpreters, however, find the possibility of an earlier association. The earliest use of "we" occurs in some texts of Acts 11:27–30, the passage concerning Agabus's prophecy. This was at Antioch. According to Acts 13:1, one of the church leaders at Antioch when Paul launched his mission to the Gentile world was a "Lucius of Cyrene." The texts with the "we" reading at this point are not the best of the Western texts, and the identification of Luke with this Lucius is far from certain, but as early as the fourth century Ephrem Syrus understood the two to be the same.

In Romans 16:21 Paul refers to a Lucius as a kinsman. From Acts 20:2–6 it appears that Luke was present in Corinth with Paul when he wrote the Roman letter. This, too, is a doubtful identification since Lucius appears to be a Jewish kinsman (though it is not certain), and Luke was a Gentile. This is indicated by Paul's listing Aristarchus, Mark, and Jesus called Justus as the only Jews among his fellow workers (Col. 4:10–11). He then listed the other fellow workers (Gentiles) Epaphras, Luke, and Demas (Col. 4:12–14).

Luke nowhere in Acts names himself. Apart from personal modesty, that is strange since, according to Paul's own Epistles, Luke was so very much a part of Paul's work. It is strange, too, that Titus who also was so much a part of that work is not named in Acts. This, with Paul's references in 2 Corinthians 8:18 and 12:18 to his sending with Titus "the brother who is famous among all the churches," has influenced interpreters from as early as Origen and Jerome to identify Luke as "the brother" and the brother of Titus. The Greek definite article does sometimes carry the force of a possessive, i.e., Titus and "his brother." These are possibilities which cannot be demonstrated. As a definite starting point for Luke's association with Paul the Acts 16:9 ff. passage must serve.

For definite knowledge of Luke the person, we must look to the Pauline letters. In Colossians 4:14 Luke is identified as an associate of Paul, as "the beloved physician," and one who sends greetings to the Christians in Colossae. In the Epistle to Philemon, written about the same time as Colossians from Paul's Roman imprisonment, Luke is identified with others as one of Paul's fellow workers. In Paul's second letter to Timothy, written near the end of his life and ministry, Paul has the intriguing line "Luke alone is with me" (2 Tim. 4:11). Only in these three places in the New Testament is Luke named.

Stimulated by the Colossian reference to Luke as "the beloved physician," scholars have sought evidence of medical terminology in Luke-Acts, and some are convinced they have found it. Others challenge such findings, saying that the terminology could have been used by any writer. This may well be.

It is also possible that evidence for the author's being a medical man may be found in his areas of interest more than in any specifically medical terms. For instance: Of all New Testament writers, this one is most interested in the virgin birth of Jesus (Luke 1–2). In the account of Jesus' healing Simon

Peter's mother-in-law (Matt. 8:14–16; Mark 1:29–31; Luke 4:38–39) Matthew and Mark report that the woman had a "fever"; Luke reports that it was a "high" or "great" fever, that is, a bad case. When she was healed, Matthew and Mark report that she served the guests, literally "started serving them"; Luke adds significantly that "immediately she started serving them"— in other words there was no convalescence. Mark reports the healing of the woman with the hemorrhage (5:25–34) saying that she had suffered many things under the treatment of many physicians, that in the process she had spent all the money she had, and instead of getting better she got worse. When Dr. Luke reports the same event (8:43–48), he writes that she had for twelve years suffered from an *incurable* sickness!

The reference to Luke in Philemon 24 reflects only that Luke, who had started his association as a fellow worker with Paul so many years before in Troas or Macedonia (around A.D. 50), was still with Paul (around A.D. 62– 64) in Rome. The time reflected in 2 Timothy 4:11 must be about A.D. 66– 67. At that time Luke alone of the many missionary associates of Paul was with him. He had been the loyal fellow worker and probably the medical attendant of the apostle for fifteen or more years.

## DATE

Scholarly opinion on the date of the Gospel of Luke ranges from the early sixties to some time in the second century. For the most part the opinion is divided between two dates: the early sixties (around A.D. 61–63) or a few years after the destruction of Jerusalem in A.D. 70—perhaps around A.D. 80. The latter date is the more commonly accepted one today.

The argument for the earlier date follows the line of evidence used by Adolph Harnack.[1] This approach begins with Acts 28:30–31, moves back to Acts 1:1, and on back beyond that to the previously written Gospels to which Luke refers. For the last eight chapters of Acts, the reader is brought to a fever pitch of excitement wondering what will be the end of Paul's series of trials before the Jewish Sanhedrin, Felix, Festus, Herod, and Nero. But the book closes without giving the final results—Paul is nearing the end of a two-year imprisonment in Rome, but there is no word of the end. Why? Harnack and those following this approach have theorized that when Luke ended Acts, Paul was still a prisoner awaiting trial; hence a date of around A.D. 64.

The next step in the argument for the early date goes to the statement in Acts 1:1. There can be no doubt that the reference is to the Gospel which Luke had written previously. In it he had reported what Jesus did and said before his commission to the apostles to witness from Jerusalem to the ends of the earth. The Book of Acts reports that witness from Jerusalem to Rome. This would place the writing of Luke some time before Acts. How long before?

To find the earliest date that Luke could have been written, we must begin with the Gospel of Mark. Since Luke contains 350 verses of Mark it must have been written after Mark. Assuming that Mark was written after the Christian community became largely composed of Gentiles (who used the

1. Adolph Harnack, *The Date of Acts and the Synoptic Gospels* (New York: G. P. Putnam's Sons, 1911).

written method in teaching rather than the oral method of the Jews), a safe date for Mark would be the late fifties. Hence Luke is dated a few years after Mark and a few years before Acts. A date in the early sixties is as close as one may get. Two rather imposing presuppositions serve as the foundations for this date. The one at the beginning is the presupposition of A.D. 55–60 for the writing of Mark. The one at the end is that Paul was still in prison when Luke wrote Acts around A.D. 64. For many scholars these presuppositions are too great to allow comfort in the earlier date.

The argument for the later date, around A.D. 80, relates to the advanced stage of the life of the church and Christian thought as these are reflected in the Gospel of Luke. Some interpreters find evidence in Luke 21:20 for a date after the destruction of Jerusalem in A.D. 70. The passage is part of Jesus' Mount of Olives discourse late on Tuesday afternoon before his death on Friday. In response to the disciples' comment on the beauty of the Temple, Jesus answered that the time would come when all of that would be destroyed. Silenced by his statement, the disciples left the Temple with Jesus and started toward Bethany. On top of the Mount of Olives, with the Temple in dramatic view across the Kidron Valley and with the sunset as a backdrop, they asked Jesus to explain his statement. Mark reports that Jesus said, "But when you see the desolating sacrilege set up where it ought not to be . . . then let those who are in Judea flee to the mountains" (13:14). Luke, on the other hand, reports that Jesus said, "But when you see Jerusalem surrounded by armies, then know that its desolation has come near" (21:30). This so definitely describes what happened to Jerusalem under the Roman armies that some interpreters have dated Luke after A.D. 100, holding that he used Josephus's account. Many other interpreters have rejected that view but have held that Luke's account was written after and colored by the event, making clear what Jesus meant in the saying reported by Mark.

There are other and better reasons for the date around A.D. 80. Three clear ones are the following:

(1) The use of the title "the Lord" with a force practically equivalent to a name was a development through the apostolic period. Cullmann[1] has made the definitive study of the use of the Greek word for "lord" *(kurios)* and the Hebrew words for "lord" *(adon* and *mar).* He has demonstrated that *kurios* was used in several ways in general practice. It was a term of respect, similar to "sir." It was used as a term for the many gods in the pagan religions. It was also a term for a particular one of these gods or "lords" who assumed a supreme role, such as in emperor worship when the Roman emperor came to be worshiped as "the Lord."

With only rare exceptions (such as Matt. 7:21 and John 13:13) the term *kurios* was used of Jesus in the days of his earthly ministry in the sense of rabbi; he was the respected and loved teacher. In the earliest Christian use after his death and resurrection the term *kurios* was used of him in the sense of *The Lord.* It was in Jesus' death and resurrection "that God . . . made him both Lord and Christ" (Acts 2:36). And it was in his death and resurrection that God "highly exalted him and bestowed on him the name which is above

---

1. Oscar Cullmann, *The Christology of the New Testament* (Philadelphia: The Westminster Press, 1959), pp. 193–237. See also A. M. Hunter, *The Message of the New Testament* (Philadelphia: The Westminster Press, 1944), pp. 39–51.

every name . . . Lord" (Phil. 2:9, 11). Paul was firm in his assurance to the Corinthians that there were "so-called gods," indeed there were "many 'gods' and many 'lords,'" but he affirmed "for us there is one God, the Father, . . . and one Lord, Jesus Christ" (1 Cor. 8:5, 6). For those early Christians, Jesus, through his death and resurrection, had come to be the only one who deserved the title "The Lord." That term which was so firmly fixed in that meaning at the time of his writing, Luke applied to Jesus in Gospel events which preceded such use.

(2) The need for a Gospel putting the work and teaching of Jesus positively on the basis of God's redemptive purpose for all men, specifically the Gentiles, reflects a later period, but one still earlier than the Gospel of John. The idea appears in some places in Matthew; Luke is saturated with it.

(3) The eschatological outlook embedded in Luke is not anticipation of an early return of Christ such as marked the very early church and the writings of Paul in the fifties and sixties. The anticipation has not given way to despair. It is still present, but in place of importance it has given way to the necessity of constant witness to a pagan world in order to bring them to a knowledge of Jesus Christ as Lord.

## PURPOSE

The later date and its relation to the church situation calls for a consideration of Luke's purpose in writing and how he carried out that purpose. The theme of the Gospel is well phrased as "Jesus, the Universal Savior." There are reflections in Matthew—the Great Commission for example (Matt. 28:19–20)—of the fact that what God did in Jesus Christ was for all men. In the Gospel of John fifteen to twenty years later there will be more reflections of it. Luke, however, has this as the continuous thread of his Gospel. The exposition to follow will make this clear. The extent of it may be profitably observed here.

In Simeon's song, when the infant Jesus was presented in the Temple, he is called "a light for revelation to the Gentiles" (2:32). At the beginning of his ministry Jesus was rejected by his fellow villagers in Nazareth because he implied that his role as the Anointed One and his message were for Gentiles— he reminded them that God's favor had been bestowed on Gentiles as well as, even in some cases more than, Jews (4:21–30). His association with spiritual and social outcasts was a part of his purpose in the world (5:29–32 and many others). Only once in Luke's Gospel does Jesus commend a person for *great* faith, and that person was a Gentile (7:9). It was a despised Samaritan who stopped to help a wounded man in one of Jesus' most beautiful parables (10:29–37). Men (Gentiles) will come from east, west, north, and south to share in the kingdom of God (13:29). When those originally invited (Jews) refuse the invitation to the great banquet, the invitation is extended to others (Gentiles) who accept (14:16–24). A cleansed Samaritan leper returns to give thanks to Jesus while nine cleansed Jewish lepers do not (17:12–19). Jesus' time with the disciples between his resurrection and his ascension was spent in explaining to them the redemptive significance of his suffering and their responsibility to take this message of God's forgiveness for man's sin "to all nations" (24:44–49).

Luke's view of Jesus as the Savior for all people without regard to race or life condition extends beyond this emphasis on mercy for Gentiles. It is clearly reflected in his choice of both narrative and teaching materials embracing Jesus' great concern for social outcasts, for women, for those labeled "sinners" by their fellow Jews because they had ceased to conform to the way of God as it was interpreted by the religious leaders of Israel. To such a society Jesus came with an offer of the compassionate love of God for all men, and at the same time a demand for undivided loyalty to God on the part of those who commit themselves to him. This is the "Good News According to Luke."

# OUTLINE OF LUKE

## Theme: Jesus, the Universal Savior

PREFACE (1:1–4)
1. Multiple Attempts at Gospel Writing (1:1)
2. Gospel Writing Based on Eyewitness Oral Accounts (1:2)
3. Intimation of Luke's Research (1:3)
4. Use of Gospel Writings in Public Instruction (1:4)

I. THE ANNUNCIATION AND THE EARLY YEARS OF JESUS (1:5–2:52)
1. The Promise of the Birth of John the Baptizer (1:5–25)
2. The Promise of the Birth of Jesus (1:26–38)
3. The Visit of Mary to Elizabeth (1:39–56)
4. The Birth of John the Baptizer (1:57–80)
5. The Birth of Jesus (2:1–7)
6. The Visit of the Shepherds (2:8–20)
7. The Circumcision, Naming, and Dedication of Jesus as the First-Born (2:21–39)
8. The Childhood Years of Jesus (2:40–52)

II. PREPARATION FOR THE MINISTRY OF THE UNIVERSAL SAVIOR (3:1–4:13)
1. The Role and Ministry of John the Baptizer (3:1–20)
2. The Baptism of Jesus (3:21–22)
3. The Genealogy of Jesus (3:23–38)
4. The Wilderness Temptation of Jesus (4:1–13)

III. THE MINISTRY OF THE UNIVERSAL SAVIOR IN GALILEE (4:14–9:50)
1. Rejected at Nazareth (4:14–30)
2. Accepted at Capernaum (4:31–44)
3. A Call to Four Fishermen (5:1–11)
4. Healing a Leper (5:12–16)
5. Healing a Paralytic (5:17–26)
6. A Call to a Publican (5:27–32)
7. Teaching Concerning Fasting (5:33–39)
8. Teaching Concerning Sabbath Observance (6:1–5)
9. Healing on the Sabbath (6:6–11)
10. The Call and Appointment of the Twelve (6:12–16)
11. The Sermon on the Plain (6:17–49)
12. Healing a Centurion's Servant (7:1–10)
13. Raising the Widow's Son (7:11–17)
14. Answering the Messengers from John the Baptizer (7:18–23)

[15]

27. The Parable of the Lost Sheep (15:1–7)
28. The Parable of the Lost Coin (15:8–10)
29. The Parable of the Lost Son (15:11–32)
30. The Parable of the Shrewd Steward (16:1–13)
31. A Rebuke to the Insincere (16:14–18)
32. The Rich Man and the Beggar (16:19–31)
33. Offending and Forgiving (17:1–4)
34. Believing and Serving (17:5–10)
35. Healing Ten Lepers on the Border of Samaria and Galilee (17:11–19)
36. The True Nature of the Kingdom of God (17:20–21)
37. The Day of the Son of Man (17:22–37)
38. An Unjust Judge and a Just God (18:1–8)
39. The Parable of the Pharisee and the Publican (18:9–14)
40. Little Children and Kingdom Children (18:15–17)
41. The Rich Ruler and the Way to Eternal Life (18:18–30)
42. The Third Passion Prediction (18:31–34)
43. Healing a Blind Man Near Jericho (18:35–43)
44. The Salvation of Zacchaeus in Jericho (19:1–10)
45. The Parable of the Pounds (19:11–27)

V. THE MINISTRY OF THE UNIVERSAL SAVIOR IN JERUSALEM (19:28–23:56)
1. Sunday—a Day of Triumph (19:28–44)
    (1) Entering Jerusalem as the messianic king (19:28–40)
    (2) Weeping over the city (19:41–44)
2. Monday—a Day of Authority (19:45–48)
    (1) The cleansing of the Temple (19:45–46)
    (2) Beginning a week of Teaching (19:47–48)
3. Tuesday—a Day of Controversy and Teaching (20:1–22:6)
    (1) The controversy with the Sanhedrin over authority (20:1–19)
    (2) The controversy with Pharisees and Herodians about taxes (20:20–26)
    (3) The Controversy with Sadducees about the resurrection (20:27–40)
    (4) The controversy with Pharisees about the Messiah (20:41–44)
    (5) Denouncing the scribes and Pharisees for hypocrisy (20:45–47)
    (6) Commending the pauper widow (21:1–4)
    (7) Teaching about judgment on Jerusalem and the world (21:5–36)
    (8) Summary statement of Jesus' activity during the week (21:37–38)
    (9) A reference to Jesus' approaching death (22:1–2)
    (10) Judas's preparation for the betrayal (22:3–6)
4. Wednesday—a Day of Rest in Preparation for Passover?
    (No record in New Testament of Wednesday activities)
5. Thursday—a Day of Joy and Sorrow (22:7–54a)
    (1) The preparation for the Passover Supper (22:7–13)
    (2) Observing the Passover Supper (22:14–18)

(3) Instituting the Memorial Supper (22:19–23)
(4) The dialogue around the table (22:24–38)
(5) The agony and prayer in Gethsemane (22:39–46)
(6) The betrayal and arrest (22:47–54a)
6. Friday—a Day of Trial and Death (22:54b–23:56a)
(1) Peter's denial (22:54b–62)
(2) The preliminary hearing before Caiaphas (22:63–65)
(3) The formal hearing before the Sanhedrin (22:66–71)
(4) The hearing before Pilate (23:1–5)
(5) The hearing before Herod Antipas (23:6–12)
(6) The hearing before Pilate—sentenced to die (23:13–25)
(7) Crucified and buried (23:26–56a)
7. Saturday—a Day of Rest (24:56b)
8. Sunday—a Day of Triumph (24:1–43)
(1) The angelic announcement of his resurrection (24:1–12)
(2) The appearance on the road to Emmaus (24:13–33)
(3) The appearance to Simon Peter (24:34)
(4) The report by the two from Emmaus (24:35)
(5) The appearance to the group (24:36–43)
CONCLUSION (24:44–53)
1. A Summary of Jesus' Teachings Between His Resurrection and His Ascension (24:44–49)
2. The Final Appearance and Ascension (cf. Acts 1:6–14) (24:50–53)

# COMMENTARY

# Jesus, the Universal Savior

## PREFACE (1:1–4)

The opening lines of the Gospel of Luke are without parallel in the New Testament. They are the only instance in which a Gospel writer indicates his method of research and the nature of his research sources. Therefore Luke's brief initial paragraph is of inestimable importance in any approach to an understanding of all of the New Testament Gospels. It gives the reader an insight into the kind of materials available for Gospel-writing, the way these materials were being used by the Christians, and the writer's purpose in his particular use of the materials.

## 1. Multiple Attempts at Gospel-Writing (1:1)

*Inasmuch as many have undertaken to compile a narrative:* Luke begins his Gospel by stating that others preceded him in this endeavor. By the time of his writing, Gospel-writing had become an established practice. Depending on the date of this writing (see Introduction), from thirty to fifty years had elapsed since the events contained in these gospels. The desire of the people to know the works and words of Jesus resulted in many attempts at Gospel-writing. To Luke's readers, the word "compile" meant to "line up" the available component parts of a whole. Basic to all understanding of the four Gospels is the evident fact that what Jesus did and said was first circulated among the Christians as largely disconnected units—miracles performed, parables told, sayings on certain occasions, controversy with opponents, instruction to followers. The task of the Gospel writer was to "line up" these materials into a *narrative*—a telling or narration of all the events available to the writer. Luke's word may be transliterated through Latin into the English word "digest." While "narration" is a better translation, the word "digest" suggests that each of these Gospels was just that—no writer had available to him all the works and words of Jesus. He used what he had and framed his arrangement for his purpose.

*The things which have been accomplished:* This is an accurate translation; the events and the teachings were matters of past action. Another translation however, may reflect the early Christian outlook better: "the things which have been fulfilled." The early Christians did not look at the life and ministry of Jesus in isolation. They understood it to be the fulfillment of all that had preceded it in the religious history of the Hebrew people. This was the fulfillment of God's promise to provide a Savior for sinful men. The events recorded in these Gospels were the climax of God's redemptive action.

[19]

*Among us:* This relates to the people of the fulfillment time. The early Christians had the same sense of being a corporate people of God which had marked the Hebrew people in their history. The writer was what would be called today a "second generation" Christian; he was not one of the original circle of Jesus' followers (v. 2), but he felt himself to be a part of that people of the fulfillment time.

## 2. Gospel-Writing Based on Eyewitness Oral Accounts (1:2)

In this verse Luke indicates the human agents who served as the repository for the information about Jesus and passed it on to others.

*Just as they were delivered:* Luke assures the reader that he has been faithful and careful in passing on the information he has gathered. The verb *delivered* could be translated literally "given over." The original recipients gave the information over to those who followed them. At first the materials concerning Jesus were circulated in oral form: the Christians used them in their worship, in defending their position when challenged by opponents, in explaining their position in the making of converts, and in the instruction of new converts. A case can be made for a very early written collection of some of the sayings of Jesus (v. 3), but even if that is granted, the amount was relatively small. The materials were mainly used orally, following the Hebrew method of teaching, for about a quarter of a century. Gospel-writing came to fruition when the Gentiles, who used the written method of teaching, became predominant in the Christian community.

*Those who were from the beginning eyewitnesses and ministers of the word:* The original conveyors of the material in the Gospels had themselves seen the things which Jesus did and were ministers of the word which he proclaimed. The expression *from the beginning* points to the very earliest years of the religious movement in Israel which ultimately became the Christian movement. These original eyewitnesses and ministers were basically the Twelve, the group most responsible for passing on the witness of Jesus' works and words. Luke's linking of his Gospel with his second volume, the Acts of the Apostles, makes it clear that the Twelve were the original agents. They were not alone, however, in passing on their witness; it was a trusteeship shared by all of Jesus' followers.

## 3. Intimation of Luke's Research (1:3)

In the four expressions which follow, Luke gives the clearest insight into his motivation and method.

*It seemed good to me also:* To speak of Luke's motivation is not to discount the movement of the Holy Spirit in inspiration; it is rather to include it. In the total circumstances of the multiple narratives which were being produced, Luke came to the conclusion that the wise, fitting, or appropriate thing for him to do was to write a gospel. By what process of logic or compulsion of the Spirit he reached that conclusion he did not state.

*Having followed all things closely for some time:* While Luke does not state explicitly that he used some of the written Gospels which had preceded his, he implies as much. A careful analysis of the content of this Gospel makes possible the identification of several written sources. The Gospel of Mark appears to have been one of his sources. Of the 661 verses in the Gospel of Mark, 350 are in the Gospel of Luke. They are mostly narrative material relating to the works of Jesus to which Luke added teachings of Jesus from other sources.

Luke has 272 verses in common only with Matthew. By their nature, these verses suggest an early Christian treatise on discipleship and appear to form a written source used by both Luke and Matthew. Since they are teachings of Jesus, the section is frequently referred to as "Logia" (teachings). At other times it is designated as "Q" (for the German word *Quelle*—source).[1]

This leaves 527 verses in Luke which are not in Matthew and Mark. In scholarly writings this section is frequently designated "L". It is sometimes referred to in different units. For example, Luke's infancy narratives of John the Baptizer and Jesus (1:5–2:52) bear marks of a written source (perhaps an Aramaic one). His account of Jesus' Perean ministry (13:22–18:34) bears marks of a written source. His account of Jesus' last week in Jerusalem (19:28–24:53) reflects a source different from the other Gospels. All oral and written material available to him he used.

*An orderly account:* Luke's purpose was to write a well-ordered account of Jesus' life and teachings as they could be known from his available sources. As such it would differ from some of the narratives already in circulation. Rather than an unrelated collection of deeds or of sayings, it would be an ordered account extending from the announcement of the birth of Jesus' forerunner to Jesus' death, resurrection, and ascension.

*For you, most excellent Theophilus:* Luke addressed his Gospel to *Theophilus*. The address may have been something akin to the custom of dedicating a book to some honored person. The expression *most excellent* was a title of respect and may refer to Theophilus's position or status as a Roman official. Some interpreters find only a symbolic reference in the word *theophilus* which means "lover of God." From this viewpoint the Gospel would be addressed to all Christian readers. The fact that Luke uses the identical address in his second volume (Acts 1:1), however, lends strong support to the idea that Theophilus was an individual. He may have been a friend; he may have been an inquirer into the Christian faith; he may have been a new convert to the Christian faith (v. 4); he may have been a Roman official charged with the responsibility of knowing the truth about the Christians, who were accused by many in Luke's day of being enemies to the Roman state.

## 4. Use of Gospel Writings in Public Instruction (1:4)

There is much in this verse which suggests that Luke was addressing himself to a situation in which Theophilus had been receiving instruction in matters relative to the Christian faith.

*That you may know the truth:* Whoever Theophilus was and whatever his interest in the Christian faith, Luke wanted him to have accurate knowledge about it. This is the reason for the careful research and the orderly account referred to in verse 3. The word translated *truth* is not the usual word for truth

---

1. For further reading on this "Logia" see William Barclay, *The First Three Gospels* (Philadelphia: The Westminster Press, 1966), pp. 130–40.

as a philosophical or religious concept. It is rather the word for certainty or reliability; hence, "in order that you may know the certainty."

*The things of which you have been informed:* Theophilus had some knowledge of Christian foundations from previous sources. Luke apparently regarded the content of that knowledge as dependable, and was writing to assure him of its accuracy. The Greek word translated *informed* may be very precisely translated "instructed" and has come over into English as "catechetical" or "catechism." Its primary reference is to courses of instruction. The oral materials and the subsequent written materials of what Jesus did and said were used in courses in public instruction of both inquirers and new converts. This is largely the basis for the idea that Theophilus may have been such an inquirer or convert (v. 3).

# I. THE ANNUNCIATION AND THE EARLY YEARS OF JESUS
## (1:5–2:52)

A comparison of the New Testament Gospels reveals interesting and instructive differences in the opening part of each. John begins his Gospel with the words "In the beginning," taking the reader back to Genesis 1:1 when the creative Word of God went forth to bring order and light and life out of chaos and darkness. John shows how, once again, the creative Word of God has gone forth, incarnate in human form this time, to bring spiritual order and light and life out of spiritual chaos and darkness and death. Mark even uses the word *genesis,* "beginning," to introduce his Gospel. For him, the appearance of John the Baptizer as a wilderness voice proclaiming the imminent coming of the Messiah is "the beginning of the gospel of Jesus Christ" (1:1). Matthew begins his Gospel with the genealogy of Jesus as the Son of David descended from Abraham.

Luke begins with the announcements of the coming births first of the forerunner of the Messiah and then of Jesus. This introductory section of his Gospel effectively links the Christian movement with all that preceded it in Hebrew religious history—the touch of the historian! Included in this section are all the infancy and childhood matters needed to set Jesus in his proper place in the history of God's redemptive work. The narrative delineates his birth, his identification with the covenant people of God, his presentation in the Temple as a first-born son, his appearance in the Temple again when, as a boy of twelve, he engaged in meaningful discussion with the leaders of the Temple services and the interpreters of the Hebrew faith. Except for Matthew's record of Jesus' birth in Bethlehem, chapters 1 and 2 of Luke have no parallel in the New Testament.

## 1. The Promise of the Birth of John the Baptizer (1:5–25)

Luke 1:5–25 prepares the way for the story of the birth of Jesus by relating the promise of the birth of the forerunner to prepare the way for his messianic ministry.

### (1) Historical setting and persons (1:5–7)

With a careful historian's interest in historical setting and related details, Luke introduces the birth narrative of Jesus' forerunner, giving the physical lineage, spiritual status, and domestic life of the parents.

*Verse 5: In the days of Herod, king of Judea:* This was Herod the Great

[23]

(see Matt. 2:1–21). The Herodian family spanned the two eras B.C. and A.D.[1] In the mind of the Romans, Herod the Great was a successful ruler; in the minds of his own people, the Jews, he was a mixture of benefactor and traitor. His descendants who continued his rule occupied a most important place in the first years of Christian history.[2]

*A priest named Zechariah of the division of Abijah:* The man destined to be the father of the forerunner of Jesus was a priest of the Hebrew religion descended through the priestly lineage *of Abijah.* Historically, twenty-four "classes" of priests had been set up to carry out all the sacrifices of the Temple on a rotation basis (1 Chron. 24:7–18; 2 Chron. 8:14). Each class served one week at a time, permitting two periods of service each year except for the Feast of Tabernacles when all twenty-four classes served. The class of Abijah was eighth in the list (1 Chron. 24:10). Elizabeth his wife also was *of the daughters of Aaron;* that is, she, too, was of priestly descent. The forerunner of Jesus was to come from a family solidly placed in the religious structure of Israel.

*Verse 6: Righteous before God:* In later Christian use, particularly Pauline, the word *righteous* took on a connotation of *rightness* with God through faith commitment to Jesus Christ rather than through obedience to legal requirement. Here, however, it relates to uprightness before God, and is connected with *walking in all the commandments and ordinances of the Lord blameless.* Zechariah and Elizabeth were all that sincere Jewish worshipers of God should be. The nature of their religious outlook and devotion will be more clearly reflected in later responses: the song of Elizabeth (1:42–45) and the song of Zechariah (1:68–79).

*Verse 7: They had no child:* For a marriage to be fulfilled in the production of children was regarded as a sign of God's favor and blessing. To be childless was regarded as a sign of God's disfavor.

*Because Elizabeth was barren:* Through all the years of their married life when conception had been the normal expectation, Elizabeth had not conceived. According to the customary Jewish outlook, this failure was blamed on sterility on her part. The possibility of sterility on the part of the man does not appear to have occurred to them.

*Both were advanced in years:* They had reached the point where childbearing was not the normal expectation. This does not mean that they were incapable of sexual union, only that they had now ceased to hope for a child.

### (2) Zechariah's service and vision (1:8–20)

An extended passage details Zechariah's priestly service and vision on the

---

1. For comprehensive reading on the Herods, see Stewart Perowne's two volumes, *The Life and Times of Herod the Great* and *The Later Herods* (Nashville: Abingdon Press, 1956 and 1957) and Samuel Sandmel, *Herod: Profile of a Tyrant* (Philadelphia: J. B. Lippincott Company, 1967).

2. Other members of Herod's family appearing in New Testament events are *his sons* Archelaus (Matt. 2:22), Herod Philip (Mark 6:17), Herod Antipas (Luke 3:1; Mark 6:17), and Philip the Tetrarch (Luke 3:1); *his grandchildren* Herodias who first married Herod Philip and later Herod Antipas (Mark 6:17); Herod Agrippa I (Acts 12:1); *his great-grandchildren* Salome, the daughter of Herodias and the wife of Philip the Tetrarch (Mark 6:17); Herod Agrippa II, and his sister, Bernice, popularly regarded as his consort (Acts 25:13).

occasion of the announcement of the coming birth of the forerunner.

*Verse 8: When his division was on duty:* There were so many priests in the system at that time that they served in rotation by families, and even by divisions or ranks within the families.

*Verse 9: It fell to him by lot* reflects the manner of choice for the varying services to be carried out. The lot may have been drawn by names or by some even more mechanical method.

*Burn incense:* The burning of incense was an established part of the ritual of sacrifice (see Exod. 30:1–8). The sweet odor of the burning incense was a dramatic contrast to that of the burning flesh on the altar, and went up as a pleasing smell to God. It came to be an essential part of the service of prayer. It was in this atmosphere that Zechariah received the assurance that his prayer for a son had not gone unheeded (v. 13).

*Verse 10:* While the chosen priest—Zechariah in this instance—carried on the prayer and incense-burning service within the Temple, the gathered people prayed just outside until the service was finished and the priest dismissed them. This was a routine and continually repeated experience—but on this occasion the ending was far from routine.

*Verse 11:* As the prayer-incense ritual was in progress—likely as it was about to end—Zechariah became aware of the presence of another.

*An angel of the Lord:* Angels appear very infrequently in the Old Testament. The doctrine of angels developed extensively in the intertestamental period. From the beginning of the events of the New Testament, angels were very much in evidence. In biblical thought they are an order of messengers serving the purpose of God. To the Jewish people they represented an order of creation higher than the human order. Jewish teachers spoke of them as "the higher family." They were understood to have knowledge superior to that of human beings, and it was generally accepted that God took them into his counsel regarding his purposes and action.

*Verse 12: Zechariah was troubled:* He was perplexed at the visitation. Awesome or reverent fear came over him. There is no indication that Zechariah had had previous visitations. To have reacted any other way would have been abnormal.

*Verse 13:* This was not God's angel of judgment; he was God's angel of mercy. His first words were to relieve anxiety. The text indicates a face-to-face conversation opening with the angel's words, *Do not be afraid.* More exactly the construction means, "stop fearing," i.e., "calm your fears." The upright man has nothing to fear when the messenger from God comes.

*Your prayer is heard:* This may have related to Zechariah's prayer in that very service, or it may have related to prayer in the past—prayer through the years. The word translated *prayer* is the word for a petition or request that an inferior humbly makes of a superior.

*Elizabeth will bear you a son:* This specific prayer answer suggests that the prayer in focus was the prayer over the years for a son. Likely Zechariah now had not enough hope to pray for a son. God had heard; in his own time and purpose he had answered. Now was the time for Zechariah and Elizabeth to have a son. What Paul later called "the fulness of time" (Gal. 4:4, KJV) was about to dawn.

*You shall call his name John:* Among the Jewish people names were significant. The Hebrew name meant "one whom the Lord has graciously given."
This one was to be God's gift when human hope had failed.

Verses 14–17 have the structure of poetry, the cadence of song, and take
their place with similar responses of others involved in this total event: Gabriel
(1:32–33, 35); Mary (1:46–55); Zechariah (1:68–79). These verses reflect
a liturgical nature and use of the materials. The "song" of Zechariah is clearly
identifiable in the ancient literature of Israel (see comment on 1:67). It is
entirely possible that Mary's "song" was a worship form in the religion of
Israel, a song which she used as spontaneously as one today might use Psalm
103 or "Majestic Sweetness Sits Enthroned."

*Verses 14–15:* The birth of this child was to be an occasion of rejoicing, not
only for Zechariah and Elizabeth, but also for many others. The rejoicing
would extend through John's whole ministry as a voice of God, because he was
destined for greatness before God.

*No wine nor strong drink:* John's life would be characterized by self-denial.
He would not indulge in the stimulus of alcohol. *Wine* here is the product of
grapes; strong drink *(sikera)* was an intoxicant made from other fruits, vegetables, grains, or honey. Abstinence from them was a mark of genuine piety.

*Filled with the Holy Spirit:* Through all his life John's stimulus would be the
Holy Spirit. A special working of the Holy Spirit would cause the womb of his
mother Elizabeth to receive creatively the seed of his father Zechariah. The
working of the Holy Spirit within him would be evident all through his life.

This contrast between the stimulus of the wine with its destructive result and
the stimulus of the Holy Spirit with its redemptive result is used elsewhere in
Scripture (by Peter at Pentecost, Acts 1:13–17; by Paul in Eph. 4:18–20).

*Verse 16* is a comprehensive statement of John's role. His ministry would
turn many Jewish people—*the sons of Israel*—to a meaningful relationship
with God. The evidence of his accomplishing this is clear in the accounts of his
ministry (see Mark 1:2–11; Matt. 3:1–17; Luke 3:3–22).

*Verse 17:* In more detailed terms this part of the angel's announcement
presents the distinctive ministry which John would perform.

*He will go before him:* Before whom is not clearly stated, but the immediate
antecedent of the pronoun "him" appears to be God (v. 16). When his actual
time to serve arrived, John went before Jesus as forerunner to announce his
coming. Luke's earliest readers were not confused by the ambiguous pronoun.

*In the spirit and power of Elijah:* John was a *priest* by family lineage, but he
would perform the ministry of a *prophet* in his service to God. With a burning
commitment and a devotion to his duty which disregarded personal safety,
like a new Elijah he would challenge both common man and king to examine
their lives. The return of Elijah to prepare the way for the Messiah by calling
people to repentance in the face of God's judgment was a common expectation
based on prophetic word (Mal. 4:5–6). Later Jesus, in speaking to his disciples of this expectation, would say that John's coming was the fulfillment of
that promise (Matt. 17:12–13). The angel here gave to Zechariah the same
interpretation. John was to be the new Elijah whose ministry would, in repentance and restoration of relationship, *turn the hearts of the fathers to the children* (Mal. 4:6 includes "and the hearts of children to their fathers"). This
probably refers to peace or unity between fathers and children as a result of

response to John's call to repentance. He would turn many from disobedience to the wise obedience which characterizes the just, that is, the upright.

*To make ready for the Lord a people prepared:* John would have the approval of God upon him and would perform his ministry faithfully. The product of his ministry would be *a people prepared* for God's purpose. From the perspective of Christian history, we know this purpose was the coming of God's Anointed One, Jesus. It is not clear that Zechariah so understood it at the moment. In the months that would follow as he and Elizabeth considered Gabriel's words, they would come to see the messianic significance involved. That conclusion would be reflected in Elizabeth's greeting to Mary (1:42–45) and in Zechariah's praise when the eight-day-old child received his name (1:68–79).

Verses 18–20 reflect Zechariah's continuing perplexity which left no room for faith in God's promise. The angel identified himself more exactly and imposed a convincing sign of the authority of his words.

*Verse 18:* Zechariah asks how it is possible, since he and Elizabeth are past the years of normal expectation of parenthood, and have been childless, that they should have a son. Why should they expect any change in that condition so late in life?

*Verse 19: I am Gabriel, who stand in the presence of God: Gabriel* means literally "God's strong man." This was no ordinary angel. His customary position was standing before God always ready to do his bidding.

*I was sent to speak . . . to bring you this good news:* Wherever the angel Michael is mentioned in Scripture, he is ready to fight (Dan. 10:31, 21; 12:1; Jude 9; Rev. 12:7). Wherever Gabriel is mentioned, he is ready to make a speech (Dan. 8:16; 9:21; Luke 1:9, 26). This special angel sent on this special mission was God's official spokesman, bearing God's words. God's word was considered an extension of God's person in Hebrew thought. So for Zechariah not to believe the message of good news meant he did not believe God.

*Verse 20:* The sign Gabriel gave Zechariah was an appropriate one. Because Zechariah did not believe Gabriel's *words* (which were really God's words), he would not be able to speak any words until Gabriel's words became reality! That was real punishment; it proved to be convincing.

### (3) Reaction of the people (1:21–22)

The people outside the Temple were waiting for the benediction, and wondered at the delay. When Zechariah came out, unable to speak, they understood from his signs that he had experienced a vision, and departed with no spoken benediction. Zechariah completed the days of his appointed service in the Temple in silence. The sign he had requested *(How shall I know this?* v. 18) was working.

### (4) Elizabeth's conception and praise (1:23–25)

When Zechariah had finished his service in the Temple, he returned to his home, which appears to have been in the hill country outside Jerusalem (see v. 39), and some time later *Elizabeth conceived* (v. 24).

This birth story does not belong in the same category with the story of Mary's conception, but rather with the Old Testament story of Abraham and

Sarah. The child was conceived by Zechariah's union with Elizabeth, but God worked to bring fruit to the fruitless who were past the time for conception and childbearing.

*Verse 24:* Elizabeth withdrew from social life for five months. This was a time of contemplation on her experience and of rejoicing in her sense of fulfillment.

*Verse 25: Thus the Lord has done:* It was only natural that this dramatic conception would be interpreted as the work of God. In common with the people of their day, Zechariah and Elizabeth probably had interpreted their childlessness as an indication of God's displeasure, his punishment for some reason unknown to them. This is not our view today. Our understanding of the body and its functions or malfunctions is far beyond that of their day. In Jewish thought God was so involved in his creation that everything that happened was understood in some way as the *direct* act of God.

*To take away my reproach:* God had seen fit to look upon this priestly couple, to remove his displeasure, to give his blessing in the form of a son. The removal of his displeasure was in itself an occasion of rejoicing. To experience motherhood after long years of yearning was blessing added to blessing.

## 2. The Promise of the Birth of Jesus (1:26–38)

The annunciation of the birth of John is followed immediately by the annunciation of the birth of Jesus. The stories have a definite structural parallel until they diverge at the conclusion. Gabriel made a startling appearance. Mary, to whom he appeared, was perplexed. Gabriel explained his mission and message. Mary in faith accepted the message in obedience to the will of God.

### (1) Gabriel's appearance and Mary's reaction (1:26–29)

The same angelic spokesman was sent from God to announce the birth of the Savior.

*Verse 26: In the sixth month:* It is clear from the preceding verses as well as from verse 36 that the reference is to Elizabeth's status. Her conception came six months before this announcement. This point will be important later in estimating the relative ages of John and Jesus.

*A city of Galilee named Nazareth:* Galilee was known as Gentile territory, but in the New Testament time it was predominantly Jewish in population. The Jews of Judea looked upon it as inferior to Judea and its people as uncultured people. There is New Testament evidence that the village of Nazareth may have held a place of particular scorn in their thinking (John 1:46).

*Verse 27: To a virgin . . . Mary:* The Greek word translated "virgin" is the usual one for a sexually pure person.

*Betrothed to a man:* Initial betrothal or engagement arrangements were usually made by the parents. They may have been made in Mary's very young childhood. They were considered binding and the final marriage ceremonies would come in due time.

*Joseph, of the house of David:* Luke tells us nothing of Mary's betrothed except his name and his lineage—he was of the royal line of King David. Unlike Matthew, who saw in Joseph a man of dreams (like his Old Testament namesake) who went to Egypt and back under God's purpose, Luke expresses no interest in the man or his name itself. His interest was in the matter of the Davidic lineage since that was an important part of the birth of Jesus in David's city, Bethlehem.

*Verses 28–29:* To Gabriel's *Hail, O favored one, the Lord is with you,* Mary responded in perplexed wonder at the meaning of the greeting. Jewish girls married very early. Mary was probably in her early teens. In her song in Elizabeth's home (1:46–55) she appears as a gentle, humble, deeply pious person. It was only natural that such a visitation would startle her.

## (2) Gabriel's announcement and explanation (1:30–37)

Much of this section is in poetic form.

*Verses 30–31:* Gabriel assured Mary that as one favored of God she was not to be disturbed by God's messenger and message. The simple message was that she was going to conceive and bear a son.

*Jesus:* The Hebrew word from which the word *Jesus* comes is the name "Joshua." This honored name of historic significance in Israel means "deliverer" or "savior." Matthew notes its significance in his account of the announcement made to Joseph: "You shall call his name Jesus, for he will save his people from their sins" (Matt. 1:21). As Joshua of old delivered his people from their enemies and brought them into the land of God's promise, so Jesus would deliver his people from sin.

*Verses 32–33:* Mary's son would occupy an exalted place of honor and rule, which Gabriel described in lofty terms. He would be *great.* He would be called *Son of the Most High,* a favorite title or name for God (Mark 5:7; Luke 1:35, 76; 6:35; Acts 7:48; Heb. 7:1). He would receive from God *the throne of his father David.* Some interpreters understand this to mean that Mary, too, was descended from the lineage of King David. They find support for the view in Romans 1:3. This may be true but not necessarily so. As the son of Mary whose husband was of Davidic lineage, Jesus would have the same right to that throne as a son physically born of Joseph. His rule and his kingdom would be never-ending. Others before him had occupied thrones but they had always been temporary. Jesus' rule would be different.

*Verse 34:* Mary reflected lingering perplexity at one point. Since she was unmarried, how was she to become a mother? Her question related to the natural process of motherhood, and reflected inability to understand, not unwillingness to experience the event.

*Verse 35:* Gabriel's explanation related her experience to the power of the Holy Spirit. The all-encompassing presence of the Most High, the power of the Holy Spirit, would, in Mary's experience, work the conception apart from relationship to a human male. The child to be born of Mary would be called *holy, the Son of God.* The word *holy* means set apart for God's purpose. The exact grammatical construction "God's son" gives further emphasis to the fact that Jesus was not conceived of human paternity. What Mary was to experience was unique. While other births had been brought about through God's working in unusual circumstances (Abraham-Sarah; Zechariah-Elizabeth), this was of a different category. It would be a conception by the power of the Holy Spirit apart from human paternity.

*Verses 36–37:* Gabriel gave further assurance to Mary by reporting to her that her kinswoman Elizabeth, long known for her sterility, had now conceived a son and was in the sixth month of her pregnancy.

*For with God nothing will be impossible:* This rendering, identical with the KJV except for the changing of "shall" to "will," is true to the meaning of the passage, but it is not really a translation. Literally the text must be translated "for shall not be powerless any word from God." The idea is again that of the word of God as an extension of his person. (Compare v. 19, comment.) No word which God sends forth into the affairs of his creation will be powerless to execute its end. God has given his word; what he has said will take place, whether or not the finite human mind can understand the "how" of it.

### (3) Mary's obedient acceptance (1:38)

What Mary could not understand by rational power she was well able by faith to accept. In her response, *"I am the handmaid of the Lord,"* Mary voiced the essence of her outlook on life. She was here in the world as the servant of God. With a fine sensitivity which grasps its simplicity, Moffatt translates the statement "I am here to serve the Lord."

*Let it be to me according to your word:* Having accepted by faith the experience which Gabriel foretold, and having given recognition of her one purpose for being in the world, Mary voiced her obedient acceptance of the role. Moffatt has caught her spirit in his translation: "Let it be as you have said."

While the virgin birth of Jesus is affirmed in only two places in the New Testament—here and in Matthew—its place in Christian faith has a long and solid history.[1] Its acceptance is a commitment of faith as it was for Mary herself. Where understanding stops, faith does not stop.

There are multiple elements in the New Testament accounts of the incarnation of God in Jesus Christ: *when* it took place; *where* it took place; *how* it took place; *why* it took place; all of these have their relative importance. Probably most interpreters will grant that the last one named is of greatest importance. *Why* God became incarnate seems to be of greater importance than when and where and how. That does not rule the other questions out of a place in Christian faith. The when and the where and the how were matters of God's wisdom and choice, just as the why was. But one does need to guard against becoming so engrossed in either or all of the others that one forgets the primary one, *"Why did God become man?"*

### 3. The Visit of Mary to Elizabeth (1:39–56)

In this section the relative roles of the two unborn sons are further delineated by the meeting of the two expectant mothers.

The length of time between Gabriel's visit to Mary and Mary's visit to Elizabeth is not indicated. Two matters are implicit in this account: Mary

---

1. For further reading on the virgin birth of Jesus, see J. Gresham Machen, *The Virgin Birth of Christ* (New York: Harper and Brothers, Publishers, 1932); James Orr, *The Virgin Birth of Christ* (New York: Charles Scribner's Sons, 1907); Dale Moody, "The Virgin Birth," *Interpreters' Dictionary of the Bible,* ed. George A. Buttrick (New York: Abingdon Press) IV, 789–91.

had conceived before she went to visit Elizabeth; her conception was very soon after Gabriel's announcement.

*Verse 39:* Zechariah and Elizabeth lived in an unidentified town in the hill country of Judea approximately sixty-five miles from Mary's home in Nazareth of Galilee. Gabriel's mention of the power of God at work in Elizabeth probably prompted Mary to go to visit her older kinswoman for consideration of their common experience.

*Verses 40–41:* When Mary greeted Elizabeth, the sound of her voice coincided with a marked movement of Elizabeth's baby. Since Elizabeth was in her sixth month, this was certainly not her first consciousness of the movement of her baby. Probably it was a remarkably strong movement which she associated with Mary's greeting.

*Filled with the Holy Spirit:* This is the explanation for Elizabeth's response to Mary's greeting and the baby's movement.

Verses 42–44 have been called the song of Elizabeth. In part it has poetic structure and in part it does not; hence, it is not as clearly a song as the other passages in this section. It is really a response of blessing followed by an explanation of the response.

*Verse 42:* Here are two blessings in parallel. *Blessed are you among women* expresses much the same thought of Gabriel's greeting (v. 28). It proclaims the exalted privilege of Mary. *Blessed is the fruit of your womb* is a natural parallel. The child born to such a woman is a blessed child.

*Verse 43:* Elizabeth's humility is expressed in her wonder that she should be so honored that *the mother of my Lord should come to me.* This statement provokes a question as to the source of Elizabeth's perception. Some interpreters relate it directly to the motivation of the Holy Spirit (v. 41).[1] It appears more likely that it was the end of a growing apprehension of all that had been taking place in her experience as she and her husband had considered it in reverent wonder. Gabriel had indicated to Zechariah that John would be like a preparatory Elijah to prepare for the day of the Lord. It would naturally follow that somewhere there would come the Anointed One for whom John was to prepare the way. Jewish people attributed conscious action even to unborn babies. When the sound of Mary's voice struck Elizabeth's ears her unborn child *leaped for joy* (v. 44). By some such train of thought Elizabeth arrived at her joyful conclusion that Mary was to be the mother of the one for whom her son was to prepare the way. The Holy Spirit confirmed that conclusion for her.[2]

*Verse 45:* A final blessing was pronounced by Elizabeth. Mary was blessed because she had believed that there would be a fulfillment of all the things which had been spoken to her. It reflects Elizabeth's perception that Mary, too, had received God's promise of a mighty work in her experience. Mary's presence reflected faithful acceptance and prompted the beatitude.

Verses 46–56: Mary's song of praise reflects her character and her emo-

---

1. For example, R. C. H. Lenski, *The Interpretation of St. Mark's and St. Luke's Gospels* (Columbus, Ohio: Lutheran Book Concern, 1934), p. 532; and B. H. Carroll, "The Four Gospels," vol. 1 of *An Interpretation of the English Bible* (New York: Fleming H. Revell Company, 1916), p. 90.

2. George R. Bliss, "Commentary on the Gospel of Luke" *The American Commentary* (Philadelphia: American Baptist Publication Society, 1884) II, 34.

tional response to God's mighty work in her life and in the life of the people of Israel. It is poetic in structure and makes free use of Old Testament language, showing evidence of much contemplation on the part of Mary as she weighed all the things which Gabriel told her. Now her meeting with Elizabeth brought additional confirmation to her faith that God was working a most unusual event in her experience.

*Verses 46–47* constitute a parallelism:

> *My soul magnifies the Lord,*
> *and my spirit rejoices in God my Savior.*

No categorical distinction can be made here between the words *soul* and *spirit*. They appear to be synonyms referring to that which constitutes the real person. The total of Mary's "inner being" expressed itself in praise.

The parallelism is carried forward by the two verbs. *Magnifies* literally means "make great." The Latin translation of this text has given to Mary's song the title "The Magnificat." Her soul dwelt on the greatness of God and on what he was doing in his people. *Rejoices* expresses her inner state of joyful well-being as she contemplated her experience.

The third area of the parallelism is in the words *Lord* and *God my Savior*. Here, too, no categorical personal distinctions are to be made between the two names. The redeeming God of Israel, who was the Lord of Mary's life, was the object of her joyful praise.

*Verses 48–49* point out the particular work which God had accomplished in Mary; verses 50–55 point out the work which he had accomplished in Israel, the people of his redemptive purpose. Verses 48–49 constitute a four-line stanza: lines 1 and 3 show what God had done for Mary; lines 2 and 4 give the results—praise for Mary (line 2), and praise to God (line 4).

> *for he has regarded the low estate of his handmaiden.*
> *For behold henceforth all generations will call me blessed;*
> *for he who is mighty has done great things for me,*
> *and holy is his name.*

Mary recognized her humble station in life; yet the God of Israel had chosen her as the mother of his incarnate Son. For this the people of generations to come would speak their blessings upon her. Because the mighty God had worked in this marvelous way, his *name,* and his very nature, would be recognized as *holy,* completely set apart and awesome.

*Verses 50–55* indicate the work of God in the affairs of men. His purpose had been accomplished as he put down the great and lifted up the small. The background of this statement is the history of Israel from Abraham to Mary's day. The more prominent part of that history was the exodus and its subsequent events. The structure of the passage is that of dramatic contrast through parallelism. *The proud . . . the mighty . . . the rich.* These were world rulers who had opposed the purpose of God by pursuing their own purposes—Pharaoh of the exodus, for instance. *Those of low degree . . . the hungry . . . his servant Israel . . . our fathers . . . Abraham and his posterity.* These all had immediate reference to the insignificant slave people whom God delivered from Egypt, provided for through forty years of nomadic life in the wilderness, and finally brought to this event in the life of Mary, all as a part of his merciful and redemptive purpose.

The entire song is a psalm of praise to God in recognition of his redemptive purpose as it had worked itself out in history and was still working itself out in Mary's experience.

*Verse 56:* Mary remained with Elizabeth three months before returning to her own home. This suggests that she left just before the birth of Elizabeth's baby; the announcement to Mary that Elizabeth was to bear a son had come in Elizabeth's sixth month.

## 4. The Birth of John the Baptizer (1:57–80)

This section concludes the matters related to the birth of Jesus' forerunner.

### (1) Birth, circumcision, and naming (1:57–66)

The birth of any son was an occasion of rejoicing among the Jewish people. This particular child, born to a childless couple who had passed the time of normal expectation of parenthood, occasioned even greater rejoicing. Verses 57–58 relate the rejoicing of neighbors and kin. The birth was an event shared by the entire community as the corporate people of God—this newborn child was a part of all of them. Verses 59–63 give the details of a significant but commonplace practice among the Jews—the circumcision and naming of a child—but given more significance in this case.

*Verse 59: The eighth day . . . circumcise:* The mark of the covenant people from the time of Abraham had been the circumcision of every male child. A hygienic practice among many of the people of that day, it had a religious significance for the Jews. It symbolized the putting off of the filth of the old life, and a commitment to the way of God. Soon after the people of Israel came up out of Egypt under Moses' leadership, there was a service in which all the males (children and adults) who had not been circumcised (due either to Israel's neglect or to Egypt's prohibition as a suppressive measure) were circumcised. This event was spoken of as a day of God's "rolling away" from them the filth of Egypt. They were God's covenant people (Josh. 5:2–9). It was a meaningful rite which historically came to be set on the child's eighth day.

*They would have named him:* The giving of the name was of great importance in Israel. The name stood for the character, the very person of the individual. Some present-day interpreters of Jewish customs understand this practice to indicate that "personhood" was given in the giving of the name.

*Zechariah:* It was only natural that a first-born son, particularly of an old man who would not likely have another, be given the name of his father. This was the intention of those present. Elizabeth intervened to indicate that the child was not to be named for his father, he was to be named *John.* This was not even a family name among the kin of Zechariah and Elizabeth (v. 61). Her suggestion was so inappropriate, that the group would not accept it.

*Verse 62: They made signs to his father:* There is no reason to believe that when Zechariah had been deprived of speech nine months before, he had been deprived of hearing also. There probably was a well-recognized practice of using signs (even when accompanied by words) in communicating with one who spoke only through signs.

*What he would have him called:* The husband and father, as the head of the family, had the final authority. The neighbors and kin were expecting the father to confirm their intention and to tell them to give his name to his first-born son. Zechariah was a significant name, meaning "one whom the Lord remembers." But it was not significant enough for this child.

*Verse 63: Writing tablet:* The Greek word *pinakidion* is a diminutive form derived from the word for pine tree. It was a small piece of flat wood on which Zechariah could mark his meaningful words—*his name is John.* The vision, Elizabeth's conception, the nine months of speechlessness had convinced Zechariah! Now he indicated that he believed the words spoken by Gabriel.

*Verses 64–66: His tongue loosed:* While the people wondered at Zechariah's agreement on this unusual name, his power of speech returned. His first words were words of praise *blessing God.* The sense of *fear,* reverent awe, which fell on the gathered community was passed on to others as the report of these things went out to the surrounding area—*all the hill country of Judea.* As the people considered them their consensus was voiced in a question, *What then will this child be?* reflecting their sense of wonder as to the ultimate role of one whose birth was accompanied by such portentous events. The closing sentence in verse 66 does not appear to be a part of their question. It is rather Luke's comment on their wonder. It was clear to the community that God was working some purpose in this child.

### (2) Zechariah's song of praise (1:67–79)

Verse 64 indicates that Zechariah's first words were words of blessing God; logically this song belongs there, since it begins, *Blessed be the Lord God of Israel.* But for Luke to have placed it there would have broken the continuity of the narrative, so he finished his story before giving Zechariah's song.

*Verse 67:* Zechariah was *filled with the Holy Spirit,* i.e., so completely under the Spirit's control that his words had their source in the Holy Spirit.

*Prophesied:* By derivation of the word as well as by the nature of the message it is clear that the prophet in Israel was the one who "spoke for" God. He spoke for God, whether his message related to past event, present circumstance, or future development. He was not necessarily a foreteller of future events, but he might be. Zechariah's words related both to the past action of God in Israel (vv. 68–75) and the future action of God through the ministry of John (vv. 76–79). It was fittingly labeled prophecy. All of it related to God's redemptive work in and through Israel.

The structure of Zechariah's song is that of poetry. The language is that of the Old Testament and the worship forms of the people of Israel. Large parts of the passage are recognizable in an ancient prayer known in varying forms and sometimes called "The Eighteen Benedictions."[1] Under the motivation of the Holy Spirit, out of his memorized treasures of Scripture and song, Zechariah praised God.

*Verses 68–69: He has visited and redeemed his people:* God's past work of redeeming Israel merges into the present events: *he has raised up a horn of salvation for us in the house of his servant David.* In Hebrew thought the *horn* was a symbol of strength, probably from the idea of an animal's strength being demonstrated in its horns.

*In the house of his servant David:* The reference is clearly to the idea that

---

1. Alfred Edersheim, *The Life and Times of Jesus the Messiah* (Grand Rapids: Wm. B. Eerdmans Publishing Company, 1940) I, 158.

the Redeemer-King would be descended from David. If John was to be the forerunner of the Messiah, God's redemptive work was reaching its climax in this total event. In this way Zechariah could refer to it as something which God had already done; in his purpose it was already an accomplished fact.

*Verses 70–75:* This redemptive work of God is related to prophetic promise (v. 70). God's spokesmen of old had assured Israel that God would give them victory over all who opposed them as they followed God's leadership to their destiny (vv. 70–71). He had assured them that he would keep his redemptive covenant with them (v. 72), establishing them as a nation to worship him and serve his redemptive purpose (vv. 73–75).

*Verses 76–79* turn the emphasis in God's redemptive purpose to the role of this child, John. He would be *called the prophet of the Most High.* He was of priestly descent, but he assumed the role of prophet when he began his ministry preaching in the wilderness country of Judea. Later Jesus would say of him that he was the greatest of the prophets (Luke 7:26–28).

He would *go before the Lord* as Gabriel had indicated. In so doing he would prepare the way by giving the people *knowledge of salvation . . . in the forgiveness of their sins* (v. 77) *through the tender mercy of our God* (v. 78).

*Verse 78* brings John's mission up to the coming of the one for whom he was preparing the way.

*When the day shall dawn upon us from on high:* This rendering in the Revised Standard Version is not a translation. It is a smooth paraphrase of a Greek expression which translated literally would be "in which shall shine upon us the light rising from on high." The coming of the Redeemer would be like the sun coming at dawn. It would mean light and life to a world enshrouded in *darkness* and *death* (v. 79). This one would conduct the world's people along the *way* or the road *of peace.*

While couched in Hebrew religious terms, Zechariah's song is thoroughly "Christian" in its force. It grasps the history of the Hebrew people from Abraham to John and Jesus as one redemptive act of God.

### (3) John's hidden years (1:80)

In one brief verse Luke distills thirty years. John probably began his ministry when he was about thirty years of age.[1] From his birth to that point, nothing is said other than that he developed physically and spiritually and that he grew up, not in the usual place for the son of a priest, the shadow of the Temple, but *in the wilderness.* In solitude he would come to an understanding of the nature of his role and the message he was to proclaim.

## 5. The Birth of Jesus (2:1–7)

These verses contain two parts of the narrative: the journey from Nazareth to Bethlehem, with the reasons for the journey; the birth in Bethlehem.

### (1) The journey to Judea (2:1–5)

*Verse 1:* The occasion of Joseph's going from Nazareth in Galilee to Bethlehem in Judea was an enrollment required by the Roman government. Since

---

1. Jesus was about thirty when he went to be baptized by John (Luke 3:23). Interpreters are in agreement that he did so soon after John began his ministry. John was probably six or eight months older than Jesus.

the Jews were not subject to military conscription, this was most likely an enrollment for a new tax. The emperor in Rome was Augustus Caesar. He ruled from about 30 B.C. to A.D. 14. Here, as in other places in his Gospel, Luke evidences his interest in setting the event of Jesus' birth into the historical (Roman) and religious (Jewish) situation.

*Decree:* Literally translated the word is a "dogma." It was an official order with all the power of Rome, mightiest nation in the world in that day, behind it.

*All the world should be enrolled:* The literal meaning of the word "world" is "the inhabited earth." It was a technical term used freely to refer to the Roman Empire. To the Romans their empire was "the inhabited earth"; all other parts of the world were to them relatively unimportant. The entire empire, of which Palestine was a part, was to *be enrolled*—to have a census taken, which would be used in collecting taxes. The journey to Bethlehem was for the purpose of registering for the tax, not for the paying of the tax. Outside of Luke's report there is no exact mention of such a universal census at the time indicated, although there are some inscriptional evidences suggesting such a possibility. The evidence is inconclusive and is rejected by some and accepted by others. Arguments which have been lodged against Luke's accuracy at this point have been largely arguments from silence.

*Verse 2:* Two major problems face the interpreter of this verse: (1) What is meant by *first enrollment?* (2) When was Quirinius the governor of Syria? The problem is due in part to inadequate secular records of the period. It is clear from Roman history that Quirinius was the governor of Syria in A.D. 6, subsequent to the death of Archelaus. Only in Luke 2:1 is there an indication that he was the governor in 6 B.C., about the time of the birth of Jesus. It is clear from Roman history that about that time (7–6 B.C.) Quirinius was in control of the military forces and the foreign policy of Syria under the rule of Varus. In this capacity, he would have directed any census for taxation. This may be Luke's intention in the Greek expression which exactly means "Quirinius governing in Syria."

*This was the first enrollment:* The Greek word *prote* means first in a series. It does not seem likely, then, that Lenski is right in holding that it meant that never before had such a census been decreed.[1] It is more likely that it is Luke's way of referring to a taxation census (of which there is no other record) under Quirinius's control at the time of the birth of Jesus, in contrast to one while Quirinius was governor in his own right in A.D. 6. The second one was well attested in history because it caused the revolt of the Jews under the leadership of a certain Judas (Acts 5:37) and the rise of the revolutionary party of Zealots.

*Verse 3: All . . . each to his own city:* This was the way everyone in Palestine enrolled. In other parts of the empire the method customary to those people would be used. The Jewish custom of census enrollment was for a man to enroll in the town regarded as his native city. The enrollment likely required name, occupation, property, and kindred.

*Verse 4: Joseph . . . Bethlehem . . . lineage of David:* Joseph had historical connections with Bethlehem, though at the time of this event he lived in Nazareth. The historical connection may have been only through his ancestral

---

1. Lenski, op. cit., p. 556.

lineage back to David. Or he may have lived there before going to Nazareth. Some elements of the Matthew-Luke infancy narratives indicate that when Joseph and Mary went to Bethlehem they were considering it a permanent move. The Greek word *tektōn* applied to Joseph in the New Testament designated one who lived by working with his hands—a carpenter, a stone-mason, and even a farmer in some papyri. Bethlehem was the historical headquarters for the stonemason's guild and therefore a more natural residence than Nazareth for a builder.

*Verse 5: With Mary:* The construction may mean that he journeyed with Mary or that he enrolled with Mary. Actually, it was both. Although the physical union of their marriage was not consummated until after Jesus was born (Matt. 1:25), the official ceremonies had been concluded and Mary was his wife (Matt. 1:24). She would have to be listed in the census. The possible reasons for her going at a time so close to the birth of her child have been debated—whether she was required to go; whether Joseph could have registered her in her absence; whether this was part of an intention to make Bethlehem their permanent residence. The answer must be sought in many small bits of evidence. Luke's main concern was to let Theophilus know why Jesus was born in Bethlehem but grew up in Nazareth, and to set the related events solidly in the center of Hebrew religious history including the Temple and its sacrificial service.

*With child:* The word, used only here in the New Testament, means simply "pregnant," with no reference to the stage of pregnancy. We know that Mary was near the end of her pregnancy, however, not from the KJV translation "being great with child" but from the circumstance described in the next verses.

## (2) The birth of Mary's first-born (2:6–7)

The birth of Jesus apparently came soon after the arrival of Joseph and Mary in Bethlehem. They had not found a place to live. The fact that the journey took only a few days indicates that Mary was near the end of her term when they undertook the journey, and therefore suggests some urgent reason for her making it.

*Verse 7: Her first-born son:* The term naturally suggests that Mary had other children later, and the Gospels name four men as Jesus' "brothers" and also refer to his "sisters" with no indication of the number. "First-born," however, does not necessarily mean that there were other children; an only child would also be a "first-born." Luke's phrase means literally, "she gave birth to her first-born, a son." The birth of Jesus was a natural physical birth with the customary labor and birth pains. The conception was supernatural, not the birth.

*Swaddling cloths:* Every newborn Jewish baby was wrapped in cloths provided for the purpose. Dainty gowns and frilly dresses were not used for babies in that day. For some time the baby would live in the first-century equivalent of receiving blankets!

The fact that Mary is the subject of the verbs *wrapped* and *laid* does not indicate that she alone did these things without the help of a midwife or her husband. This was simply Luke's way of reporting the essential event.

*Inn:* A "lodging place" or very literally a "loosing-down place" where pack animals would have their packs removed and their owners would take shelter for the night. Some have argued for a lodging place with some of Joseph's relatives. Others have argued for a public place of accommodation for travelers. The latter fits the total scene much better: a small town; a small lodging place for travelers; more people than could be accommodated (due to the census?); an inn-keeper who provided the best place he could for a bit of privacy for a woman approaching childbirth. These animal shelters were usually an uncovered enclosure adjoining the inn. Around the enclosure there were porch-like shelters formed either by natural rock overhang or by man-made structure. In these humble surroundings, Jesus was born.

*Manger:* This may mean the stall for the animals in contrast to the lodging place for the people, or it can also mean the eating place of the animals. The latter appears more likely; soft hay was the first resting place for the one who as a man would say he had "no place to lay his head" when night came. The setting was a dramatic contrast to the heavenly annunciation which follows.

## 6. The Visit of the Shepherds (2:8–20)

This section presents an elaborate scene of divine announcement of the birth of Jesus. An intriguing facet of the infancy narratives is that Luke, who wrote with the Gentile interest in the foreground, reports the announcement of Jesus' birth as it was made to Jews (the shepherds), while Matthew, who wrote with the Jewish interest in the foreground, reports the announcement as it was made to Gentiles (the Magi). Each had his own purpose.

*Verse 8: There were shepherds:* No further identification is given. They were clearly Jewish shepherds who had a special interest in the Son of David-Messiah concept in Israel. One might conjecture that their sheep-raising was related to the sacrificial Temple services in nearby Jerusalem.

*In the field:* The shepherds were out away from the town in the open country. According to custom they likely had temporary structures for safe enclosure of their flocks at night and for some shelter for themselves. It is not possible to argue for or against the modern calendar date of December 25th for the birth of Jesus by referring to this setting. Luke's interest was not in the time of year.

*By night:* The night darkness made the brilliance of the angelic appearance all the more vivid.

*Verse 9: An angel of the Lord:* Here again a special messenger of God appeared. The concept of an order of created messengers ranking above the human level was well fixed in Hebrew thought.

*Glory . . . shone around them:* The word translated "glory" is used in many ways in Scripture and it almost defies definition. Here it takes the form of supernatural light as the messenger of God addressed the shepherds. *They were filled with fear*—a reverential awe, not a cowering fear. Awe-struck they waited.

*Verse 10: Be not afraid:* Whatever element of foreboding lingered in their awe was dispelled by the angel's words—literally "stop being afraid." There was no basis for fear; the messenger brought them *good news* which meant *great joy,* not for the shepherds alone but for everyone.

*Verse 11: To you is born this day . . . a Savior . . . Christ the Lord:* The day for the Jews started at sunset; the implication is that Jesus was born at night and the angel appeared to the shepherds that same night. *Savior* means "deliverer"; *Christ* means "anointed one"—*christos* in Greek, "messias" from the Hebrew; *Lord* means ruler and ultimately would be a title used by Christians almost as a proper name. Its use is characteristic in Luke. The entire expression had a definite messianic connotation: a Davidic Anointed One—Savior and Lord.

*Verse 12: Sign:* This newborn Savior would be identified to them as a baby swathed in the customary cloths but cradled in a manger. *Wrapped in swaddling cloths* would not have distinguished the baby from any other, but *lying in a manger* would.

*Verse 13: Multitude of the heavenly host:* The word translated *host* is the word for army. In rabbinic writings *heavenly host* meant an army of angels. In the Old Testament it sometimes was used poetically to refer to the stars as objects of worship in non-Jewish religions (Jer. 8:2; 2 Chron. 33:3, 5). Here it must be used in the sense in which it was used in the rabbinic writings, an army of angels praising God.

*Praising God and saying:* Although Luke says the angels praised by saying the lines of poetry, traditionally this has been interpreted as praise through singing. That may well be. The word translated *praising* carries no indication either of singing or not singing. The words have been spoken of as a "song." This is also true of Mary's "song" and Zechariah's "song," though there is no indication that they sang. To minds accustomed to group praise as musical praise, the scene in verses 13–14 naturally suggests an angelic musical chorus praising God.

*Verse 14:* The words are definitely poetry and may be arranged in several ways depending on varying textual readings in different manuscripts.

(1)  *Glory in the highest places to God*
     *and on earth peace to men of* (God's) *good will.*
In this arrangement there is the rhetorical pattern of "chiasmos," that is, the arrangement of four parts on the Greek letter X (Chi).

                Glory           in the highest to God
         in the earth          peace           to men
"Glory" and "peace" balance "in the highest" and "in the earth." The major difficulty in this is that it must omit the Greek preposition "among" before men; while the manuscripts vary, the preposition is well attested.

(2)  *Glory in the highest places to God*
     *Peace in the earth*
     *Good will among men.*
For this three-line reading one must follow a text which has the word "good will" in the nominative case. There are such readings, but not in the best manuscripts, which have the genitive form, "of good will."

When the different readings and possibilities are carefully compared, the result appears to be a two-line poem with one part relating to heaven and God and one part relating to earth and men, specifically men with whom God is pleased.

(3)  *In the highest places, glory to God*
     *On the earth, peace and* (God's) *good will to men.*
This arrangement makes the different parts easier to see. The first line confesses the praise of the heavenly host for God for what he has done in bring-

ing a Savior into the world. The word order of the Greek text with *glory* the first word and *God* the last word in the line is even more emphatic.

God's action in bringing the Savior into the world meant *peace* among men. Paul would later write that Jesus "came and preached peace" (Eph. 2:17), more, that "he is our peace" (Eph. 2:14). The word translated *with whom he is pleased* (RSV) or "good will" (KJV) is never used in the New Testament of man's good will or pleasure; it always relates to God's good will or pleasure. The translation sometimes used "among men of good will" is from the Latin Vulgate, not the Greek text. Peace between men and good will upon men are God's gifts through this Savior.

*Verses 15–20* indicate that immediately after the angelic announcement was made, the shepherds went to Bethlehem, found the family in the stable, and reported the visit and message of the angels. *All who heard* the report of the shepherds were amazed. They are not identified. The reference may be to people to whom the shepherds spoke as they sought the baby or to people at the inn where the baby was born. Luke singles out Mary's reaction (v. 19). She stored the shepherds' words in her heart for thoughtful consideration in the days ahead. The shepherds returned to their flocks speaking their praise for and to God for all they had heard and seen. *As it had been told to them* appears to refer to the angel's message. There is no indication that Mary and Joseph shared with the shepherds the remarkable event of Jesus' conception and birth.

## 7. The Circumcision, Naming, and Dedication of Jesus as the First-Born (2:21–39)

This section describes three Jewish practices which were customary for infant boys. (1) On the eighth day of the boy's life a service in the home would include circumcision and naming. (See discussion on 1:59.) (2) After at least thirty-one days of a first-born boy's life he would be presented in the Temple as the first-born, holy to God; the "ransom" price would be paid according to ancient custom (Exod. 13:2–15; Num. 18:15–16), and he would be taken back home for rearing. This did not have to be on the thirty-first day; it could be any time a Temple visit was possible after thirty-one days. (3) After at least forty-one days (eighty-one for girl babies) the parents would go to the Temple for purification or dedication in the light of their new responsibilities. They would make an offering of a lamb for a burnt offering and a dove (or a pigeon) for a sin offering, or, if they could not afford a lamb, they could offer two doves (or pigeons) (Lev. 12:1–8). Luke 2:22–24 indicates that both of these Temple services were cared for in one visit to the Temple; hence, after Jesus was at least forty-one days old.

*Verse 21: He was called Jesus:* This was in accordance with Gabriel's announcement to Mary (Luke 1:31) and to Joseph (Matt. 1:21). The name means "one who delivers" or "one who saves." (See discussion on Luke 1:31.)

*Verse 22: The time came for their purification . . . they brought him:* Mary and Joseph appear to have performed both of the Temple services in one visit. They were apparently still living in Bethlehem.

*Verse 23: Every male . . . holy to the Lord:* The reference to Exodus 13:2,

12, 15 is not an exact quotation. The Exodus passages make it clear that it was first-born males who were to be counted holy to God and who had to be "ransomed." The ransom price was only a token, perhaps two or three dollars by present-day standards. Having been bought back (ransomed) from God, the first-born son would be reared in the home as any other son.

*Verse 24: A pair of turtledoves, or two young pigeons:* Again, the quotation is only a fragment of Leviticus 12:1–8. Mary's offering of two doves (the offering of the poor) is an indication of the financial status of the family into which Jesus was born and reared.

Verses 25–35 record a significant event on the occasion of Jesus' presentation in the Temple.

*Verses 25–27:* There was present a man named Simeon, described as one who was *righteous, devout,* and *looking for the consolation* (comfort) *of Israel.* The last phrase indicates his yearning and waiting for the messianic deliverance anticipated in Israel. He had experienced a revelation from the Spirit of God that he would live to see the Messiah, *the Lord's Christ.* Just how that revelation was made to him is not indicated. Nor is it indicated just how the Spirit made it known to him that this baby boy was that Messiah. In some way he knew.

*Verses 28–32:* He took the child in his arms and spoke his praise to God in what has been called the "Song of Simeon" or, from the liturgical form of the Latin text, the "Nunc Dimittis" from the opening line, "Now dismiss, Lord, thy servant in peace" (v. 29, literal translation).

Simeon was ready to be dismissed from this life; he had lived to see God's salvation (v. 30) or deliverance realized in the coming of the Messiah, even though that Messiah was only an infant. This was a salvation prepared for all people (v. 31)—the child would be a revealing light to the Gentiles and a redeeming glory to the Jews (v. 32). Here, again, Luke's universal outlook appears.

*Verses 33–35:* Simeon also spoke words of blessing to Joseph and Mary. He spoke of the fact that this child was destined for unusual things.

*The fall and rising of many in Israel: fall* for those rejecting him and falling before God's judgment; *rising* for those accepting him and experiencing God's salvation.

*A sign that is spoken against:* He would become an object of hostility and slander by many. The suffering of her son would be like a sword in Mary's own heart (v. 35). This statement appears to be a parenthetical one. The last line, *that thoughts out of many hearts may be revealed* (v. 35), appears to go back to the statement regarding the reviling and hostility he would face. These would reveal the real inner character of many.

*Verses 36–38* record another unusual occurrence on this same occasion. A very old woman named Anna, described as a prophetess who spent all of her time in the Temple, was there. The language of verses 36–37 is ambiguous. It is not clear whether she was a widow eighty-four years old, or whether she had been a widow for eighty-four years.

In the Temple she devoted herself to prayer and fasting (v. 37), indications of genuine devotion. *Coming up at that very hour* appears to refer to the actions and words of Simeon (vv. 28–35). She added to his words her own words of thanks to God. She spoke *of him* (v. 38). The nearer antecedent is *God* but, since the infant Jesus is the central one in this total passage, it is more likely that he is the one of whom she spoke to all those present (Simeon, Joseph, Mary, and others) *who were looking for the redemption of Israel* (v. 38), i.e., the anticipated messianic redemption.

*Verse 39* indicates that after the performance of all these services (the circumcision and naming in the home; the presentation of the first-born in the Temple; the purification of Joseph and Mary in the Temple) the family returned to Nazareth. This is the natural movement of the story: residence in Nazareth; journey to Bethlehem; birth of the baby; performance of the customary services related to childbirth; return to Nazareth where Jesus was to live until he began his public ministry at age thirty. If Luke were the only Gospel, there would be no complication.

There is complication for readers of both Matthew and Luke. The Gospel of Matthew contains the story of the family's flight from Bethlehem to Egypt to escape the wrath of Herod the Great, a subsequent return from Egypt but still not free from danger, since Archelaus (as cruel as his father) had succeeded Herod, and a consequent journey on up the coastal road to Nazareth where Jesus was reared (Matt. 2:13–23). Matthew has no indication of a previous residence of Joseph and Mary in Nazareth, but takes up the birth account at the time of the visit of the Magi (when Jesus was probably around eighteen months old) and tells of the flight and ultimate journey to Nazareth. Luke reports previous residence in and the return to Nazareth. Both report that Jesus grew up in Nazareth, living there until he started his public ministry. Why did Luke not record the flight to Egypt? Of the multiple answers which have been suggested, one of these two would appear to be the most plausible: either Luke's research materials did not contain the story, or if they did it did not meet his purpose in setting the birth in Bethlehem but the home in Nazareth. Since essential parts of a definite "harmonizing" account are lacking in both Gospels, conjecture is the only possible approach. The subjective nature of any conjectural approach cannot assure a solid solution.

## 8. The Childhood Years of Jesus (2:40–52)

*Verse 40:* In Nazareth Jesus grew from babyhood through childhood and youth to the maturity of manhood. His development—physical *(became strong),* mental *(filled with wisdom),* and spiritual *(the favor of God)*—is noted in a summary statement.

There was one experience of vital importance to Luke's account, the beautiful and moving story of Jesus' visit to the Temple at age twelve. It is important because it reflects Jesus' awareness of his unusual relationship to God and to the religion of Israel and the Temple services at that early age.

*Verse 41: Passover:* This ancient festival was a memorial to the deliverance from Egypt in which God began the transformation of a slave people into a people for his redemptive purpose. In reality the people did not think of it merely as a "memorial." They thought of themselves as participating with their ancestors in that mighty act of God. Joseph and Mary made the annual pilgrimage to share the week in Jerusalem.

*Verse 42: When he was twelve:* In many religious things a Jewish boy assumed the responsibility of a man when he became twelve. In reckoning popu-

lation for building synagogues, a boy of twelve was counted as a man. At
twelve he became a "son of Torah" (son of the law) and was expected to
learn it and live by it. This journey to share the Passover in the Temple area
was an experience to be coveted.

*Verses 43–45: When the feast was ended:* Luke's interest here is not in
the events of the week; at the end of Jesus' life there will be another Passover
journey to Jerusalem with a week of events which will bring about his death.
On this occasion the week ended and the caravan of kindred and neighbors
started the return to Galilee (v. 43). Joseph and Mary assumed that Jesus
was with other children in the caravan (v. 44). When night came and the
caravan broke up into family camp groups it became evident that Jesus was
not in the caravan (vv. 44–45). Joseph and Mary returned to Jerusalem and,
after three days of searching, found him in the Temple (vv. 45–46). One
might imagine that it took three days because the last place one would seek
a twelve-year-old boy in the fascinating scenes and markets of Jerusalem
would be the Temple!

*Verses 46–47: Sitting among the teachers:* These were the teachers of the
law—the interpreters of the Jewish Scriptures, history, and religion. The
teaching was usually carried on in the many sections of the covered porches
around the inside walls of the Temple enclosure.

*Listening . . . asking them questions:* Jesus was listening to their teachings.
He was asking questions for further information. Verse 47 indicates that he
was also responding to their questions. They were amazed at his discernment
reflected both in the kind of questions he asked them and his responses to
their questions.

What was the subject of this teaching, questioning, answering? Was it the
law with its multiple phases? Was it the Passover festival which they had
observed? Could it have been the sacrificial services of the Temple and its altar
and Jesus' desire to understand the full purpose of it all? The record gives
us no clue.

*Verse 48: Son, why have you treated us so?* A mother's question! Why have
you done this to us? Why have you caused us all this distress? She was *aston-
ished* to find him so engaged with the teachers. Her anxiety was real and
normal—a boy of twelve lost in Jerusalem for three days on his first visit
from a small village. This was a very human part of the event.

*Your father and I:* Joseph shared Mary's anxiety. Some have found Mary's
reference to Joseph as Jesus' "father" to be inconsistent with the virgin birth
story. It is not. This was the only normal way for her to refer to the relationship of the three of them. Besides, in every way other than physical paternity
Joseph was the father of Jesus.

*Verse 49:* Jesus responded with a question, *How is it that you sought me?*
It can hardly be that he was so lacking in discernment or so insensitive to their
concern that he was surprised that they had sought him. His question may have
meant, "Why did you continue looking for me elsewhere?" In his mind *this*
was the only place they should have expected to find him.

His next question by its construction anticipated the answer "yes." The
question was literally, "You were aware, were you not, that I must be in the
things (or, in the places) of my Father?" Two matters stand out in this question. First, there is an implied distinction between Jesus' relationship to Joseph

as father (Mary's use) and his relationship to God as Father (Jesus' use). He did have a father-son relationship to Joseph, but there was a higher Father-Son relationship which he sustained to God. Second, while the Greek term is ambiguous ("in my Father's places" if it is masculine—"in my Father's affairs" if it is neuter), the reference is unquestionably to God. "In my Father's places" would refer to the Temple buildings; this was God's house; he was God's Son; he belonged here. "In my Father's affairs (or things)" would refer to the religious service and work of God; he belonged in it.

Eighteen years later, after his baptism, the voice from heaven, and the wilderness temptation, he would reflect a full and mature consciousness of his role in relation to God and God's redemptive purpose among men. Luke's only purpose in including this story must have been to show a growing awareness on Jesus' part, even at this age, that he sustained an unusual relationship to God and God's work.

*Verses 50–52:* Joseph and Mary could not grasp the full import of Jesus' words. Mary stored them up in her heart to add to the growing mass of food for meditation. Jesus returned to Nazareth as an obedient boy of twelve. The earlier statement (v. 40) of his growth and development is repeated in verse 52. One phrase is added, *and man.* Among his townsmen he was looked upon with favor.

The eighteen years, the so-called "hidden years," from this age to age thirty can be recovered only hypothetically. Many have tried to ferret out what those years were like. Two sources supply the material for such search: first, what can be known about life in the home of a carpenter, in a village like Nazareth, in the first quarter of the first century A.D.; second, what can be gathered out of the teachings of Jesus which would reflect on the nature of his life during those years—home scenes, community scenes such as funerals and weddings, market scenes, etc. No final answer may be found but the search can be exciting and rewarding.

Here are a few examples: Jesus' parable of the children playing in the marketplace (Luke 7:32) and disagreeing over whether to play "funeral" (making sad music) or "wedding" (making joyful music) may well recall his own experience as a child. He used it to chide the Pharisees for their inconsistency in rejecting John the Baptizer for his nonpublic life and at the same time rejecting Jesus because of his public life. A woman using yeast in making bread (Matt. 13:33; Luke 13:21), the remarkable growth of a tiny mustard seed (Mark 4:30–32; Luke 13:19), a fisherman sorting his catch (Matt. 13:47–50)—these are like pages out of Jesus' life.

## II. PREPARATION FOR THE MINISTRY OF THE UNIVERSAL SAVIOR (3:1–4:13)

There are four elements of preparation for Jesus' public ministry given by Luke: the role and ministry of John the Baptizer; the baptism of Jesus; the genealogy of Jesus; the wilderness temptation. These are the necessary preliminaries for an understanding of Jesus' ministry. The first three are in chapter 3.

### 1. The Role and Ministry of John the Baptizer (3:1–20)

The parallel between John and Jesus which was started in chapters 1–2 continues in chapter 3. John appears first as the one preparing the way for God's Anointed One. The political and religious setting is given.

*Verse 1: Tiberius Caesar:* In Rome the ruler was the Emperor Tiberius who, after thirty years of engagement in military affairs became emperor in A.D. 14. Luke indicates that John started his ministry in the fifteenth year of Tiberius's rule; hence, by his reckoning, A.D. 29.

*Pontius Pilate:* When Herod the Great died in 4 B.C., he left a will which divided his territory into three unequal parts with three of his sons as the rulers. Archelaus received the most important part, including Judea, and assumed the title "ethnarch" meaning "ruler of the nation." He had extreme difficulty in assuming his rule; he was bitterly opposed by his half-brother Herod Antipas and by the Jews in Judea. Finally, due to extreme brutality to the Jews and the Samaritans, he was banished to Gaul in A.D. 6. In place of the Herod family, Rome set up a series of governors or procurators in Judea. Pontius Pilate was the fifth in the series. The duration of his position (A.D. 27–37) indicates that from the viewpoint of Rome he was a competent ruler. From the viewpoint of the Jews his rule was marked by charges of incompetence, insult, violence, and injustice. This was characteristic of the Jews' outlook on all their Roman rulers.

*Herod being tetrarch of Galilee:* Herod Antipas was the son of Herod the Great by his Samaritan wife, Malthrace. *Tetrarch* means ruler of a fourth part; that was about the proportion of the total territory which his father left him. He is best known in the New Testament in relation to the death of John the Baptizer and as one involved in the several hearings in Jesus' trial. Galilee was immediately north of Archelaus's inheritance.

*Philip tetrarch of . . . Ituraea and Trachonitis:* Philip was the son of Herod the Great by his Jerusalem wife, Cleopatra. He is not to be confused with still

[45]

another half-brother, Herod Philip, whose wife (and niece) Herodias left him to marry Herod Antipas and influenced her daughter Salome to request the death of John the Baptizer. Salome was the daughter of Herod Philip and Herodias and, to confuse the family ties a bit more, she later married Philip the tetrarch, her stepfather! Ituraea and Trachonitis, Philip's fourth of the territory, were northeast of Galilee and not as clearly defined as Galilee.

*Lysanias tetrarch of Abilene:* The identity of Lysanias is uncertain. If he had family connections with the Herod line, it is not known. In 40–36 B.C. a Lysanias, son of Ptolemy, had ruled in Ituraea. Some have thought that Luke was referring to him and was therefore wrong. This is most unlikely. An inscription dated between A.D. 14 and 29 identifies a man named Nymphaios as the freedman of the tetrarch Lysanias. That is all that is known of him. This is likely the one to whom Luke referred. *Abilene* was another loosely defined territory north of Ituraea and a bit west-northwest of the modern Damascus.

*Verse 2: In the high-priesthood of Annas and Caiaphas:* This is a strange expression. Annas was appointed high priest by Quirinius in A.D. 7 and held the office until A.D. 14. One of his successors was a son, Eleazar; his son-in-law, Caiaphas, held the office from A.D. 18 to 36. Later, four other sons of Annas held the office. This family record in the office reflects the honored place which Annas held in the minds of the Jews. He was apparently a man of continuing influence following his actual high-priesthood. When Jesus was arrested, his first hearing was before Annas, who questioned him briefly and informally before sending him on to Caiaphas for the official hearing (John 18:12–13).

*The word of God came to John:* It was in this historico-politico-religious atmosphere in Palestine that the messianic movement under John's leadership started. *The word of God came* is a prophetic formula used in the Old Testament of the prophets—"the word of the Lord came" to Micah, Isaiah, Jeremiah, Ezekiel, and others. (See for instance Jer. 1:2, 4; 2:1, etc.; Ezek. 3:16; 6:1.)

*In the wilderness:* Putting together the accounts in all four Gospels, we learn that John's appearance was in the uninhabited territory just north of the Dead Sea, at approximately the point where a much-traveled highway crossed the Jordan River connecting Judea with Galilee and other northern areas. Attempts to associate John with the covenant group at nearby Qumran have not been successful. The important thing was that here was a priest who disassociated himself from the priestly service in the Temple, assumed the role of a prophet, and called the people to spiritual renewal.

*Verse 3: Preaching a baptism:* Baptism was not new to the Jews. Gentiles who adopted the religion of the Jews were required to accept baptism as a part of the initiation. Of the men three things were required: baptism, to symbolize cleansing from the old life; circumcision, to symbolize acceptance into the covenant people; a sacrifice, to indicate that they were giving themselves to the God of Israel. Gentile women were required baptism and a sacrifice. The new and dramatic element in John's message was that he was calling upon *Jews* to be baptized.

*Repentance:* The baptism which John demanded was a baptism marked by *repentance*. The root meaning of the word *repentance* relates to a complete change of mind and, correspondingly, a complete change of conduct. It represents an entirely new outlook on life, conduct, values, and motivations. While the idea of "sorrow for sins" was not a part of the word itself, it was a natural association, and Paul would write later, "For godly grief produces a repentance that leads to salvation . . ." (2 Cor. 7:10).

*For the forgiveness of sins:* The purpose of repentance was to secure *forgiveness.* The Greek word means dismissing or sending away. In common use it was applied to the releasing of water from a reservoir, or to releasing race horses from the starting gate of a race. The word was used in translating the Old Testament from Hebrew to Greek to indicate God's work in separating the penitent from his sins or in covering over his sins. *Sins* is the word for man's personal failure to meet God's requirement for him. This failure was grounded in man's placing his own will and desire above the will and desire of God.

*Verses 4–6:* John identified himself with Isaiah's *voice of one crying in the wilderness* (40:3–5). It is significant that this is a part of the Suffering Servant section of Isaiah. Jesus later identified himself as the Suffering Servant. The imagery of the Isaiah passage is that of citizens preparing a road over which their king would travel to visit their part of his realm. In preparing the road they would tear down the high places—*every mountain and hill shall be brought low*—and use the soil to fill up the low places—*every valley shall be filled.* The road would be made straight—*the crooked shall be made straight*—and smooth—*the rough ways shall be made smooth.* So John saw himself as a wilderness voice calling to the people to make a spiritual road in their hearts because the messianic king was coming.

A comparison of the use of the Isaiah passage in the other Gospels reveals Luke's interest in the universal aspect of the redemptive work of Christ. John has "make straight the way of the Lord" (1:23). Matthew and Mark both have "prepare the way of the Lord, make his paths straight" (Matt. 3:3; Mark 1:3). All three use only enough of the passage to indicate John's preparatory work. Luke adds another one and one-half verses indicating how the way is to be prepared (v. 5) and the result of the preparation (v. 6), which is that *all flesh shall see the salvation of God.* The Hebrew text of Isaiah 40:5 has at this point "the glory of the Lord." Luke is using the Greek translation of the Hebrew text, the Septuagint, here. The "glory" of God is the full shining forth of all that he is and does. The "salvation" of God is the mightiest part of his action in providing redemption. Isaiah saw this as reaching even to the Gentiles. Luke, too, saw that, and made it central in his Gospel.

Verses 7–14 show that the new messianic movement John had started met an enthusiastic welcome. People responded eagerly and *multitudes . . . came out to be baptized by him.* John detected evidences of insincerity on the part of many who came. In harsh terms he warned them of the need for sincerity in repentance and demanded a life demonstrating that sincerity.

*Verse 7: Brood of vipers:* The people hurrying to baptism reminded John of a family of snakes wriggling along ahead of a brush fire. The "brush fire" was the approaching judgment of God which would be a part of the Savior's confrontation of man with God.

*Verse 8: Bear fruits that befit repentance:* John demanded a life demonstrating the genuineness of repentance and confession (Matt. 3:6) of sin. Examples of genuineness follow in verses 10–14.

*We have Abraham as our father:* This is not a "straw man" argument. John had likely debated with many the question of whether descent from Abraham, who had a covenant relationship with God, gave them that same covenant relationship. Jesus, and later Paul, would carry on this same argument that physical descent from Abraham did not produce "spiritual sons of Abraham," that is, sons of God. With biting sarcasm, John said that God could turn the stones there in the wilderness into better *children of Abraham* than they were!

*Verse 9: Even now the axe is laid to the root of the trees:* This is a symbol of judgment. The coming of the Messiah meant both salvation and judgment.

*Verses 10–14:* Three groups of people inquired of John what he would accept as evidence of sincerity warranting baptism. He answered each with evidence related to their particular situation in life:

First, of *the multitudes* (v. 10) he required an attitude of compassion issuing in help to a needy fellowman. This is the meaning of the words, *he who has two coats, let him share with him who has none.*

Second, of the *tax collectors* (v. 12) he required honesty in carrying out their business transactions. That is the meaning of the charge, *collect no more than is appointed you.*

Third, of the Jewish mercenaries serving in the Roman army as *soldiers* (v. 14) he required that they be content with the wages agreed upon for their service and that they *rob no one by violence or by false accusation.* This, too, involved integrity in their office and honesty in dealings with their fellowman.

*Verses 15–17* reflect perplexity on the part of the people. They wondered if John might not be the Messiah for whom they waited. John made it clear that he was not the Messiah but that the Messiah was coming after him. He was so much greater, that John felt unworthy of performing for him the task of the lowest in a staff of household servants, i.e., the untying of his sandals.

John had been baptizing the people with *water* to symbolize the cleansing from sin after turning from disobedience to obedience. The one coming after him would baptize *with the Holy Spirit and with fire.* Opinion is divided on the meaning of this expression. Some interpreters understand one baptizing: *with the Holy Spirit and with fire* meaning baptism in the purifying Holy Spirit— an act of salvation. Other interpreters understand two baptizings: baptism with the Holy Spirit, meaning salvation; baptism with fire, meaning judgment.

In the Scriptures fire is used as a symbol both of God's presence and of judgment. Because of the judgment illustration in the following verse (v. 17), it seems to be a judgment reference here. For some the coming of the Messiah meant salvation (baptism with the Holy Spirit); for some it meant judgment (baptism with fire). John used the illustration of the threshing floor. This was a level place on a hill in order to catch the breeze. The grain was beaten or trampled until well broken up. Then the farmer would toss it with his *winnowing fork* so the wind would blow the chaff to one side and the wheat could be gathered into the granary. The chaff would then be burned. *Unquenchable fire* is fire than cannot be extinguished. In other places the phrase appears as one of the dreadful expressions related to the punishment of those who reject God. The coming of the Christ faced men with decision; their decision determined whether their relationship to him was one of salvation or judgment.

*Verses 18–20* serve as a summary statement concerning John's ministry and destiny at the hands of Herod Antipas. Verse 19 is a preview of John's arrest, imprisonment, and execution, which came some time later. Just how much later is uncertain; the Gospel writers relate it in connection with the guilty fears of Herod when he heard of Jesus' success—he thought Jesus was John the Baptizer alive again! (The account is in Mark 6:14–29, Matt. 14:1–12, Luke 9:7–9.)

## 2. The Baptism of Jesus (3:21–22)

Luke reports the baptism of Jesus very briefly. Interesting additional elements are in the other Gospels but cannot be considered here.

Jesus went from Nazareth to ask baptism at the hands of John. Perhaps two motives prompted his action: he wanted to identify himself with the new messianic movement John had started; he wanted to take his place with sinful humanity whom he had come to redeem.

Luke states that Jesus *was praying* at the time of his baptism. This information is absent from the other three Gospels, and points up another characteristic of the Gospel of Luke: it contains more on Jesus' prayer life than any other Gospel.

At Jesus' baptism startling phenomena took place. The heaven was opened; the Holy Spirit descended upon Jesus; God spoke to him. The Greek word translated *heaven* is practically equivalent to our expression "the skies." The imagery is that of the skies opening like a curtain. Through that opening, as if from heaven itself, *the Holy Spirit descended . . . in bodily form, as a dove.* All four Gospels report the Holy Spirit's descent as a dove, but only Luke has the phrase, *in bodily form.* That may be Luke's way of indicating to his readers just how the Holy Spirit became visible. Matthew reports that Jesus saw the Spirit's descent (3:16), and John reports that John the Baptizer saw it (1:32). No indication is given of others witnessing it.

The dove is a fitting symbol of the Holy Spirit. The first reference to the Spirit of God in the Bible (Gen. 1:2) is to his hovering like a bird over the chaos out of which God brought light and order. The dove held a very prominent place in the Jewish sacrifices.

*A voice came from heaven:* This experience was to be repeated several times in the life of Jesus. Probably it was what the rabbis referred to as the Bath Qol, a Hebrew term meaning "daughter-voice" or "daughter of the voice." In our experience the closest concept is the word "echo"—a voice which comes strangely from the atmosphere around us but cannot be located. The Jewish people held generally that with the cessation of the prophets God had ceased to speak to men. Many of the rabbis did not accept this. They insisted that God still spoke to men and reported experiences in which he spoke to them. Their description of what it was like was that of the Bath Qol defined above. Whether or not this was the manifestation, we must not become so fascinated by the phenomenon of the voice that we miss the words which were spoken. That is the important part of the experience.

*Thou art my beloved Son; with thee I am well pleased:* While there is much debate about the origin and significance of these words, their source appears to be two passages of Hebrew Scripture generally regarded as in some sense messianic—Psalm 2:7 and Isaiah 42:1. If this is the case, they identify Jesus as the Suffering Servant (Isa. 42:1) Son of God (Ps. 2:7).

The experience of Jesus in the Temple at age twelve showed that even then he possessed an awareness of an unusual relationship to God and to the sacrificial services of the religion of Israel. Now he had come to identify himself with the new messianic movement. The voice indicated to him the precise nature of his relationship to God and to the religion of Israel. He was to realize his role as the Son of God after the pattern of the Suffering Servant described by Isaiah. It was through his suffering that the redemptive work of God would reach its dramatic climax. With that consuming realization, Jesus withdrew from the company of men after his baptism for forty days in the wilderness.

### 3. The Genealogy of Jesus (3:23–38)

While Mark and Matthew proceed immediately to the wilderness experience of Jesus, Luke inserts a statement of Jesus' age at this time—about thirty (v. 23)—and his genealogy. From the earliest days of Gospel study, interpreters have been challenged by and have debated the meaning of the strikingly different genealogies of Jesus in Matthew and in Luke. Matthew's (1:1–17) is introduced by the statement that Jesus Christ was the son of David. It then begins with Abraham and traces the lineage through David and Solomon down to "Joseph the husband of Mary, of whom Jesus was born, who is called Christ." Luke, on the other hand, begins with Jesus—supposedly the son of Joseph—and traces the lineage from some man named Heli back through Nathan to David, on through Abraham, and all the way back to *Adam, the son of God* (v. 38). At only a few names do the two lines touch.

Many interpreters have concluded that there is no satisfactory solution to the problem of reconciling the two, and that it is not worthwhile to try. Many others have regarded an understanding as valuable and have worked out different solutions.

(1) The view that Matthew gives Joseph's *physical* lineage and Luke gives his *legal* lineage. Julius Africanus, who died about A.D. 240, wrote a letter to Aristides explaining his interpretation of the genealogies. Only a few fragments of the letter are extant but the fourth-century church historian, Eusebius, endorsed the view and explained it in his famous history of the church. Africanus used the Jewish custom of levirate marriage by which a man would marry his brother's widow to have children by her *for his brother*. He started with Jesus and moved backward:

Matthew's list: Jesus—Joseph—Jacob—Matthan.
Luke's list: Jesus—Joseph—Heli—Melchi.

Africanus's copy of Luke either did not have two who in our New Testament stand between Heli and Melchi (Matthat and Levi) or he omitted them to make his system work.

By his reckoning, Matthan and Melchi were brothers by the same mother but different fathers. Matthan married a woman whose name by tradition was Estha. By her he had a son named Jacob. After Matthan died, his brother Melchi married Estha and by her had a son named Heli. In time Heli married and died. His half brother Jacob married his widow and by her had a son named Joseph. *Physically* Joseph was the son of Jacob; *legally* he was the son of Heli since Jacob's levirate marriage to the widow was to have children *for Heli*.

Jacob traced his lineage to Abraham through David's son, Solomon. Heli traced his lineage to Abraham through David's son, Nathan. This accounts for the difference in the two lists and indicates that through both the *physical* line of Joseph (through Jacob) and the *legal* line of Joseph (through Heli) Mary's son, Jesus, had a rightful claim to the throne of David.

In addition to endorsing this view, Eusebius held that Mary's line, though not given, was also through David since by Mosaic law people had to marry within their own tribe. He does not cite his authority. It is probably Numbers 36:6-12, which contains laws requiring marriage within one's own tribe in order to keep the girl's inheritance within her tribe. This related to the division of the land when Israel entered Canaan following the exodus. Later, the need no longer existed, and after the Babylon captivity and the fragmentation of the tribes, it is extremely doubtful if it was practiced.

(2) The view that Matthew gives Joseph's *legal* lineage and Luke gives his *physical* lineage. As in Africanus's view, the purpose of this approach is to indicate Jesus' rightful claim to the throne of David. By it Solomon's line failed in Jechoniah, according to Jeremiah 22:30. In Matthew's list, that line crossed over to Nathan's line in Shealtiel and Zerubbabel (1:12), who are to be identified with Zerubbabel and Shealtiel in Luke 3:27 so from that point on the lines are the same. At the Jacob-Heli point in the two lines the levirate marriage law is again used but with the result that the "Heli line" was the *physical* line and the "Jacob line" was the *legal* line of Joseph.

(3) The view that Matthew gives *Joseph's physical* line through his father, Jacob, and that Luke gives *Mary's physical* line through her father (or grandfather), Heli. Robertson[1] states that this view is found as early as Eusebius. The citation which he gives in Eusebius, however, is *not* this view; it is the Julius Africanus view explained above. Eusebius's only statement concerning Mary is that she, too, must have been descended through David, due to the Mosaic inheritance laws of marriage within one's own tribe. The Eusebius explanation clearly understands both genealogies to be through Joseph. A major reason for this view is that in Luke's list Joseph's name appears without the Greek article—"of Joseph," not "of the Joseph,"—while every other name in the list has the article, i.e., "of the Heli," "of the Matthat," all the way back to "of the Adam." By usual Greek usage this places Joseph in a category separate from all the other names. If this is the case, his name belongs within the parenthesis. The reading will be *Jesus . . . being the son (as was supposed, of Joseph) . . . of Heli, the son of Matthat,* etc. The meaning will be that while Jesus was thought of as the son of Joseph he was really descended through Mary and her male line began with Heli, her father or grandfather. It was common practice to reckon a woman's lineage through the male side of her family.

It is difficult to endorse any of the views and feel fully satisfied. The third one has the least complications. The major pitfall to be avoided is that of becoming so engrossed in this question that one misses the purpose which each Gospel writer had in the genealogy he used. Matthew desired to show Jesus as the son of David and thus to demonstrate his rightful place as the messianic king. Through David he traced Jesus back to Abraham, the father of the Jewish people and their religion. This was meaningful for the Jews, and Jesus'

1. A. T. Robertson, *A Harmony of the Gospels* (New York: Harper and Brothers Publishers, 1922), p. 3, footnote.

claim to the throne would be official through Joseph as Jesus' "foster father" just as though Joseph were his real father.

On the other hand, Luke desired to show Jesus' relationship not just to the Jewish people and Abraham, but to the entire human race. For that reason he traced the line on back beyond Abraham to Adam, the father of the human race and *the son of God*. This is another indication of Luke's universal interest.

## 4. The Wilderness Temptation of Jesus (4:1–13)

Immediately after his baptism, Jesus withdrew into the wilderness for a forty-day period of retirement from people. He wanted to be alone while he wrestled with the significance of the words, "Thou art my beloved Son; with thee I am well pleased" (3:22), seeking to know the nature of his messianic role.

*Verse 1: Full of the Holy Spirit . . . led by the Spirit:* These expressions indicate the motivation in Jesus' withdrawal. *Full of the Holy Spirit* everywhere in the Scriptures means to be completely controlled by the Holy Spirit. Mark's characteristically abrupt style says that the Spirit "drove him out into the wilderness" (1:12, literally, "cast him out"), while Matthew states that he "was led up into the wilderness *by* the Spirit" (4:1, author's translation). Luke, however, has "he was being led *in* the Spirit in the wilderness" (author's translation). Of the three, Luke's total expression most clearly indicates voluntary action in Jesus' following the Spirit's leading, rather than being compelled to do what he did not wish to do.

*Verse 2: Forty days in the wilderness:* No particular significance is indicated in the *forty days*. Through frequent appearance in Jewish religious history it had come to be a rather stylized term for "a long time." Here, however, there is nothing to indicate that anything other than forty days is meant. *In the wilderness* is not definitely located geographically. The place of withdrawal for meditation was somewhere in the general area of the baptism experience.

*He ate nothing in those days:* Mark's very brief account contains nothing of Jesus' experience other than that he was tempted by Satan and served by angels (1:13–14). Matthew 4:2 uses the religious word "fasted." Luke 4:2 uses the emphatic Greek double negative "he did not eat nothing" to make a very strong positive assertion. Some interpreters understand that the reference is to food in the ordinary sense, and that Jesus did eat whatever was naturally available to him—fruit, nuts, etc. Luke's statement, however, suggests total abstinence from food. It does not appear to be a planned action—that is, denying his physical appetite and need as a means to a spiritual end. It was rather that matters of the spirit weighed so heavily upon him that physical need was not in his consciousness. The question of how long a person can survive without food belongs in a category different from this experience of Jesus.

At the end of this period, Jesus became keenly aware of his hunger and need for food. At that point both Matthew and Luke report the temptation to turn stones to bread. They have a different order for the other two temptations. Matthew—turn stones to bread; leap from the Temple wall; bend the knee to the devil; Luke—turn stones to bread; bend the knee to the devil; leap from the Temple wall. Luke's order is more natural in geographical sequence, i.e., the first two in the wilderness, the third in Jerusalem. Matthew's order is

more natural in *logical* sequence; Jesus moves from the lowest level of temptation at the point of physical hunger to the highest level of temptation at the
point of the question of supreme authority in his life—God or Satan.

There is little profit in exploring these temptations as to their objective or
subjective nature. Did the devil appear to Jesus as objectively as the appearance reported by Martin Luther who threw his inkwell at him? Did the devil
lead Jesus objectively and actually up to Jerusalem and to the wall of the
Temple? Did he lead him to the top of some mountain from which Jesus could
objectively and physically see all the kingdoms of the world at his feet and himself the ruler over all of them? The temptations were just as real and as
significant whether they happened in fact, or were all a part of Jesus' meditation, wrestling in his mind with the idea of fulfilling his role as the Messiah
after the pattern of the Suffering Servant of Isaiah. This is the important part
which must not be lost in consideration of other areas of interest.

### (1) Temptation at the physical level (4:3–4)

*Verse 3: If you are the Son of God:* The grammatical construction is that of
taking for granted a fact rather than raising doubts. Precisely, the translation
is, "Since you are the Son of God." The temptation was not to doubt that he
was the Son of God; it was to use his power as the Son of God in such a way
as to avoid the way of suffering.

*Command this stone to become bread:* The round, flat, brown stones in the
wilderness had the size, shape, and color of the bread used then. To a hungry
man the stones brought up the vision of bread. The temptation was that as the
Son of God Jesus should not have to suffer hunger as other men did; he could
relieve that suffering by the power that was his.

*Verse 4:* Jesus' response is a quotation from Deuteronomy 8:3. While the
grammatical construction, *it is written,* is a way of introducing quotations from
the Hebrew Scriptures, it also carries a very strong assertion of the abiding
truth of that which was quoted—precisely, "it has been and it stands written."

*'Man shall not live by bread alone':* By this quotation Jesus indicated that
bread was important to him; he had to eat just as other men did. But *bread
alone* was not the important thing, there was something more important. Luke
did not include what that "something" was, but Matthew did. It was "every
word coming from the mouth of God." The most recent *word* from God was
that voice from heaven indicating Jesus' way as the way of suffering. Jesus
interpreted this temptation as temptation to avoid that way of suffering. As a
man he would trust himself to God's way as other men had to do.

### (2) Temptation at the power level (4:5–8)

This temptation was at the level of political power. In imagery, see Jesus on
a high mountain looking far out over the landscape with his mind going on to
envision the political kingdoms of the world at his feet. That was the kind of
Messiah the people wanted, one who would lead them in revolt against Rome
to give their nation the important place they desired it to have among the
nations of the world.

*Verses 6–7: To you I will give all this authority:* It was commonly held that
the devil's area of authority and operation was in the world. Whether he
actually had the authority and power he claimed is a debated question. There

are times when his claim is rather convincing! His offer was that he would deliver the world to Jesus for him to rule. His condition was that Jesus come to the place of authority by the devil's way—*if you, then, will worship me*—that is, "yield to my will, accept my way."

Jesus recognized the temptation and its import. He was here in the world to win men to be in reality the sons of God. Could he not win them more easily by yielding to their desire for a political, revolutionary Messiah who would deliver them from Rome and establish them as a nation as they had been in the golden days of David and Solomon? But this would have been to turn from the hard way of suffering pointed out at his baptism as God's way for him.

*Verse 8:*

> 'You shall worship the Lord your God,
> and him only shall you serve.'

Jesus' response was another quotation from Deuteronomy, this time from 6:13. Two things stand out in the answer. One, only to God is man to bend the knee; two, only to God is man to render service. As God is undivided, he wants an undivided worshiper and servant. Jesus knew that he could not take two ways to his messianic role. It was either take the power structure desired by the people, or take the harder way, the way of suffering which was God's way. He chose God's way.

### (3) Temptation at the spectacular level (4:9–12)

This might be labeled the "Faith Level" because it focused on Jesus' committing himself in trust to God's way. All the temptations, however, are related to his committing himself to God's way. This one was the temptation to make a spectacular display of himself and his power in order to win the people to follow him.

*Verses 9–11:* The scene was the Temple in Jerusalem with Jesus standing on the highest point and the people in the open court far below. There they were in their half-hearted seeking for God and longing for his Messiah. The temptation came in the words of one of the most beautiful of their worship songs, Psalm 91:11–12. If he would leap from the wall, God would charge the angels to bear him up so he would float softly down into the midst of the people without the slightest injury. They would acclaim him as the Messiah who had come right out of the heavens. Some interpreters have understood that Jesus' place on the *pinnacle of the Temple* was a place occupied every morning by a priest who scanned the heavens to see if the Messiah might be appearing on that day and, if so, to announce it to the people below.

*Verse 12:* Jesus interpreted this as another temptation to take the easy way and avoid the way of suffering. He rejected the temptation by another quotation from Deuteronomy (6:16), *you shall not tempt the Lord your God,* that is, you shall not presume upon God's favor by putting him to a test to see if he will keep his word. Jesus was a better interpreter of the Scripture than the devil was. He knew that spiritual ends can but rarely be accomplished by unspiritual means. He knew that the promise in Psalm 91 was not for one who made a display of himself or challenged God. It was for one committed to the hard way which God had appointed him, and its assurance was of God's presence and help as he walked that way. Jesus rejected every temptation to take an easy way.

*Verse 13* indicates that when Jesus had successfully met and rejected the temptations, *the devil . . . departed from him until an opportune time.* The Greek text precisely reads "unto a season." This was not the only time Jesus faced the temptation to take the easy way. We are shown other instances when he faced such temptations as these; the devil would return.

Some interpreters understand this temptation section to be a representative summary of all the temptations Jesus faced throughout his ministry. Others understand it to be one experience immediately following his baptism and the final step to the beginning of his public ministry. The latter appears to be the more likely. Having rejected every temptation to avoid the way of suffering, Jesus set his feet upon that road of suffering which led ultimately and inevitably to Jerusalem and the cross.

## III. THE MINISTRY OF THE UNIVERSAL SAVIOR IN GALILEE
### (4:14–9:50)

In amount of material, the part of Luke which covers Jesus' ministry is far out of proportion to the other sections. It contains the entire sweep of his public ministry from its Galilean beginning to its Judean ending. For this reason, the ministry of Jesus has been divided into three sections (see outline). The time covered by his ministry has been the subject of much debate. Some interpreters have held that, going by the synoptic Gospels, the entire ministry may have been a year or less. When, however, the Gospel of John is taken into account, the time appears to have been much longer; the length of his ministry involves the difficult problem of John's several Passover events. How many Passovers did Jesus attend during the course of his ministry? Two? Three? How were they related to the beginning of his ministry? Depending on the answers to these questions, his ministry may have covered something over three years. A period from two and one-half years to three and one-half years as the outside limits is about as close as one may hope to arrive with satisfaction.

In John 1:35–2:11 there is a report of Jesus' beginning a ministry in Judea immediately after his baptism, and of his gathering an initial group of disciples before he returned to Galilee. This is not in the synoptic Gospels, whose earliest record of Jesus' ministry begins in Galilee. Luke's account of it is in 4:14–9:50.

### 1. Rejected at Nazareth (4:14–30)

Luke 4:14–15 reports Jesus' return to Galilee and his being empowered by the Holy Spirit. He taught in the synagogues in Galilee and the report of his work and teaching *went out through all the surrounding country.* This is a summary report with no synagogues named. John 2:1–11 contains a report of Jesus' action in Cana, and 2:12 contains a report of a brief stay in Capernaum. How and whether these can be fitted into the Lukan reference is not certain. These are the only possible references to a ministry prior to his return to his hometown.

Luke 4:16–30 records the very important appearance of Jesus in Nazareth. It is important because it reflects Jesus' understanding of his role as the Anointed One and the nature of the message he was sent to proclaim. It was that understanding and message which caused his hometown people to reject him and infuriated them to the point that they attempted to stone him to death.

*Verse 16:* Upon his return to Nazareth after his baptism and the beginning of his ministry, he went to the synagogue on the sabbath *as his custom was,* that is, either as he had done all of his life there or as was his custom in his public ministry—to make the synagogue his base of operation. Apparently at the place in the service for the "lesson"—sometimes referred to as a "brief sermon"—he was asked by the superintendent to take the service as a guest rabbi would have been asked.

*Verses 17–19:* He unrolled the scroll of Isaiah until he came to the part now marked 61:1–2. Whether this was providentially the scheduled passage from the prophets for that sabbath or whether it was Jesus' deliberate selection is not clear. In either event, it was a perfect passage for his purpose. The quotation in Luke is from the Greek Septuagint. The Septuagint version was a rather free translation of the Hebrew text, and Luke's version is a rather free reading of the Septuagint text. This accounts for the differences in the wording between Luke and Isaiah.

The following major emphases in the Isaiah text stand out in Jesus' use. The Spirit of the Lord had anointed his messenger; the message was one of good news to the downtrodden; the work was that of release to those bound in all the miseries of life; the proclamation was that this was a time acceptable to God for man's release and liberty. Jesus stopped reading in the middle of verse 2 in Isaiah, omitting the reference to judgment. He would include that later.

*Verses 20–22:* Having finished the reading, Jesus returned the scroll to the attendant and sat down according to the custom in teaching. All the people were watching intently because they knew him and had heard of his ministry in other places.

*Today this scripture has been fulfilled in your hearing:* With this startling announcement he began. They were seeing the fulfillment of that Scripture. *He* was the Anointed One of whom the prophet wrote. *He* was the one who was to carry out all of this ministry.

At first their response was one of wonder. They were impressed by the *gracious words*—words of grace, or beauty—which came from him. They wondered that he—known to them as *Joseph's son,* the carpenter's son—should be the one to fulfill the role of the servant in Isaiah. Likely they were accustomed to him, too, as an artisan, probably a carpenter, in the village. Their reaction changed from wonder to fury when they came to understand what he was saying and what he meant by it.

*Verses 23–24:* Jesus recognized that people would be skeptical about his claim and his work. He used two proverbs and applied them to himself in this situation: *Physician, heal yourself;* and *No prophet is acceptable in his own country.* The second one is in the other three Gospels (Mark 6:4; Matt. 13:57; John 4:44); the wording is slightly different in all four Gospels and three different settings are involved: in Luke, Jesus' first visit to Nazareth; in Mark and Matthew, Jesus' last visit to Nazareth; in John, Jesus' leaving Samaria to go into Galilee.

The first proverb is recorded only by Luke of the New Testament Gospel writers, but both are in the recently discovered Coptic Gospel According to Thomas (Logion 31):

> No prophet is acceptable in his village;
> No physician heals those who know him.

The difference between the Thomas version of the "physician" proverb and Luke's version is thought-provoking. Did Thomas have a separate source for it or did he change Luke's version for some reason?

Jesus referred to reports of his work in Capernaum and the probable desire of the people of Nazareth to see him do the same things in his hometown. There is no indication that he did any works in Nazareth to please or satisfy them. Throughout his life he refused to do unusual works merely to satisfy the curiosity of people.

*Verses 25–27* demonstrate Jesus' understanding of the message he was to proclaim. In essence it was that God's favor and mercy were for Gentiles as well as Jews. He used Jewish history to illustrate instances in which God's mercy was bestowed upon Gentiles *rather than* Jews. Elijah had been sent by God to help a Gentile widow in Sidon; even though there were many Jewish widows, not one of them was included in Elijah's ministry (1 Kings 17:1, 8–16). Elisha also had been sent by God to help the Gentile leper, Naaman of Syria; even though there were many Jewish lepers, not one of them was included in Elisha's ministry (2 Kings 5:1–14).

This was an unusual use of events in the history of God's dealings with men through his prophets. Now, Jesus was saying that God had anointed him to go and proclaim his mercy to men, and that included the Gentiles. God's mercy was not to be limited to the Jews.

*Verse 28* indicates that the villagers understood Jesus' message and were infuriated. They could not accept the idea of God's favor and mercy for any except the Jews. They had departed from God's purpose in making them a people to whom he would reveal himself in redemptive work and through whom that revelation would be passed on to their Gentile neighbors.

*Verse 29:* The villagers likely regarded Jesus' words as blasphemy and, hence, worthy of death by stoning. Although the carrying out of a sentence of capital punishment had been taken away from the Sanhedrin and reserved for Roman official action (John 18:31), there are evidences of mob violence intending death in several places in the New Testament (John 8:59; Acts 7:54–60). This appears to be what they intended to do in this instance. They rushed Jesus from the synagogue and out to a steep hill from which they could hurl him downward, as though into a stoning pit prepared for that purpose. When the body was broken and helpless from the fall they would continue hurling stones until life was beaten from the body, and the pile of stones would be his burial place, a silent and gruesome warning to others to avoid the conduct which resulted in such a death.

*Verse 30:* That was their plan. *But passing through the midst of them he went away:* It is not clear whether Luke understood this as a miracle in which they were prevented from carrying out their purpose, or whether it was his way of abbreviating the account, thus emphasizing that the experience terminated in rejection. One can well imagine that if John had included this event in his Gospel, he would have written, "For his hour was not yet come!"

### 2. Accepted at Capernaum (4:31–44)

As previously indicated (see comment on 4:14), John 2:12 mentions a short visit of Jesus to Capernaum with his mother, brothers, and disciples.

If that is related to this trip to Capernaum it is not clear. If it has a parallel in Luke, it is likely the one of Luke 4:23 before the Nazareth episode. Matthew does not contain the Nazareth episode, but he reports that after John the Baptizer was arrested Jesus went to Galilee and then he adds, "and leaving Nazareth he went and dwelt in Capernaum" (4:13), suggesting permanent residence. Matthew relates the move to Isaiah 9:1-2, "Galilee of the Gentiles—the people who sat in darkness have seen a great light . . ." (Matt. 4:15–16). Luke makes no reference to this as a permanent move but it appears to have been such. This was the center of Jesus' traveling about until the fateful journey to Jerusalem.

*Verses 31–32:* He taught in the synagogue every sabbath. The people were moved by his teaching and the personal sense of authority which distinguished it from the teaching method of the rabbis who cited long lists of rabbinic authorities to support their teaching.

Verses 33–37 contain the first of the many miracles in the Gospel of Luke. These miracles belong to several categories: (1) physical sickness of many different types—fever, leprosy, paralysis, blindness, speech impediment, hemorrhage, seizure, dropsy, spinal curvature; (2) nature—stilling a storm; feeding the five thousand; a catch of fish; (3) mental and/or spiritual condition—the Gadarene; (4) death—widow's son; Jairus's daughter. The concept of miracle in the New Testament is *an event in which God acts in a way that transcends normal operation of natural law.* In Jesus' use, miracles had a twofold thrust: they relieved human need and suffering; they stimulated faith that God was working through Jesus as the Messiah. The first of these meanings is emphasized in all the Gospels; the second is rarely pointed out in the synoptics, but it is a major emphasis in John.

Acceptance of miracle required a commitment of faith even for those who witnessed them. Jesus' "Beelzebul controversy" with the Jewish religious leaders (Luke 11:14–26) came about because they *saw* his miracles—they could not deny that supernatural power was producing them—but they were so opposed to him that they would not *admit* that God's power was behind them, so they attributed them to the power of Satan. Acceptance of miracle as a part of Jesus' work still requires the commitment of faith. The late C. S. Lewis liked to say that when you posit the kind of God revealed in the Old and New Testaments, you run "the risk of a few miracles."[1] So it is in Luke.

*Verse 33* describes a man in the synagogue at Capernaum as one *who had the spirit of an unclean demon.* This introduces the phenomenon of "demon possession." While it is a marked phenomenon elsewhere in the New Testament (Mark, for example), there is a minimum of it in Luke. An approach to the total phenomenon requires a study of all the New Testament passages on it; that is not possible in this exposition of Luke. It is necessary to observe that all of the "demon" stories in the New Testament do not fit into one category. In some of them the people attribute simple physical illness to demons. For instance, a person having a fever would attribute it to an evil spirit, that is, an outside agent causing it. Our medical understanding today would say he had a germ, or a virus, or "a bug." So it was with many cases of blindness, paralysis, deafness, etc.

---

1. C. S. Lewis, *Miracles* (New York: The Macmillan Company, 1947), p. 128.

But not all the accounts of demon possession can be fitted into that category. There are cases in which the condition appears to be more spiritual than physical. In other cases the person has been so given over to evil that it has affected his mental or physical actions. So the search for a complete solution to the problem of demon possession is still open-ended.

*Verse 34:* Probably through Jesus' teaching in the synagogue, this man detected in Jesus one who was set against all of .the "uncleanness" that was in him, the "demon" that drove him in his own conduct.

*What have you to do with us . . . ?* This was an idiom of the day meaning "what do we have in common?" Here was the Anointed One of God face-to-face with one driven by evil. What, really, did they have in common? They had this: Jesus had come into the world to destroy the very evil which drove this man.

*Have you come to destroy us?* The man recognized Jesus as *the Holy One of God.* He knew that in that presence his evil stood condemned. The word *us* appears here to refer only to people like this man, not to a plurality of demons as in some of the miracle stories. He and all like him stood condemned and deserving judgment from *the Holy One of God.*

*Verse 35:* Jesus rebuked the man and charged him to stop his crying *out with a loud voice* (v. 33) and disturbing the people present. Then Jesus appeared to address himself directly to the personalized evil within the man: *come out of him.* The man fell to the floor probably in a convulsion-type of seizure. When he recovered, all evidence of the presence of the demon in him was gone and there was no evidence of physical harm from the convulsion.

In what category does this story belong? Is it a case of physical malfunction of some sort attributed to a demon? Is it a case of mental aberration of some sort attributed to a demon? Is it a case of one so given over to evil that the result has become a matter of physical or mental function? Evidences for a total and unqualified answer are not available. This is clear: in the presence of Jesus, evil of every type was challenged.

*Verses 36–37:* The people who witnessed this event were amazed at the *authority and power* of Jesus. They deliberated over the kind of *word* from Jesus that brought such healing. The report spread far and rapidly.

*Verses 38–39* contain another miracle of a very different kind. From the synagogue Jesus went to the home of Simon Peter. *Simon's mother-in-law was ill with a high fever.* Mark and Matthew simply report "a fever"; Luke alone reports the serious nature of the case. *They*—apparently the family—*besought him for her.* If he had healed others, even a man with convulsions, they believed he could heal her of her fever. He did so, and her recovery was so complete that no convalescence was needed: *immediately she rose and served* those present. Again, Mark and Matthew simply report her healing and service. It is Dr. Luke who reports the immediacy of recovery without need of any convalescence.

*Verses 40–41* report additional healing by Jesus *when the sun was setting.* The healing of the man in the synagogue and of Simon's mother-in-law in the home took place on the sabbath. By Jewish traditional laws it was illegal to practice healing of any kind on the sabbath. To complicate the matter, it was also illegal to carry a burden of any kind on the sabbath. But the sabbath ended at sunset. When it was legal to carry their sick ones, many people came to Simon's house bringing those sick *with various diseases*. He healed them with a touch of his hand.

According to the many healing stories in the Gospels, Jesus' method varied. Sometimes he only spoke; at other times he touched a person as a stimulus to faith. Sometimes by action he focused the attention of the individual on what he proposed to do: touching blind eyes, lifting up a paralyzed arm, thrusting his fingers into deaf ears to indicate his intent to "open" them. The very variety of method lends credence to the stories as authentic.

*Verse 41:* Among those healed that night were others who were described as having demons. He silenced their crying out that he was the Son of God. Perhaps it was their intuitive contrast of their characters with his which caused them to identify him. It is an interesting phenomenon that often the sinful people recognized Jesus' true character when the religious leaders did not.

*He . . . would not allow them to speak:* For some reason Jesus did not welcome their crying out that he was the Anointed One. His reasons are not stated. Theological implications of far-reaching significance have been found in the idea of a "messianic secret" in the synoptics. The "messianic secret" idea has developed along two lines. One is the view that Jesus himself kept his messiahship a secret until he was ready to reveal it, first to the Twelve, and then to the people. Another line of thought is that the messianic secret did not originate with Jesus at all but was a product of Mark in developing the view that: (1) Jesus at first did not think of himself as the Messiah; (2) he looked for the coming of another as the Son of Man; (3) only near the end of his ministry did he come to think of himself as the Messiah.

In 1901, W. Wrede published a work entitled *Das Messiasgeheimnis in den Evangelien* ("The Messianic Secret in the Gospels"). While, in the form in which Wrede presented it, his thesis has been largely rejected, it still continues to exert a great influence on the study of the synoptic Gospels in general and the Gospel of Mark in particular. The idea of a messianic secret has been based on the instances in which Jesus tried to silence the idea that he was the Messiah. Some examples: the silencing of demons which were shouting his identity (Mark 1:24–25, 34; 3:11–12); silence imposed in relation to the reporting of miracles (Mark 1:44; 5:43; 7:36; 8:26); the silencing of the disciples after the confession at Caesarea Philippi (Mark 8:30); and the transfiguration (Mark 9:9). There is also the withdrawal of Jesus from the crowd (Mark 7:24; 9:30), and his delivery of "the mystery of the kingdom" to the disciples only through the miracles (Mark 4:10–12). Vincent Taylor has a brief but cogent refutation of the theory in his commentary on Mark.[1]

Whatever may be the problem in the total of the Gospels, this instance and some similar to it seem to reflect no more than the growing inconvenience of the crowds which were responding to reports about Jesus and were following him to see him perform miracles—following in such increasing numbers that they made it necessary for him to withdraw from the crowded streets into the open country. He wanted to discourage *erroneous* messianic ideas, not the idea that he was the Messiah.

---

1. Vincent Taylor, *The Gospel According to St. Mark* (London: Macmillan and Company, Ltd., 1952), pp. 117–24.

*Verses 42–43* are summary in nature. After the night of healing, Jesus withdrew to *a lonely place.* On other such occasions the indication is that during periods of great popularity, Jesus withdrew to be alone and pray. Indeed, Mark 1:35 reports that on this occasion Jesus withdrew and prayed.

*The people*—led by Simon Peter according to Mark 1:36—sought and found Jesus. When he indicated that he would not go back into the town with them, they *would have kept him from leaving them.* He told them that he had to go on to other cities and fulfill his appointed purpose of proclaiming *the good news of the kingdom of God* (v. 43). That may have been what he was praying about when they found him.

The manuscripts of Luke are divided on the reading in verse 44. The best ones have, *he was preaching in the synagogues of Judea.* The RSV adopts this because it has the best manuscript support. Indeed, the support cannot be seriously challenged. Other manuscripts have that he was preaching *in the synagogues of Galilee.* Whatever the original reading, it was *in Galilee* that he continued his preaching, teaching, and healing at this time.

### 3. A Call to Four Fishermen (5:1–11)

In the synoptic Gospels the first disciples called in a vocational sense were two sets of brothers: Andrew and Simon; James and John. They and Zebedee, the father of James and John, were partners in a fishing business (Luke 5:7–10; Mark 1:16–20; Matt. 4:18–22). Although John 1:44 identifies Bethsaida as "the city of Andrew and Peter," Luke 4:38 locates Peter's home in Capernaum; it was apparently there that this call was extended.

According to John 1:35–51, Jesus' first contact with these men was in Judea, before he returned to Nazareth after his baptism. Simon, Andrew, Philip, and Nathanael accompanied Jesus on that return. Andrew and another disciple of John the Baptizer (unidentified) had spent several hours with Jesus. Andrew went to find his brother Simon and to bring him to Jesus. While there are insoluble problems of identification involved, it is almost universally understood that the unidentified disciple was John the son of Zebedee and that he, too, brought a brother (James) to Jesus. The assumption is that the men returned to their businesses. If this is the case, the event in Luke 5:1–11 represents a meeting some time later when Jesus called the four fishermen to leave their business and accompany him as "fishers of men."

*Verse 1:* The growing popularity of Jesus resulted in crowds following him to the extent that it was difficult for him to work. Such was the scene when *the people pressed upon him* along the shore of the sea. *Gennesaret* was another name for the Sea of Galilee.

*Verse 2:* In the shallow water near the shore were two fishing boats. The owners *were washing their nets* ("mending," Mark 1:19 and Matt. 4:21) in preparation for work that night.

*Verse 3:* Jesus requested Simon, the owner of one of the boats, to permit him to use the boat. They pushed out far enough that the stretch of water prevented the people from pressing upon them, and from there Jesus taught *the word of God* (v. 1) which they desired to hear from him.

*Verses 4–7:* When he finished teaching, Jesus told Simon to push out farther into deeper water and cast his nets. Simon responded that they had toiled all the previous night without catching anything. This suggests an early morning scene. He would, however, at Jesus' word try once more. The result was a catch so big that the nets were in danger of breaking. They signaled for help from their partners. *They* indicates the presence of Andrew in the boat with Jesus and Simon. There may have been servants, too (Mark 1:20). The catch loaded the boat until it sank down about to the level of the water.

*Verses 8–9: Simon Peter* was overwhelmed. John 1:42 records that the first time Jesus met Simon he gave him the nickname *Peter,* meaning "rock." The name is introduced naturally here, assuming that the first readers of the Gospel were acquainted with it. Even "The Rock" had weak knees in the presence of such an event. *He fell down at Jesus' knees* and in humility confessed his sin and his unworthiness to stand in Jesus' presence—*Depart from me.*

*Verse 9* points out that the reason for Simon's reaction was the astounding catch of fish. It is also significant that Luke has this as the next major event after the healings in Simon's home (4:38–41). Every succeeding event increased his sense of wonder.

*Verse 10:* This sense of wonder also characterized James and John. Although Jesus used the singular in his word to Simon—*henceforth you will be catching men*—the other three felt themselves included in this call. Verse 11 states that they *brought their boats* to the shore, *left everything and followed him.* Mark and Matthew do not include the story of the catch of fish. They report that Jesus found Andrew and Simon "casting their nets" and James and John "mending their nets" and that he said, "Follow me, and I will make you fishers of men." They left their father, Zebedee, and hired servants with the boats and followed Jesus. This was a permanent commitment on their part. In every listing of the Twelve in the New Testament, these four are named first. Three of them were destined to form the inner circle with Jesus —Peter, James, John. Andrew would come to be known for bringing people to Jesus: his brother Simon (John 1:40–42); the boy with the loaves and fish (John 6:8); the Greeks who sought an interview with Jesus (John 12:20–22).

## 4. Healing a Leper (5:12–16)

Verses 12–16 contain another healing miracle. In this case the sickness was leprosy. The pattern of action and result is similar to other stories: Jesus healed some person; the report spread; many others came to hear him and to request healing; he withdrew to be alone and to pray.

*Verse 12: In one of the cities:* The particular city is not identified. Identification would have added nothing to the event.

*A man full of leprosy:* Leprosy was a greatly dreaded disease. It was loathsome in its end result of rotting flesh and ultimate loss of hair, fingers, eyes, and other parts of the body. Too, it was often used as a symbol for sin and in many minds probably interpreted as punishment for sin. *Full of leprosy* indicates the seriousness or extent of the case.

*Lord, if you will:* The term translated *Lord* was in general use a title of respect or honor, like our word "Sir." In Luke it is definitely a title for Jesus as the Anointed One. The man had apparently become acquainted with what

Jesus was doing and was convinced that God's power was working through him. *If you will* means literally "if you wish." He was convinced of Jesus' power and was submitting to Jesus' willingness to heal.

*You can make me clean:* In other healing stories the expression is "to make whole" or healthy. The nature of leprosy makes the expression *make me clean* appropriate.

*Verse 13: He . . . touched him:* To touch a leper was to become ceremonially defiled and to require separation from society. Jesus did not follow many of the ceremonial laws. He did not hesitate to do the unthinkable—to touch a leper. He believed that love and help for the needy take precedence over ceremonial laws.

*I will; be clean:* The will and the power brought cleansing. There were immediate indications of healing.

*Verse 14:* Jesus charged the man to report this only to the Jewish religious authorities. Negatively, this may have been for the purpose of minimizing the growing reports and increasing messianic enthusiasm of the people whose views of the Messiah did not agree with Jesus' views. Galilee was a hotbed of messianic hope, but for a revolutionary deliverer. Jesus did not want to encourage that. Positively, Jesus encouraged the man to follow the custom in cases of the healing of leprosy (Lev. 13, 14). After showing the priest indications of healing and making an offering of thanksgiving, the healed leper would cleanse his body, change his clothes, and become an accepted part of society again. Jesus' instruction that he show himself *to the priest* does not necessarily suggest a Judean setting for the incident. Matthew locates it near Capernaum, by putting the incident between the Sermon on the Mount and the healing of the paralytic in Capernaum (Matt. 8:1–5). Priests lived throughout Palestine and went to Jerusalem when their time of service arrived. The action which Jesus ordered for the man could have been done in almost any town in Galilee.

*Verse 15* indicates that in spite of Jesus' caution to the leper, the report of the healing *went abroad* with the usual result of the crowds of people multiplying.

*Verse 16:* As on other occasions of great popularity and demand by the people, Jesus *withdrew to the wilderness and prayed. The wilderness* was any part of the country where there would be no people and Jesus could be alone. He could no more afford to yield to the voice of the people in their desire for the wrong kind of Messiah than to the voice of the devil in the earlier wilderness experience. Both were the voice of temptation to take the easy way. In prayer he found the strength to say "No."

## 5. Healing a Paralytic (5:17–26)

While Luke does not identify the town in which this healing was done, Matthew (9:1) identifies it as "his own city," and Mark (2:1) gives the name "Capernaum." In the house where Jesus was, a great crowd gathered. It is doubtful if Mark's "at home" really implies that this took place in Jesus' home. The literal translation is "in a house," so no particular house is indicated. Some have understood it as another healing in Simon's house. Among those present were Pharisees and teachers of the Jewish religious law from Jerusalem and Judea as well as Galilee.

*Verse 17:* Pharisees were a pious religious group among the Jews. While Jesus chided them for their extreme attention to external obedience to the law and their neglect of the more important inner and spiritual requirements of God, they were the most religious people among the Jews. They were careful guardians of both the Mosaic law and the thousands of traditional laws which had been built about it.[1]

*Teachers of the law:* These were the official interpreters of the Jewish Scriptures and religion. With the Pharisees they had heard the reports of Jesus' teachings and deeds and had come to witness them for themselves.

*Verses 18–19:* In the course of Jesus' teaching, four men (Mark 2:3), unable to carry a paralytic friend through the crowd, went up to the roof, opened the ceramic *tiles,* and lowered the man into the presence of Jesus.

*Verse 20: When he saw their faith:* The immediate antecedent to the pronoun *their* is the four men who exercised such determination in bringing their friend to Jesus. There is no indication of the paralytic's faith or lack of it unless his permitting them (or perhaps encouraging them) may have implied it. The element of faith as a prerequisite to the performance of a miracle is a variant in the healing stories. Sometimes it is stated; sometimes it is not.

*Man, your sins are forgiven you:* These words were addressed directly to the paralyzed man. It is extremely doubtful if this means a causal relationship between the man's spiritual condition (sin) and his physical condition (paralysis). On other occasions Jesus refused to enter upon that type of debate (Luke 13:1–5; John 9:1–7). The words demonstrated Jesus' compassion for the total man in the total situation. Such faith in God's messenger had its inevitable result in God's forgiveness.

*Verse 21:* The teachers of the law (v. 17) are here identified as *the scribes.* Originally this was a group of professional copyists of the Scripture. From their association with the Scripture, they came to be the professional interpreters of the Scriptures and the religion of Israel. They joined the Pharisees in strenuous objection to Jesus' pronouncement of forgiveness to the paralytic.

*Who is this that speaks blasphemies? Who can forgive sins but God only?* Logically, their first question grew out of the second one. They believed that the forgiveness of sins was the prerogative of God only. Therefore, for anyone else to assume to forgive sins was for him to assume the work of God and, hence, to blaspheme or revile God. Their approach was a syllogism:

Major premise:  Only God can forgive sins.
Minor premise:  For man to claim to forgive sins is to blaspheme.
Conclusion:  Therefore, this man is blaspheming God.

What Jesus did next had the force of changing their syllogism:

Major premise:  Only God can forgive sins.
Minor premise:  This man evidently forgives sins.
Conclusion: Therefore, he must be God—or at least God's power must be working through him.

*Verse 22: Jesus perceived their questionings:* In the midst of the crowd and the excitement, he understood what they were saying and what it implied.

*Verse 23: Which is easier, to say . . . . :* The implication was that it was as

---

1. For helpful material on the Pharisees, see Matthew Black, "The Pharisees," *Interpreter's Dictionary of the Bible,* op. cit., III, 774–81; and Samuel Umen, *Pharisaism and Jesus* (New York: Philosophical Library, 1963).

easy for him to heal spiritually (forgive sins) as to heal physically (cure the paralysis). Whatever he *said* would take place. His words were the creative extension of his person.

*Your sins are forgiven you . . . rise and walk?* He could say either and whichever he said would take place.

*Verse 24: But that you may know:* They could not see objectively the result of his pronouncement of forgiveness; they could not see the man's sins leave him. They could see objectively the result of his command *Rise and walk.*

*The Son of man:* This title—much disputed as to both its origin (Daniel, Psalms, or 1 Enoch) and its meaning—was a messianic term and Jesus' favorite designation for himself. In John's Gospel Jesus' most frequent reference to himself is the first-person pronoun "I"; in the synoptics it is a third-person reference, the Son of Man.[1]

*Has authority on earth to forgive sins:* Here the point of emphasis is not one of power—what he can or cannot do. It is rather a question of what *authority* he has or has not. He was God's authorized agent for granting forgiveness of sin, and that required no more exercise of authority or power than to heal physical bodies.

*Rise, take up your bed and go home:* This is an imperative calling for obedient response. In other instances Jesus healed a paralyzed arm, or gave hearing, or sight, or healing to some part of a man's body. This was a man totally immobile from paralysis, a healing of the total man. The *bed* was a simple pallet-like piece of cloth.

*Verse 25* indicates the man's response. He arose, picked up his pallet, and went home *glorifying God.* He attributed his healing directly to God and praised God for it and probably for the healing as well.

*Verse 26* indicates the response of the witnesses. *Amazement seized them all:* This appears to include those who a few minutes before had accused Jesus of blasphemy. His healing the man simply by speaking a word convinced them of his ability to forgive the man's sins simply by speaking a word. Filled with awe, they said, *"We have seen strange things today."*

### 6. A Call to a Publican (5:27–32)

*Verse 27: After this he went out:* At the end of the teaching-healing event, Jesus left the house, *and saw a tax collector.* These tax collectors—translated "publicans" in other versions—were Jews who had secured the office of collecting taxes for the Roman government. That alone made them a despised people in the eyes of the rest of the Jews. Added to that onus was the custom of bidding and paying for the office and then setting and collecting higher taxes, as far as possible above the price paid; the difference was their profit for the office. In social and religious life they were ranked by the ordinary Jew with prostitutes and others who rejected the Jewish law and customs.

*Levi:* Mark 2:14 indicates that his father was named Alphaeus. Matthew 9:9 identifies him by another name, Matthew. He *was sitting at the tax office*

---

1. For a comprehensive treatment of the expression "Son of Man," see O. Cullmann, op. cit., pp. 37–92.

—the tax collection place, most likely a bench and table arrangement, perhaps with balances for weighing merchandise. Tax offices were located on main roads at the edges of towns and cities. There he collected taxes from farmers, merchants, and caravans. When Jesus extended the call *"Follow me,"* Levi left everything and joined Jesus and the four fisherman. The expression *follow me* is used regularly in the Gospels to indicate following in the vocational sense. Those who responded committed themselves to a ministry, in association with Jesus, of proclaiming the kingdom of God. Those who rejected it did so because they found the conditions of following too severe.

*Verse 28:* In a similar way the expression *left all* regularly indicates affirmative response and enlisting in the ministry of Jesus.

*Verse 29:* Levi gave a dinner for Jesus and the disciples (Matt. 9:10). To it he invited many *tax collectors and others.* Matthew and Mark identify the others as "sinners," a word used for religious and social outcasts. No doubt the occasion was for introducing Levi's new friend and leader to his old friends and associates.

*Verse 30: The Pharisees and their scribes murmured:* The expression *their scribes* reflects the practice of both main religious parties—Pharisees and Sadducees—to include scribes as members to interpret the law and the traditions for them. When these strict observers of all traditional laws saw Jesus and his disciples eating with spiritual and social outcasts they whispered to each other their accusations against Jesus and his disciples.

*Why do you eat and drink with tax collectors and sinners?* To share the table with others was to have the closest fellowship with them. It indicated acceptance of the other persons and enjoyment of the mutual experience. To the Pharisees it was unthinkable that one who professed loyalty to the way of God could associate himself with those who had rejected the way of God.

*Verse 31:* Jesus answered them with a parabolic or proverbial saying: *Those who are well have no need of a physician, but those who are sick.* It is doubtful that the people of Jesus' day knew or practiced the modern idea of "preventive therapy." They went for the physician's aid when they were sick, not to ward off sickness. The proverb was clear; it needed no explanation. Jesus gave an application to the immediate situation.

*Verse 32: I have not come to call the righteous, but sinners to repentance:* To ask if this means that Jesus regarded his questioners as righteous is to miss the point of his proverb. They regarded themselves as righteous and, hence, did not consider that they needed repentance. They were the first to grant that the tax collectors and sinners (v. 30) were unrighteous and needed repentance. Jesus took them on their own grounds in an *ad hominem* form of argument: Let us grant that you are righteous and do not need me and my message. If this is true, leave me to bring my message of repentance to those who *do* need it, the tax collectors and sinners.

Jesus understood himself as representing a God who was concerned about sinners. He had come for the very purpose of calling sinners to repentance. To do that he accepted their invitation to table fellowship and used the occasion as a means of reaching them for God. What the Pharisees considered to be a discredit to him, he considered to be his very purpose in life. They had no answer to that.

### 7. Teaching Concerning Fasting (5:33–39)

Verses 33–39 contain a continuation of the dialogue between Jesus and the Pharisees and their scribes. They turned the question from the matter of eating with sinners to the matter of abstaining from eating—fasting. They pointed to the practice of the disciples of John the Baptizer and the disciples of the Pharisees in fasting and to the failure of Jesus' disciples to fast. Jesus answered by using three incisive illustrations to show that the old forms (practices) of the Jewish religion were inadequate to contain the new approach to God which he was offering.

*Verse 33: Fast often and offer prayers:* Fasting was ideally an indication of genuine concern about spiritual matters, and was characteristically accompanied by prayer. This was a standard practice of the Pharisees and evidently of the disciples of John the Baptizer. With those who had joined his movement, John continued to minister up to his imprisonment and death. At that point some of his disciples may have associated themselves with Jesus (Matt. 14:12) while others continued a separate ministry.

*But yours eat and drink:* The implication of the Pharisees was that Jesus' disciples did not fast and pray but gave themselves to a life of indulgence. This was not true. Jesus did not reject fasting. He did point out the meaningless and even hypocritical manner in which it was practiced by many (Matt. 6:16) and counseled his hearers as to its proper and meaningful practice as a part of the worshiper's personal relationship to God, not as a display for men (Matt. 6:17). He also practiced prayer, and taught his disciples the proper motives for and attitudes of prayer (Matt. 6:7–15). This charge of the Pharisees may have been responsible for later misunderstanding of Jesus' teaching. Logion 14 in the recently discovered second-century Coptic Gospel According to Thomas quotes Jesus as teaching that fasting, praying, and giving are sinful. The Gnostics who produced this book rejected all forms of worship. In this logion the three practices which Jesus commended in Matthew 6:1–18 are reversed both in order and in interpretation. That may have been influenced by this charge of the Pharisees that Jesus' disciples rejected fasting and by his response. If so, it was misunderstanding on their part.

*Verses 34–35:* Jesus used the happy occasion of a wedding to illustrate his disciples' omission of fasting. During the wedding festivities the *wedding guests* rejoiced in the association with the bridegroom. It was not a time for sorrow and fasting. When the wedding ended and the bridegroom left, his friends would have ample time and occasion for sorrow and fasting.

The surface meaning of the illustration was clear. Jesus' disciples had come to understand that life in God's way was a life of rejoicing not of mourning. Christians reading the illustration against the background of the cross and the sorrow of Jesus' disciples in his leaving them see in Jesus' words a veiled reference to his death. If he intended that, it was reflection of his own understanding; neither his disciples nor the Pharisees had any background at that time for such understanding.

*Verse 36:* Jesus used the illustration of the futility of patching an old garment with a piece of new cloth. Luke calls it a *parable*. It is not a parable in the sense of a story; it is a parabolic saying which, with imagination, can be expanded to an amusing story. The saying is also in Mark 2:21, Matthew 9:16, and the Coptic Gospel According to Thomas, Logion 47. These four present three versions of the saying, which are as follows:

Mark and Matthew quote Jesus as saying that no one sews a *new* piece of cloth on an *old* garment because to do so would be futile. The new and, hence, unshrunken piece of cloth would shrink at the next washing. Because the old cloth could shrink no more, the result would be a bigger hole in the old garment than the original one.

Thomas quotes Jesus as saying that no one sews an *old* patch on a *new* garment because the failure of the old to shrink in washing would tear a hole in the new garment.

Luke quotes Jesus as saying that *no one tears a piece from a new garment* in order to patch an old one. To do so would be to ruin the new garment and to have an undesirable old garment with colors that did not match.

The three versions point to the nature of proverbial sayings and how they come to be used by different people for different purposes. The slight changing of the saying does not change its basic meaning but it may provide an emphasis for a distinct purpose. In Luke's version the meaning is that no one could take the joy away from his disciples and compel them to conform to the old practices of the Jews. It would not only mean ruining the new *(he will tear the new),* but it would be futile because the new and the old just did not fit one another *(the new will not match the old).*

*Verses 37–39* contain the illustration of the futility of storing new wine in old wineskins. The result is similar to that in the illustration of the patch— a total loss. This illustration is also in Mark, Matthew, and the Gospel According to Thomas with instructive parallels and differences.

Mark, Matthew, and Luke emphasize the futility of putting new wines into old wineskins. The old wineskins had stretched as far as they could be stretched when the original wine expanded in fermentation. New wine put into the old wineskins would expand in fermentation but the old wineskins could stretch no more. They would burst and both the old skins and the new wine would be lost. This is the total of Mark's account (2:22). Matthew adds that putting new wine into new wineskins is to preserve both (9:17). Luke omits that but he adds another item omitted by Mark and Matthew: *No one after drinking old wine desires new; for he says, 'The old is good.'*

Thomas includes this last Lukan item with a very slight alteration, and then adds another item about not putting *old* wine into *new* wineskins (Logion 47)!

What did Jesus mean by the illustration? He meant that the *old forms* of the Jewish religion (fasting, ceremonial observances, etc.) were inadequate for the *new content* which he was offering. The new content (his way of life) could not be forced into the old forms (the Jewish way of life). To try to force such conformity would be to lose the significance of both.

Some interpreters have concluded that Luke's verse 39 was not a part of Jesus' saying, and that by adding it, Luke missed the entire point of Jesus' illustration. This is an unwarranted conclusion. The place of verse 39 is textually secure. The only variant in the manuscript is that some have "the old is better," while the best manuscripts have "the old is good." Too, the presence of this part of the saying in the Thomas gospel argues for his getting it from Luke or a source which he had in common with Luke.

Another and convincing argument for its genuineness is the presence of the same teaching in another form in the miracle of the water turned to wine in John 2:1-11. In both Luke (5:34-35) and John the setting is a wedding feast. In both of them the teaching is the same—the old forms of the Jewish religion could not contain the new content of what Jesus was offering. In Luke the old forms were wineskins; in John they were the ceramic jars used for the religious cleansings. From the same "source" from which their "water" came Jesus provided the "best wine," and his disciples were convinced that they had committed themselves to the right leader.

One of John's themes is Jesus' chiding the religious leaders for rejecting his teaching and clinging with satisfaction to the old. Luke 5:39 has the same force. Jesus chides the Pharisees for "tasting" his "new wine" but rejecting it and clinging to the "old wine" of Judaism and saying, *"The old is good* enough."

## 8. Teaching Concerning Sabbath Observance (6:1–5)

*Verse 1:* The occasion was a sabbath. Jesus and his disciples were walking along one of the public paths through the grainfields. They plucked some of the heads of grain, rubbed them in their hands to separate grain from husk, and ate the grain. According to Deuteronomy 23:25 it was lawful to eat grain in this way when walking through another man's field. The hands could be used but not a sickle.

*Verse 2:* Some Pharisees observed the disciples' action and charged them with violating the sabbath laws. What they were doing was legal, but the action was interpreted as labor and, hence, a sabbath violation. The exact nature of the violation was not explained. It may have been regarded as "harvesting" or it may have been regarded as "carrying a burden." A scribe copying the Scriptures might stop at the close of day, put his pen over his ear, and go out to observe sunset and the beginning of a new day. If, however, the sunset was ushering in the sabbath, the scribe would leave the pen on the writing table lest he violate the sabbath prohibition on "carrying a burden" by carrying the pen back into the room after sunset. With this kind of interpretation, even conveying grain from the stalk to the mouth could be a sabbath violation.

*Verses 3-4:* Jesus reminded them of violations of religious laws allowable in other situations where man's need was involved. Specifically he cited a situation in which a priest gave David the sacred bread from God's altar when David and his men were hungry and on a mission for the king (1 Sam. 21:1-7). This bread was sacred, to be eaten only by the priests, and not to be used as "common bread." But need took precedence over ceremony. The Pharisees could hardly say that the priest, David, or his men had sinned in the event.

*Verse 5:* Jesus then stated a principle which guided him and his followers in sabbath observance: *"The Son of man is lord of the sabbath."* God had given the sabbath for man's benefit. Jesus was God's authorized messenger. Jesus assumed the responsibility of determining the proper use of the sabbath in line with the original purpose of God. God meant for the sabbath to serve man's physical and spiritual need; he did not mean for man to serve the sabbath's need (Mark 2:27). This interpretation Jesus followed in every situation in which sabbath observance and genuine human need came into conflict.

## 9. Healing on the Sabbath (6:6–11)

The occasion was another sabbath and the setting was a synagogue. The scribes and Pharisees watched to see if Jesus would heal a man's withered hand. He took the initiative by impressing on them the priority of the sabbath over all days as a day for doing that which was good. He healed the man, but the Pharisees were not convinced by his argument and were furious.

*Verse 7: So that they might find an accusation against him:* Hostility against Jesus was growing. The people received him with great enthusiasm. The Pharisees and scribes considered him a threat to the total religious structure in Judaism. They considered him a lawbreaker and could not believe that a lawbreaker came from God. So they watched for evidence to use against him. By their traditional laws it was illegal to practice medicine, healing, or surgery (except circumcision) on the sabbath.

*Verse 8: He knew their thoughts:* This required no special knowledge on his part. They were perfectly obvious in their intentions. Their eyes going from him to the lame man and back were evidence of their train of thought.

*The withered hand* could have been a defect from birth or a result of attrition following paralysis. Although it is not stated, it would have fitted their views to have attributed the man's condition to God's punishment for sin (see John 9:1–2).

*Verse 9:* Having called the man to stand in a prominent place in the group so his condition could be clearly seen, Jesus posed a question regarding the right or wrong way to use the sabbath. The question has the balance and parallelism of poetic structure.

> "Is it lawful on the sabbath
> to do good or to do harm,
> to save life or to destroy it?"

Given that choice, the Pharisees were shut up to one answer—it is lawful to do good, not harm; it is lawful to save, not destroy. Saving a life or saving a limb represented doing good on the sabbath, not doing evil.

*Verse 10:* When Jesus commanded the man to stretch out his hand and arm, he did so; the withered hand was healed.

*Verse 11:* The Pharisees could not answer Jesus' logic, but they could not approve his action. *Filled with fury* they started discussing what they might do to Jesus. There is no indication that they desired to kill him—a theme so frequent in John's report of the religious leaders in Jerusalem. On the surface the discussion of this group appears to have had the goal of finding a way of stopping him or discrediting him with the people who were accepting him.

## 10. The Call and Appointment of the Twelve (6:12–16)

In Jesus' ministry the time arrived for a larger outreach than he could accomplish alone. Out of all his followers he called Twelve who would work closely with him, so that he could send them out in working groups.

*Verse 12: In these days:* This meant at this point of his need for an enlarging ministry.

*All night he continued in prayer:* His withdrawal into the hills to pray all night reflected the burden which he carried. The time had come when he needed special help. He prayed all night before making his choice.

*Verse 12: Disciples:* This word means "learners." They were people who followed him to learn his understanding of God's way for men. Both the Pharisees and John the Baptizer had disciples (Luke 5:33).

*Verse 13: Twelve, whom he named apostles: Apostles* means "ones sent with a message." In Mark 3:14 the purpose of Jesus is specifically stated along two lines: "to be with him, and to be sent out to preach . . . ." Jesus wanted human companionship in this work; he wanted men whom he could send to do the same work he was doing.

The Twelve are listed four times in the New Testament. The similarities and differences in the four listings reflect organization for working purposes.

| *Mark 3:16–19* | *Matt. 10:2–4* | *Luke 6:14–16* | *Acts 1:13* |
|---|---|---|---|
| Simon Peter | Simon Peter | Simon Peter | Simon Peter |
| James | Andrew | Andrew | John |
| John | James | James | James |
| Andrew | John | John | Andrew |
| | | | |
| Philip | Philip | Philip | Philip |
| Bartholomew | Bartholomew | Bartholomew | Thomas |
| Matthew | Thomas | Matthew | Bartholomew |
| Thomas | Matthew | Thomas | Matthew |
| | | | |
| James, son of Alphaeus | James, son of Alphaeus | James, son of Alphaeus | James, son of Alphaeus |
| Thaddaeus | Thaddaeus | Simon the Zealot | Simon the Zealot |
| Simon the Cananaean | Simon the Cananaean | Judas, son of James | Judas, son of James |
| Judas Iscariot | Judas Iscariot | Judas Iscariot | |

In each list the Twelve are divided into three groups of four each. In each group the same man is named first—Simon Peter, Philip, James the son of Alphaeus. After that there are different orders within the groups. Simon Peter is always listed first and Judas Iscariot is always listed last with a comment about his being the traitor. In the listing in Acts, Judas Iscariot is omitted because he had committed suicide prior to the event being reported.

This comparison suggests that the Twelve worked in groups; later, when Jesus sent out the seventy he sent them "two by two" (Luke 10:1). The place of the two sets of brothers in the first group is in line with the record of their being called first and their frequent presence with Jesus when the others were left behind. The place of Judas Iscariot and the mention of his treachery reflect the opinion in which he was held by the early church.

Lengthy consideration of the variation of names in the four lists cannot be undertaken here. A few suggestions for study are in order. There is no question about the identity of Simon the Cananaean in Mark–Matthew and Simon the Zealot in Luke–Acts. *Cananaean* was an Aramaic word meaning "an enthusiast" or "a zealot." The Zealots were a political group desiring a revolution against Rome and self-government for the Jews. They were constantly planning such a revolution and searching for the right leader. It is possible that others in the Twelve were of the same persuasion—Judas Iscariot, for instance, or the fiery Zebedee sons whom Jesus nicknamed "Sons of Thunder."

By position of names and comparative linguistic studies, some interpreters have attempted to identify Thaddaeus of Mark–Matthew with Judas son of James of Luke–Acts. The evidences are fragile. In like manner some have attempted to identify Bartholomew of these four accounts with Nathanael of John 1:45–50. In the four lists, Bartholomew stands next to Philip, and in John, Philip brought Nathanael to Jesus. Such attempts represent interesting suggestions but can never be conclusive.

In all lists James, who heads the third group, is distinguished from any other James by the designation *son of Alphaeus*. Nothing more is known of Alphaeus. It is not likely that the reference is to Alphaeus the father of Matthew. Had that been the case, this James would have been more clearly identified as the "brother of Matthew." In Luke–Acts the Judas who does not appear in the Mark–Matthew lists is distinguished from Judas Iscariot by the identification "son of James." This third James in the complex is not further identified. The name was common; it is the equivalent of the Hebrew name Jacob.

## 11. The Sermon on the Plain (6:17–49)

*Verses 17–19:* Jesus came down from the mountain with the newly appointed Twelve and was met by a crowd of people from as far south as Jerusalem and as far northwest as Tyre and Sidon who had come *to hear him and to be healed* by him. They *sought to touch him, for power came forth from him and healed them all*. This appears to reflect healing by bodily contact with Jesus, similar to the later case of the woman with the hemorrhage (Luke 8:43–48).

It was to this mixed group including other disciples as well as the Twelve that Jesus gave the teaching which has been called "The Sermon on the Plain" *(a level place)* in contrast to "The Sermon on the Mount" of Matthew (chapters 5–7). The question of the relationship of the two passages has been thoroughly examined with no agreement as to conclusions. The Matthew passage contains one hundred eleven verses. The Luke passage contains only twenty-nine verses. This means that only about one-fourth of the Matthew material is in the Luke passage. Many of the teachings in the Matthew passage are in other teaching sections in Luke. There are some verses in Luke which are not in Matthew. The point of emphasis in Luke is different from that in Matthew. Matthew's point of emphasis is more spiritual; Luke's is more social.

A search for a satisfying answer to the problem of relationship must follow certain questions as guidelines:

a. Did Jesus deliver the teaching on two different occasions, one reported in Matthew and another in Luke?

b. Did Jesus deliver the teaching on one occasion only and Matthew and Luke had different sources for it?

c. Or, if they had the same sources, did they select some materials, omit others, and interpret others according to their different purposes?

d. Have Matthew and Luke collected teachings of Jesus from multiple occasions and grouped them in these places according to their purposes?

Of the four questions, the third appears to promise more fruitful conclusions.

Verses 20–26 present "Blessings" and contrasting "Woes." A comparison with Matthew reveals that Matthew omits the "Woes," includes a larger number of the "Blessings," and puts a different emphasis on the "Blessings" which are also in Luke.

*Blessed:* Jesus' use of this word of congratulation reflects the paradoxical nature of the sayings. They appear to state the very opposite of what is commonly accepted as worthy of congratulations. Congratulations, you who are poor. Congratulations, you who are hungry . . . you who weep . . . you who are hated! The second part of each saying must be understood and accepted if the first part is really to be accepted.

*Woe:* This is the very opposite of "blessed." It means misery and suffering. The same paradoxical structure is in the woes: Woe, you who are rich . . . well fed . . . laughing . . . enjoying the praise of men. The second part of the woe must be understood if the first part is to have meaning.

**The Four Blessings:**

*Verse 20: Blessed are you poor, for yours is the kingdom of God:* In Matthew's version the qualifying phrase "in spirit" places the emphasis on the spiritual: that is, the one who recognizes himself as a spiritual pauper is the one who comes to possess the spiritual treasures of the kingdom. In contrast, Luke's emphasis is on the socially and economically downtrodden. Precisely, "the kingdom of God is your own." In the main, the first followers of Jesus were of this level of society. That was not in itself a blessing. But to consider their treasure, the kingdom of God, was to realize their true wealth. A distinction between "kingdom of heaven" (Matthew) and "kingdom of God" (Luke) cannot be argued with cogency. Whatever its ultimate nature in the purpose of God, the kingdom was first of all the spiritual reign of God in the hearts of his worshipers. This was blessing surpassing the misery even of the poor.

*Verse 21a: Blessed are you that hunger now, for you shall be satisfied:* One of the strongest and most insistent of the natural drives, hunger, is here reckoned as a blessing. While it is starkly stated and lacks the spiritual qualifying phrase that appears in Matthew—"hunger and thirst *for righteousness*"—the spiritual likely comes to override the physical even in Luke's version. There was hardly a future prospect of abundant food to promise relief of physical hunger. The land was overpopulated and underproductive, and the majority of people on the lower economic level rarely had a satisfying meal. Jesus, who in his own experience knew the necessity of bread, knew of the higher hungers of life and that one had to experience that spiritual hunger before he could experience spiritual satisfaction.

There is dramatic contrast in the word translated *shall be satisfied*. It was a word for fattening cattle, for making sleek. Transported to the area of spiritual hunger, it promised "you shall be filled to satiation."

*Verse 21b: Blessed are you that weep now, for you shall laugh:* Whether weeping for one's own sin or sorrowful state, or weeping in sympathy for others in that state, the one who knows weeping can, under God's reign, anticipate transforming joy. Jesus later used this in specific application to the Twelve. He said that when he was taken from them by the cross, they would weep and mourn, but their mourning would be transformed into joy. That transformation to joy they experienced in his resurrection.

*Verses 22–23: Blessed are you when men hate you:* To be hated by others, excluded from the company of and worship with others, reviled by others— these are not ordinarily considered grounds for rejoicing or recognized as blessings. *On account of the Son of man* indicates that Jesus' reference is to persecution because they were his followers. Hostility to Jesus was increasing; soon it would engulf both him and those identified with him.

*Rejoice in that day:* that is, the day when they would be mistreated because of their identity with him. *Leap for joy* is a stronger expression than *rejoice*. Two reasons were to motivate them. In heaven their reward was great, and what they gained there was exceedingly more important than what they suffered here. On earth they were classed with the prophets who had been persecuted by the "fathers" of those now persecuting them. The prophets were the most honored men in Jewish history. To be classed with them was blessing.

### The Four Woes:
The woes are the opposite of the blessings.
The poor (v. 20) versus the rich (v. 24).
The hungry (v. 21a) versus the full (v. 25a).
The weeping (v. 21b) versus the laughing (v. 25b).
The persecuted (v. 22) versus the praised (v. 26).

*Verse 24* pronounces woe on the rich because they had already received their *consolation*. Their consolation was in their consciousness of having everything and needing nothing. There was no anticipated blessing in their future.

*Verse 25a* pronounces woe on those who were full. The future held no promise of fullness; they already possessed that. Only *hunger* was promised them. This probably anticipated their coming to a state of recognized emptiness and finding nothing to bring them satisfaction.

*Verse 25b* pronounces woe on those who spend their time in laughing. This is not a sentence pronounced on wholesome laughter. It reflects a way of life characterized by self-sufficiency and satisfaction with the physical and material. For such ones the promised future is mourning and weeping. They would come to sense the emptiness and futility of what they had known as life. Jesus' parable of the lost son (15:11–32) would be a good example of joy transformed to sorrow.

*Verse 26* pronounces woe upon the praised, and compares those of whom *all men speak well* to the praised false prophets rather than the persecuted true prophets (v. 23) in the history of Israel. Amos, for instance, had been condemned while Amaziah was praised. But in the end Amos was vindicated and Amaziah was carried into captivity where he had no place to perform religious service (Amos 7:10-17). To be praised by all men may be an indication of failure to follow the hard way of God's people.

Verses 27-42 are a group of sayings dealing with the general area of person-to-person relationships in society. The connections between some of the sayings are not always obvious, and the interpreter must either search carefully for the connection, or else understand them as isolated sayings included here without clear connections to the general theme of the passage. Verse 40 is an example.

Within this larger section, verses 27-36 deal with the difficult theme of love for one's enemies. While it is not stated here as it is in Matthew's version, the background of the teaching is undoubtedly the Jewish teaching "You shall love your neighbor and hate your enemy" (Matt. 5:43). To love their neighbors was a definite command from God (Lev. 19:18); to hate their enemies they regarded as an allowable implication. In fact, however, to hate one's enemies was forbidden to their fathers in regard to the Edomites and the Egyptians (Deut. 23:7). Jesus took it for granted that they would love their neighbors. He focused on the necessity of loving their enemies.

*Verse 27: Love:* Two Greek verbs are regularly translated *love* in the New Testament. One, *phileō,* relates basically to a warm, personal affection for its object. The other, *agapaō,* is used to mean rational good will and recognition of the value of its object. It is this second word which is used throughout this section. Even one's enemies must be regarded from the viewpoint of the recognition of their value as persons and a rational good will which desires what is best for them.

*Enemies:* The word is not further defined. To Jesus' hearers the first application was probably to the suppressing Romans in particular and the Gentiles in general. But it was not limited to them. Even among the Jews there were many whom one might consider his enemy—one whose relationship in religious, social, or economic life was marked by hostility. Even for this one, Jesus' followers were to exercise rational good will, desiring what was best for him.

*Do good:* Exercise positive action expressing love even for those who express hate to you.

*Verse 28: Bless:* Return blessing for reviling received.

*Pray:* Pray for those whose conduct toward you is abusive.

Jesus' followers were not and are not to live on the level of getting even and striking back. They are to adopt a positive-action approach at every point of experience. This is elaborated in the verses which follow. Some of the practices reflected in the passage were well known to Jesus' hearers but sound strange in twentieth-century society. The follower of Jesus is to seek in these teachings a principle of conduct, and then conscientiously follow that principle.

*Verse 29: To him who strikes you on the cheek, offer the other also:* The background of this is the ancient law of retaliation (Exod. 21:23-24; Lev. 24:19-20; Deut. 19:21). It was given to a people who, as slaves, had not experienced self-government and now as free were living in a community in which they had to learn self-government. The law was given as a step toward justice. If in conflict a man knocked out another man's tooth, the injured man was permitted by law to knock out a tooth of his injurer. But only one —"tooth for tooth." Jesus regarded it as a law which served its purpose in its day, but that day had passed, and men had grown to a higher level of relationship. To turn the other cheek rather than to return a blow to the cheek was to use an unusual and dramatic way of showing that Jesus' follower was not living by the principle of getting even.

*From him who takes away your cloak do not withhold your coat as well:* The *cloak* was the long outer garment worn when needed but put aside when it interfered with work. The *coat* was the next garment which would be worn at all times. Jesus pictured an imaginary situation in which a person's cloak was seized when it had been put aside and was easily taken. To the thief the owner should call, "Wait, I'll give you my *coat,* too." This would indeed dramatize the fact that the owner was not living the grasping life but rather enjoyed the giving life.

*Verse 30* continues that very strong language: give to every beggar; do not insist on the return of material goods taken by another. It is not likely that even in that day of a rather simple life of material possessions, these sayings were to be taken as literal actions. They were moral aphorisms. Every person is to find the principle which is the foundation for the conduct of Jesus' people: live the *giving* life, not the *grasping* life. Then in his own life situation he applies that principle honestly and conscientiously.

*Verse 31* is a positive statement of a Hebrew wisdom saying at least as old as the book of Tobit which dates from the second century B.C.—"What you hate, do to no one" (Tobit 4:15). The Gospel According to Thomas quotes Jesus as saying this in a similar negative form—"Do not what you hate" (Logion 6). When Rabbi Hillel was challenged by a Gentile to teach him the entire law while he stood on one foot, Hillel quoted the Tobit saying and then added, "This is the Law and the Prophets; everything else is commentary." Both in Matthew 7:12 and Luke 6:31, Jesus makes it a positive statement: *"as you wish that men would do to you, do so to them."* This is the climax of the positive actions of verses 27–31 as contrasted with an attitude of retaliation.

Verses 32–36: As verses 27–31 show that it is wrong to return evil in place of evil and right to return good in place of evil, verses 32–36 show that there is no spiritual dynamic in returning good in place of good. That is a commonplace practice even by those who are not followers of Jesus. In his Sermon on the Mount (Matt. 5:17–48) Jesus taught that his followers must go beyond the usual, the commonplace, in demonstrating a level of ethical conduct which is higher than the conduct of those who are not his followers.

*Verse 32: Sinners,* those who do not follow God's way, return love to those who love them. Jesus' followers must go beyond that; they must love those who do not love them (see Matt. 5:43–48).

*Verse 33:* Those who do not follow God's way return good actions for the good actions which their fellow sinners do for them. For Jesus' followers to do the same has, therefore, no merit or commendation for them. They must return good actions for evil actions done them. In so doing, they demonstrate the superior conduct anticipated in Jesus' disciples.

*Verse 34:* Sinners lend money to the needy. Their action is not necessarily one of concern for the needy. It may be that their motive is solely that of profit through interest. To demonstrate the higher ethical life, Jesus' followers are to give to the needy, to give because they share Jesus' concern for the needy.

*Verse 35* summarizes the three actions, loving, doing good, giving, practiced without expectation of the return of the love, the good, or the gift. Such conduct has a twofold return.

*Your reward will be great:* This is a moral maxim without qualification. It is not a matter of loving and being loved. It is a matter of loving because that is the right way for the followers of Jesus Christ. It brings its own reward in the sense of well-being in having done what was right.

*You will be sons of the Most High:* To conduct one's life in this way is to exhibit the character of the sons of God. God is graciously disposed to men whether or not they merit it. He is *kind,* gracious, to the *ungrateful,* who are ungracious, lacking in gratitude for benevolence. *Selfish* means grasping. If Jesus' followers are to exhibit the characteristics of sons of God, they must conduct themselves as God does.

*Verse 36* gathers up the total—*Be merciful, even as your Father is merciful.* The Greek word used here is not the usual New Testament word for mercy, but is a word meaning compassionate, pitying. In the plural form it is sometimes translated "tender mercies." The Father is compassionate toward all men; so must his children be. *Even as* translates a word expressive of manner—after the manner of God's character, so exhibit your character as his sons.

Verses 37–42 are usually labeled "Judging Others." While this is a natural heading because of the opening words, it does not appear to get to the heart of Jesus' words. Jesus is talking about an effort to help a fellowman in difficulty that is frustrated because the helper is involved in the same difficulty. Pointing out areas needing improvement in another's life is to leave one's self open to counterexamination for areas needing improvement.

*Verses 37–38:* The initial caution about judging is given in four expressions, two negative and two positive: *judge not, condemn not, forgive, give.*

*Judge not:* literally, stop judging. This does not mean that Jesus' followers are never to form an opinion about another. Later Jesus pointed out that the only way to determine the good or bad nature of a tree is to examine its fruit (vv. 43–44). The kind of judging referred to here is the type of disparaging criticism which tries to attain moral superiority by pointing out the vices or moral inferiority of others. This is a cheap way of attaining superiority. Jesus saw it as a poor way because it merely opened the accuser to the same type of charge.

*Condemn not:* literally, stop condemning. The idea is the same as stop judging, but the expression is stronger. The word is a compound meaning "stop passing sentence on" or "stop assigning penalty to." It is the next step after judging. After we judge someone guilty we tend to pass sentence upon him. But we are not to do that. Both commands are followed by a very emphatic double negative: "you will never be judged in return; you will never be sentenced in return." The idea is summarized later in the sentence: *For the measure you give will be the measure you get back.*

*Forgive:* This is the first of the positive statements. It is not the usual word for God's forgiving sins, but is a word which means "to pardon" or "to set free." It may revert to the idea of injury received (vv. 28–30). Rather than cherishing the memory of injury with hope of revenge, we should pardon the one who injured us by setting him free. In this we will experience a return of the same pardon.

*Give:* This second of the positive statements is not qualified. The total passage indicates a generous spirit in dealing with the weaknesses of others or with injury growing out of that weakness. The illustration is of measuring grain—it is piled up, shaken down to a solid pack, and then more poured in until the container overflows. This is the kind of generosity which men will return for generosity shown them.

*Verse 39:* Just as the result of one blind man's trying to guide another blind man along a path is that both miss the path and fall into the ditch, so one man trying to help another may find frustrating failure if he has the same weakness or problem. This will be elaborated in other illustrations in verses 41–42.

*Verse 40:* It is not clear just how this verse fits this passage. In another context Jesus used this saying to warn his disciples of coming persecution. If he, their Lord and Master, had faced hostility and evil treatment, they could anticipate the same (Matt. 10:24–25; John 15:20–21). In this passage, however, that can hardly be the relationship of verse 40 to verse 39. It could conceivably be the relationship of verse 40 to Jesus' own example in responding to the kind of evil treatment discussed in verses 27–38. He had met hate with love, mistreatment with kindness, reviling with blessing. His disciples should follow their teacher's example.

In his warning about coming persecution as recorded by John, Jesus reminded the disciples that once before he had told them, "A servant is not greater than his master." He was no doubt referring to the occasion earlier that same evening when he washed the disciples' feet and used it as a lesson on humility (John 13:16), reminding them that they were not above him. The two uses that evening did not have the same meaning; the earlier use could have a very similar meaning to the use in Luke if it relates to the general area of humble service even in face of resistance and hostility.

*A disciple is not above his teacher:* In all three uses of this saying two applications are permitted. (1) If the teacher performs humble service for others (John 13:16), the disciple is not above such service. (2) If the teacher is reviled and persecuted, the disciple can anticipate the same thing; he cannot expect to be immune from persecution (Luke 6:40; John 15:20–21).

*Every one when he is fully taught will be like his teacher:* This, too, permits two applications. To be fully taught is to learn to follow the teacher's example both in humble service and in acceptance of persecution. The acceptance will not be one of negative resignation to an undesirable fate. It will be one of positive aggression in using the situation to the glory of God. The saying is very similar to one in Matthew 10:25: "it is enough for the disciple to be like his teacher, and the servant like his master."

Verses 41–44 are almost identical with Matthew 7:3–5. While the two use some differing words, the translation into English is the same. In the original text, Luke's version is more emphatic. Where Matthew has "how will you say," Luke has "how can you possibly say." Where Matthew has "the log in your eye," Luke has "the log in your own eye." In both Matthew and Luke the teaching is connected to the "judge not" passage and deals with the same vice, i.e., ignoring one's own greater faults while assuming to help another's lesser faults.

*Verse 41: Brother:* The word was customarily used in the general sense of one's fellowman. It was not restricted to a blood brother or even to a brother in a religious group.

The illustration is exaggerated for the sake of dramatic effectiveness. A man with a huge log protruding from his eye looks at the tiny speck in the eye of his brother, and has the boldness to suggest that he could help to remove the speck from his brother's eye, all the while ignoring the huge log in his own eye. The ridiculous nature of the scene has led some interpreters to suggest that Jesus said "spring" rather than "eye." The Aramaic word for eye is also the word for a spring of water. The imagery is that of a man offering to get a small twig out of his neighbor's spring while back home his own spring is polluted by a big log and he does nothing about it. That would be a more natural illustration, but Jesus did not always use a natural illustration. He frequently exaggerated the illustration to make it more effective.

*Verse 42* definitely reflects the "eye" imagery rather than the "spring" imagery. Both Matthew and Luke have an emphatic form of the verb for seeing. "First take the log out of your own eye, and then you will see clearly to take out the speck that is in your brother's eye."

*Hypocrite:* This word comes directly from the Greek theater. It means to wear a mask and play a part. An actor could portray one type of character while beneath the mask he was a different kind of person. In Matthew's version of this sermon the word is used to describe those who put on a theatrical performance in giving, praying, and fasting (Matt. 6:1–18). In Luke's version, Jesus meant that it is playacting to try to help another in his fault when one's own faults are greater. We can be concerned about our brother's problem and desire to help, but we can help effectively only after we have cleared up our own greater problem.

Verses 43–45 continue the kind of contrast in character which marks this entire sermon.

*Verse 43* bears the kind of reverse parallelism referred to earlier. (See discussion of Luke 2:14.)

Good tree ⟍ ⟋ bad fruit
Bad tree ⟋⟍ good fruit.

*No good tree bears bad fruit:* It is the nature of a tree to produce fruit corresponding to that nature. Some interpreters cite exceptions to this due to drought, worms, etc. These are results from outside causes, not from the nature of the tree.

*Nor again does a bad tree bear good fruit:* It is the nature of a bad tree to bear bad fruit. Two trees may grow in the same orchard: a "native" tree and a "cultivated" tree. The fruit they bear corresponds to their inner nature —small or large fruit, sweet or sour fruit.

*Verse 44* opens with a transitional expression—*each tree is known by its own fruit*—which points back to the preceding illustration and forward to the next illustration. A thorn tree does not bear figs. A briar bush does not bear grapes. Fig trees bear figs; grape vines bear grapes. The gospel of Thomas adds that thorns and thistles bear no fruit at all (Logion 45), only thorns and stickers!

*Verse 45* contains Jesus' application of these illustrations. Like a good tree, a good man produces good. Like an evil tree, an evil man produces evil. This is because of the inner nature of the two. That which they show external-ly is due to what they are internally—good *heart* or bad *heart*. What they are internally is reflected even in their words. The mouth opens; the words come out; they reflect what is on the inside. There is an ancient Chinese proverb which states that the heart of man is a well and the mouth of man is a bucket and that what is in the well of the heart comes up in the bucket of the mouth. Jesus' saying precisely translated has the same idea—"because his mouth speaks from that which fills his heart."

Both Luke and Matthew conclude their account of the sermon with the vivid illustration of the two builders (Luke 6:46–49, Matt. 7:21–27). The illustration is the same, but each has some details which are more vivid than the other's. Both introduce the illustration with a reference to calling Jesus *Lord* but not following his lordship. Luke has the shorter reference—*Why do you call me 'Lord, Lord,' and not do what I tell you?* (v. 46). While the larger company of hearers were addressed by the question, it was also for the Twelve. Even they gave evidence of conduct which was not consistent with their profession of Jesus as the *Lord* of their lives. A lord is to be obeyed. To the degree to which the first-century or the twentieth-century disciple fails to obey, he fails to demonstrate the truth of his profession that Jesus is his Lord. The illustration relates lordship to hearing and doing.

*Verse 46: Every one who comes to me and hears my words:* This relates both to those who hear and accept his words and those who hear but reject his words (v. 49). The expression *my words* refers immediately to the teach-ings in this sermon. Since the sermon is on the theme of the nature of dis-cipleship which Jesus presented in all his teachings, it is accurate to apply the term to the total of his teachings as the foundation for life.

*Verse 48:* The one who hears Jesus' words and *does them*—acts their demand out in life—Jesus compared to a man building a house on a rock ledge.

*Dug deep:* He did not build on the soft surface. He dug down to solid rock and even into the rock; literally, "he dug and went deep." On that rock he laid the foundation and built his house.

*When a flood arose, the stream broke against that house:* The picture is that of a flash flood with a torrential stream striking the house. At this point Matthew adds more vivid detail—"the rain came down on top, the floods came up under, the winds blew against the sides of that house" (Matt. 7:25).

*Could not shake it:* The house was thoroughly tested but the torrents could not shake it down.

*It had been well built:* Some manuscripts of Luke have *for it was founded on a rock* (the Matt. 7:25 reading), but this is the better reading. It was a simple and obvious fact.

*Verse 49* presents the other type of man. He, too, was a builder, but of a different character.

*On the ground without a foundation:* This means simply on the surface.

One might extend the detail legitimately by indicating that this man did not dig down through the soft surface and into the solid rock. He took the easy way.

While Matthew's account (7:27) repeats the testing of rain pouring down on the roof, flood waters coming up beneath, and winds beating against the sides of the house, Luke has simply that the torrent reached it and *immediately it fell.* The imagery is that of a man building a house on the smooth sand of a dry ravine—a *wadi,* to Jesus' hearers—which, in the rainy season, becomes a raging torrent; the house quickly crashed in ruin.

The contrast is dramatically apparent. Two men hear Jesus' words. One accepts them and builds his life on them though it is a hard task. The other rejects them and takes the less difficult way of life. Inevitably both lives are tested by the reversals of life and the judgment of God. One stands; one falls. The difference is the foundation.

## 12. Healing a Centurion's Servant (7:1–10)

Following the sermon on the plain, Jesus went into Capernaum again. While he was there he healed the sick slave of a Roman centurion. A similar story is given in John 4:46–54, and some scholars make the two identical. The differences in details, however, far outnumber the similarities. The event in Matthew 8:5–13 is the same as the one in Luke, but again the details vary so much that either Luke had a different source or each writer framed the story to make clear a different emphasis. The second alternative is the more probable.

*Verse 2: A centurion:* The man was a Roman officer in charge of a company of soldiers (the title indicates one hundred) stationed in Capernaum to maintain law and order.

*A slave:* Slavery was a social practice of the day. While it was degrading in society as a whole, there were exceptional instances of honorable relationships between slaves and masters. This was such a case, as the next phrase shows.

*Who was dear to him:* The RSV marginal reading "valuable" may suggest commercial value. This was not likely Luke's meaning. In all other uses of the Greek word in the New Testament, the word means "to honor," "to hold in high esteem" (Luke 14:8; Phil 2:29; 1 Pet. 2:4, 6).

The slave was gravely ill, near death. Having heard of Jesus and his arrival, the centurion sent leaders of the Jews to request that Jesus come to heal his slave (v. 3). This was not for devious reasons, or to apply pressure. He states his reason for not going personally in verses 6–7.

*Verses 3–4: Elders:* The word means literally "older men." These were men of maturity, who had won the respect of their fellows and had been entrusted with leadership in the synagogue. They made the request (v. 4) and added their own encouragement because the Roman officer was *worthy* of Jesus' merciful ministry. This may reflect their own doubt as to whether Jesus would minister to a Gentile. They did not know his attitude and his concern for men regardless of race.

*Verse 5:* The Jewish leaders offered two evidences of the centurion's worthiness:

*He loves our nation:* The word translated *love* is the usual one for willing and desiring the best for the object of one's love. The centurion recognized the importance of the Jews and looked upon them with good will. This was a rare outlook for a Roman.

*He built us our synagogue:* The Greek pronoun is emphatic—*he himself built us our synagogue.* This hardly means that the centurion paid for the synagogue personally. It is more likely that his leadership had made possible the building of the synagogue at Roman expense. The centurion may have been an interested inquirer into the Jewish religion. The New Testament contains several references to such Romans.

*Verses 6–8: Jesus went with them:* It was a rare event when the synagogue leaders joined Jesus in an errand of mercy. He went because of the call for help, however, not because he was moved by Roman generosity. As they neared the house, the centurion sent friends to stop Jesus from coming further.

*I am not worthy to have you come under my roof:* The centurion knew that it was forbidden to Jews to go into the house of a Gentile. Too, he regarded himself as unworthy of going into the presence of one of Jesus' character and reputation. That was the reason he had sent the Jewish leaders rather than going personally (vv. 3, 7). He explained (v. 8) that as a man accustomed to having his orders obeyed, he knew that all Jesus had to do was give the order and the slave would be healed. This confidence was based on his acquaintance with what Jesus had done in healing others. Several cases had been in Capernaum.

*Verse 9: When Jesus heard this he marveled:* It was most unusual to have such confidence from anyone. Up to this point there is no record of Jesus' healing a person in absentia. The centurion knew authority and he had confidence in Jesus' authority.

*Not even in Israel have I found such faith:* Jesus' amazement was that such an expression of faith came not from a Jew (who supposedly knew and worshiped God), but from a Gentile (whom the Jews regarded as pagans and who were outside the religion of Israel). Not even among the Jews had Jesus encountered such an expression of faith. While Jesus many times spoke of faith, there are only two recorded instances of his having commented on the *greatness* of a person's faith. Both were Gentiles: this Roman centurion and the Syro-Phoenician woman (Matt. 15:28).

*Verse 10:* There is no indication of what Jesus did to accomplish the healing. The concluding statement is simply that when the friends returned to the centurion, they found the slave healed. (For an interesting possibility of what Jesus may have done, compare John 4:50.)

## 13. Raising the Widow's Son (7:11–17)

The New Testament records three instances of Jesus' bringing a dead person back to life: this youth (only in Luke); the daughter of Jairus (Luke, Mark, Matthew); Lazarus of Bethany (only in John). They involve differing lengths of time in which the person had been dead: Jairus's daughter, probably a few minutes; this youth, probably a few hours; Lazarus, four days. The end result was the same in all cases. By including this event at this place in his Gospel, Luke indicates that Jesus could not only prevent death (the centurion's slave) but he could also counteract it after it had taken place.

*Verse 11: Nain* was a town a few miles southeast of Nazareth. Accompanied by *his disciples and a great crowd,* Jesus approached the *gate of the city.* From what remains of the ancient city, there is no indication that it was ever a walled city. *Gate* must refer to the road entrance into the city. The city was in the hills, and many caves which served as burial places are still evident near the modern village of Nein.

*Verse 12: A man who had died:* The phrase is one word in the Greek, a participle. The tense makes it clear that the person was dead. Furthermore, the people were carrying the body out of the city to the place of burial. Custom dictated burial as soon after death as the necessary preparations could be made. This is the basis for the statement made above that this man had been dead a few hours.

*The only son of his mother . . . a widow:* Nothing in the words used here gives a clue to the age of the dead person. The word *man* in the RSV is not in the Greek text; the participle indicates simply a dead male. Because of Luke's stress on the fact that this was the only son of a widowed mother, interpreters have been influenced to understand this as a young man to whom the mother looked for support. Jesus used the word *young man* (v. 14), when he called him back to life. The term "only son" is the term used in John 3:16 in reference to God's giving his "only Son." Luke's use of this term and his stress on the fact that the mother was a widow may be a clue to Jesus' particular interest in this case. The absence of Joseph after the episode in the Temple when Jesus was twelve is cited by many interpreters as one of several bits of evidence that at this time Mary, too, was a widow.

*A large crowd:* The translation *large* may be misleading. While the Greek word sometimes is used for a large crowd, it actually means "a sufficient number." Men were needed to carry the body. People in a number sufficient for respectable "mourning" would be needed, whether paid mourners or neighbors and relatives. A widow who had lost her only means of support could not likely afford a large company of mourners. The group was "sufficient" but not necessarily *large.*

*Verse 13: When the Lord saw her:* "The Lord" is Luke's usual way of referring to Jesus. The use of the term developed historically after Jesus' death. The natural title for Jesus at this time was "teacher." Luke wrote from the later historical perspective in which the almost universal term used by Jesus' followers was "Lord" or the double title "Lord Jesus."

*He had compassion:* Jesus was always moved by human suffering, sorrow, and need. Luke emphasizes this characteristic more than the other Gospel writers. If Mary, Jesus' mother, was indeed a widow at this time, Jesus' feeling for this sorrowful widow would have been all the more acute. He showed his concern for her later by committing her to the care of the beloved disciple rather than his half brothers (John 19:26–27), who at this time seem not to have believed that he was the Messiah (John 7:5). It is easy for Christians to see a parallel between this incident at Nain and Mary's sorrow over the death of her "only Son." If Jesus foresaw this parallel, however, Luke gives no indication of it.

*Verse 14:* Bidding the mother to stop her weeping Jesus *came and touched the bier.* This was a startling action. To come into contact with a corpse in any way was to become ceremonially defiled and to require ceremonial purification before returning to the synagogue for worship. The bearers of the corpse had to experience such defilement. It was not necessary for Jesus to do so. His action was another indication of his rejection of those ceremonial laws which he regarded as valueless.

*Young man, I say to you, arise:* In the performance of miracles, Jesus followed no set pattern. Sometimes he touched the person; sometimes he only spoke; sometimes he did both. At the raising of Lazarus (John 11), Jesus used the occasion to teach that where he was present the authority of life over death was already in operation. No such teaching accompanied this event, but the truth of the principle was in operation.

*Verses 15–17: The dead man sat up, and began to speak:* Again Luke affirms the reality of death; precisely translated the phrase reads, "the corpse sat up and started talking." No longer was it a corpse; now a living person gave physical evidence of the return of life. So Jesus *gave him to his mother.* Luke does not report the naturally joyful reunion. He reports the *fear,* that is, "reverent awe" which seized them all. They gave the glory to God in such expressions as *A great prophet has arisen among us* and *God has visited his people.* In the history of Israel a *prophet* was God's authorized spokesman. He spoke and acted for God. Sometimes he performed miracles (Moses, Elijah, Elisha). Jesus did both. The people accepted his work as validation of his ministry as God's prophet. Their report spread all the way to Judea (v. 17).

## 14. Answering the Messengers from John the Baptizer (7:18–23)

*Verse 18:* The report of *these things*—specifically the healing of the centurion's slave and the raising of the widow's son—reached the disciples of John the Baptizer. Generally, the phrase embraces all the things Jesus was doing. John's disciples reported the events to him in prison. Herod Antipas, displeased at John's preaching that Herod's marriage to Herodias was illegal and, hence, adulterous (Mark 6:14–29; Matt. 14:1–12; Luke 9:7–9), had arrested and imprisoned him. John sent two of his disciples to question Jesus.

*Verses 19–20: Are you he who is to come . . . ?* "The Coming One" was a common reference to the promised and anticipated Messiah. John's question must be considered in the light of the total circumstance. He had understood his role as the one who prepared the way for the Coming One (Luke 3:4–6, 15–17). He had identified Jesus as that Coming One (John 1:29–36). Now John, the preparatory one, was in prison for his preaching, and the one for whom he had prepared the way was experiencing tremendous success and was being called *a great prophet* (v. 16). It would have been unnatural if John had not wondered about this complex of ideas and events.

*Shall we look for another?* If Jesus did not prove to be the Coming One, John had been wrong in his identification, his commission to prepare the way for the Messiah remained to be carried out, and in prison he was helpless to do anything. Other than the normal problem brought up by John's adversity and Jesus' prosperity, what could have caused John to wonder and doubt?

John may have anticipated that the coming Messiah would set up the kind of kingdom the people desired, that he would lead a revolution against Rome and restore Israel to a place as a nation among the nations. While Jesus was experiencing tremendous popularity with the people and success in his work, he had made no move toward establishing such a kingdom. Still clinging to his anticipation of such a kingdom, John may have wondered if Jesus was or was not the one to set it up.

*Verse 21:* Jesus did not give an immediate answer to their question. He continued a ministry which included casting out evil spirits, and healing the blind and many others who had various *diseases*.

*Verse 22:* When he answered their question, it was not with a categorical "Yes, I am the Coming One." As in other cases, he left them to draw their own conclusion. He told them to report to John what they themselves had seen him do and what they had heard that he was doing: healing the blind, the lame, the lepers, the deaf; raising the dead; preaching the good news. According to Isaiah 29:18–19; 35:5–6; 61:1, these things were a part of what God was expected to bring about in the glorious future for his people. Jesus indicated that in him and his work they had become reality. In him the kingdom of God had indeed broken into history and the age to come—the age of the Messiah—had arrived.

*Verse 23: Blessed is he who takes no offense at me: Takes no offense* means precisely "never stumbles." Jesus' action was not to make it harder for one to accept the idea that the Messiah had come. All that he was doing was to make it easier for men—including John in prison—to understand that the kingdom of God had been inaugurated even though it was not the kind they had expected.

### 15. Jesus' Appraisal of John the Baptizer (7:24–35)

*Verses 24–25:* Jesus sensed that the people who had confidence in him might be tempted to blame John for lacking their confidence. Jesus spoke to remove such thoughts and to give his high appraisal of John. He reminded them that when they responded to reports and went out into the wilderness to see this man John, they did not see a *reed* blown back and forth by the shifting winds. They did not see *a man clothed in* the *soft raiment* which characterized those who lived the soft life of the king's palace. The words have an element of the scorn of rugged men for the "sissies" at the *king's courts*.

*Verses 26–27:* They saw *a prophet . . . and more than a prophet.* The unbending, rough-clad man they heard was a prophet—spokesman from God—but not an ordinary prophet. He was the one sent from God to *prepare* the *way before* the Messiah (v. 27; see Mal. 3:1). In this Malachi passage God promised to send his messenger to prepare the way for the sudden appearance of the Lord in his Temple. This Lord would be God's messenger of his redemptive covenant with men. His coming would mean the purifying of the Temple, God's ministers and their service to God. Jesus saw himself as that one and John as the one who prepared the way for him.

*Verse 28:* Jesus said that among those born of women there was no man greater than John. This was not a contradiction of John's statement that the one coming after him was so much greater than he that he was not worthy to loosen the lace of his sandal (Luke 3:16). Nor did it indicate that John was the greatest man who had been born. The immediate reference is to God's prophets. The prophets were the most honored men in the history of Israel. Jesus said that John was the greatest of them all, the one anointed of God to prepare the way for God's Messiah. This made him not only the last in the series, but the greatest in the series.

*Yet he who is least in the kingdom of God is greater than he:* Interpreters are divided in their understanding of this statement. The division may be summarized in two major views.

Some understand Jesus as speaking from the viewpoint of religious privilege. John stood at a unique place in the scale of religious privilege. He stood above all those who had looked forward to the coming of God's messianic king, but below those who actually experienced that king and his kingdom. So he was greater than all those who had preceded him in anticipation, but he was less than even the least one of those who followed him in realization. The first part of this view is convincing; the second part leaves a sense of incompleteness.

Others understand that Jesus was speaking from the viewpoint of the nature of the kingdom of God. John thought of the kingdom as apocalyptic, external, material, political. Like the people of his day, he expected the Messiah to lead the kind of revolution against the Romans which Judas Maccabaeus had led against the Greeks, to establish Israel as a political kingdom. When Jesus did not do that, John was perplexed (vv. 18–20; see comment above). On the other hand, Jesus understood the kingdom of God to be inner, spiritual, and eternal rather than external, material, and temporal. The *least one in the kingdom of God* who understood that nature was superior to John who, even with all his greatness, misunderstood. This second view is more convincing.

*Verses 29–30:* The difference of this passage from what precedes and what follows it and its absence from Matthew's parallel account indicate that it is Luke's explanation of the way people reacted to John and to Jesus in their corresponding roles. The common people and the tax collectors had accepted John's call to repentance and baptism. They had accepted Jesus as the one for whom John was the forerunner. They welcomed Jesus' appraisal of John and *justified God*—that is, they judged that God was right in sending John with the call to repentance, confession, and baptism.

On the other hand, the Pharisees and teachers of the law *rejected the purpose of God.* The word translated *purpose* is the word for "counsel" or "plan." As the leaders of the religion of Israel they were a part of God's plan or purpose in John and Jesus. The word translated *rejected* means to "treat with contempt," "to spurn," and is antithetical to *justified.* Each helps to interpret the other. *For themselves,* that is, as far as they were concerned, they spurned John's call to repentance and baptism. They did not regard it as applicable to them. They rejected John; they rejected Jesus; and they rejected Jesus' appraisal of John as the greatest of the prophets.

*Verses 31–35:* The long introduction to this parabolic illustration is typical of the introductions which the rabbis used. *To what then shall I compare . . . what are they like? They are like children . . . .*

*Verse 31: The men of this generation:* i.e., the people who could not make up their minds about John and Jesus. Was John like a reed bent by the changing winds? Or was he the greatest of the prophets? Was Jesus really the Coming One? Or was John wrong in so identifying him?

*Verse 32: Like children sitting in the market place:* The scene was a common one—children joining in games while their parents shopped. But they could not agree on what they wanted to play. One group wanted to play "wedding," so they made gay music expecting the others to dance. The other group wanted to play "funeral," so they made sad music and expected the others to mourn. The couplet is poetry which, in the Aramaic language of Jesus and his Jewish listeners, possessed the cadence of song, including rhyme.

*Verses 33-34:* Jesus applied the parable to the people's appraisals of John and Jesus. John came *eating no bread and drinking no wine.* The reference is not just to eating and drinking, but to a way of life. John withdrew from social life and all its expressions and lived an ascetic life in the wilderness. *The Son of man*—Jesus' favorite reference to himself—came *eating and drinking.* Again the reference is not to eating and drinking per se. Whether or not Jesus drank wine should not be argued on the basis of a charge by those who were trying to discredit him. The reference is to a way of life different from John's. Jesus went into the towns; he entered into the social life of the day; he banqueted with sinners.

The people accused John of madness which drove him to live in the wilderness, the haunt of evil spirits. They held that a normal person would mix with people in social life. But when Jesus mixed with people in social life they threw what amounted to curse words at him: "glutton," "drunkard," "friend of tax collectors," "friend of sinners." The compassionate person portrayed in the Gospels denies the first two charges but looks upon the second two as a part of what God had sent him to do.

*Verse 35* contains a proverb—*Yet wisdom is justified by all her children.* The RSV translation *yet* makes a difficult saying more difficult, suggesting some sort of contrast. The Greek text has the simple connective "and"—a more understandable translation.

*Wisdom* is the ability to make the right choice when faced with multiple choices. What is chosen indicates the nature of the wisdom. In this proverb *wisdom* is personified as a mother, and what she produces is personified as her *children* (Luke), or her deeds (Matt. 11:19). The mother is *justified* in having made the right choice (or failed to do so) by the nature of what she has produced (child or works).

If this is correct, the people and the tax collectors (v. 29) were wise, and their choice of accepting John and Jesus justified their wisdom. The Pharisees and teachers of the law (v. 30) were not wise, and their foolishness was demonstrated in their rejection of John and Jesus. It is a wise person who can produce consistent decisions.

### 16. Anointing by a Sinful Woman (7:36–50)

Luke follows the charge against Jesus of consorting with tax collectors and sinners with an incident in which Jesus ate with a Pharisee. Jesus accepted the company of all who invited him. He used this occasion to teach a lesson on forgiveness.

*Verse 36: Sat at table:* The Greek reads "reclined on a couch at the table." This was a formal dinner and followed the Roman custom of reclining.

*Verse 37: A woman of the city, who was a sinner:* Literally, "a woman who by her nature was a sinner in the city." The nature of her sin is not indicated. It has been generally understood that she was a harlot. Some understand that Luke's very silence about the nature of her sin indicates that. Attempts to identify her with Mary Magdalene from whom Jesus cast out seven demons (not one of her demons is named, however, harlotry or otherwise—Luke 8:2), or this incident with the anointing by Mary of Bethany (John 12:1–8) have been unsuccessful.

Some commentators have interpreted this incident as taking place in an open court to which the public had easy access to observe the banquet. Even if this were the setting, it was a most unusual thing for such a woman to venture upon the property of a Pharisee. Nevertheless, when she learned that Jesus was at the dinner, she went in taking a cruse of perfumed oil. Whether or not she had met or heard him previously is not indicated.

*Alabaster flask:* This was a delicate container of finely polished stone or marble made with a long neck and sealed. In order to use the contents, the neck would have to be broken with the result that all the perfume would have to be used at one time.

*Ointment:* This was a highly scented oil used for perfuming the body. The fact that it was in an alabaster cruse indicates its value.

*Verse 38:* The woman stood behind Jesus and over his feet as they stretched back from the table. His feet were bare; the sandals by custom had been left at the door.

*Weeping:* From what she knew of Jesus' character, she was convicted of sin in her own character. Some interpreters understand that she had experienced forgiveness at a previous meeting with Jesus. Her tears fell on his feet and she wiped them off with her unbound hair. The loose flowing hair is regarded by some as an indication of immodesty. Two opposite characters met in the event.

*Kissed his feet:* The tense of the Greek verb indicates that she fervently kissed his feet. By dramatic contrast, when Judas identified Jesus to the arresting officers, he too "kissed him fervently." She broke the neck of the cruse and poured the aromatic oil on Jesus' feet. How different from the purpose for which she may have been keeping it, to anoint her own body.

*Verse 39:* Although the Pharisee had invited Jesus into his home, he looked on him with suspicion. When he observed that Jesus did not shrink from the woman's presence, he felt that his suspicion was confirmed. He knew that this woman was a sinner. Surely, if Jesus were indeed a *prophet,* his insight would sense the woman's character. It did not occur to him that Jesus knew her character but still did not shrink from her.

*Verses 40–41:* Jesus told a story to his host Simon. A creditor had two debtors. One owed him *five hundred denarii;* the other owed him *fifty.* The Roman silver denarius was worth about eighteen cents. Its relative value is more readily grasped in the fact that it was the normal day's wage for a working man. These debts were both large ones for a working man—five hundred days' work, and fifty days' work. When the debt was due to be paid and neither debtor could pay, the creditor graciously canceled both debts.

*Verses 42–43:* Jesus used parables and example stories to confront men with decision and response. So he asked his host, *"Which of them will love him more?"* Simon gave the obvious answer, "I am of the opinion that the one who had the larger debt canceled."

*Verses 44–46:* That obvious answer made clear Jesus' application of the story to the situation of the three. Simon and the sinful woman were set in contrast. When Jesus entered Simon's house, Simon did not appreciate him enough to extend the common courtesy of having a servant wash Jesus' feet. But the woman washed them with her tears and dried them with her hair. Simon did not appreciate Jesus enough to bestow the customary kiss on his forehead or cheek. But the woman kissed his feet. Simon did not appreciate Jesus enough to provide ointment for the hair. But the woman lavishly anointed his feet.

*Verse 47:* The woman had a consciousness of great sin. Great forgiveness adequate to care for all the sin elicited the response of great love in return. Jesus' statement, *"her sins . . . are forgiven,"* has prompted some to hold that she had previously experienced forgiveness and now was expressing her love and appreciation. That would be a natural sequence and would parallel the story. The man's love followed the cancellation of his debt, not preceded it.

In contrast, Simon had little or no consciousness of sin. He had sought no forgiveness. He would not have believed Jesus capable of forgiving sin. He did have a little appreciation and had indicated that by inviting Jesus into his home. But he knew nothing of love and the joy of sins forgiven.

*Verses 48–50: Your sins are forgiven:* If the woman had previously been forgiven, these were words of reassurance to her—the kind of reassurance often needed by the newly forgiven sinner. If she had not been forgiven in some previous meeting, Jesus detected in her action the kind of consciousness of sin and commitment to God which made forgiveness possible. The details of the parable story would not parallel so well in this case. The application would be made in reverse.

*Verse 49: Those who were at table with him:* These were probably other guests whom Simon had invited. If so, they would be of the same opinion as Simon on matters of sin and forgiveness. Some may have been members of Simon's family. Simon does not appear to be included, though he probably had the same problem about Jesus' pronouncing forgiveness.

*Who is this, who even forgives sins?* The objection implicit in their question was the same one voiced when he pronounced forgiveness to the paralyzed man (5:21). There they called Jesus' words blasphemy because only God could forgive sin. They interpreted Jesus' words to mean that he was claiming to do that which only God could do. So he was.

*Verse 50: Your faith has saved you:* There had been no expression of faith. Luke's report suggests that Jesus had understood *faith* in the woman's boldness in coming into Simon's house and sincerity in weeping and lavishing devotion upon him. For Luke to have omitted the saying would have suggested salvation without faith. At the time of Luke's writing, salvation by faith had become so axiomatic that salvation without faith would have been incomprehensible.

## 17. Beginning a Second Tour of Galilee (8:1–3)

*Verse 1: Soon afterward:* These words connect with the last event in chapter 7—Jesus in the house of Simon the Pharisee.

*He went on through cities and villages:* Only one of the events of this tour can be definitely located geographically—the healing of the demoniac in the *country of the Gerasenes* (v. 26). Matthew 13:1 and Mark 4:1 locate the teaching in parables (Luke 8:4–15) "beside the sea," but no more definitely than that.

*Preaching and bringing the good news:* While this tour included some miracles, it was more a preaching and teaching tour than the previous one. Jesus was accompanied by the Twelve, who had been with him for most of the previous tour, and by a group of women, all of whom had experienced some kind of healing (v. 2). Only one healing is mentioned specifically, however, and that requires some interpretation.

*Mary, called Magdalene, from whom seven demons had gone out:* Little is known about this Mary apart from her loyalty to Jesus. She was apparently from the town of Magdala, and that name was used to distinguish her from other women named Mary (Mark 15:47; 16:1; Matt. 28:1). Whether *seven demons* refers literally to seven maladies which had been cured all at one time or on seven separate occasions, or whether *seven* refers symbolically to the completeness or fullness of her condition before Jesus healed her is not clear. Nor is the nature of her problems indicated, as it is in other cases related to demons (epilepsy, Matt. 17:14–21; a deaf and dumb condition, Mark 9:17–29; blindness, Matt. 12:22). Attempts to prove harlotry have not been convincing.

The other women named are Joanna, who was the wife of Herod's steward Chuza, and Susanna. Joanna is mentioned only one other time in the New Testament as part of the postresurrection events (Luke 24:10). Susanna is not mentioned elsewhere. Besides these there were *many others,* all apparently women of influence and financial means. They accompanied Jesus and the Twelve and supplied necessary funds *out of their means* (v. 3).

## 18. The Parable of the Sower (8:4–18)

This parable is included in Matthew and Mark as one of Jesus' parables told by the sea. Luke comments only that it was given to a crowd of followers which grew from town to town (v. 4). From the earliest records of Christian thought, the parables of Jesus have occupied interpreters. It is generally accepted that they are at the heart of Jesus' teaching. Outstanding works are available on the parables alone. To know the very heart of Jesus' teaching and the early church, those works must be studied.[1]

Parables are almost totally absent from the Old Testament. The rabbinical writings, however, covering the rabbinical teaching from about 100 B.C. to

---

1. For further reading on parables, see C. H. Dodd, *The Parables of the Kingdom* (New York: Charles Scribner's Sons, 1956); J. Stanley Glen, *The Parables of Conflict in Luke* (Philadelphia: The Westminster Press, 1967); A. M. Hunter, *Interpreting the Parables* (Philadelphia: The Westminster Press, 1960); Joachim Jeremias, *The Parables of Jesus* (New York: Charles Scribner's Sons, 1962); Ray Summers, *The Secret Sayings of the Living Jesus* (Waco: Word Books, 1968); Dan O. Via, *The Parables* (Philadelphia: Fortress Press, 1967).

A.D. 200 abound in parables. Every spiritual, ethical, or moral teaching was explained by a parable. Jesus' parables follow the rabbinical pattern. He was using an effective and well-known method of teaching.

Verses 5–8: The scene was a familiar one—a farmer in spring planting time walking through his field, reaching into a bag or a basket, scattering seed by the handful. After the seed was scattered the ground would be ploughed to cover the seed with soil.

*Verse 5: Along the path* suggests "beside the path." The Gospel According to Thomas has "on the path." That, precisely, was what Jesus meant. The paths were made by people walking through the fields after harvest. When planting time came, the farmer simply scattered the seed and ploughed the fields, including the paths, to cover the seed. In Jesus' parable, birds ate that easy-to-find seed before it could be ploughed under.

*Verse 6: Some fell on the rock*—that is, on the very shallow soil barely covering a sheet of flat rock. This seed sprouted, but because there was no moisture from deep soil, it withered and did not reach maturity.

*Verse 7: Some fell among thorns*—brambles that infested the corners and borders of the fields. The Greek word for thorn is *akantha,* recognizable in the word for the red-berried garden shrub, pyracantha, that is "fire-thorn." The thorns grew right along with the grain and choked it out so it bore no fruit.

*Verse 8: Some fell on good soil:* This was that part of the field free of rock and thorns and having depth of soil. There the seed sprouted, grew, and produced fruit in the proportion of one hundred to one—an abundant harvest indeed. Mark 4:8 has varying yields—thirtyfold, sixtyfold, a hundredfold. Matthew 13:8 has the reverse—a hundredfold, sixtyfold, thirtyfold. The Thomas gospel has sixty to one and one hundred twenty to one. In every case, it was an impressive harvest.

*He who has ears to hear, let him hear:* This expression frequently follows a teaching of Jesus. Sometimes, as here, it is clearly the words of Jesus. At other times it appears to be the writer's appeal to his readers. It means simply that the hearer with the power of spiritual discernment should listen, understand, and apply the teaching in his own experience.

*Verse 9:* Later, the disciples—apparently the Twelve—asked Jesus to explain the meaning of the parable. To the modern reader their request seems to reflect dull minds. The meaning appears to be so obvious. That, however, is because we already know the explanation of the parable (vv. 11–15). Without that explanation, there would be few clues for the modern reader's understanding.

*Verse 10,* with much fuller parallels in Mark 4:11–12 and Matthew 13:11–17, has been the source of much perplexity for interpreters. In rabbinical use, parables were for the very purpose of making the teaching easier to understand. Whatever these verses in Mark, Matthew, and Luke mean, it is obvious that Jesus' main purpose in using parables was for the same reason—to make his teaching easier to grasp. It is nonsense to say that it was not. Why, then, did Jesus seem to say that in the case of some listeners he spoke in parables so they would *not* understand?

Some interpreters understand Mark 4:11–12 as a saying of Jesus about his teaching in general (rather than just the parables) and the reaction of many —particularly the Pharisees and scribes—in rejecting it. Mark's placing it here in relation to the parables has led to the confusing idea that Jesus used parables so that only the Twelve could understand them and for others they would be interesting stories with no particular significance. Matthew and Luke followed Mark's text, thus leaving the same impression. Matthew, in fact, elaborates on the idea to the extent of quoting Isaiah 6:9–10 about the discouraging prospect Isaiah faced in proclaiming God's message to a people who would continue to reject it.

In line with this interpretation, it is interesting to note that in the rabbinical writings, every instance of the use of this passage from Isaiah has understood it to hold out the hope that *if* they will but see and hear and turn, they will be healed. In the total purpose of Jesus, that view is more fitting. The Pharisees and scribes were so set in their opposition to Jesus and his message that the more he taught the more they hardened themselves against him and rejected his message. In the Matthew setting, this statement about parables follows immediately the charge that Jesus was in league with Beelzebul (12:24) and the request for a sign which would force them to believe against their will and apart from spiritual perception (12:38–42). It is likely that Jesus had in mind the continuing hardening of the Pharisees against him so that even simple parabolic teaching was beyond their acceptance. There was always on his part the willingness to accept and forgive any who did see, hear, and turn.

Verses 11–15: The interpretation of the parable is more along the line of allegory (in which the details have major importance) than parable (in which only the central idea is of major importance). There is a central idea which is true to the nature of a parable—the result of the sowing depends on the condition of the soil. But in the interpretation the details are explained allegorically. Some interpreters understand the interpretation to be not the words of Jesus but an addition after the early church had used and interpreted the parable and had experienced among its members these various results. Others see in it nothing which would not have applied to the people who listened to Jesus and responded in different ways.

This latter view is very natural if one considers the setting in verse 4. A crowd of followers grew as Jesus and his disciples moved from town to town. As Jesus observed them he considered the fact that some would become fruit-bearing followers and others would not. Some would come to live the genuinely spiritual, upright life which he desired for his followers. By life and by word they would become his witnessing people, and through their witness others would come to the same kind of experience and life. Still others, however, would simply hear his teaching and continue in the same old way of life. Jesus saw himself as the sower, the people as the field, and the seed as the word of God. He considered the discouraging fact that so many would not receive the word to become fruit-bearing followers. But he also considered the encouraging fact that some would receive the seed fruitfully and there would be a harvest. Isaiah 6 ends on that same encouraging note (see 6:10).

*Verse 11: The seed is the word of God:* Matthew has "the word of the kingdom" (13:9). The word of God which Jesus was proclaiming was the good news of the kingdom of God breaking into history. Men heard the same word but responded in different ways.

*Verse 12:* Some people heard the word, but there was not even enough depth of soul to give it lodging. As birds picked up the seed from a hard path through the field, the devil took away the word before it could find lodging. Such hearers bore no fruit.

*Verse 13:* Some people heard the word and received it joyfully, but their nature was too shallow. They gave initial evidence of faith and promises of fruit-bearing, but when the real testing time came, they proved incapable of living up to that promise. They bore no fruit.

*Verse 14:* Some people who heard the word and received it had sufficient depth of character to produce fruit, but they also had an inordinate concern about the material cares and pleasures of life. Like thorn bushes, these cares and pleasures choked the growing new life.

*Verse 15:* Some people who heard the word and received it possessed depth of character—*an honest and good heart.* The seed planted in good, prepared soil with patience grew, developed, and produced fruit. Jesus said of them that they were "of such a nature" that they had *an honest and good heart.*

In every case the sower is the same, Jesus; the seed is the same, the word of God. The difference lies in the kinds of soil, the people. So Jesus saw the crowds who followed him. To try to apply this to the idea of salvation—those who are never saved, those who are saved but fall away, those who are saved but bear no fruit, those who are saved and bear fruit—is to make this a twentieth-century allegory which would have been meaningless to Jesus' followers. They did not have the background of centuries of debate over the question of whether or not salvation in the New Testament sense of the word includes the ideas of "losing one's salvation" or of "being saved but not bearing fruit."

### 19. Responsibilities in Hearing and Serving (8:16–18)

Both Luke and Mark (4:21–25) relate Jesus' saying about not concealing a lighted lamp to this parable of the sower, and continue with a caution about how one hears. Matthew includes the illustration of the lamp in the Sermon on the Mount (5:15). Luke's association of the two is very natural—as it is the nature of seed to grow in the soil and produce fruit, so it is the nature of a lighted lamp to serve by illumination. One illustration (the lamp) illustrates another (the seed and soil).

*Verse 16: Lamp:* This was the shallow dishlike earthen lamp which burned oil. A piece of flax or cloth might serve as the wick.

*Vessel:* Mark and Matthew have a word specifically used for dry measure such as grain or similar products. Luke has a more general word used for either dry or liquid measure. Both types of vessels were commonly used in the homes of Jesus' hearers.

*Bed:* The word means a couch of any sort. It is the root from which our word "clinic" comes.

*Stand:* This was an elevated resting place for the lamp.

Together the terms form a graphic scene. No one would enter a dark room, light the dimly burning lamp, and then cover it with a household utensil or put it under a couch. Rather, he would put it up on a stand where its light would be most effectively dispersed.

*That those who enter may see the light:* This idea is only in Luke. It is generally interpreted as a reflection of Luke's interest in the Gentiles and their coming into the light of God as he was known and worshiped by the Jews, and then as he carried out his redemptive work in Jesus. Jesus desired his followers to bear fruit, like seed in good soil, and to illumine all men, including the darkness of Gentile life.

*Verse 17* is a wisdom type of saying which may be applied in varying situations. Paul used it to illustrate the impossibility of concealing evil (Eph. 5:13). Here it appears to refer to the inevitable demonstration of one's true nature. Good soil will cause the seed to bear fruit; a lighted lamp will illumine not only those already in the circle of its light but also all those who enter that circle.

*Verse 18* summarizes the central lesson of the two illustrations. Jesus cautioned the Twelve to take care how they heard the word and responded. The effectiveness of their service depended on such care. This same saying is used as part of Jesus' explanation of why he taught in parables (Matt. 13:12), and in the conclusion of the parable of the money (Luke 19:26; Matt. 25:29). It is the kind of saying which permits multiple applications in teaching whether by Jesus or his followers.

*To him who has will more be given:* This means that demonstrations of wise hearing, receiving, fruit-bearing, warrant one's being entrusted with more and greater responsibility. The long arm of opportunity reaches out to lay hold of the one who has demonstrated his fitness for greater responsibility and service.

*From him who has not, even what he thinks that he has will be taken away:* To prove unworthy of trusteeship and incapable of rendering the service anticipated by the trusteeship, is to lose the opportunity of service—fruit-bearing or light-bearing.

## 20. Qualifications for Kinship to Jesus (8:19–21)

The place of this brief reference to Jesus' family suggests that his mother and brothers were a part of the crowd mentioned in verse 4. If this is not the case, Luke's reason for using it at this point is conjectural. The most likely reason is to point up the non-fruit-bearing nature of his brothers. That reason may not have applied to his mother. There is nothing else in the Gospels to indicate her opposition to what he was doing.

*Verse 19: His brothers:* Some understand these to be the sons of Joseph by a previous marriage, believing that the physical union of Joseph and Mary was never consummated and that, hence, she had no child except Jesus. This ignores Matthew 1:25 which records that the physical union was not consummated until after Jesus' birth. There is no reason to think that theirs was not a normal union with other children born after that. Others understand these brothers as Jesus' half brothers, born of Mary and Joseph while Jesus was born only of Mary.

Little is known of these men. Matthew 13:55–56 refers to four brothers: James, Joseph, Simon, and Judas; there is the additional reference to "all his sisters." John 7:5 indicates that at that time in Jesus' ministry, Jesus' brothers "did not believe in him." Later, Paul refers to "James the Lord's brother" (Gal. 1:19) as a leader in the Jerusalem church and to "the brothers of the

Lord" as traveling missionaries who took their wives with them on their travels (1 Cor. 9:5). Acts 1:14 refers to his brothers as part of the group in the upper room.

*Verse 20: Desiring to see you:* There has been much conjecture as to why they came. Mark reports (3:21) that some of Jesus' friends believed he had lost his power of reason. The religious leaders from Jerusalem charged that he was in league with the devil (Mark 3:22). Add to this the fact that his brothers did not believe in him, and it appears that they came because of their concern for his welfare, and probably to discourage him in his work and to seek his return to the carpenter's trade in Nazareth. Mary's concern would be normal. Whether or not she, too, sought to discourage him and to try to get him to return to Nazareth is conjectural. Jesus did include her in the same sweeping statement about his brothers (v. 21). There is no other indication in the New Testament that she tried to oppose him in his work.

*Verse 21:* In his response Jesus pointed to a different order of kinship. Those were his mother and his brothers who were hearing and obeying the word of God. In this manner the family is related to the parable of the sower. To hear and do the word of God is to bear fruit, to illumine, the dark, to be part of Jesus' real family which transcended physical kinship.

### 21. Stilling the Storm (8:22–25)

This miracle of Jesus' mastery over the forces of nature is placed by Mark at the end of a day of Jesus' teaching in parables, which included the parable of the sower (4:35). Matthew includes it in a setting of different kinds of miracles (8:18, 23–27). If his setting is to be considered chronological—which is very doubtful—it follows Jesus' healing of Simon's wife's mother in Capernaum. It is of importance that Matthew interpreted the event as a retirement of Jesus to get away from the crowds. Luke gives no indication of setting. He simply reports that it came about *one day* (v. 22). The obvious indication is that it was one of the days of Jesus' ministry about the shores of the Sea of Galilee. His purpose in reporting it was to show the reaction of the Twelve to such power (v. 25).

*Verse 22: Boat:* This was the type of boat used by the fishermen in Galilee which could easily accommodate Jesus and the Twelve. If they were leaving from Capernaum—a possibility from Matthew's account—the boat probably belonged to the fishing company of Zebedee, John, James, Simon, and Andrew.

*The other side of the lake:* From any of the towns in the area of Jesus' activity on the western shore of the sea, *the other side* would be the eastern shore in the Gerasene territory (v. 26).

*Verse 23: He fell asleep:* Wearied from the work of the day, relaxed from the pressure of the crowd, in the relative quiet of the few miles across the sea, Jesus went to sleep. One of the meaningful touches of the humanity of Jesus is the frequent reference of the Gospel writers to his being hungry, thirsty, tired, sleepy, and lonely.

*A storm of wind came down:* To the north of the Sea of Galilee snow-capped Mount Hermon towers 9,200 feet high. To the west are the Horns of Hattin, 2000 feet high. To the northwest the mountains near Safed are 2,750 feet high. The surface of the Sea of Galilee is 700 feet below sea level. This makes a natural setting for very sudden and vicious storms caused by cold winds coming down and striking the hot air over the surface of the sea. On this occasion, the waves were dangerously close to swamping the boat.

*Verse 24:* The three accounts of this event afford an interesting study in the different words used by the writers to report it. Mark 4:38 has "Teacher [*didaskalos*], do you not care if we perish?" Matthew 8:25 has "Save, Lord [*kurios*], we are perishing." Luke 8:24 has "Master, Master [*epistatēs*], we are perishing." Almost the same variation occurs in their reporting of what Simon Peter said at Jesus' transfiguration. Mark 9:5 has "Rabbi," the equivalent of "Teacher"; Matthew 17:4 has "Lord"; Luke 9:33 has "Master." Scholars are not agreed on why Matthew should use the word "Lord" in these two incidents which is Luke's characteristic term for Jesus, while Luke uses a different word, "Master." This may be merely an optional word in Luke's vocabulary, since he uses it six times (5:5; 8:24, 45; 9:33, 49; 17:13), and he is the only New Testament writer who does use it.

Comparing these three versions shows that the Gospel writers were not representing their quotation of the disciples' words as verbatim sayings. They were relating the event—the disciples' fear, their cry for help, and Jesus' response. It is quibbling and an erroneous understanding of the nature of the Scriptures to hold that different disciples said different things and that each writer reported what at least one of them said. The variety of expression is evident in the remainder of the story. All three writers report a twofold rebuke by Jesus but not in the same order. Matthew places Jesus' rebuke of the disciples for their lack of faith first and his rebuke of "the winds and the sea" second. Mark has first the rebuke of "the wind and the sea" and then the rebuke of the disciples. Luke has the same order as Mark but uses still different words in the first one—"the wind and the wave of water" (literal translation). The accuracy of their report does not depend on precise agreement in words used or order followed.

*Rebuked:* The basic meaning of the Greek word is "to find fault with," and by uses derived from that, "to chide," "to censure severely," and ultimately, "to restrain" violence or ferocity. This last use is intended in this case. All three writers use the same word.

*They ceased, and there was a calm: The wind and the raging waves* stopped their violence, and a calm "came to be" (literal translation). As quickly as the storm had come, "a great calm" came, as Matthew and Mark report. To the Twelve it probably seemed that they had never known such quiet.

*Verse 25: Where is your faith?* Again, compare the three accounts. Matthew, "Why are you afraid, O men of little faith?" (8:26). Mark, "Why are you afraid? Have you no faith?" (4:40). Luke, "Where is your faith?" Which did Jesus say? A more important question is, "What did he mean?" The answer is obvious. He was chiding them for having such little faith that they could not trust God to take care of them while they were engaged in God's work. They were God's people; they were engaged in God's work; it was God's weather. Why not trust him?

All outside the boat was calm and then a storm broke inside the boat— twelve men turning from fear to wonder and asking one another, *Who then is this, that he commands even wind and water, and they obey him?* Matthew reports that they asked, "What sort of man is this . . . ?" They knew him to be a man who got tired, sleepy, hungry, and thirsty; who could heal fever, paralysis, leprosy, and cast out evil spirits. They were amazed to see him exercise power even over the forces of nature. A clue to the unspoken answer to their question lies in their own words as Luke reports them: they said *"he commands."* This verb has the same basic stem *(epitassei)* as the word Luke uses in verse 24—"Master, Master." Jesus was a "Commander" not just for his disciples but also for the destructive forces which threatened them. Why should they not have faith rather than fear?

### 22. Healing the Gerasene (8:26–39)

*Verse 26:* Following the storm, the group reached *the country of the Gerasenes.* Luke locates it loosely but accurately as *opposite Galilee.* It is impossible to locate it more definitely than somewhere along the southeastern shore of the Sea of Galilee because of problems both in textual evidence and in archaeological evidence.

From the viewpoint of textual evidence, the different manuscripts of Luke contain three different readings: Gerasenes, Gergesenes, Gadarenes. The same three words appear in different manuscripts of Matthew and in different manuscripts of Mark. From the accepted principles of determining correct readings, the conclusion is that Matthew originally had "Gadarenes" and Mark and Luke originally had "Gerasenes."

From the viewpoint of archaeological evidence there are ruins of two towns, Gadara and Gerasa, on the eastern shore of Galilee that date from New Testament times. The town names do not appear in the New Testament, only the names designating the people: "Gadarenes" or "Gerasenes." Besides this, at a later date, there were two other towns by these names: Gadara, thirteen miles southeast, and Gerasa, forty miles southeast of what is judged to be the approximate site of this New Testament event. So, in the territory of the people known as Gadarenes or Gerasenes, somewhere near the shore, and where the hills were precipitous, the event may be located.

*Verse 27: A man from the city:* This man had previously lived in one of the towns nearby—Gadara or Gerasa. But now he lived *among the tombs,* in the caves which were used as burial places. *For a long time he had worn no clothes:* He had abandoned the company and the customs of men. Matthew omits altogether and Luke inserts later Mark's detailed account of the ineffective efforts of men to "tame" (dominate) him and of his continual screaming night and day as he cut himself among the rocks of the cliffs. Matthew—who reports two men rather than the one in Mark and Luke—adds the detail of extreme ferocity which prevented anyone from approaching.

*Who had demons:* This simple explanation indicates the motivation of the man for abandoning human company and living in such a repulsive place, condition, and manner. (See Luke 4:33 for a discussion of demons and demon possession.) This Gerasene man appears to have been a case of insanity associated with a complete dominance of evil. Whether the evil had driven him to his state of mental aberration or the mental aberration had driven him to his state of evil is not indicated. The outcome was Jesus' healing of both conditions, and that is the important part which must not be lost in some of the mystifying details.

For a better understanding of the event it is wise first to consider verse 29 which indicates the reason for the man's actions and words in verse 28.

*Verse 29:* Jesus *commanded the unclean spirit to come out of* the man. To have a "demon" or to have an "unclean spirit" mean the same thing. The stories of Jesus' dealing with demoniacs differ. Sometimes Jesus speaks to the person; at other times he speaks to the evil spirit within the person. Sometimes the person is represented as speaking; at other times the evil spirit in the person is represented as speaking. All occur in this incident. Jesus speaks to the man and he replies (vv. 29, 30, 38). The demons also speak to Jesus, and he speaks to them (vv. 31, 32).

*Verse 28:* In response to Jesus' command for the evil spirits to come out, the man fell down before Jesus and cried loudly, *What have you to do with me?* that is, "What is there between us?" or "What do we have in common?" The expression *Jesus, Son of the Most High God* implies that the man had some kind of knowledge of Jesus. There is no clue as to its source: previous knowledge of Jesus or his reputation; present identification of Jesus to the man; insight which, by contrast with his own evil nature identified Jesus as under the control of a good Spirit, God. These and other conjectures have been offered. They can be only conjectures. Matthew (8:29) has the thought-provoking addition that the demon-driven men (Matthew has two) asked Jesus, "Have you come here to torment us before the time?" The suggestion is that they were rational enough to know that ultimately they would experience "torment" for their evil, and were fearful that Jesus was going to bring that torment on earlier than was due.

*Verse 30:* The contrast between the man's words and Jesus' words is dramatic and instructive. The man called Jesus *Son of the Most High God.* Jesus asked the man, "What to *you* is a name?" (literal translation). The pronoun is emphatic—"*You,* what name fits *you.*" (In Jewish thought, the name meant the real person, his character.)

*And he said, "Legion"; for many demons had entered him:* The man's answer showed recognition of his demon-driven character. It was not a name, but a nickname describing his nature. While the number in a Roman legion varied from one historical period to another, after Augustus (B.C. 27–A.D. 14), it came to be 6000 foot soldiers with some units of cavalry added at times. This unfortunate man's cry had the sense of, "Call me Six Thousand." He felt that many demons were tearing him apart. It is rewarding to note that Jesus' method of dealing with the man at this point is in line with modern practice in dealing with mental cases by establishing identity—"Tell me about yourself; who are you?"

Verses 31–33: Embedded in this healing story is another short miracle story —the strangest of all those reported of Jesus and so far beyond our understanding that some have denied it as a true miracle story and have sought a rationalistic understanding of it.

*Verse 31: The abyss:* The word means a pit unlimited in depth and, hence, "bottomless pit." In Romans 10:7 it seems to refer to the place of the dead. In Revelation 9:1; 11:7; 17:8; 20:1, 3 it refers to the dwelling place of evil spirits. That is apparently the meaning in this passage. The demons are represented as recoiling from that terrible destiny even when they recognize Jesus' authority to make them come out of the man (v. 29).

*Verses 32–33:* This territory was inhabited by a mixed populace of Jews and

Gentiles. If the swine herdsmen were Gentiles, there was nothing irregular about their trade. If they were Jews, their trade was illegal if the swine were for their own consumption and at least irregular if they were only preparing them for the Gentile market. In either case the presence of a herd of swine in this territory was a common matter.

*They*—the demons—begged Jesus to let them enter the swine. If they could not live in men, they preferred to live in hogs rather than in the abyss. Jesus *gave them leave,* literally, "permitted them" to transfer their dwelling place from the man to the swine. Under the control of the demons, the swine acted as violently as the man had. They rushed down the steep hill and were drowned in the sea. It is ironic that *abyss* was sometimes used of the depth of the ocean. They did not want the depth of the bottomless pit, but they got the depth of the sea!

Matthew's version differs from Mark's and Luke's at this point. When the demons said to Jesus, "If you cast us out, send us away into the swine," Jesus replied "Go," literally, "Be gone" (Matt. 8:32)—in modern colloquial "Get out of here," or perhaps even "Scram!"

There is an ethical problem in the destruction of the swine. What right did Jesus have to destroy the property of others? Some have solved the difficulty by the simple expedient of holding that Jesus did not destroy them; the demons did. This is inadequate for serious consideration of the language of the Gospels. Some have avoided the entire problem by saying that whatever Jesus did as the Son of God was right, even though we may never understand the reason for it. This ultimate and comprehensive approach may fit the action of a sovereign God but it is an unsatisfactory way of dealing with the type of detailed action involved in this event.

Some interpreters understand that Jesus did not actually grant the permission but simply said, "Go," meaning, "Go where you belong, the abyss." The demons misunderstood, thought they had permission, and entered the swine with the disastrous results indicated.

Other interpreters, using the same Matthew reading, have taken a different approach. When Jesus said, "Be gone," the crazed man went into convulsions (as happened in other cases of people so afflicted). These actions frightened the swine, they stampeded, and were drowned.

Such interpretations may be plausible on the basis of the Matthew account. There is no possible way they can be based on the Mark and Luke accounts in which Jesus permitted the demons to do as they had requested. Some interpreters have suggested that this was a means of letting the man know that he was really experiencing healing. The sight of the swine acting as he had formerly acted convinced him that he was free of his legion of demons.

The ethical problem has been faced from the viewpoint that Jesus, as a good Jew, considered the herdsmen's trade illegal, regardless of whether they were Jews or Gentiles. The destruction of the swine was strictly legal by his standards, and it also served as a means of convincing the man that he was really healed; the unclean spirits could not return, but had been destroyed with the unclean animals in the depth of the sea. This appears to be as plausible as any and more plausible than some of the attempts to deal with a complex and perplexing event. A pitfall to be avoided is that of interpreting an event in a very different culture in the first century in the light of the requirements of law and order in the twentieth century. Today, a man may consider his neighbor's making counterfeit money or illegal liquor wrong and deserving destruction. But he becomes guilty of law-breaking if he takes the destruction into his own hands. He must follow constituted law enforcement channels to bring about the destruction of the nefarious trade. So twentieth-century man imposes his method on a first-century event. This is an unproductive approach to understanding the message of the Gospels.

*Verses 34–39* report the total result of the event by indicating the reaction of different persons. *The herdsmen* fled the scene in fear and reported what had happened. *The people* from both city and country came out to see both the man they had known and feared because of his ferocity and the one who had healed him. *The man* was sitting at the feet of Jesus—the traditional position of a pupil in relation to his teacher. He was clothed. He was sane. All of this was in dramatic contrast to his previous state.

*They were afraid:* Interpreters are divided on the significance of this expression. Some understand it to mean that the Gerasenes feared they, too, would lose commercially if Jesus continued destroying swine. They preferred their swine to a Savior. This is unlikely unless they, too, were "demon possessed," and there is no indication of that. Others understand that they were afraid of one who exercised such power. This is more likely. It was not the kind of reverent awe which Jesus could use constructively; it was a terror which repelled. They begged Jesus to leave their territory.

Likely because he sensed the lack of any foundation for helping the people, Jesus left. But he left behind a witness. The man who had been healed desired to go with Jesus (v. 38), but Jesus told him to stay, to go to his home and *declare how much God* had done for him. The man obeyed, but he did not restrict his testimony to his home. He went about the entire city publicly *proclaiming how much Jesus had done for him* (v. 39). He had been told to report what *God* had done for him; he reported what *Jesus* had done for him. There are theological overtones in this, whether it reflects the man's terminology or that of the Gospel writers; both Mark and Luke use it. What Jesus had done was the action of God working through him.

## 23. Raising Jairus's Daughter (8:40–56)

Luke contrasts the Gerasenes' rejection of Jesus and the welcome Jesus received on his return to the west shore of the sea. In this section, one miracle story—the healing of a woman—is embedded within another miracle story—the raising of Jairus's daughter.

*Verse 40: When Jesus returned* refers to his having left the crowd (Matt. 8:18) to go to the east side of the sea (Luke 8:22). He came back to the same place—most likely Capernaum (Matt. 9:1—"his own city") which had been his headquarters since the rejection at Nazareth (Luke 4:31). Mark 5:21 places the scene "beside the sea" and includes it in the chain of events following Jesus' teaching in parables "beside the sea." Luke gives no definite location but follows Mark's order, while Matthew departs from that order and places here several other events previously given by Luke: the healing of a paralytic; the call of Matthew; the visit with the messengers from John the Baptizer. The order of Mark and Luke is most likely correct.

*Verse 41: A man named Jairus* sought Jesus in the crowd which surrounded him. He was *a ruler of the synagogue.* These rulers were men who had proved their capacity for effective management of the affairs and services of the synagogue. This prominence in the life of the city accounts for the rare preservation of the man's name (Mark 5:22) and its use by Luke (v. 41).

*Falling at Jesus' feet* was not unusual demonstrativeness in oriental culture. It indicated the man's great distress and his genuine desire that Jesus come and heal his twelve-year-old daughter who *was dying.* Luke uses the imperfect tense, indicating that she was not dead but had what appeared to be terminal sickness. Matthew and Mark each use words and tenses differing from Luke and from each other, and both indicate that the daughter was already dead and that Jairus was requesting that Jesus raise her. Since Mark and Matthew have no prior instance of Jesus' raising a dead person and Luke has (7:11–16) it is likely that if the daughter had been dead, Luke would have been the one to stress that fact. Jesus went with Jairus with the intention of staying the sickness and preventing the impending death.

*Verse 42:* Matthew states that the disciples went with Jesus and Jairus; the reference appears to be to the Twelve, although only Peter, James, and John went into the room with Jesus. Mark indicates that a great crowd followed as Jesus went. Luke is the most graphic. His expression, *the people pressed round him,* means literally that they were suffocating him. It is a detail which makes clearer how the woman could approach and touch him without being observed.

*Verse 43:* The woman *had had a flow of blood for twelve years.* Mark reports that she had suffered much from many physicians, that she had spent all her money for their treatment, but instead of getting better she continued to get worse. Matthew omits all that. Luke, the doctor, states the case professionally; hers was an incurable case! The King James Version's reference to her experience in paying physicians for treatment is so poorly attested in the manuscripts of Luke that it cannot be regarded as a part of the original and is rightly omitted from the RSV text. It was an interpolation by a later copyist influenced by Mark's passage.

*Verse 44:* In her condition the woman was reluctant to approach a strange man in a public crowd and ask for his help. Too, ceremonial law meant ceremonial uncleanness for Jesus if he touched her. She believed so strongly that the power of God was working through Jesus that he would not have to touch her. If she could only touch him, she would be healed. With such faith (v. 48), when her fingers touched the edge of his robe, she was conscious of the cessation of her hemorrhage.

*Verse 45:* Jesus was conscious that *power* had *gone forth from* him to heal. Since he had not consciously touched anyone for that purpose, he knew that someone had touched him for that purpose. This is likely another indication that the healing miracles Jesus performed drained his energies. It was part of his reason for frequent retirement for rest in prayer. The disciples could not understand Jesus' question. When the people around Jesus denied touching him, Peter exclaimed that in the pressure of the people they were all touching him.

*Verses 47–48:* When she knew that Jesus knew that healing had occurred, the woman knelt before him, admitted her action, and explained why she had done it. Jesus related her healing directly to her faith, and the event can be understood only in that light. There was no healing power in Jesus' robe, nor in Simon Peter's shadow (Acts 5:15), nor in handkerchiefs and aprons brought to Paul from people too sick to attend his services in person (Acts 19:12), but people experienced healing in all these contacts. The only satisfactory answer in accepting the phenomenon of such healing is that God has sometimes seen fit to honor a faith so simple that it must make contact with his power in some tangible, objective, even material way. But it has been a combination of man's faith and God's power which has produced healing.

*Verse 49:* A man from the house of Jairus came at that point to report to Jairus that the daughter had died and that there was no further need to *trouble Jesus.* The word means to weary or harass.

*Verse 50:* In Jesus' words to Jairus there is something of the ring of his words to Martha and Mary on the occasion of their brother's death (John 11); where Jesus was present, the power of life over death was already operative—*Do not fear; only believe*—literally, "Stop fearing; believe." Jairus had believed in Jesus' power to save the daughter from dying. He was not to lose that belief. He would see Jesus' power to save the daughter from death.

*Verses 51–53:* At the home Jesus permitted Peter, James, John, and the parents to enter the room with him. At the door he paused to quiet the mourners with the words, *"she is not dead but sleeping"*—a metaphorical reference to the quiet which death brings to the turmoil of life. (See John 11:11, 14; 1 Thess. 4:13; 1 Cor. 15:20, 51. The Jews referred to one who had died and was buried as "sleeping with his fathers.") On this occasion the people scoffed at Jesus. They knew the child was dead; he would find out for himself when he entered the room. Doubtless, they went on with their wailing.

*Verse 54:* Taking the little girl by the hand—this time the conscious touch of power was his—he said, *"Child, arise."*

*Verse 55: Her spirit returned:* That part of her which animated the body returned to renew that animation. There is unquestionable evidence that people in that day believed that a person's spirit lingered about for three days after death hoping to get back into the body, but on the fourth day when the natural processes of death had definitely taken over the body, the spirit would go away. That was Martha's meaning when, concerning Lazarus, she said, "Lord . . . he has been dead four days" (John 11:39). Her concern was not so much with the unpleasant situation of opening the cave after those processes had started as it was with the fact that *it was too late* to help Lazarus. She, too, learned that when Jesus is present, it is never too late.

The word translated *spirit* is also the word for wind or breath. It is not definite whether Luke uses it in this simple sense, that is, "her breath returned," or whether he uses it in the more refined sense of the spirit—sometimes called "soul"—as that which gives life and animation to the body. The latter fits the event better.

The raising was instantaneous, *she got up at once.* As calmly as a doctor ordering sustenance for a patient who is recuperating after long illness, Jesus ordered that food be given to the child. Some have understood that this was to demonstrate the reality of her return to life. That is not at all likely. Jesus requested and ate food to prove to his disciples that he was a flesh-and-bones body and not just a "ghost" after his resurrection (Luke 24:40–43), but these parents had no such need.

*Verse 56:* Jesus requested that the amazed parents not report to anyone what he had done. He appeared to be satisfied for the people to go on believing that the child had not really been dead but in a coma of sickness from which he had healed her. Why this secrecy? It may be that there is a very simple reason. Everything Jesus did increased the crowds, even to the point of limiting effective service on his part. Galilee was a hotbed for revolutionary messianic expectations. Jesus' understanding of his role as the Messiah was entirely different from theirs. He continued his ministry, but he tried to subdue any fanning of the messianic flame which threatened.

### 24. Beginning a Third Tour of Galilee: The Mission of the Twelve (9:1–6)

These verses report Jesus' sending the Twelve on a mission of preaching and healing in the villages of Galilee. Mark has the same mission. Matthew has a much longer section on Jesus' instructions to the Twelve, with an added note that after Jesus had sent them out, he too started on a tour of Galilee. It appears to have been a division of labor in order to reach more people.

*Verse 1:* He gave them both the *power* and the *authority* over demons and different kinds of sickness. The word *diseases* translates a general word for various types of illness. The association with the word *demons* may indicate authority and power to heal sickness attributed to the presence of evil spirits in a person.

*Verse 2: He sent them out to preach the kingdom of God and to heal.* Jesus regarded his own healing miracles as a sign of the presence and power of the kingdom of God among men. Their work as his authorized messengers meant the same thing. Mark 6:7 indicates that they were sent in pairs "two and two." How they were divided is not indicated. Fairly safe conjecture would put Peter and Andrew together, James and John together, and then the other two sets of four each (see discussion on 6:13–16) broken down into four teams of two each. There is no ground for attempting to name the teams.

*Verse 3:* It must be remembered that the disciples were not being equipped as foreign missionaries for a term of several years. They were going into villages where most of them were well known and in many cases where they had previously been with Jesus. They were going among their own people (the Jews) and in many cases likely their own kin. The assignment was very limited in space, time, and persons. On previous journeys, Jesus had been with them. On this one, they went without him. What they had learned from him they were now to practice in their own experience.

They were to make no elaborate provision for their comfort, food, or shelter. They were to live with the people whom they served, receiving nothing for their services, paying nothing for their hospitality.

*No staff:* This was a walking stick, not a club for protection. There is no apparent reason for the prohibition. The conjectural reason is that they were to carry nothing that would encumber them or need looking after—not even a staff or a second robe. Mark 6:8 reads that they should take nothing "except a staff." He cannot have had in mind a different kind of staff since all three Gospels have the same word. Some interpreters understand that Jesus permitted them to take the staff they already had (Mark) but not to secure a new one (Matthew and Luke). There is no evidence in words or grammar for this interpretation, which is a straining attempt at harmony. All the evidence is that Mark reports Jesus' instruction to take nothing except a walking stick, and Matthew and Luke report that he told them to take nothing that would get in their way.

*Nor bag:* Interpreters are divided on this word. Some understand it to mean that they were not to take any bag for carrying provisions. Others understand it to refer to a bag such as a beggar or traveling teacher would carry for receiving coins from those who passed or stopped to listen. This is probably influenced by Matthew 10:8, "You received without pay, give without pay." The former view is the more probable. They would eat in the homes where they stayed; they would need no bag for provisions.

*Do not have two tunics:* The tunic was the inner garment beneath the outer robe. To wear two was to have additional comfort against the cold. This suggests that the season was not winter. To carry an extra tunic in order to have a change would be to have something requiring looking after, or might even suggest concern or anxiety about material comfort. This instruction must not be considered in relation to our twentieth-century affluence with our multiple changes of clothing from day to day. The working people in Jesus' day probably had one outfit of clothing at a time. Even in 1954, trouble developed at a hospital in Jordan because the wife of the gatekeeper had two dresses and the wives of the other workers had only one each which they got when they married; they would not get another until the first one was worn out.

*Verse 4:* They were to make one home in a village their headquarters for the duration of their stay. No reason is given for this. Matthew 10:11 indicates that when they went into a village or town they were to seek for someone in the town who was "worthy" and stay in that home. It is not clear as to what constituted being "worthy." Probably it meant one who, knowing their mission, would give them hospitality.

*Verse 5* may clarify the identity of those who were not worthy. Jesus told them that when they were not received they were to go on to the next town. When they left the town which had rejected them they were to stop outside the town, stamp their feet as if to remove even the dust of the town, and then go on to preach in a town which would receive them. Their shaking off the dust of the town was a witness that the town had rejected the messengers and message of God; they were now free of responsibility for that town but were not to stop their preaching. Other towns would receive them and their message.

*Verse 6:* They departed and followed Jesus' instructions. Their success was reported upon their return (v. 10).

## 25. Herod's Disturbance Over the Identity of Jesus (9:7–9)

It may be that Luke's placing this little episode here indicates that the ministry of the Twelve increased the excitement over Jesus and what he was doing.

*Verse 7:* Herod Antipas, the ruler—tetrarch—of Galilee and Perea, heard the reports of what Jesus was doing and was perplexed. Some people were reporting that Jesus was John the Baptizer alive and preaching again.

*Verse 8:* Some were reporting that Jesus was *Elijah.* The miracles may have been responsible for this rumor. Elijah was noted for his miracles and he was expected to come back as a forerunner of the messianic age (Mal. 4:5). Others were saying that Jesus was certainly one of the ancient prophets returned to the earth but they did not know which one.

Mark and Matthew quote Herod as repeating and half-believing that John had come back to life. His executing John at the request of his stepdaughter Salome upon the instigation of his wife Herodias had bothered him. He had not wanted to do it but he had allowed himself to get into such a position that he had to to sustain his pride (Mark 6:17–28; Matt. 14:3–11).

*Verse 9* quotes Herod as saying, *"John I beheaded; but who is this about whom I hear such things?"* Jesus was preaching the same message of repentance and the presence of the kingdom of God which John had preached. Had God perhaps brought John back to life to continue what Herod had stopped? Herod started seeking an opportunity to see Jesus. So far as the record reveals it, he did not get that opportunity until Pilate sent Jesus for Herod to try on the charge that he was a disturber and revolutionist (Luke 23:6–12).

### 26. Feeding the Five Thousand (9:10–17)

Of all the miracles which Jesus performed, only this one is in all four of the Gospels. It made a tremendous impression on the followers of Jesus and the early church. The writers used the event in different ways. In Luke it is little more than an indication of Jesus' concern for the tired and hungry people. In Mark and Matthew it is definitely an indication of an attempt at a wilderness revolution in which the people sought to make Jesus the leader; he even had to dismiss the Twelve before he could break up the crowd. In John it serves as the perfect foundation for Jesus' speaking of himself as the life-giving bread from heaven in contrast to the physical bread which Moses, and he as the prophet like Moses, had given in the wilderness.

*Verse 10:* The Twelve returned from their mission and reported their success. The indications are that he had appointed the time for the return of all of them. Luke uses a word that indicates a full and detailed report. Jesus detected need for a period of retirement with the Twelve. It may have been for rest or for further instruction or for both. Matthew indicates that the news of John the Baptizer's death had something to do with it (14:12–13). The plan did not succeed. The people learned where he had gone and followed for more of his teaching and healing.

They went into the vicinity of *Bethsaida,* a town on the shore of the Sea of Galilee, just east of the place where the Jordan River flows into the sea. It was a fishing town; the name itself means either "house of the fisher" or "house of the hunter." John 1:44 gives it as the home of Philip, Andrew, and Peter, though later than that Peter clearly had a home in Capernaum. Bethsaida (also known as Bethsaida Julias) was at the most western point of the territory of Herod Philip, who had named it in honor of Julia, daughter of Augustus Caesar.

Since it was clearly outside of Galilee, some confusion has arisen over the statement in John 12:21 that Philip was from "Bethsaida in Galilee." To compound the confusion, while Luke 9:10 states that Jesus and the Twelve went to Bethsaida *before* the miracle of the loaves and fishes, Mark 6:45 states that *after* the miracle Jesus directed the Twelve into a boat and told them to "go before him [i.e., ahead of him] to the other side, to Bethsaida." All of this has influenced some interpreters to theorize that there were two towns involved: Bethsaida Julias on the northeast shore of the Sea of Galilee and Bethsaida on the northwest shore, perhaps a suburb of Capernaum. This cannot be substantiated except conjecturally on the basis of these different references to Bethsaida. If one must have a clear solution to the problem, he must wait; it simply is not available now.

*Verse 11:* When the crowds arrived, even though his time with the Twelve was cut short, Jesus *welcomed them, spoke to them of the kingdom of God,* and healed some of them.

*Verse 12:* Near the end of what appears to have been a day spent in teaching, the Twelve suggested that Jesus dismiss the people to go into the villages and secure food and lodging. *We are here in a lonely place* indicates the sort of place to which Jesus had taken them for the retirement.

*Verse 13:* Jesus suggested that the disciples feed the people. They responded that unless they went to buy food, they had only *five loaves* of bread and *two fish.* The loaves were the common small flat loaves, approximately the size of a thin hamburger bun. There is no indication about the size of the fish, except that in John 6:9 the bread and fish appear to be a boy's lunch, and a diminutive form of a word is used for the fish, implying that they were small fish. That word is not used for fish at any other place in the New Testament, but it was in common use at the time as indicated by other writings of the period.

The combined presentation of the four Gospel accounts is that the Twelve had no resources for feeding the people—not enough food, and not enough money to buy food, if there were places to shop (John 6:7). Beneath the surface is the fact that there were available to them resources of which they had taken no cognizance. Jesus was there.

*Verses 14-15:* Jesus commanded the disciples to seat (literally, "cause to recline," as for dining) the five thousand in one hundred groups of fifty each. In Mark's account this action has military overtones which are not in Luke. Mark uses it with several other details to emphasize the attempt of the people to start a revolution with Jesus as the leader.

*Verses 16-17:* Jesus took the bread in the presence of the people. Like a father at mealtime, he asked God's blessings upon it. Like a father, he broke the bread, dividing it among the Twelve with orders that they should pass it on to the people. All ate to their satisfaction, and each of the Twelve returned a basketful of unused food.

Attempts have been made to rationalize the story by giving a "natural" explanation of it. Some have suggested that Jesus used the little boy's willingness to share his lunch (John's account only) to shame the people so that others, too, produced food for sharing. Jesus blessed it before it was distributed. The surplus of twelve baskets of food has been regarded as a detail which grew in the telling of the story.

Some have suggested that Jesus had previously stored food there in a cave. He took the Twelve's supply (or the boy's, in John) and added his to it to feed all the people.

Such attempts ignore one thing. The people who recounted and used this story so freely believed that Jesus had performed a miracle. It was that which made the event meaningful to them and caused them to cherish it. From the viewpoint of Mark's account with all of its detail related to an attempt at revolution, it was precisely Jesus' miracle which caused the people to attempt to make him their leader. In time of war, it would be of inestimable value to have a leader who could provide in such a way. Because of overpopulation and underproduction, it has been estimated that likely three-fifths of the crowd had never had a really satisfying meal before this one.

### 27. Peter's Confession (9:18–21)

All four Gospels contain a confession about Jesus by Simon Peter. In John 6:66–69 it follows the departure of many of Jesus' followers because they would not accept his teachings about the necessity of his death. In Mark, Matthew, and Luke it precedes Jesus' statement about his death; in fact, it paves the way for that statement and results in the Twelve's perplexity and resistance to it.

Luke's account of Peter's confession is shorter than Matthew's (16:13–20), and is given with an introduction which differs from both Matthew and Mark (8:27–30).

*Verse 18:* The testing of the Twelve came after Jesus had been engaged in a session of prayer, just as his calling the Twelve came after a night of prayer (6:12–16). On this occasion Jesus asked the Twelve what they had heard as to people's opinions concerning him. Apparently several answered this question reflecting divided opinion. The responses were the same as the opinions voiced in the reference to Herod's perplexity (vv. 7–9). *John the Baptist* was a preacher of repentance and a proclaimer of the kingdom of God. So was Jesus. *Elijah* was a great miracle-working prophet of God. So was Jesus.

*Verse 19: One of the old prophets:* Which prophet is not identified, but Matthew 16:14 includes the opinion of some that Jesus was Jeremiah returned to life. Jeremiah was the weeping, compassionate prophet of God. So was Jesus.

The point of interest is the opinions of men as to the kind of person Jesus was and the kind of work he was doing.

*Verse 20:* Jesus wanted to prepare the Twelve for what was ahead for them and for himself, and such opinions were inadequate for that purpose. He therefore separated the Twelve from other men when he asked, *"But who do you say that I am?"* The language is emphatic—"But *you* in distinction from all the others, who do you say that I am?" He wanted their personal opinions as conclusions drawn from association with him, listening to his teachings, and observing him at work.

Only one answered this question, Simon Peter. All evidence indicates that he voiced their group judgment. As a group they had considered and had reached a consensus: "You are the Christ" (Mark 8:29); "The Christ of

God" (Luke 9:20); "You are the Christ, the Son of the living God" (Matt. 16:16). It is obvious that Peter said only one thing. Either he said one thing and all three Gospel writers interpreted this meaning in the term they used. Or he said one of the three and the other two writers interpreted his meaning in the term they used. The decision is subjective. To this writer, Mark's version appears the most likely with the other two as interpretive variations.

What they confessed was that they had concluded that he was the Messiah (Hebrew), Christ (Greek); both words mean the Anointed One, promised of God as redeemer and inaugurator of his messianic kingdom. Mark and Luke lack the Matthew 16:17 blessing of Jesus upon Simon and his indication that it was an opinion reached not by human reasoning, but by divine revelation. They also lack what has been called the most disputed passage in the Gospels, Matthew 16:18–19. All three include his command that they not report that he was the Christ (v. 21). He was still finding it necessary to discourage popular opinion which would lead to the revolution the people desired.

## 28. The First Passion Prediction (9:22–27)

Mark and Matthew permit a sentence break between Jesus' instructions that they were not to report that he was the Christ and his beginning to speak to them of his approaching death. Luke permits no break. His interpretation of the event is accurate, and his linking *their confession* that he was the Christ to *his confession* as to what kind of Christ he was catches dramatically the spirit of exultation followed by sorrow.

This experience marked the turning point in Jesus' life. Up to this point he had been with the crowds in joyful proclamation of the kingdom of God and in a ministry of mercy. While the crowds were present in the months which followed, Jesus spent more and more time with the Twelve, trying to prepare them for his death, his resurrection, and their continuing witnessing. They were slow and reluctant learners.

*Verse 22:* One reason Jesus did not want the disciples to report that he was the Christ was that the people would not have understood what kind of Christ he meant. Even the Twelve did not.

*The Son of man:* As previously noted (5:24), in the synoptic Gospels this is Jesus' favorite term for himself. It embraces the idea of reaching exaltation through humiliation and was the appropriate term to use on this occasion.

*Must suffer many things:* In the common view, the Christ would be an exalted conqueror. Suffering was not a part of his lot. From the voice from heaven at his baptism and the subsequent wrestling in the wilderness, Jesus had been moving forward to that Suffering Servant realization. The word translated *must* is an impersonal verb involving a necessity if a desired end is to be reached. The desired end was the completion of the mighty acts of God in bringing redemption to men. If that desired end was to be realized, *the Son of man must suffer many things.*

*Rejected by the elders and chief priests and scribes:* These were the leaders of the sacrificial services of the religion of Israel and the official interpreters of that religion. For a long time, events had clearly indicated that Jesus was on a collision course with those leaders. His rejection by them was inevitable. They could never accept his view of the Messiah or of the true nature of God and religion.

*Be killed:* Jesus spoke of the prophets of old as true spokesmen for God who were rejected and killed by their own people (see 11:47–51). Stephen's defense in Acts 7 was a tracing of Hebrew history around in terms of this theme. For the reader of Luke alone (or even of Mark, Matthew, and Luke together), there is little preparation for the violent reaction as that which Jesus predicted of the leaders. The Johannine accounts of Jesus' trips to Jerusalem, the hostility of the leaders and their attempts to kill Jesus make these words of Jesus believable.

*On the third day be raised:* From this point Jesus spoke repeatedly of his coming death. In each recorded instance he spoke also of his resurrection on the third day. The failure of the Twelve to accept his teaching partly explains their reluctance to believe the reports about his resurrection when the events did take place.

It must be noted that some interpreters do not regard these predictions of Jesus' death as authentic. Because of the difficulty of believing that Jesus could foresee the events so clearly, and because some details bear the marks of a "post-Easter" setting, they reject the words as having come from Jesus. They regard them as creations of the church at a later date. In response to this view it must also be noted that one may accept the sayings as genuine sayings of Jesus and still grant some evidences of coloration or clarification added at a later time. For example, in Matthew's account (16:21), Jesus said on this occasion that his suffering and death would take place in Jerusalem. Mark and Luke have no indication of where it would take place, though, considering the Johannine events, Jerusalem was the natural place to anticipate such action. Most likely Jesus did not say "Jerusalem," and Mark and Luke are correct. The passage is aided, not injured, by Matthew's addition of the word in the light of the history of the event. Mark indicates that Jesus said he would rise after three days. Matthew and Luke change this to *on the third day* in the light of the history of the event. The details vary; the saying is authentic.

Verses 23–27: If we did not have the accounts of Mark and Matthew, these verses would be more difficult to understand in their sequence, because Luke's account has a missing link. Even with Mark and Matthew there is some difficulty.

Mark and Matthew describe the vigorous reaction of the Twelve to Jesus' prediction of his violent death—they would not accept it. As Peter had led the group's confession, so he led in the objection to this prediction: "God forbid, Lord! This shall never happen to you" (Matt. 16:22). It should be remembered that when the time came, Peter drew a sword—or butcher knife —and did all he could to prevent Jesus' death. Both Mark and Matthew indicate that Jesus rebuked Peter for getting in his way—like a stone in the road he traveled, like Satan in the wilderness trying to turn him from the hard way. He told Peter that now he was not speaking by revelation from God as he had in the confession, but by human motivation.

All three of the Gospels insert this saying of Jesus about cross-bearing at this point. Mark states that Jesus called the crowds and the Twelve together and gave them this teaching (8:34), and his introduction suggests that the teaching was given on a different occasion but is inserted here because it fits so well—as Jesus is to bear a cross, so his followers must be prepared to bear crosses.

But does it fit so well? Nothing in what Jesus said about his death indicated death by crucifixion. All that he said indicated mistreatment, rejection, and death by the Jewish religious authorities. That would have been death by stoning—illegal indeed, but still occurring occasionally. There was no clue that his death would be by the cross until the fourth saying concerning his death (Luke 18:22; Mark 10:33; Matt. 20:19). On that occasion, as they were nearing Jerusalem, Jesus told them that when they arrived, he would be arrested by the Jewish leaders, turned over to the Romans (Gentiles), and crucified. From that time on talk about the cross would be meaningful.

What about this teaching on cross-bearing (vv. 23–27)? It may be understood in this setting, but the transition is not easy. It is more understandable as a saying of Jesus later, during the week in Jerusalem, or even after his death and resurrection as he talked with them about their future witnessing when he would no longer be with them. That witnessing would entail suffering, but so had his. The worthy disciple would accept whatever suffering was inevitable in the road God had chosen for him. This was what the cross meant to Jesus. Whether Jesus gave the teaching here or gave it later and the Gospel writers used it here, the meaning is the same.

*Verse 23: Deny himself:* i.e., deny anything which would prevent complete commitment. The expression is the type of saying which must be interpreted individually in each person's case. An easy life, ambition, even a hard but honorable way of life must be denied if that is not God's will.

*Take up his cross:* This must not be weakened, as it has sometimes, to apply to sickness, family trouble, business reversal, and a thousand other important things. To Jesus the cross meant one thing—what God desired for him as a part of his plan, in his case, death. So for his follower it means commitment to his way even if that means death. It cannot stop short of that and be the cross.

*Daily:* This emphasizes the continual, never-let-up nature of the commitment. The cross was not something which Jesus could carry and lay aside and pick up again. From the time he set himself to the obedient acceptance of the way of the Suffering Servant, the cross was there. Service to God after the cross-pattern of Jesus is a full-time service.

*Verse 24:* The cross with its suggestion of death may repel. Jesus told his disciples, however, that to avoid the cross was what really meant death. There is a double paradox in this verse, with the second reversing the first but relating to the same truth:

*For whoever would save his life will lose it;*
*and whoever loses his life for my sake, he will save it.*

*Life:* There is no English word for expressing precisely the meaning of the Greek word *psychē*. Sometimes it is translated "life," sometimes "soul." In the usual English sense of these two words, it is neither, but more like a combination of both. It is not just "life" in the sense of physical life as opposed to death. Nor is it "soul" in the sense of some spirit which animates the body. It means all that makes up "the real self."

If one is so fearful of losing his real self that he refuses to take up his cross and follow Jesus lest that mean death, he is certain to lose that "real self" and find that he has come to the worst sort of "death"—worse than physical death—because even while living physically he is living without meaning.

On the other hand, one who is willing to face death and the loss of self because of his relation to Christ will find that rather than losing his real self he has saved it. He denies everything which might be considered the good life and commits himself to Christ and the cross. He does not lose; he gains.

*Verse 25:* Continuing that line of thought, Jesus challenged his followers to consider the matter of profit and loss.

*He gains the whole world:* This is hyperbole. No person could gain the whole world with all its treasures of wealth, pleasure, position. But assume that he could. Grant that as a basis for argument. In so doing, he *loses or forfeits himself*—his real self, his best self. *What does it profit a man?* That is no bargain, only total loss.

So the Twelve faced the prospect of committing themselves to follow Jesus in such a way as to anticipate the worst sort of death—the cross. But Jesus assured them that this did not mean loss; it meant gain; it meant the realization of life at its most meaningful and best. All except Judas experienced that. He decided to take the loss and found "death" in spite of it.

*Verse 26:* With powerful appeal Jesus painted two scenes. In one, men here in this life are ashamed of him. They refuse to be identified with him. For them the cross is a scandal. In the other, Jesus returns in the glory of the Father and the angels. Those who were ashamed to identify with him in his humiliation find that they cannot be identified with him in his glory. As their character did not measure up in the earthly state, it does not measure up in the heavenly state. The choice was and is every person's, and only the person can make it.

Unquestionably this coming *in his glory and the glory of the Father and of the holy angels* is a judgment-coming of some sort. Attempts to relate it to the "glory" of his transfiguration a week later when Moses and Elijah appeared, or the "glory" of his resurrection which was announced by angels, or the "power" with which the Spirit came at Pentecost have not been convincing. What judgment, then, is he referring to?

*Verse 27:* Except for this verse it would not be so difficult to interpret verse 26, which on the surface is a natural reference to judgment at the consummation of God's purpose for the world and man. The part which causes the greatest difficulty is Jesus' statement, *there are some standing here who will not taste death before they see the kingdom of God.* Mark has, "the kingdom of God come with power" (9:1). Matthew has, "the Son of man coming in his kingdom" (16:28). This difference does not help to clarify the matter. Mark's and Luke's statements could be applied to other events; Matthew's is another clear reference to the consummation.

In the total of Jesus' teachings in the synoptic Gospels, two "judgment days" stand out: judgment on Jerusalem in A.D. 70; judgment on the world at the consummation. Can either of these fit both verses 26 and 27?

Some of those present did live to A.D. 70 when Jerusalem was destroyed. That coming in judgment might fit Luke and Mark; it hardly fits Matthew. Too, there is the question of what possible understanding the Twelve could have had of that event at this time. In the Gospels, Jesus' discussion of that event came on Tuesday of the week of his death in Jerusalem. The idea appears to have been completely new to the Twelve, as if they had not heard of it prior to that time.

His coming in glory at the end of the world best fits the entire judgment scene. It, however, certainly did not take place in the lifetime of any of his hearers! If that was what he meant, he was anticipating the end too soon. On another occasion he said that he simply did not know when the end of the world would be; God had not made that known to men or angels (Mark 13:32). On that occasion he made a similar statement: "This generation will not pass away till all has taken place" (Luke 21:32; Mark 13:30; Matt. 24:34). Although the idea is greatly disputed, his reference seems to have been to his coming in glory and judgment at the end of the world. He knew the nature of history and the end of history, but he did not know the extent of history. That was known only by the Father.

There is another possibility. Mark 9:1 begins with the words, "And he said to them." This is the mark of a separate saying. It suggests the possibility that Jesus gave this saying in another setting and with another reference (the transfiguration which follows in Mark 9:2–8?). When Matthew and Luke dropped the connecting words "And he said to them," the result was a different setting and reference—and a very difficult one.

### 29. The Transfiguration of Jesus (9:28–36)

One week after the confession experience, Jesus took Peter, John, and James up on a mountain to pray. What followed is commonly referred to as Jesus' transfiguration. It has a direct link with the confession of the Twelve, the prediction of Jesus' death as a part of his role as the Messiah, and the inability of the Twelve to accept his prediction. The transfiguration must be understood as a part of that whole.

*Verse 28: On the mountain:* The mountain is not identified in any of the Gospels. Mark 9:2 and Matthew 17:1 have "a high mountain." No indication is given as to why Jesus retired to a mountain. This is the first of several details which relate the event to the "new exodus," a theme which appears frequently in the Gospels. As examples, note the following: it took place on a mountain; the face of Jesus took on a rare brilliance; Moses was there; they talked about Jesus' "exodus" (the Greek word Luke uses for "death"); the Shekinah cloud of God's presence was there; the voice of God spoke out of the cloud; Peter related the event to the Feast of Tabernacles which memorialized the life of Israel in the wilderness.

*Verse 29:* While Jesus was praying, *the appearance of his countenance was altered. Appearance* translates a word which means "visible form or expression." *Countenance* translates the Greek word for "face." *Was altered* could be translated "became another" meaning "different." Hence, "the visible expression of his face became different." Matthew indicates the difference; "his face shone like the sun" (17:2). Luke's reference in verse 37 to "the next day" after the transfiguration leaves the impression that this took place at night.

*His raiment became dazzling white:* This suggests that the light of his face was reflected on the robe which he wore; hence, that the robe was white and a natural reflector. If this is not the meaning, the impression is that his whole body took on the same light as his face, and it shone through the garments, making them appear translucent. Nothing else in the description fits that, and Mark's detail about the brightness of Jesus' clothes fits the other view. If it was night, the effect would have been all the more striking. No explanation of this event is given in the New Testament. Some interpreters have understood it as a preview of Jesus' resurrection body. Some have interpreted the passage as a creation of the church after his resurrection interpolated back into the account of his life before the cross. One interpreter has explained it as Jesus' deity shining through a humanity which could not contain it. Such division of the divine and the human in Jesus does not make the theologians happy.

The Gospels leave the experience with an air of mystery. As the face of Moses took on a rare radiance while he talked with God on the mountain about the exodus of Israel, so Jesus' face took on a rare radiance as he talked with God on the mountain about his "exodus."

*Verse 30: Moses* was the representative of the law. *Elijah* was the representative of the prophets. The significance of their presence rather than some other great men out of Israel's history becomes evident later (see discussion on vv. 35–36). To question in what form or state they appeared and what implications that has for the nature of life after death is to get outside the purpose and meaning of this event. They appeared *in glory.* This may mean with the same sort of radiance which characterized Jesus. On the other hand, it may mean only a state beyond that which had been theirs as mortal men.

*Spoke of his departure, which he was to accomplish at Jerusalem:* The word translated *departure* is the Greek word *exodon*—"exodus." Only Luke tells us what the three talked about—his death in Jerusalem. Jesus had tried for a week to discuss his death with the Twelve; they could not sympathetically or understandably discuss it with him. The three disciples most capable of understanding him and entering with him into a consideration of his death, he took apart to pray about it—Peter, John, and James. But they went to sleep. Moses, representing the law which dealt with sin, and Elijah, representing the prophets who revealed God's promise of a Savior to deal with sin, talked with Jesus about his death. His death would be a type of "new exodus" by which God would create a new Israel.

*Verse 32:* Only Luke reports the sleep of the disciples. The text permits two translations. Alford[1] and the RSV render the central part of the verse *those who were with him were heavy with sleep* [bebarēmenoi] *but kept awake* [diagrēgorēsantes], *and they saw his glory.* Twenty-eight other versions translate the phrase to indicate that those who were with him were burdened down with sleep and saw the transfigured Christ with Moses and Elijah only after awaking. Of more than thirty commentaries checked, only one (Alford) understands that the disciples remained awake in spite of their sleepiness.

The verb which is translated "kept awake" *(diagrēgoreō)* is found nowhere else in the New Testament. Nor is it found in the Koine Greek papyri. It is

1. Henry Alford, *The New Testament for English Readers* (Chicago: Moody Press, nondated reprint of original 1863 publication), p. 350.

strictly a classical Greek verb. Wherever it is found in this particular tense it has the force of "stay awake." Never in classical Greek, however, is it found in a context with the specific word for "sleep" *(hupnos)* as it is here in Luke. That fact makes precise meaning difficult.

The conclusion is that while the RSV rendering *were heavy with sleep but kept awake* is permissible, in the total structure of verse 32 it is unnatural. The natural sense is that the three disciples fell asleep and missed what Jesus, Moses, and Elijah talked about, but when they awoke they saw Jesus with the radiance on his face and Moses and Elijah with him.

*Verse 33:* In Luke's understanding of the event, the conversation was over and Moses and Elijah were about to leave—*were parting from him.* There is no hint of this in Mark and Matthew. The three Gospels are in complete accord that Moses and Elijah actually departed while the cloud enshrouded the group (v. 36).

Again, Peter spoke, continuing the link with his confession (v. 20) and his resistance to Jesus' prediction of his death (Matt. 16:22). On the other two occasions he represented the group and led in their confession and remonstrance. It is not clear that he did so here; he seems to have spoken his own view. Mark 9:6 indicates that all three of the disciples were awestruck, literally "they had become filled with fear." What Peter said represented another attempt to prevent Jesus' going to Jerusalem where he had said that he would die.

The entire "exodus-tabernacles" motif of the passage, combined with Peter's proposal, suggests that the time for the Feast of Tabernacles was near—late September. Tabernacles was one of the six holy seasons which Jesus is known to have attended (John 7:2, 10, 14, 37). The disciples wanted to stay out of Jerusalem (John 11:7–8, 16).

*Master:* Luke again uses this word *(epistata)* which he alone uses for Jesus (8:24). Mark uses "Rabbi," the equivalent of "Teacher" (9:5, cf. 4:38). Matthew uses the same word "Lord" which he used in the account of the storm at sea (8:25).

*It is well that we are here:* Peter regarded it as fortunate that they were there on the mountain in the company of Moses, with whom the Feast of Tabernacles had originated. They could observe the festival better there than in Jerusalem.

*Let us make three booths:* The Feast of Tabernacles memorialized the forty years between the exodus and the entrance into the promised land, when the Hebrew people had lived a nomadic life. The festival was a week of living in temporary structures such as *booths* or tents along the roads into Jerusalem, the streets of Jerusalem, or even on the flat rooftops of the houses. It was a joyous time of sharing the life of their ancestors in that most meaningful period of their history.

*Not knowing what he said:* This is a rather literal translation. Mark 9:6 has, "he did not know what to say." Matthew omits that comment on Peter's action. The probable meaning was that Peter was awe-struck and perplexed by all the events and was not thinking the matter through clearly as he made his proposal. All the chain of events, however, support the idea that he was trying to avoid Jerusalem by suggesting that they observe the Feast of Tabernacles there on the mountain.

*Verse 34:* Even as he was speaking a cloud came over them and "was enveloping them in its shadow" (author's translation). To be suddenly surrounded by a cloud on a mountain is an eerie experience even when it is only a natural circumstance. The unusual circumstances of this occasion made it all the more eerie. Some understand that the cloud, too, was luminous as the face and raiment of Jesus were. The exodus motif of the event suggests the Shekinah cloud of God's presence as in the original exodus. *They were afraid*—awed—*as they entered the cloud.*

*Verse 35:* As God had spoken to Moses on the mountain during the exodus, he spoke here. This was another instance of the "daughter-voice," or voice from heaven, which came at Jesus' baptism. (See the discussion on 3:22.)

*This is my Son, my Chosen:* Mark and Matthew have, "This is my beloved Son." Some manuscripts of Luke have "beloved," but they are not the best ones. The reading *Chosen* is unquestionably the original word in Luke. This, too, adds to the parallel with the exodus in which the Hebrews came out of Egypt as the "chosen people," to be agents in God's work of redemption for men.

*This is my Son* indicates that the voice spoke to the three disciples and for their benefit. In the baptism experience the same phrase had been used (from Ps. 2:7), but it was directed to Jesus; undoubtedly Mark and Luke there have the correct reading and Matthew's "this is" (Matt. 3:17) has been influenced by this quotation at the transfiguration. At the baptism, the voice said to Jesus, "You are my Son"; at the transfiguration it said to the disciples, "This is my Son."

*Listen to him:* The tense of the imperative indicates continuous action—"keep on listening to him." The chain of events starting with Peter's confession indicates that the command to listen referred to their listening to what Jesus was saying about his death. They had confessed faith that Jesus was the Son of God, and now the voice from heaven—right out of the cloud of God's presence—confirmed that confession. But when Jesus said that his sonship involved death in Jerusalem, they rejected it and would not listen to him. Even now when Moses and Elijah had appeared to talk about his death, Peter had proposed that they not go to Jerusalem. The voice from heaven was saying essentially, "Keep on listening to what he is saying about the necessity of his death."

*Verse 36:* Matthew reports that when the voice came the disciples fell upon their faces in prostrate awe and that Jesus touched them, calming their fear and bidding them arise. This explanation, not in Mark and Luke, makes more understandable the statement of all three that when the cloud had disappeared Moses and Elijah also had disappeared and *Jesus was found alone.* Although there are so many differences in the details of the three accounts, all three Gospels close the account with the words precisely translated, "Jesus only."

This is an important and significant phrase. Moses was the representative of the law; Elijah was the representative of the prophets. Together the law and the prophets represented the total concept of God's authority in the Hebrew religion. Moses and Elijah disappeared; "Jesus only" remained; the voice from heaven said, "Listen to him." As God had spoken authoritatively through the law and the prophets, so he now was speaking and would continue to speak through Jesus—his *Son,* his *Chosen.* Jesus is God's word of authority. The disciples were to listen to what he said—even when and especially when he spoke of the necessity of his death as a part of his work as the Christ.

*They kept silence and told no one in those days:* Both Mark and Matthew indicate that Jesus told the disciples not to report this experience until after his resurrection from the dead. While Luke did not include the instruction, he probably had that in mind in his words *in those days.* The experience was not reported then; it was reported after Jesus' resurrection.

The command to silence is probably in line with the previous commands to silence; the reporting of a spectacular event would have encouraged the people in their determination to make Jesus their kind of revolutionary leader. Even with their reluctance to accept the idea of his death, the disciples did have a background which made Jesus' reference to reporting the event "after his resurrection" understandable. He had told them that he would be raised on the third day after his death.

## 30. Healing the Epileptic Boy (9:37–43)

Whether or not the transfiguration took place at night, this healing took place *on the next day.* Upon coming down from the mountain, Jesus and the three were met by a crowd of people including a man who begged Jesus to heal his afflicted son, an *only child,* that is, the father's only hope for perpetuating his family.

*Verse 39:* The RSV of Matthew 17:15 quotes the father as saying that the boy was "an epileptic." The verb so translated literally means "be moonstruck" or "a lunatic." This indicates ancient man's understanding of epilepsy; its coming and going seemed in many instances to be seasonal and related to the waning of the moon. Luke, however, did not use that word. He quotes the father as saying that the son had sudden seizures, by *a spirit,* when he would cry out incoherently, be shattered by convulsions including foaming at the mouth. These seizures were of long duration—*will hardly leave him.* Doubtless the condition was epilepsy.

*Verses 40–41:* At the man's request, the disciples who had not gone with Jesus up the mountain had tried to heal the boy but had been unsuccessful. Their failure at this time when they had successfully healed at other times (v. 6) may be an indication of the severity of this case. Mark and Matthew indicate that the disciples' faith was inadequate to deal with this case. They had not believed that they could heal him. Luke suggests the same reason, though it is not so pointed a reference to the disciples.

*Verse 42:* While the man was bringing the son to Jesus, the convulsions returned. Jesus healed him as he had so many other cases and restored him to his father. The same language is used here as in other cases. The condition was attributed to the work of an evil spirit. Jesus rebuked the evil spirit, and it bothered the boy no more. He was healed. The case was in line with their understanding and the cure was in line with their understanding. Modern man does not treat epilepsy as demon-caused. But neither does modern man completely understand its nature or its cure.

*Verse 43:* As in other cases, Luke registers the amazed reaction of the people. They attributed what Jesus had done to *the majesty of God.* Less poetically than the RSV translation, they attributed it to "the greatness of God."

## 31. The Second Passion Prediction (9:44–45)

In all three Gospels this is a brief statement of Jesus' about his death. Mark and Matthew gave it no particular sequence other than its taking place during the Galilean tour. Luke relates it specifically to the chain of events beginning with the disciples' confession of their faith that he was the Messiah. There is an indication in Mark 9:31 that this was more than one short saying. Mark used the imperfect tense "he was teaching," meaning either a teaching extended over some period or a teaching repeated over and over. The latter is more likely. Jesus used the closing weeks of the Galilean ministry to speak often of his coming death.

The saying is introduced by the last half of verse 43 closing the account of Jesus' healing the epileptic boy. *While they were all marveling at everything he did, he said to his disciples* . . . . In the midst of the amazed reaction of all who had witnessed the event, Jesus brought the minds of his disciples back to the fact that even with all that power, he *was* destined to die shortly.

*Verse 44: Let these words sink into your ears:* This took all of them back to his prediction of his death at their confession (v. 21), and it took Peter, John, and James back to the voice from heaven saying, "Listen to him" (v. 35). They were not to let his merciful ministry to the needy cause them to forget about his death.

*The Son of man will be delivered into the hands of men:* That is the total of the saying in Luke. *Delivered* means given over in any way. Later the word is used of Judas both from the viewpoint of his being a "betrayer" and from the simple viewpoint of his formal identification of Jesus in order that a legal arrest could be made. While Luke reports only this brief reference to his death, Mark and Matthew both report a longer statement, similar to his earlier one, including that he would be killed, and then raised to life on the third day. The *men* into whose hands he was to be delivered are not identified. Unquestionably the reference is to the elders, chief priests, and scribes of the earlier occasion (cf. v. 22). The Twelve had no indication from either reference that death would be by anyone other than the Jewish religious leaders.

*Verse 45:* The reaction of the Twelve to this saying—or to these repeated sayings as Mark indicates—was not the vigorous resistance they registered at the former saying (Mark 8:32–33; Matt. 16:22–23). On this second occasion Matthew reports that "they were greatly distressed" by it (17:23). Mark says that "they did not understand the saying and they were afraid to ask him" (9:32). They grasped only enough to distress them and make them fear what Jesus would say if they asked him for further discussion.

Luke reports the same twofold reaction as Mark but he also comments that *it was concealed from them, that they should not perceive it.* There is no indication who or what had concealed it. Since every detail of the related events makes it clear that Jesus wanted them to understand, it can hardly be intended that it was God who had concealed it. Most likely it was their own unwillingness to accept his death or admit its necessity which had clouded their ability to understand what Jesus was talking about. "There is no one so blind as the man who refuses even to look." This proverb was certainly true in their experience. The construction of the phrase *that they should not perceive it* most often expresses purpose, but in this case it expresses result, and was so used frequently. The word translated *perceive* is used only this one time in the New Testament. In common use it meant to understand by the senses. Their refusal to listen was dulling their understanding of what Jesus was trying to get them to see about his coming death and resurrection.

## 32. Teaching on Humility (9:46–48)

This teaching of Jesus on humble service has no introduction in Luke. The implied connection is clearly the contrast between Jesus' trying to get the Twelve to accept his death as a part of the work in which they were engaged and their arguing in the shadow of death over the question of their own relative greatness as his followers. Mark 9:33–34 helps us to understand the connection. From the transfiguration of Jesus and the healing of the epileptic boy, the Twelve and Jesus went to Capernaum. On the road, Jesus observed that the Twelve were engaged in lively discussion over some subject. When they settled down in Capernaum, he asked what they had discussed along the road. They did not want to tell him because they had been discussing their relative rank as his followers when they should have been trying to arrive at an understanding of his references to his death.

*Verse 46: And an argument arose among them as to which of them was the greatest.* Several details of recent events served as a background for their argument. From the beginning of their association, Peter had apparently held first place. Peter had also led in their resistance to Jesus' saying about his death and he had been severely rebuked by Jesus. Was he losing his position? Even after that rebuke Jesus had taken Peter, John, and James apart from the others for a night of prayer as he had taken them into the room when he raised the daughter of Jairus. Peter had led in suggesting that they stay on the mountain for the Feast of Tabernacles, but his suggestion had been rejected. It is not clear as to whether that experience was concealed from the other nine disciples as it was from the public. The nine who had been left behind had lacked the faith to heal an epileptic. One can almost hear Peter saying, "Now if *I* had been there . . . !" Was it time for a reorganization and realignment of rank in their group?

*Verse 47:* When Jesus understood the trend of their thinking, he used a little child to illustrate true greatness. Matthew uses the phrase "greatest in the kingdom of heaven" in the opening part of his account (18:1), but the "in the kingdom of heaven" part drops out, and the account ends in Matthew on the theme of pastoral concern in the worshiping community (18:5–7). In Mark and Luke the emphasis is on concern for relative greatness in the small circle of the Twelve.

*Verse 48:* Jesus gave his view of their relative greatness in three related statements leading to a climax: The first and third statements relate specifically to the theme of greatness, moving from the lowest level—service to a little child—to the highest—the one who is really great. The second part puts receiving Jesus and receiving God on the same level, as one act.

*Whoever receives this child:* To accept the responsibility of service to a little child was to accept humble service. On another occasion, when mothers brought their babies to Jesus for his blessing, the Twelve were indignant that Jesus was asked to give attention to babies (Luke 18:15–17). But Jesus rebuked the disciples and reminded them that childlike humility was a characteristic of kingdom citizens.

*In my name:* This was a common expression for the idea "as one's representative" or "in one's place." To receive and serve a little child as Jesus would have done if he had been the one involved is to act as Jesus' representative, to act in his place. Such humble service is not too menial for Jesus. Nor is it too menial for his disciples. To accept a child in humble service is to accept Jesus; he identified himself with the humble.

*Him who sent me:* God had sent Jesus as his servant. To accept the role of a servant is to accept Jesus in his role as a servant, and that means to accept God who sent him in that role. Luke accurately understands that the disciples' accepting the role of servants was directly related to Jesus' suffering and death.

*He who is least among you all is the one who is great:* From the viewpoint of man generally and the Twelve specifically, this is a paradox. It seems to be the very opposite of what men regard as true. To be great is to be served—the more servants one has, the greater he is. Jesus reverses this—the more people one serves, the greater he is. Therefore, to serve all is to outrank everyone else in service for who could do more than that? Jesus never discouraged ambition for greatness, but he redefined greatness. In place of the love of greatness, he substituted the greatness of love—love expressed through humble service.

### 33. On Working Together (9:49–50)

This brief section is only loosely connected with the preceding one. The common theme linking them is that of service to God in relation to Jesus. The words *in your name* (v. 49) link it to the preceding *in my name* (v. 48).

*Verse 49: John answered:* Luke connected this as a response to Jesus' saying about receiving him and receiving the one who sent him. John had rejected one who was working "in Jesus' name" but was not one of the Twelve, and he wanted to know if he had done the right thing in stopping the man.

*We saw a man casting out demons:* The *we* may refer to all or part of the Twelve. When they had seen this is not indicated. It may have been on the recent preaching and healing tour. From the event in the next paragraph (vv. 51–56), one might conjecture that the brothers John and James were the ones who saw and stopped this man who was healing.

*In your name:* This man was working as one of Jesus' followers, doing his work as the representative of Jesus.

*We forbade him, because he does not follow with us:* The disciples (John was one of those involved) had stopped the man from healing. They thought he could not really be working in Jesus' name since he was not identified with their group. John was not reporting boastfully what they had done. Whatever pride he may have had in stopping the man had now been replaced by concern lest he had done wrong in rejecting one who was working in Jesus' name. Did that alter John's relation to Jesus (v. 48)?

*Verse 50:* Jesus administered no rebuke to John and his associates. He used the plural form of the imperative when he responded, *"Do not forbid him."* The construction literally means, "Stop forbidding him." This man—and any future cases like him—was not to be stopped from working in Jesus' name just because he was not one of the attending company.

*For he that is not against you is for you:* Luke gives this short general principle—if a man is working, but not against you, he is automatically working on the same side with you. Mark includes an additional reason—no one could be doing mighty works in Jesus' name one moment and then speak evil of him in the next moment (9:39). The timeless warning is against refusal to recognize as genuine work for Jesus Christ that which is done by one who belongs to another company of followers. Whatever his label, if his work is for Christ, it is a part of the same work every other worker is doing.

## IV. THE MINISTRY OF THE UNIVERSAL SAVIOR ON THE JOURNEY TO JERUSALEM (9:51–19:27)
### (including events in Samaria, Galilee, Perea, and Judea)

Logically the next "chapter" division of Luke should begin at this point. There is a major break in the Gospel here.

### 1. Departure from Galilee (9:51)

It is of major importance in Luke's understanding of the movements and teaching of Jesus at this period, that very soon after the confession and transfiguration experiences with his emphasis on his death, Jesus started the journey to Jerusalem where he would die. Luke, therefore, indicates the beginning of Jesus' journey to Jerusalem at 9:51, even though Jesus does not reach Jerusalem until 19:28. In this long section of material, however, Jesus is not represented as moving on a straight course to Jerusalem (as in Mark 10:32 and Matt. 20:17). Luke includes material representing in sequence: (1) Jesus in Samaria at the outset of the journey; (2) later material back up in Galilee; (3) material in Perea on the way to Jerusalem; (4) material at some place on the border between Samaria and Galilee; and (5) material in Judea as they near Jerusalem. If this constitutes a problem relative to Luke's claim in 1:3 that he proposed to write "an orderly account," it must be resolved in the larger controlling purpose of Luke's theological theme; that is, after the confession of the disciples and Jesus' prediction of his death, there was one thing which loomed above everything else and took precedence over everything else—the journey to Jerusalem where death awaited him.

### 2. Journey into Samaria (9:52–56)

This briefly recorded journey into Samaria includes no record of a ministry of Jesus there. Jesus and the Twelve started to Jerusalem by way of Samaria. They were rejected by one village and went on to another; whether it, too, was in Samaria or back across the border in Galilee is not clear. Apparently nothing else transpired in Samaria.

*Verses 51–53:* Jesus *sent messengers ahead,* probably to arrange overnight accommodations in a Samaritan village. When Jesus and the others arrived they found that the Samaritans would not allow them to stay in their village *because his face was set toward Jerusalem.* The hostility between the Jews and the Samaritans had a long history. The Samaritans were a hybrid people

descended from the intermarriage of Jews left in Palestine at the time of
the Babylonian captivity and non-Jews who came in to occupy the land. When
the Jews returned to the land for the rebuilding of the Temple and their
culture, the Samaritans wanted to help. The strict Jews rejected their help
because of the intermarriages and hybrid offspring. The Samaritans went
home and built their own temple on Mt. Gerazim, and the bitter hostility
which started then has not yet ended.

Because the direction of Jesus and his disciples indicated that they were
going to Jerusalem for worship, the Samaritan villagers rejected them. There
is here a very dramatic contrast between this event and that reported in the
last section in which John and some others had rejected a man who was
working on Jesus' side. It is possible that this event actually came much later
and that Luke put it here in order to dramatize the acceptance-rejection
motif. The impression left was that they started to Jerusalem but had to
turn back; hence, the Galilean material which follows. The problem has not
been solved.

*Verse 54:* James and John reacted with what seems to have been a characteristic suggestion. They may have been the two who stopped the man in
the previous event (v. 49). They asked Jesus if he wished them *to bid fire
come down from heaven and consume* the Samaritans. Most likely what they
had in mind was lightning. They were ready to become Elijahs and pray
for God to send down fire and blast the village which had rejected Jesus
(see 2 Kings 1:9-12). Not without a reason had Jesus given them the nickname "Sons of Thunder" (Mark 3:17).

*Verse 55:* Jesus rebuked James and John for their suggestion. The word
translated *rebuked* means literally "to intimidate," and in general use meant
to refuse or reject. Jesus rejected their suggestion as unworthy in motivation.
Some manuscripts of Luke record Jesus' rebuke as, "You do not know
what kind of spirit you are. For the Son of man came not to destroy the lives
of men but to save them." The reading is poorly supported and must be a
much later addition to excuse the immature understanding or too-zealous
spirit of James and John, and to give Jesus' spirit in contrast.

*Verse 56: They went on to another village.* The village is not identified.
The impression is that it was another Samaritan village on up the road toward Jerusalem. Jesus practiced what he had instructed the Twelve to do on
their preaching tour—when he was refused hospitality, he moved on to another village which would extend it.

### 3. Counseling and Calling Disciples (back in Galilee?) (9:57–62)

The theme of this brief section is discipleship. It contains an instance in
which Jesus cautioned one man about the cost of discipleship and two instances of his calling men who were reluctant to follow him.

*Verse 57:* Luke gives no certain setting for the event but says it took place
*as they were going along the road.* The first impression is that it took place
in Samaria because of the setting of the preceding paragraph. Two matters
argue against the Samaritan setting. First, the Matthew parallel includes it
in a series of events in Capernaum (Matt. 8:5, 19-22). That setting is not
conclusive, however, because Matthew, as well as the other Gospel writers,

frequently places his materials where they best fit his purpose. Of greater force is the fact that, except for the brief Samaritan event, Luke is continuing a teaching on discipleship begun in verse 46 which is linked with materials that Mark 9:33–50 has in a Capernaum setting. Also Luke's next section (10:1–24) continues the theme of discipleship. The conclusion is that this event is a part of the Galilean ministry. The language belongs to the category of proverb and wisdom teaching.

*I will follow you wherever you go:* Luke does not identify the person who so addressed Jesus but Matthew calls him a scribe—one of the professional interpreters of the Jewish religion (8:19). Neither writer reports what prompted the scribe's proposal. A background of acquaintance with the teaching and ministry of Jesus is most likely. *Wherever you go* indicates his readiness to accompany Jesus with the Twelve. It is not likely that the statement has theological overtones, such as, "I will follow you even to Jerusalem and death." There is no indication that the man knew that phase of Jesus' teaching to the Twelve.

*Verse 58:* Jesus' answer was a strong word of counsel that contained the possibility of discouraging the man from joining this ministering group. Since Jesus' usual practice was to encourage people to follow him, he must have detected an overzealous spirit in the scribe. He called the man's attention to the cost of committing himself to such discipleship. Jesus never extended a call to easy discipleship.

*Foxes have holes, and birds of the air have nests:* Wild animals have their accustomed place of rest—dens to which foxes return for daytime rest after their nocturnal activities, roosting places to which birds return for nighttime rest after their daily activities. Even little animals and birds know where they will live and rest.

*But the Son of man has nowhere to lay his head:* By contrast, Jesus had no place which could be called his "home" after he committed himself to public ministry as the Suffering Servant of God. He went where the Father led him. When night came, he slept where he found a welcome, even as he had instructed the Twelve to do when he sent them out. Thus, he cautioned the scribe to consider the life he would be giving up and the life he would be accepting if he did indeed follow Jesus wherever he went.

*Verses 59–62:* In contrast to his cautioning the overzealous scribe, Jesus extended a call to two men who responded with willingness to follow but with some reservation about immediate commitment. Jesus challenged them to recognize relative values in what he asked them to give up and to accept.

*Follow me* was a call to commitment to a continuing ministry as one of Jesus' associates. It was the call extended to the four fishermen, who left their fishing business, and to Matthew, who left his tax business. It was a call to break ties which bound one to an old life and to establish new and unrestricted ties to a new life as Jesus' follower.

*Lord, let me first go and bury my father:* On the surface this was a reasonable request. The man was willing to become Jesus' follower, but there was something he thought he had to do *first*—something which had priority in his life. He was willing to fulfill *that* prior claim and *then* he would follow. Jesus' answer was framed to correct the man's views of "priorities"—of what should be *first* in his life.

*Leave the dead to bury their own dead:* The answer is so abrupt as to appear unfeeling. If the man's father had just died and the burial was impending, or if his father was seriously ill with death impending, Jesus' answer was indeed abrupt and lacking the compassion which characterized him. If either condition was true, Jesus was using strong, dramatic, almost insensitive language to direct the man's attention to priorities, calling him to a service related to life, not death—which looked forward, not backward. Whatever it cost one to make that commitment, the end justified the commitment.

There is nothing, however, in the account to indicate that the man's father was either dead or in terminal illness. The man may have been offering an excuse for delaying. In Jewish custom, filial responsibility dictated that the son should see that his father had whatever he needed in this life, and an honorable burial when he came to the end of this life. This man was putting filial responsibility to his earthly father in temporal matters above responsibility to his heavenly Father in eternal matters. Jesus used strong language to call his attention to that.

There is a play on words in Jesus' saying, *leave the dead to bury their own dead*. The first *dead* is metaphorical; obviously those literally dead can bury no one. Jesus is referring to those concerned about matters related to this physical life and its end—important matters unquestionably. The second *dead* refers to those literally dead or facing that end. Leave even important matters relating to life and death in the hands of those who have experienced no call to a higher responsibility. What they do is important, but it is secondary in importance to one thing—commitment to the will and call of God.

*But as for you, go and proclaim the kingdom of God:* The subject of the imperative is emphatic, meaning, "as for your primary concern." It was a reminder that he had received a call to something which takes precedence over earthly and temporal concerns. That which was to have the priority in the man's life was the proclaiming of the kingdom of God. The eternal had broken into the temporal, the heavenly had broken into the earthly, the powers of life had broken into a world of death. The proclamation of that good news was primary; it could not be secondary, even where family ties were involved. In a sense this was what Jesus had done where his mother and family were concerned. He called this man to do the same.

*Verse 61:* Another man expressed willingness to follow Jesus, but he too had a recognized priority. He did not ask to hold on to human ties and responsibilities. He asked only, *let me first say farewell to those at my home.* On the surface the request was simple enough. He did not ask to wait until death severed earthly ties; he only asked time for a farewell. Two items, however, point beneath the surface. One, his farewell likely indicated the prolonged festive occasion of one who was leaving on some extended journey—not just a simple kiss and good-bye. Two, the word *first* is significant. The man was establishing something else as first, making commitment to the service Jesus proposed second.

*Verse 62:* Jesus accepted the man's willingness to follow, but changed the order of his priorities: *No one who puts his hand to the plow and looks back is fit for the kingdom of God.* The saying has the unmistakable character of a proverb. Whether a folk-saying commonly used or a proverb original with Jesus, it has a new application in Jesus' use. Usually this is understood as a plowman's pride in plowing a straight furrow and the impossibility of doing so by looking back to where he has been rather than forward to where he is going. This may be true. Another idea, however, is more fitting. The man who puts his hand to the hard toil of plowing in seedtime but looks back to the comfort or pleasure of house or town, will gather no fruit in harvest. So one who would commit himself to plowing and sowing with Jesus but looked longingly back to what he had left was not fit for the kingdom of God. The word translated *fit* means literally "well-placed," indicating that which is "useful" for task or movement. The emphasis is not on moral or spiritual fitness but on practical usefulness. To be "useful" in the proclamation of the kingdom of God, one must recognize that plowing the field in anticipation of harvest has priority over everything else.

### 4. The Appointment and Mission of the Seventy (10:1–20)

This appointment has no parallel in Mark and Matthew. Some of the instructions which Jesus gave this group are identical with those he gave the Twelve (Matt. 9:36–11:1). The identity of the seventy is not clearly established. They were from the large company of Jesus' followers and may or may not have included the Twelve.

*Verse 1: The Lord appointed seventy others:* The word *others* naturally suggests that these were a different group from the Twelve who were sent out previously. It has good support in the ancient manuscripts of Luke. Other good ancient manuscripts, however, have that Jesus sent out seventy "others also." The *also* suggests that they were sent in addition to the Twelve. This reading has better support except that one manuscript—the third-century Bodmer manuscript—does not have the word *also*.

There is one further complication. Some good ancient manuscripts of Luke have "seventy-two others." The support is about equally divided between this and the "seventy others," except that the Bodmer manuscript has "seventy-two." In a case of this kind the rules of evidence for establishing the correct text turn to the matter of probabilities. "Seventy" was a good Jewish number made by multiplying two numbers for completeness, seven and ten. This recommends it as the probable original. "Seventy-two," however, was another good Jewish number for completeness. The number "twelve" indicated completeness in the religious sense, such as twelve patriarchs in Israel, twelve apostles of Jesus. "Seventy-two" would indicate six additional teams of twelve, making, with the Twelve, seven teams of twelve each. It is easy, then, to understand why some copyist would raise the number to seventy-two. There is no good reason for a copyist's reducing such a good number to seventy. Therefore, the probability is that this commissioned company was seventy, and that they went ahead of Jesus and the Twelve in teams of two; Jesus and the Twelve followed them (v. 1). It was an enlarging of the witnessing company on a much grander scale.

*Verse 2:* Except for the reversal of one verb and object in the Greek, the introductory statement of Jesus is identical with his word to the Twelve (Matt. 9:37–38).

*The harvest is plentiful:* Jesus took many of his illustrations from rural or village life. The eager people were like a ripe field ready for harvesting.

In the same way Jesus saw the Samaritans as an "unexpected harvest" ready to be gathered (John 4:35–42).

*The laborers are few:* Compared to the masses of people to be reached, those willing to reach them were discouragingly few. This has been the history of the gospel.

*Pray therefore the Lord of the harvest:* God directs the laborers into the part of the field he wants harvested.

*Verse 3: Go your way:* The call to pray for laborers is immediately joined by the commission of those praying to go themselves as laborers in the harvest. This, too, has been the history of the gospel; those who have prayed for laborers have often found themselves called to go.

*I send you out as lambs in the midst of wolves:* Jesus did not appoint them to an easy life and work. By this time he had encountered many who were set against him and were vicious in their opposition to him. His witnesses would face the same danger. As it had not stopped him, they were not to let it stop them.

*Verse 4:* These instructions against careful provision for their material needs differ little from those Jesus gave the Twelve on the earlier occasion (Matt. 10:9–15; Luke 9:3–5). They emphasized the limited time and place of the journey and the urgent emergency of their task. Nothing was to encumber or detain them.

*Purse:* The word indicates a small bag for carrying money.

*Bag:* This was a larger bag such as a shepherd or traveler would use for carrying food or clothes.

*Sandals:* Certainly they were expected to *wear* sandals. They were not to *carry* an extra pair. This parallels the 9:3 instruction not to take an extra tunic.

*Salute no one on the road:* No discourtesy or lack of cordiality was meant. The Jewish "salutations" were long, formal, and involved. The urgency of the mission demanded the omission of any such delay for social amenities.

The instructions in verses 5–8 relate to their physical provisions of food and shelter. Briefly summarized, they were to live as guests in the homes of those who received them as they served.

*Verse 5: Peace be to this house:* When they entered a house they were to pray the traditional prayer of God's peace—*shalom*—upon it. Their prayer was a blessing upon the home.

*Verse 6: Son of peace:* One who is of a peaceable character or nature; the construction indicates character. Such a person would accept the prayer for peace and be blessed by it—*your peace shall rest upon him.* But if the head of the house was not peaceable, hence, lacked the character to receive the blessing of the prayer for peace, *it* (your peace) *shall return to you.* This strange saying probably refers to the Jewish idea of words as extensions of the person to accomplish a desired purpose. If so, it means that no prayer for God's peace and blessing is wasted or fails in its purpose. If the one upon whom the blessing is pronounced rejects it, it will return to bless the one who sincerely offered it.

*Verse 7:* The home which received Jesus' appointed messengers was to serve as their base of operation while they were in that town. They were to accept its hospitality as payment for services rendered.

*Verse 8:* Wherever they went they were to eat whatever food was served them. Paul gives the same advice for Christians regarding eating in the homes of nonbelievers (1 Cor. 10:27), and it is included also in the Gospel According to Thomas (Logion 14). It anticipates the possible reluctance of some to eat foods which traditionally they had regarded as unclean. They were to understand that food was a physical and material matter and to eat what they were served without causing inconvenience to their host by requiring "kosher" food.

*Verse 9:* Two duties were assigned to the seventy. They were to *heal the sick* and to proclaim, *The kingdom of God has come near to you.* The latter may be translated "has come upon you" or "among you"—opinion is divided over the force of the verb. Did Jesus mean that the kingdom of God was approaching and was almost upon them? Or did he mean that in his presence among men the kingdom of God had indeed arrived? Did he mean that the kingdom was a "realized" event, or was it an "anticipated" event? Was it "present" or "future"? When all of Jesus' teachings are examined, the conclusion is that there was in his thinking an element of both "now" and "not yet." The kingdom had experienced a beginning—an inauguration—in his presence and work, but at the same time it anticipated a consummation in the total purpose of God.

*Verses 10–11:* The same instruction was given in 9:5. (See discussion on that verse.) The only difference is the addition of verse 11b: *nevertheless know this, that the kingdom of God has come near.* In spite of their rejection, the kingdom was at hand, and they were under judgment for their rejection.

Verses 12–16: These warnings of judgment are not included in Luke's account of the sending of the Twelve. Matthew includes them as a part of the large section on the sending of the Twelve, but also includes Jesus' criticism of the attitude of the people, the Pharisees, and the Galilean towns. Matthew's use is a very general one. Luke, on the other hand, makes a specific application at this point.

The major problem relates to the woes upon the towns (vv. 13–15). Because of the similarity between verses 12 and 14, some interpreters have held that these woes were originally given by Jesus in some undetermined setting and that Luke has given them a specific setting in relationship to the mission of the seventy. Others have held that Jesus gave them where Luke has placed them, near the close of the Galilean ministry after he had experienced growing opposition to his view of the nature of the kingdom of God and of the Messiah. This appears to be the more likely solution. Matthew does not include the mission of the seventy, but he does include the woes on the towns as a part of Jesus' reaction to the opposition he had encountered.

*Verse 12:* To emphasize the dire consequences of rejecting him and his message, Jesus compared the fate of the rejecting people with the Old Testament town, Sodom. Its sin had been so revolting that its name has come down through history as a name of shame. Its judgment had been so devastating that it was a byword. But the towns which had rejected the person, presence, and message of Jesus had committed greater sin than had Sodom.

*It shall be more tolerable:* That is, "more endurable." There are degrees of guilt and degrees of responsibility related to guilt. There are degrees of punishment for guilt directly related to the degrees of responsibility. Both Sodom of the Old Testament and the rejecting towns of Jesus' day were guilty and faced judgment, but the towns of Jesus' day bore greater guilt than Sodom.

*On that day:* This unquestionably refers to the day of God's ultimate reckoning with man, "the day of judgment" (Matt. 10:15). Throughout the Scriptures there is the concept of judgment in which ultimately man, the creature, will answer to the Creator for what he has done with the trustee-ship of life and opportunity. It is presented in many ways in the New Testament. Two of the most graphic ones are the sheep and goat judgment scene (Matt. 25:31–46) and the great white throne judgment scene (Rev. 20:11–15).

*Verses 13–15:* Jesus singled out three towns for reprimand for their rejection of him and the kingdom: Chorazin, Bethsaida, and Capernaum. These were predominantly Jewish, with a background for understanding Jesus' message. He compared them with two Gentile towns—Tyre and Sidon—which lacked that background.

Chorazin was a town just two miles north of Capernaum. It is mentioned in the New Testament only in this one instance (Matt. 11:21; Luke 10:13). Jesus' reprimand suggests that he had performed miracles there—*mighty works*. These are not recorded in the New Testament.

Bethsaida was a town about five miles east of Capernaum. It is mentioned several times in the New Testament: the home of Andrew, Peter, and Philip (John 1:44; 12:21); the place near which Jesus performed the miracle of feeding the five thousand (Luke 9:10); the village where Jesus healed a blind man (Mark 8:22–26).

On what occasion had Bethsaida rejected Jesus? Two occasions may be in the background of this reference. First, when the blind man asked Jesus to touch him and heal him, Jesus led him outside of the village before he healed him, and then instructed him not even to go back into the village. This could reflect a rejection of Jesus. More likely it reflected their rejection of the nature of the kingdom and the Messiah as Jesus understood them. Second, the day after Jesus fed the five thousand, people from that location near Bethsaida (John 6:22; Luke 9:10) followed him to Capernaum (John 6:24) and engaged him in a discussion as to what kind of Messiah he claimed to be. Moses had given their fathers "bread in the wilderness" (the manna). Did Jesus' giving them "bread in the wilderness" mean that he was claiming to be the promised prophet like Moses (Deut. 18:15)?[1] When Jesus explained his understanding that death was a part of the experience of the Messiah, the people rejected that view as too hard to accept and refused to follow him further (John 6:41–66).

Capernaum was the center of Jesus' ministry and had witnessed more of his mighty works than any other town. Although he was joyfully received by the common people, the Pharisees and scribes consistently rejected him and his message.

These three neighboring towns were the hub of the circle in which Jesus worked in Galilee. Not only had they definitely rejected him, but they were

---

1. It is instructive to note that in his defense before the Jewish authorities, Peter interpreted Jesus as the fulfillment of that promise (Acts 3:22–26).

also representative of the nearly total rejection by the Jewish religious leaders in Galilee. As such they stood in the same position as Jerusalem and the rejection in Judea. For the rejection in Judea we are dependent upon the Gospel of John up to Jesus' last week in Jerusalem. At that point the synoptic Gospels also include his Judean rejection.

Tyre and Sidon were basically Gentile towns on the Mediterranean coast of Phoenicia—Tyre about thirty miles from Capernaum, and Sidon about fifty miles. In Jesus' day they were notorious for their wickedness, just as Sodom had been in the ancient world. The New Testament contains only one reference to Jesus' having gone into that territory and only one event on that occasion—his healing the afflicted daughter of a Canaanite woman (Mark 7:24–30; Matt. 15:21–28). When she appealed for help, Jesus responded that he had been sent "only to the lost sheep of the house of Israel" —a ministry to the Jews—and she was a Gentile. When she persisted, Jesus responded that it was not fitting "to take the children's bread and throw it to the dogs." Jews typically regarded Gentiles as "dogs," but this was not characteristic of Jesus. Whether he took this tack to test her faith or to use her as an example for the Twelve is not explained. She answered that what he said was true, but that puppies—the word both he and she used means "little dogs"—were permitted to eat the scraps from the children's table, the leftovers. Jesus responded, "O woman, great is your faith!" and healed her daughter.

Only twice did Jesus commend a person for *great* faith, and both were Gentiles. Luke includes the case of the Roman centurion (7:9). It is strange that he did not include this one. This event, and perhaps other unreported ones like it, prompted Jesus' statement that if the quality of miracles done in Capernaum and other Galilean towns had been done in the heathen towns of Tyre and Sidon, the people would have afflicted themselves with irritating sackcloth robes, would have taken their seat on the discomforting ash heap, and would have repented of their evil ways. Therefore the day of God's ultimate reckoning with man (v. 14) will be more endurable for them than it will be for enlightened Jewish towns which rejected him.

Capernaum (v. 15) was particularly singled out for reprimand. Because Jesus had spent more time there and done more *mighty works* there, its judgment was the greater. The words of judgment are poetic:

> *will you be exalted to heaven?*
> *You shall be brought down to Hades.*

The question is introduced in the Greek by the negative particle, indicating that the natural answer is negative. "You will not be exalted to heaven, will you? No. You shall be brought down to Hades." As a major town having favored commercial, social, and religious privilege, Capernaum might think of herself with pride in anticipation of continuing honor and prosperity. Jesus did not so see her future.

*You shall be brought down to Hades:* The manuscripts are divided on the reading. Some have a word meaning simply "shall go down"; others have a causative stem, "shall be caused to come down." The simple form, "shall come down," has better support. Regardless of the word used, the meaning of Jesus was the same; he saw Capernaum under the judgment of God and destined for ruin. Her future was not to be exaltation; it was to be degradation.

*Hades:* In the King James Version, the word "hell" is used to translate two Greek words—*gehenna* and *haides.* In the subsequent major versions a distinction is made by translating *gehenna,* "hell" and *haides,* "Hades." *Gehenna* consistently means "the place of punishment of the departed wicked." "Hades" rarely means that (Rev. 20:14), but regularly means "the place of the dead," the unseen place to which the dead go. In this sense of the realm of the dead it was used for the idea of extinction.

Some interpreters understand Hades here to mean "hell," and that Jesus was pronouncing sentence of final judgment upon the inhabitants of the town of Capernaum.

Other interpreters understand Hades in the sense of the doom of death and extinction for the town itself. This is more likely. In Matthew 11:23 Jesus is quoted as saying of Capernaum, "You shall be brought down to Hades. For if the mighty works done in you had been done in Sodom, it would have remained until this day." The meaning there is clearly that Sodom ceased to be because of her shameful sin and that Capernaum will cease to be because of her sin of rejecting Jesus. By its rejection, the town had forfeited its right to remain a town.

Other interpreters understand that both of the previous views must be included in Capernaum's destiny. Sodom ceased to be, but her sinful inhabitants remained under God's judgment beyond the destruction of the city. So, too, Capernaum would cease to be, but that would not be the end of her responsibility for her sin of rejecting Jesus. The end of Capernaum as a city came as a result of the A.D. 66–70 wars of the Jews against the Romans. But the citizens who had rejected Jesus await that ultimate reckoning of man with God in final judgment. Whether or not Jesus had both ideas definitely in mind in his statement, this view is consistent with the total New Testament concept of judgment as both temporal and eternal.

*Woe* translates an interjection expressing displeasure. It could be used rather lightly: "Alas for you . . . !" It could also be used with a much more serious portent: "Calamity upon you, Chorazin! Calamity upon you, Bethsaida!" There is no doubt that it was in this later mood that Jesus spoke. What they thought wicked Gentile towns—Sodom, Tyre, Sidon—deserved, they too deserved and would receive because of their rejection of Jesus.

*Verse 16:* This judgment upon the rejecting cities was joined to the work of those appointed by Jesus as much as it was to the work of Jesus himself. The seventy were going out as his appointed and authorized proclaimers of the presence of the kingdom. To reject them and their message was to reject Jesus and his message. In so doing, they were rejecting the very God who had brought them to this day of opportunity. In rejecting that day of opportunity, they left for themselves nothing except judgment.

*Verse 17:* No indication of the length of this mission is indicated. Jesus had probably instructed them as to the time of their return. When they returned, they reported joyfully on their success. They had been sent to heal and to proclaim the presence of the kingdom. They had been successful even in very difficult situations—*even the demons are subject to us.* The word translated *subject to* is a military term for subordination. The demons lined up in submissive obedience to their commands.

*In your name:* That is, "in your stead" or "as your representative." They went where Jesus could not go, but their presence there was as his presence there. The demons were obedient to them as they would have been obedient to Jesus if he had been there. Hence, the seventy healed men as Jesus would have healed them if he had been there.

Verses 18–20: Jesus' response was joyful recognition of what their success really meant—the ultimate complete failure of Satan in his opposition to the redemptive purpose of God in Jesus.

*Verse 18: I saw Satan fall like lightning from heaven:* This saying has been joined to other Scripture references in an attempt to determine the origin, present area of activity, and ultimate destiny of Satan. Whatever may or may not be the success of such effort, what Jesus commented on here was the ultimate defeat of Satan. As dramatically as lightning flashing—Satan was doomed by Jesus' power and authority over evil. The evil forces active in the world, of Satanic origin, gave way when Jesus' representatives proclaimed his kingdom and exercised the power and authority he gave them. Already Satan's kingdom was being victoriously plundered by Jesus' kingdom. Ultimately the defeat would be total.

*Verse 19:* As Jesus' representatives went out to do his work in conflict with the powers of evil, they were to understand that victory was to be theirs.

*Authority to tread upon serpents and scorpions:* The Satan-serpent motif of Hebrew religious thought is the background for this symbolic way of assuring victory for Jesus' associates. As a serpent, Satan had first led man to rebel against God (Gen. 3:1–7). The promise of his defeat was couched in this symbolic language: like a serpent his head would be bruised by the heel of a descendant of the woman whom he had deceived (Gen. 3:15). Now Jesus assured his messengers of Satan's inability to defeat them in the same symbolic way. The dreaded serpents and scorpions of the desert, feared by travelers, served as fit symbols for the Satanic forces which would oppose Jesus' appointed workmen.

*Nothing shall hurt you:* Like the beautiful Psalm 91 which was sung so often by the troubled Jewish people, this was the poetic language of assurance. The Jew who sang that psalm knew that he was not literally immune from flying arrows, or illness and plague (Ps. 91:5, 6). But he knew that his total life was in the hands of a God who cared and who would see that his life was positively and creatively used even in trouble. So Jesus' messengers would not be literally and physically immune to danger, injury, or even the death of martyrdom. But in the overruling purpose of God all the combined forces of evil could not defeat them. To apply this literally to the presumption of "snake-handling" is to fail to understand the nature of Scripture and its meaning.

*Verse 20: Do not rejoice in this:* Jesus did not mean that they were not to rejoice in the assurance of God's care for them as they worked for him and subdued evil spirits. It was rather a way of saying that there is something far more meaningful to rejoice in: *but rejoice that your names are written in heaven.* This image of a written roll containing the names of all of the redeemed of God is a concept which finds frequent expression in the Scriptures. It emphasizes the fact of the ultimate and heavenly security of God's people regardless of the adversity of evil in this life.

## 5. Rejoicing at Certain Victory (10:21–24)

In the report of the seventy Jesus saw the long chain of the mighty redemptive acts of God reaching its climax. The powers of evil were doomed to defeat in their conflict with the powers of good. Jesus rejoiced in that certain victory, and expressed his rejoicing in a prayer of thanksgiving.

*Verse 21: In that same hour:* At the time of the messengers' report.

*In the Holy Spirit:* As the Son of God who had become flesh to live as a man among men, Jesus prayed to his Father, motivated by the Spirit (Matt. 4:1; Luke 4:1).

*Father, Lord of heaven and earth:* Jesus addressed God as the Lord of the total of creation. His lordship in heaven is unquestioned; his lordship on earth, however, is both questioned and challenged by men. But it is in fact as ultimate and complete as his lordship in heaven. In his purpose it is an accomplished fact.

*Thou hast hidden these things from the wise and understanding:* The religious leaders of Israel professed to know and understand God's purpose and plan, but by their rejection of God's Son and his kingdom they were proving that God's purpose and plan were in fact unknown to them. This was due, not to God's failure to reveal; it was the inevitable result of the leaders' failure to apprehend. If God had "hidden" these truths, it was by his giving a revelation which they rejected and refused to follow.

*And revealed them to babes:* The simple common people, who professed no wisdom of God's ways, were open to Jesus, his message, and his call. By their acceptance of him they possessed the revelation of God's victory over all evil through Jesus and those who believed in and followed him.

*Such was thy gracious will:* The RSV marginal reading is more accurate and fitting: *so it was well-pleasing before thee.* It was God's good pleasure to make his way known to and to use in his work those who accepted his Son and his message. He was pleased that *babes* had accepted even though *the wise and understanding* had rejected. He was using the readiness of the simple people.

*Verse 22* is more typical of the language of John's Gospel than it is that of the synoptics. The closest parallels are in such passages as John 8:19; 10:15; 17:3. The point of emphasis in this passage and in John is the identity of Father and Son in work and purpose.

*All things have been delivered to me by my Father:* In Matthew 28:18, Jesus says that the Father has given him "all authority." In John 17:2, it is all who have received eternal life. In Luke the *all things* may be comprehensive enough for both ideas. Because of the unity between Father and Son, the Father gave the Son authority to proclaim his kingdom and to do his work. But he gave also those who by faith accepted the Son and identified themselves with him and his work.

*No one knows who the Son is except the Father:* The wise and understanding (v. 21) did not know him; the babes did. But there is a nature of the Son which is of such greatness that it is known only by the Father. No man can ever know the fullness of the nature of the Son. It passes finite knowledge.

*Or who the Father is except the Son:* In the same way there is a depth
in the nature of the Father which cannot be known by natural man. Man
knows God in direct proportion to his committing himself and opening himself to God. In this way finite man may come to know something of the
infinite God.

*Any one to whom the Son chooses to reveal him:* The way to know God
is through the Son. But the Son chooses to reveal God only to those who
want to know him and will open themselves to him. In the Gospels there
are reports of the religious leaders requesting of Jesus some kind of sign
or demonstration which would convince them even when they did not want to
believe. He refused to do so. The only "sign" which he promised them was
that of his death and resurrection. He did not force his will on anyone. He
chose to reveal God, but only to those who were willing to believe and
accept him.

*Verses 23–24:* Jesus spoke to his messengers of the blessed privilege they
enjoyed. As they had watched Jesus work and had seen the power of God
over evil in their own work, they had witnessed things which great and
honored men had yearned to witness but had not. Standing in history at the
point of the fulfillment of God's redemptive purpose in the sending of the
promised Savior, they had seen and heard realities which kings had longed
for and prophets had dreamed of. Those great and honored men in Israel's
history had looked forward to the fulfillment of God's promise. It had not
been realized in their time. But it had come to be history in the time of
these associates of Jesus. They were seeing and hearing the fulfillment. They
were privileged and blessed beyond prophets and kings.

## 6. The Parable of the Good Samaritan (10:25–37)

The exact setting in which Jesus gave this parable is not stated. Several
elements suggest a Judean setting—Jesus' setting the story on the robber-
infested road between Jerusalem and Jericho, and his depicting a priest and
a Levite traveling along that road; Luke's introductory words in the next
paragraph relating this event to Jesus' journey and entry with his disciples
into Bethany, the village of Martha and Mary just outside of Jerusalem; the
desire of the lawyer to discuss eternal life. Since the incident and parable
are only in Luke, no appeal for aid in locating it can be made to the other
Gospels.

*Verse 25: A lawyer:* This was not a lawyer in today's sense of an advocate
in legal matters. He was a specialist in the interpretation of Jewish religious
laws. Jesus used the man's competence as an interpreter to call him to judgment and decision in answering his own question (vv. 36–37).

*To put him to the test:* This was a testing of wits in which the specialist
in the law doubtless intended to discredit Jesus among his followers by de-
feating him in theological discussion on how to attain eternal life.

*Teacher:* He addressed Jesus as a rabbinical teacher, for such he was,
though untrained in the Jerusalem rabbinical school.

*What shall I do to inherit eternal life?:* The idea of *eternal life* is a major
concept in the Gospel of John. According to John, Jesus had discussed the
idea during several visits to Jerusalem—visits not included in the other

Gospels. The proposal is all the more natural if this event took place in Judea.

*What shall I do . . . ?* characterizes the Jews' approach to being right with God. It required "works"; it was a matter of "doing" the requirements of the law.

*Verse 26:* Jesus accepted the lawyer on his own ground for argument. He asked him, *"What is written in the law?"* Torah, the total law system in Israel, was the Jews' total approach to doing what God desired and, hence, of having assurance of the highest expression of life—living on, even beyond physical death.

*Verse 27:* In Torah there were hundreds of laws regulating life and conduct. These were condensed in summary form in the Ten Commandments. The Ten Commandments are in two sections: laws regulating conduct in man's relationship to God; laws regulating conduct in man's relationship to his fellowman. The lawyer astutely included both in his answer, indicating that the law required supreme love for God (Deut. 6:5) and love for one's neighbor (Lev. 19:18). Matthew 22:34–40 contains a later scene in which Jesus, too, used these in summarizing the total of legal requirement. In Matthew's account, the event takes place on Tuesday after Jesus' arrival in Jerusalem. In Luke the event occurs at some undetermined time before the arrival in Jerusalem. If these are separate events, Jesus used the lawyer's answer in the Luke event to answer a Pharisee in the Matthew event.

*Verse 28:* Jesus agreed with the lawyer's answer. The way to eternal life is the way of supreme love for God joined inseparably with compassionate love for one's neighbor. Jesus and Paul agreed with their Jewish contemporaries that *complete* obedience to the law of God was the way to be right with God. They found that way ineffective in experience, however, because of man's inability to give complete obedience to the law. They understood that the way to life was the way of faith in God's gracious love in spite of man's inability and sin.

*Verse 29:* The lawyer's next question was the logical one. How is a man to determine who his neighbor is? That must be determined before one can love his neighbor as he loves himself. It is easy to know who is intended in Deuteronomy 6:5, since there is only one God to love. But who is intended in Leviticus 19:18? The lawyer felt justified in reserving the right to decide who his neighbor was and, hence, whom he was to love. The word for *love* is the word for evaluation. It meant to recognize and esteem as a person. Jesus' answer indicated that in this case the neighbor was a person broken and in need of help even when that help would inconvenience and cost the one who gave it.

*Verses 30–35* contain one of the Gospels' most beautiful parables. The country between Jerusalem and Jericho is very rugged with an abundance of hills and caves. These had come to be the favorite hiding places of robbers who preyed on travelers. Jesus' story was a very realistic one. A traveler on that road, by implication a Jew, was attacked by bandits who robbed him even of his clothes and beat him until he was half dead.

*Priest . . . Levite:* In the ancient religious hierarchy of Israel there were three orders: the high priest, priests, Levites. In New Testament times, the general responsibility of the priests was to make the sacrifices; that of the Levites was to care for all lesser matters, such as cleaning the buildings, washing the sacred vessels, preparing the lamps, arranging for and carrying out the musical liturgy.

Jesus pictures first a priest and later a Levite (in the order of their rank) traveling the same road and seeing the beaten and bloody man. Some interpreters say that they were returning from their Temple service in Jerusalem, since the same expression, *going down,* is used for their journey as for that of the unfortunate man who was *going down from Jerusalem.* Others understand the word to have the general meaning of "traveling"; they interpret the refusal of the Temple officers to help the wounded man as reluctance to disqualify themselves for their time of service in the Temple (which they were on the way to Jerusalem to take part in) by touching the bloody man and becoming ceremonially defiled. They valued their opportunity to serve God's Temple more than they valued their opportunity to serve God's child—a fellow Jew. This view better dramatizes Jesus' lesson to the lawyer.

The priest and the Levite *passed by on the other side.* This means that they took the opposite side of the road avoiding any possible contact with the man lest they be ceremonially defiled.

Then a Samaritan came down the same road and found the man (v. 33). On Samaritans, see discussion on 9:52–56. The Jews and the Samaritans mutually hated one another. But this Samaritan did not go on by in fear of ceremonial uncleanliness, or out of racial hatred. He saw only a man who needed help, and he provided the help because he was moved by compassion for a fellow human in need.

*Bound up his wounds, pouring on oil and wine:* Oil was used as a soothing balm, wine as an alcoholic antiseptic. Both were standard medicines in the ancient world and were recognized by the "father of physicians," Hippocrates, who used them in dressing open flesh wounds.

*Set him on his own beast and brought him to an inn:* Beyond dressing the man's wounds, the Samaritan walked in order that the wounded man might ride to a public inn. There he personally cared for the wounded man. When he was leaving the next day, he paid the innkeeper an estimated amount for the man's expenses, instructed him to provide for the man's needs, and promised to pay the remainder of the expense when he returned. *Two denarii* (two days' wages) were worth approximately forty cents in today's currency, but we must also consider the nature of the inn and the different buying power of the money in contrast to a few days at a modern hotel!

*Verse 36:* Jesus concluded his vividly drawn story by calling upon the lawyer for a decision: *Which of these three, do you think, proved neighbor . . . ?* It was characteristic of Jesus' parables that they called men to decide and to take responsible action based on the decision.

*Proved* is the word for demonstration. Which one—priest, Levite, Samaritan—two of them honored men, one a despised foreigner—demonstrated that he valued his fellowman as a person and had a compassion which prompted action?

*Verse 37:* There was only one answer, and the lawyer was both clever enough and honest enough to give it: *The one who showed mercy on him.* Implicit in the story, the question, and the answer is the answer to the lawyer's question (v. 29). The neighbor whom he is to love is the man who needs his compassion and help—regardless of physical, social, or racial status. Today, in existential encounter with human need, we must recognize that for Jesus any concern for carrying out the traditional expressions of worship which keeps us from giving compassionate help to broken humanity fails to meet the requirement of God: "Thou shalt love thy neighbor as thyself." It was to such encounter and decisive action that Jesus called the lawyer in his response, *Go and do likewise.* The tense of the imperative indicates habitual practice—"make a habit of doing as the Samaritan did." The lawyer had asked what he should do (v. 25). Jesus told him what to do —practice the demonstration of love at every opportunity where need is evident.

### 7. Visiting the Home of Martha and Mary (in Judea) (10:38–42)

This incident definitely took place in Judea. Whether or not its position subsequent to the preceding materials indicates the possible locale of those events is disputed. It appears doubtful. Luke does not appear to be using a journey sequence, though that was suggested at 9:51.

*Verse 38: As they went on their way:* This was some journey to Jerusalem. Whether it was for the final Passover week or for some other reason is not clear. *They* indicates Jesus and his traveling companions—the Twelve and perhaps others.

*He entered a village:* The emphatic use of *he* in the Greek, in contrast to *they,* suggests that Jesus stopped in this village and his companions went on to Jerusalem. The *village* was unquestionably Bethany (John 11:1; 12:1–8), which was practically a suburb of Jerusalem.

*Martha received him into her house:* She extended the hospitality of her home. Some manuscripts have only, "she received him"; some have, "she received him into the house"; some have, "she received him into her house." The use of the word *her* has led some interpreters to think that it was Martha's house and that her sister Mary, and her brother Lazarus (John 11:1; 12:1–2) lived there. This cannot be demonstrated and is of relatively little importance.

*Verse 39: Mary . . . sat at the Lord's feet and listened to his teaching:* To sit at another's feet was the position of a pupil receiving instruction from a teacher. This has led to the RSV translation, *his teaching.* The word in the Greek is not the term for teaching in the doctrinal sense. It is singular in form meaning a discourse or an account. In Luke 24:17 the plural form means "conversation" between two people. In this instance it may mean no more than Mary's intent listening as Jesus talked of his work or of the journey just ending.

*Verse 40: Martha was distracted with much serving:* The term *distracted* means to be overburdened or to be dragged about by things. As a good hostess, Martha was concerned about the many things needful for the comfort of family and guest.

*Do you not care that my sister has left me to serve alone?* The construction is almost peevish—"You do care, don't you, that my sister has left me to serve alone?" Martha did not see how Jesus could condone Mary's inactivity and her own overactivity in a crisis situation!

*Verse 41: Martha, Martha:* There was gentle and tender chiding of Jesus' in his repetition of the name. He appreciated her desire to be a good hostess, but he felt that it was causing her to miss something of greater importance. He contrasted many troublesome and distracting things with one necessary thing. The many things related to physical comfort and need were distracting Martha. The word translated *you are anxious* meant originally "pulled in two." There was one thing which stood out as a necessity and it was not related to physical comfort. It related to the inner person, to spiritual need satisfied only in fellowship and sharing. Mary had chosen that, and it was a wise choice.

*The good portion:* The word for *portion* used here is a general one for a part or division of anything. Of all that was going on in the house Mary chose her portion—to visit with Jesus and to hear him speak, in preference to anything else. Some interpreters have suggested that the word was used by Jesus as a figurative reference to food—there were many dishes provided; Mary chose the best one. That is possible; if the story were in the Gospel of John one would be certain of a double meaning. Figurative references are not commonly employed in Luke.

*Which shall not be taken away from her:* In future days of tragedy, Martha and Mary would look back to this day and its opportunities. Martha would be able to remember her distraction and the foods she had prepared. Mary would be able to cherish the memory of sitting at Jesus' feet and hearing his words. All these were important; one excelled all the others in importance.

## 8. Teaching on Prayer (11:1–13)

Some of this teaching, in a different form, is in Matthew; the rest is only in Luke. The section opens with a short version of the prayer commonly labeled "Lord's Prayer," which Matthew includes in the Sermon on the Mount (Matt. 6:9–13) but is not included in Luke's Sermon on the Plain (6:17–49). The setting is different. In this case, Jesus had been praying. When he ended his praying, one of the disciples—probably one of the Twelve is meant—requested that Jesus teach them to pray *as John taught his disciples.* The reference is to John the Baptizer; the Gospels contain no example of this teaching by John.

*Verses 2–4:* The prayer is a model for praying rather than a prayer to be prayed; however, it may be effectively used as a communal prayer. The form in Matthew indicates definitely that it was so used by the early Christians. Jesus gave it, however, as a model to indicate the attitudes which should characterize prayer.

*Father:* Some manuscripts have the longer expression, "Our Father who art in heaven." They have been influenced by the Matthew reading. Unquestionably in Luke the correct reading is simply *Father.* The attitude reflected is that of confidence. One prays to God like a child confident that his father will supply what he needs. This attitude is illustrated in the last part of the section (vv. 11–13).

*Hallowed be thy name:* The attitude is that of reverence. The name in Jewish thought stood for the person. To hold the name of God in sacred reverence was to hold God in sacred reverence. We may pray in the *confidence* of a child-father relationship. But we pray with the *reverence* of a man-God, a worshiper-Worshiped, relationship.

*Thy kingdom come:* The attitude is that of submission to the reign of God. Some manuscripts, influenced again by the Matthew reading, add, "Thy will be done." It does not belong in Luke's shorter version. The kingdom of God is the reign and rule of God. It begins in the submissive openness of the individual. One must pray for the reign of God in his own heart before he can pray meaningfully for the reign of God in society.

*Give us each day our daily bread:* The attitude is that of dependence on God to give what is needed. The petition is identical in Matthew, but the grammatical construction is different. Matthew 6:11 reads literally "Give us daily . . . ." Luke has "Keep on giving us from day to day." Interpreters are divided on the meaning of the expression translated "daily bread." Some understand it to mean, "Give us today the bread we need today"; others, "Give us today the bread we need for the next day." The latter is in the RSV marginal reading, "our bread for the morrow." In common usage the term translated "daily" referred to the necessary ration of food which a master gave his servant each day. As the work was assigned for the day, a ration of food was given to supply the energy needed for that work. If this is the meaning here, Jesus was teaching his followers to depend on God to supply their need as they did his work. There are volumes of suggestions on the nature and the practice of prayer in that meaning.

*Forgive us our sins:* The attitude is that of penitence. The word translated *forgive* also means "to dismiss, release, send away." The word *sins* is a different one from Matthew's "debts." The reference is most likely to offenses against our fellowmen which constitute sins against God. We ask God's forgiveness on the same basis as in Matthew: *for we ourselves forgive everyone who is indebted to us.* We can with confidence anticipate God's forgiveness only when we pray with the attitude of one who has already forgiven, or dismissed, the offenses committed against us by a fellowman. This is because the offenses of our fellows are so small compared to our own sins against God. We may anticipate forgiveness for the larger only when the lesser have been forgiven.

*Lead us not into temptation:* This petition has disturbed many interpreters. James 1:13 says that God "tempts no one." How are these two passages to be understood? The answer is in the attitude reflected in the petition— humility in view of human weakness. The child of God, recognizing his own weakness in the face of temptation, is to ask that God lead him in the ways where temptation does not lurk. Matthew's version helps here; it adds, "but deliver us from evil" (6:13). We pray, not only for deliverance from temptation, but also that when in the circumstances of life we are tempted, God will grant the power of deliverance from evil—the power to triumph over temptation. Sin lies, not in being tempted, but in giving way to temptation.

*Verses 5–8:* In this short parabolic illustration on confidence in praying, Jesus called upon each of his hearers to reflect on what he would do if a friend arrived unexpectedly at midnight and there was nothing in the house to feed him. He would go ask another friend for help—even at midnight. There is no special significance in the three loaves; that was simply what he needed.

Jesus described the probable reaction of the friend; he would refuse to help because it would be inconvenient. The inconvenience is indicated not only by the fact that it was midnight, but also by the reference to the sleeping children. The Palestinian family slept on pallet-like beds on the floor. The father slept next to the door. In order to get the bread, he would have to step over or around the children sleeping in the dark house. There was the risk of disturbing the sleep of the entire household. Yet, in the end, even if he would not respond to the call of friendship, he would respond to the call of human need (v. 8) and would grant the request. This, Jesus meant, is the way God responds to human need. To press one's claim humbly is to have one's need fulfilled.

The thrust of the illustration has often been misunderstood. Jesus did not mean that God does not really want to give but will if we keep on insisting so as to break down his will. He meant rather that if we can get what we need from a human friend who does not want to give it, how much more can we be sure that we will receive what we need from God, who does want to give. God has proved by his nature that he is a giving God.

*Verses 9–10* underline the idea of confidence in prayer. They have a poetic, rhetorical structure. Three imperatives in verse 9—*ask, seek, knock*—are followed by three participles in verse 10—*every one who asks, he who seeks, him who knocks.* The three imperatives of verse 9 are followed by words of promise—*it will be given, you will find, it will be opened.* The three participles in verse 10 are followed by words of assurance—*receives, finds, will be opened.*

The tense of the imperatives is the present of habitual action: "make a habit of asking . . . seeking . . . knocking." The tense of the promises is future, but only in relation to the action of the imperatives—giving follows asking, finding follows seeking, opening follows knocking. The tense of the participles (v. 10) is also present, but the words of assurance that follow them are changed from the future to the present. This emphasizes the reality and unity of the relationship—asking is receiving; seeking is finding; knocking is finding open doors.

Verses 11–13 are another parabolic illustration similar to verses 5–8, except that here the asker-giver relationship is that of son to father.

*Verse 11: What father among you:* Jesus asks each hearer to put himself in the place of a father. What would he do if his son made a request for some ordinary food: *a fish* or an egg. Some manuscripts of Luke include "bread." That is due to scribal alterations of the text influenced by the inclusion of bread in the parallel account (Matt. 7:9). The correct reading in Luke omits the word.

*Fish* was very common food, particularly around the sea of Galilee where it was no doubt a daily food. *Serpent* means just that, a snake. It is doubtful that Jesus was referring to the eel—a snakelike water animal which was not permissible as food. He was contrasting fish with serpents—that which is needful versus that which is harmful.

*Verse 12: Eggs,* too, were common food, and *scorpions* were a common danger. There is no need to strain for a relationship in the idea of a father's giving his son a scorpion's egg. The same contrast is carried out as in the fish-serpent illustration. Serpents and scorpions represent common harmful things in 10:19. They represent the same things here. Human fathers give helpful things (fish, eggs) not harmful things (serpents, scorpions) to their children.

*Verse 13:* Jesus contrasted his disciples as human fathers facing a son's request with God the *heavenly Father* facing a son's request. *Evil* here basically means "grasping," inclined to keep rather than to give. Human fathers are by nature inclined to keep, not to give. The heavenly Father, however, is by nature inclined to give, not to keep. Therefore we are encouraged to pray expecting to receive. If a grasping human father understands the matter of appropriate giving so that he gives *good gifts* to his children, how much more is it to be expected that the giving heavenly Father will give his children what they need.

*The Holy Spirit:* The most significant contrast between Matthew's version (7:7–11) and Luke's is the gift which the Father gives. Matthew has "good gifts in abundance." Luke has *the Holy Spirit.* The many ancient manuscripts of Luke have six different versions of this reading: good things; the good gift of the Holy Spirit; good gifts; a good gift; good spirit; Holy Spirit. Only the last two have good support. The third-century Chester Beatty papyri reading is "good spirit"; doubtless this means "Holy Spirit." The third-century Bodmer papyri has "Holy Spirit," and this is the reading in all the major fourth- and fifth-century manuscripts. There can be little doubt that it is the correct one. In Luke's time and in his thinking all the good gifts of God could be summed up in one big gift—the Holy Spirit. This was the thinking reflected in Acts, the writings of Paul, and the Gospel of John. To receive God's Holy Spirit is to receive the totality of God's gifts.

## 9. The Beelzebul Controversy (11:14–26)

The hostility of the leaders of the Jewish religion was nowhere more clearly evident than in this event and their charge that Jesus' power in healing came because he was in league not with God but with Satan. In Matthew 12:24 and Mark 3:22 the setting is Galilee, but the leaders are Pharisees and scribes from Jerusalem. The incident was Jesus' healing a speechless man and restoring his power to speak. The people held that it was an evil spirit which had prevented the man from speaking and that Jesus' power over the evil spirit made possible his restoration of the man's speech. In Matthew's version the man was healed of both blindness and speechlessness. Some of the witnesses asked if Jesus might not indeed be "the son of David" (Matt. 12:24)—a title for the anticipated Messiah. The Pharisees gave the sarcastic rejoinder that Jesus was not in league with God but with Beelzebul.

*Verse 15: Beelzebul:* The KJV reading "Beelzebub" is erroneous. It is from the Vulgate (Latin) text which altered the word to conform to the 2 Kings 1:2 reference to "Beelzebub." That reading probably represented a satirical pun by Elijah. Beelzebul (or Baalzebul) was the highest god of the pagan "baals." Baalzebub was a Phoenician god of decay ("god of garbage" in postbiblical Hebrew). When Ahaziah, the king of Israel, was sick, he sent messengers to the shrine of Baalzebul to ask if he would recover. Elijah met the messengers, and made the satirical suggestion that Ahaziah was sending to the "god of death"—Baalzebub—to ask about a matter of "life"; he should have asked his question of Yahweh (Israel's God) who was the God of life.

*Prince of demons:* The Hebrews contrasted the pagan god Beelzebul, the ruler of evil spirits, with God, the ruler of good spirits. Here the Jewish leaders charged that Jesus exercised authority over evil spirits because he was working in cooperation with the ruler of evil spirits.

*Verse 16: Others . . . sought from him a sign from heaven:* They wanted assurance that he was working in cooperation with God in exercising authority over evil spirits. As on other occasions, they wanted some kind of sign which would convince them against their will to be convinced.

*Verses 17–18:* Jesus first pointed out the fallacy of the charge. A *kingdom* (country) which professes unity but is divided into fighting factions loses its unity and falls. So if Satan—the ruler of evil in Hebrew religious thought—divides his forces in order that they may fight against one another, he will be engaged in destroying his own kingdom. The charge was not only false, it was also irrational and absurd.

*Verse 19:* Jesus pressed the Pharisees to apply their reasoning to their own case. *By whom do your sons cast them out?* The religious leaders of Israel claimed power over evil spirits. Was that out of cooperation with God or with Satan? This bit of irony further underlined the irrational nature of the charge against Jesus. Whether or not he granted that the religious leaders did indeed exercise such power, is beside the point. He simply asked them to look at their charge by applying it to their own case. Their sons would thus become their own judges.

*Verse 20: If it is by the finger of God:* "If" could more precisely be translated "since"—"since the situation is that I am casting out evil spirits by the finger of God." The grammatical construction affirms rather than questions the condition. *The finger of God* is a reference to the exodus miracles (Exod. 8:19) which were a test of power between the God of Moses (Israel) and the gods of Pharaoh (Egypt). The magicians of Egypt—their religious leaders—duplicated the miracles of Moses up to a point. They turned their rods into snakes as Moses and Aaron had done, but Aaron's snake consumed theirs. Snakes were gods in some forms of Egyptian worship. So that in this miracle Moses' God overcame Pharaoh's god (Exod. 7:8–13). They turned water to blood as Moses did (Exod. 7:22). They produced frogs as Moses did (Exod. 8:7). But when Moses turned the very dust of the earth into gnats (Exod. 8:18, RSV; lice, KJV), they were unable to duplicate the miracle. At this point they said to Pharaoh, "This is the finger of God"— Moses' God is the real God.

Jesus used that expression to describe what he was doing. It was no "black magic" brought about by cooperation with the evil powers of darkness. It was the genuine demonstration of the good powers of light, the indication that the very rule of God in the lives of men, his kingdom, was present. Their problem was the same as Pharaoh's. The more Moses did, the more Pharaoh hardened himself against God and his purpose. The more Jesus did, the more the Pharisees hardened themselves against him. They could not deny his miracles, nor that they were accomplished by superhuman power. But they would not grant that it was God's power. They attributed it to the only other superhuman power in their thinking—Satan's power. This reversal, in Matthew, Jesus called "the blasphemy against the Spirit" (12:31).

*Verses 21–22:* Jesus extended this statement to show what his work really implied—the ultimate complete defeat of Satan's dominion. He used the allegorical illustration of a strong man guarding his palace. As long as he is able to guard it successfully there is peace and security. But when a stronger one comes, he is able to conquer the strong man, take away his authority, and plunder his goods. The *strong man* represents Satan trying to preserve his dominion. The *one stronger* represents Jesus who came to attack Satan, to defeat him, to take away his authority, and to plunder his kingdom of its possessions. It is probably pressing the allegory beyond Jesus' original application to try to determine all the "when" and "how" and "what" of this victory over Satan, or to identify the *spoil* (v. 22)—for instance, sinful men taken from Satan by "regeneration," or the dead taken from him by "resurrection." Jesus' point was simply that what he was doing guaranteed the ultimate complete downfall of Satan and his rule in the hearts of men.

*Verse 23:* Jesus concluded his teaching with an indication that men decided which side they were on—God's or Satan's—by their response to him. Those who were not siding with him as he did God's work were against him and God's work. These were the ones accusing him of being in league with Beelzebul. The implication of their action was far from a simple negative not-being-on-his-side. If they were not with him in gathering men for God, they were positively active in scattering men from God. Evil is never a passive negative; it is always an active affirmation of destructive intent and effect.

*Verses 24–26:* This strange little parabolic story is presented in Luke as the conclusion to Jesus' answer which started in verse 17. Its meaning relates to the nature of evil and the impossibility of a strictly negative approach to good. An unclean or evil spirit that lived in a man went out and sought another place to live but found none more desirable than the former place. When it went back it found that no other spirit had taken its place in the man, so it gathered up seven other spirits of its own nature—evil—and took them to live in the house. The result was that the man in whom the spirits lived was eight times worse than he had been previously.

*When the unclean spirit has gone out of man:* Nothing is to be gained by arguing whether the evil spirit "went out" of its own volition or was "cast out" by the possessed man. The point of Jesus' story was simply that the exit of the spirit left a vacuum in the man.

*He passes through waterless places seeking rest:* The dry waste places uninhabited by human life were feared by men and regarded as the dwelling place of dangerous forms of nonhuman life: serpents, scorpions, evil spirits. But even the evil spirit found no desirable place to dwell outside of a human being.

*Swept and put in order:* When the spirit returned to its previous place of abode, it found the man still empty and, like a cleaned-out house, ready for occupancy.

*Seven other spirits more evil than himself:* The final occupied state of the man is emphasized in two ways. First, the complete number "seven" is used as the number of allies enlisted by the spirit. Second, these seven were in character even more evil than the first one.

*The last state of that man becomes worse than the first:* Formerly he was occupied by *an* evil spirit; now he is occupied by *eight* evil spirits. The central truth of the parable is clear—the futility of spiritual emptiness or negativeness. In the spiritual world as in the natural world, nature abhors a vacuum.

It is not enough for a man to be emptied of "evil." Unless "good" comes in positively to fill the emptiness, he is wide open for multiplied evil's occupancy. Reformation without regeneration is futile for effecting lasting good.

## 10. A Collection of Short Teachings (11:27–36)

There appears to be no better title for this section. These are short self-contained teachings, held together by the continuing theme of the evil of an empty and meaningless religion. At times the theme is only dimly discernible, but it is there.

*Verses 27–28:* A woman with a mother's pride in a good son raised her voice above the crowd in a natural recognition that the mother of such a son deserved to be praised.

Jesus' response on the surface was simply an affirmation that the one who deserved praise was not just the one who bore and trained good children but the one who heard God's word and responded with obedience. Positive obedience to God's word is the supreme virtue. Many in Jesus' audience were hearing the word but were not obeying it. One may also find a deeper suggestion in Jesus' answer. Was there an implied dissatisfaction with his own mother's reaction to his ministry? If so, it must be found in relation to several other small bits of evidence that Mary joined Jesus' half brothers in concern for him, his welfare, his safety in what he was doing, and entertained some hope that the inevitable result of what he was doing might be avoided. (See the previous discussion on Luke 8:19–21.)

*Verses 29–32:* Both Matthew (12:38–42) and Luke use Jesus' comparison of himself and his generation to Jonah and Solomon and their generations. They do not, however, use it in the same way, in the same sequence, or with the same central point of comparison. In both accounts, Jesus responded to the desire of the people who heard him. They wanted a *sign* that he was God's authentic spokesman—a sign which would convince them against their wills to be convinced. Jesus replied that the only sign they would receive would be *the sign of Jonah.* In Matthew, the point of comparison is Jonah's being in the belly of the whale three days and nights before coming forth with a compelling witness, and Jesus' being in the heart of the earth three days and nights before coming forth with a compelling witness. In other words, Jesus' resurrection from the dead would be the supreme sign that he was God's authentic spokesman. In a similar way Jesus gave his resurrection as a sign of his messianic authority in the Temple riddle in John 2:13–22. That was given on Tuesday before his antagonists killed him on Friday; his body—God's dwelling place on earth—was raised up on Sunday.

For Luke, the sign was not the experience but the preaching. Jonah proclaimed God's message, demanding repentance in view of God's judgment; the people of Nineveh—the ancient heathen city—responded in repentance (Jonah 3:6–9). Jesus proclaimed God's message demanding repentance in view of God's judgment; the Jewish people of his day were responding not with repentance but with rejection.

The men of Nineveh showed wisdom in responding to the preaching of Jonah. Jesus was greater than Jonah, but his generation was showing its lack of wisdom in rejecting him. The queen of Sheba (1 Kings 10:1–13) showed wisdom in going to hear the wisdom of Solomon. Jesus was greater than

Solomon, but his generation was showing its lack of wisdom in rejecting him.

*Will arise at the judgment:* The expression joins two major ideas—resurrection and judgment. In the day of God's final reckoning with men, the queen of the South will be raised up and the people of Nineveh will be raised up. Their example of wisdom in response to Solomon and to Jonah will be a silent judgment against Jesus' hearers who rejected one greater than Solomon and Jonah. If people of the ancient heathen world responded to God's messengers and message, how grave is the conduct of people in the enlightened Jewish world who were rejecting Jesus and his message!

Verses 33–36: The concept of light and darkness as symbols of good and evil was common in ancient religion and philosophy. It was well known in Persian religious-philosophical thought, and is well attested in the Hebrew Scriptures. It was a favorite idea in the Qumran community. Its presence as a major concept in the Christian Scriptures is evident.

*Verse 33:* This is the same illustration which Matthew includes in the Sermon on the Mount (5:15) and which Luke uses in another setting (8:16). There are variations in the details wherever it appears: *No one after lighting a lamp:*

> "puts it under a bushel" (Matt. 5:15);
> "to be put . . . under a bushel or under a bed" (Mark 4:21);
> "covers it with a vessel or puts it under a bed" (Luke 8:16);
> *puts it in a cellar or under a bushel* (v. 33).

In Luke 8:16 Jesus was addressing the Twelve; in this passage he is addressing the crowds.

*In a cellar:* The Greek word means a crypt, cellar, or simply a hidden (secret) place. Some interpreters have questioned whether or not Jesus said this, since cellars were much more characteristic of Graeco-Roman houses than of Palestinian houses. This needlessly clouds the teaching. Jesus may have meant no more than "a hidden place," since he was showing the real purpose for lighting a lamp—not to conceal it but to place it advantageously for illumination.

*Under a bushel:* This is the unquestioned reading in Matthew. It is in many of the best manuscripts of Luke 11:33 but is not included in a few of them. It may be authentic here, or it may have been interpolated by some copyist influenced by the Matthew reading.

*On a stand:* Whether a single concealment idea ("secret place") or a double one ("secret place" and "bushel"), the teaching is the same. A lighted lamp is not concealed; it is placed on a stand for the most effective illumination.

*That those who enter may see the light:* Luke's emphasis in both his passages, in contrast to Matthew's "all who are in the house," is another indication of his interest in the Gentiles who came from the outside to be blessed by the light which Jesus brought to a dark world.

*Verse 34:* As a lamp brings light into a dark house, so the eye lets light into a man's body; it is the window through which the light enters.

*When your eye is sound:* The word translated *sound* was used in the sense of healthy, good, operating as it should. Its basic meaning, however, is that of singleness, simplicity, sincerity. The eye operating effectively as it should causes the *whole body* to be *full of light*.

*When it is not sound:* The word translated *not sound* was used in the sense of "evil." In Jesus' illustration, it could be the opposite of "good," that is, not healthy. It could also be the opposite of "single," that is, double vision. An eye which brings into focus a single image is a good eye; it reveals that which is true and accurate. The body can act safely on that illumination. But the eye which brings into focus a blurred or double image is a bad eye; it distorts. The body cannot safely act on that illumination and so is full of darkness.

*Verse 35:* Jesus cautioned the crowds to see to it that what entered into them was light and not darkness. The caution was related to the theme of good or bad, correct or incorrect spiritual matters. He offered them *light;* their leaders offered them *darkness.* If they accepted what their leaders offered, their entire lives would be shrouded in darkness. On the other hand, if they accepted what he was offering, their lives would be full of light—as a room illuminated by a lamp. (Compare John 8:12.)

## 11. Genuine Versus Spurious Religious Practice (11:37–52)

The contrast between what the religious leaders of Israel were offering and what Jesus was offering continues through this event. Genuine religious practice is contrasted with spurious religious practice.

*Verses 37–38:* A Pharisee, into whose home Jesus had gone as a guest, was amazed that Jesus went to the table to eat without first washing his hands. The washing was not for hygienic purposes—to wash off dirt—but for ceremonial religious purposes—to wash off contamination from having touched some religiously unclean object, or even a Gentile. In a home, a father could do the ceremonial washing of his hands and all the family would be considered clean.

*Verse 39:* Jesus responded by indicating the true nature of religious cleanliness as internal and spiritual rather than external and physical. He charged the Pharisees with careful concern for external cleanliness but corresponding lack of concern for internal cleanliness. They were like people who would very carefully wash the outside of cups and dishes but would leave unwashed the inside where the real corruption was. While the Pharisees were externally clean they were internally corrupt—*full of extortion and wickedness.* The word translated *extortion* means that which one possesses by robbery or dishonesty. In Matthew's use of this teaching at another period in Jesus' life (23:23–28), this charge was associated with greed, injustice, and lack of compassion. In Luke's next few verses it has the same association. The word may mean greediness in this verse. The word translated *evil* is a more general word for unrighteousness—the very opposite of what the Pharisee sought through his careful attention to religious ceremonial practice. By basic nature this word, too, meant grasping in spirit.

*Verse 40: You fools!* The word translated *fools* does not have an evil or sinful meaning but rather means to have a head containing no thoughts. It was empty-headedness to think that God would accept external cleanliness when it was accompanied by internal corruption. The same God who made the outside and is interested in it also made the inside and is interested in it.

*Verse 41:* To *give alms* was a practice of religious piety. Here it is used for an offering to God—*give for alms those things that are within*. By this he meant that they should offer up to God as a gift their very inner selves. That would make them really clean—clean on the inside.

*Behold, everything is clean for you:* Two interpretations have been suggested for this unusual statement. It has been understood as a simple statement that, since the Pharisees already had external cleanliness, if they would offer their inner selves to God they would be totally clean—inside and outside. It has also been understood in a more complex sense—related to motivation. Make your motives right—be clean inwardly, spiritually—and you will find that *everything is clean for you*. Defilement does not come from touching things considered religiously unclean. That was what Jesus believed and practiced.

Verses 42–44: Jesus pronounced three woes upon the Pharisees. As previously observed, a woe portends judgment (10:13–15). Alas! in the day of judgment for those who make external matters supreme and neglect the more meaningful internal matters.

*Verse 42: Woe . . . for you tithe mint and rue and every herb:* According to Leviticus 27:30, when the Hebrews occupied their permanent residence in Canaan, they were to give to God as a part of their worship, one-tenth of their flocks, herds, grain, and fruit. This produce would be used to sustain the sacrificial services of their religious practice. Through the centuries the developing legalism required minute interpretation of the law and its application. The Mishna—written interpretations by the rabbis—reflects just how minute this came to be. By their interpretation, garden vegetables came to be included in that which was tithed, and finally, the herbs which were grown for seasoning. It was this scrupulous attention to legal requirement to which Jesus referred on this occasion.

*Mint* is the plant produced then and now for the use of its leaves in seasoning.

*Rue* was grown for its bitter leaves, used in medicines. According to the Mishna it was not necessary to tithe it.

*Herb* translates a general word for any type of garden vegetable produced for leaves, roots, or seeds.

In place of "rue . . . and every herb" Matthew has "dill and cummin" (23:23). Although the leaves and stems of dill might be used, these plants were grown largely for their aromatic seeds. In the Mishna, dill was specifically subject to the tithe. Cummin was a dwarf plant of the carrot family grown only for its very tiny seeds.

Both Luke and Matthew stress the meticulous care of the Pharisees in tithing. For every nine leaves of mint used, a tenth leaf was put aside for God. For every nine relatively large dill seeds or nine small cummin seeds used, a tenth one was put aside for God. Even plants not subject to the tithe in the rabbinical tradition—such as "rue"—were tithed just to be on the safe side and to run no risk of breaking the law.

Jesus was not condemning the careful stewardship reflected in the tithing of the least material possession. He was condemning a sense of values which had lost correct perspective where God's law was concerned. The law of God required tithing of material things. But it also required that man "do justice

. . . love kindness . . . walk humbly" before God (Mic. 6:8). This second requirement of the law had been abandoned by the Pharisees, and this was Jesus' major concern.

*Neglect justice and the love of God:* Matthew has, "you have neglected the weightier matters of the law, justice, and mercy, and faith." The verbs translated *neglect* are different. Luke's word means to pass along beside a thing without paying attention to it; Matthew's word means to abandon or to give up as an object of concern. Both have *justice* in first place, which basically means to do that which is right in relation to one's fellowman. Luke's *love of God*—meaning love for God—is a summary of Micah's "to love kindness and to walk humbly with your God." Matthew has "mercy and faith" as a summary of the Micah passage.

Man's relation to his fellowman and to God cannot be separated. In Jesus' understanding, to give scrupulous attention to being right with God through the tithe of material possessions, but to be wrong with one's fellowman through neglect or abandonment of justice, mercy, and love is to miss God's intent and requirement.

Matthew has "the weightier matters of the law" (23:23), a word meaning primarily that which is burdensome because it is difficult to fulfill; it had come to mean that which is "heavier" or "more important" when two objects are compared. It is much easier to try to meet God's requirement by meticulous tithing of possessions. That can be a matter of simple arithmetic —one out of ten. It is much harder to try to meet his requirement by the practice of justice, mercy, and love. That is spiritual and has to do with value judgments which can never be measured by arithmetic. But it is the more important way, and to fail to do it leaves one short of God's requirement regardless of meticulous material stewardship.

*These you ought to have done: These* refers to the spiritual matters of justice and love. Neither in Luke nor in Matthew can it refer to the tithing. *Ought* is the precise rendering of a word meaning an absolute necessity if a desired end is to be realized. Meeting God's requirement cannot possibly be realized if one leaves off justice and mercy in his interpersonal relationships.

*Without neglecting the others: The others* refers to the tithing of material possessions. A recognition of material stewardship before God is important, but Jesus seemed to think that the Pharisees' interpretation of "the seed of the land" (Lev. 27:30) as including the seasoning herbs was a bit of over-caution! He was not encouraging them to stop their tithing, but he was condemning them for ignoring and abandoning God's primary requirement of justice, mercy, and love. Apart from the positive practice of these qualities, no man can rightly claim to have met God's requirement.

*Verse 43:* Rather than practicing justice for men and humility before God, the Pharisees were completely self-centered in both the place of worship and the place of business. In the synagogues they desired *the best seat*—a circular bench at the front of the synagogue that faced the congregation. It was near the leader of the synagogue; and was a convenient place for being seen and from which to share their wisdom on questions of the Law. In the market-place the Pharisees delighted in parading in clothes with excessively large Scripture frontlets and excessively long prayer tassels (Matt. 23:5) to call attention to their piety. They valued the *salutations* they received—not mere greetings but effusive terms of honor bestowed with repeated deep bows. Like ceremonial washings and meticulous tithing these were external and physical matters rather than internal and spiritual. But they represented what the Pharisees regarded as primary.

*Verse 44:* Jesus climaxed his denunciation of the careful external legalism of the Pharisees by comparing them to tombs. The clean exterior of a burial cave gave no indication of the rottenness within. To come into contact with a burial cave was to become ceremonially defiled. During holy week in Jerusalem the exteriors of all burial caves were whitewashed lest someone unknowingly touch them and be defiled (Matt. 23:27). In Matthew's account Jesus applied the illustration more vividly. The whitewashed exterior of the tomb represented the legally clean exterior of the Pharisees. The bones and decaying flesh within the tomb represented the hypocrisy and iniquity on the inside of the Pharisees. In Luke's account the danger of contamination is more subtle. Like coming into contact with an unrecognized tomb and thus becoming defiled, men become defiled by the externally religious and deceptive Pharisees. Woe to the Pharisees for this deceptive and baleful influence.

Verses 45–52 are a continuation of Jesus' denunciation of spurious religion in response to a remark by a lawyer.

*Verse 45:* The *lawyers* were the official interpreters of both the written law and the oral law which had been developed in the process of interpreting and applying the written law. Ideally they were the ones to whom the Hebrew people looked for correct interpretation and guidance.

*In saying this you reproach us also:* The word *this* probably refers to the total of Jesus' teaching beginning in verse 39. Although many of these lawyers were themselves Pharisees, they traditionally scoffed at much of the Pharisees' practice and opinion. While they, too, engaged in minute applications of the law, they regarded themselves as being above much of the ridiculous minutiae of the Pharisees. This lawyer, however, rightly understood that the spiritual principle which Jesus used in his teaching was a condemnation of their legalism as well.

*Verse 46:* Jesus agreed: *Woe to you lawyers also,* because by their interpretation of the law they heaped upon men *burdens* exceedingly hard to bear—responsibilities exceedingly hard to accomplish. He did not explain the nature of these burdens, nor did he give an illustration. The difference between the lawyers and the Pharisees was one of degree. A lawyer might think it absurd to tithe tiny garden seeds but entirely proper to forbid a physician to administer medicine on the sabbath.

*You yourselves do not touch the burdens with one of your fingers:* The lawyers (scribes and Pharisees in Matt. 23:2) felt that they had accomplished their total purpose in setting down their interpretation of the law. They were totally unconcerned when people felt that the interpretations put impossible requirements on them and wanted the interpretations removed or changed, or asked at least for counsel in how to meet the requirements. The lawyers would not use even one finger to help lift the burden ever so slightly.

*Verse 47: You build the tombs of the prophets whom your fathers killed:* Although there are few identifiable cases of prophets who were killed because of their faith (none are mentioned here), it was traditionally held that many of the prophets had become martyrs. Jesus used that belief. Verse 48 indicates that Jesus meant that the leaders of his day shared their fathers' view that the prophets deserved to die, so they killed them to keep them from proclaiming God's word; they kept that view alive by building the memorial reminders. In doing so they indicated that their characters were the same as their fathers'—if they had been living in their fathers' day, they would have joined in the killing.

*Verses 49–51* appear to refer to some decree of God in the past. It is not, however, a quotation of any Old Testament passage. The idea as stated is embedded in 2 Chronicles 36:15–16, but it is not a quotation. In Matthew (23:24), Jesus was the one who was going to send prophets and others who would be mistreated in the synagogues and streets, some of whom would be killed. This is probably what is intended in the phrase *the Wisdom of God said*. It appears to be a roundabout way of referring to himself. (Compare 1 Cor. 1:24; Col. 2:3.) Jesus knew that sending out his prophets and apostles—spokesmen and messengers—would mean their inevitable mistreatment, rejection, persecution, and in some cases, death. In killing his prophets the religious leaders would be identifying themselves with the line of those who had killed God's true worshipers *from the blood of Abel to the blood of Zechariah*. Abel is the first recorded martyr (Gen. 4:8). Zechariah is mentioned in 2 Chronicles (24:20–21), the last book in the Hebrew Old Testament. So, from the first book (Genesis) to the last (2 Chronicles) man's murder of God's true servants has been recorded. The choice was also appropriate, since one involved the murder of a brother, and the other was murdered in the court of the priests. Zechariah's blood was thus shed in the very presence of God between the altar of burnt offerings and the Holy of Holies. In the Talmud it was regarded as one of the most terrible crimes in Israel's history. As he died, Zechariah cried out, "May the Lord see and avenge!" It was the recognition that a just God would not let such injustice go unpunished.

*It shall be required of this generation:* Jesus did not mean that his generation was to be punished because of what their fathers several hundred years before them had done. He meant that in rejecting and killing him and those whom he was sending, his generation was making up the climax of that long line of rejection and murder. They added their guilt to that of all the others. As the generation in which that guilt was culminated, they were to experience the culmination of retribution. The immediate judgment in focus may have been the coming destruction of the Temple and Jerusalem, and the dispersion of the Jews as a nation. The more ultimate judgment in focus was the final reckoning of God with man.

*Verse 52:* The lawyers faced a future portentous of judgment because they had *the key of knowledge*. In rabbinic use a "key" stood for the responsibility to interpret God's way. The lawyers had this key for opening the doors to an understanding of God's law and his requirement. Rather than using that key to gain entrance to an understanding of God's *spiritual* requirement, they restricted their use to the lower level of *physical* requirement. Not only were they failing to enter in themselves, but they were also hindering others who sincerely desired to enter. In the Coptic Gospel According to Thomas

(Logion 102), Jesus is quoted as applying to the Pharisees the fable—traditionally identified with Aesop—of the dog in the manger:

> Jesus said,
> > Woe to the Pharisees.
> > They are like a dog sleeping in the manger of the oxen.
> > He does not eat; nor does he permit the oxen to eat.[1]

A summary word on this paragraph (vv. 37–52) is in order. The Pharisees' problem of dependence on washings, tithing, honorable positions was due to their failure to grasp the basic meaning of religion as first of all inner and spiritual. Even tithing basically indicated God's ownership of the whole man—body, spirit, possessions, and relationships. To relate to God in physical and material requirements but not in spiritual requirements is to attain the secondary but fail of the primary.

## 12. The Hostility of Jewish Religious Leaders (11:53–54)

This is a summary statement pointing to the period from the time of this denunciation by Jesus to the time of his death at the hands of those whom he had denounced.

*Verses 53–54: The scribes and Pharisees began to press him hard.* They were relentless in their hostility and their determination to bring him to his death. They sought *to provoke him to speak of many things.* They were *lying in wait,* like highwaymen. What they sought was some word from Jesus which they could use to bring him to his death.

These verses could well serve as an introduction to the last week in Jerusalem when the Jewish leaders tried to trap Jesus in controversy over questions related to doctrines, practices, taxes, politics, etc. Indeed, one might anticipate that chapter 12 will begin with the arrival in Jerusalem and that fateful week. Such, however, is not the case. That arrival is delayed until 19:28.

## 13. Warning Against Hypocrisy and Blasphemy (12:1–12)

At the end of the dinner (11:37), the scribes and Pharisees initiated determined efforts to bring Jesus to his death. The opening verses of chapter 12 indicate what Jesus did when he left the dinner. Crowded by the multitudes and the Twelve, he began to speak to them about the latent danger in the Pharisees.

*Verse 1:* In the narrow street of the unnamed town, the multitude of several thousands crowded to the point of trampling one another in their efforts to get near enough to hear Jesus. He addressed himself *first* to *his disciples,* that is, the Twelve. *First* here means "primarily"—the people heard as he spoke to the Twelve.

*Beware of the leaven of the Pharisees, which is hypocrisy: Leaven,* yeast, spreads to permeate bread dough. *Hypocrisy* was this element in the Phari-

---

[1]Cf. Ray Summers, *The Secret Sayings of the Living Jesus* (Waco, Texas: Word Books, 1968), pp. 72–73.

sees which was spreading in society like yeast in dough. It was the pretense of appearing to be very religious by observance of washing, tithing, and attention to other legal practices. But in Jesus' understanding this was not really being religious; it was playacting, a staged performance for the eyes of men. That is the meaning of the word translated *hypocrisy*. Beneath the mask, concealed by the action, there was a spiritually irreligious person. *Beware:* Be on guard against contamination by adopting that hypocritical way of life.

*Verses 2–3:* Just as the mask is eventually removed from the actor's face to reveal his true hidden nature, so every type of covering is eventually removed to reveal true character. It is impossible to conceal evil completely or indefinitely. Jesus spoke particularly of the inner evil of the Pharisees which was covered over by an external show of good. His words were to be applied, however, in the experience of the listening crowds and disciples. Like the Pharisees, they would be unable to conceal successfully any evil in their lives. It is very doubtful that Jesus envisioned this uncovering as taking place in the day of final judgment when all men's lives will be laid bare before God's reckoning. He was more likely thinking of the futility of trying to conceal evil in this life.

Evil deeds covered up will become known. Evil words spoken under the cover of night will be revealed in the day that follows. Words whispered secretly in the privacy of one's own house will come to be announced publicly from the housetop. Paul used this idea when he wrote of the way light penetrates darkness and reveals what is hidden there (Eph. 5:13).

Verses 4–7 appear to continue Jesus' warning to the Twelve in particular and the crowds in general. They relate to the problem of fearing harm from one's antagonists. This was a meaningful subject of Jesus, since the scribes and Pharisees were actively seeking ways to harm him.

*Verses 4–5:* His disciples were not to fear those who had power to kill the body only—human enemies who had power to bring death to the body, but whose power stopped there. They were rather to fear the one who had power not only to kill the physical body but beyond that to cast into hell. *Hell* is the translation of the Greek "Gehenna." The name was derived from the garbage-burning Valley of Hinnom just outside Jerusalem (see Jer. 7:32), and was Jesus' (as well as his contemporaries') term for the place of eternal punishment of the wicked. Except for one place (James 3:6), the word is used in the New Testament only in the teachings of Jesus.

The meaning of the saying is clear to this extent—men are to fear the one who has power over them both in this life and beyond this life. Who is that one? Some interpreters understand it as a reference to Satan; others understand it as a reference to God. Since the words immediately following relate to God's care for men, it is probable that these words of warning also relate to God. Fear the displeasure of God (v. 5); trust the care of God (vv. 6–7). Such fear and trust would drive out fear of what men could do to them.

*Verses 6–7:* Jesus illustrated God's care for men by referring to his care for the most minute things. The very common tiny sparrow was sold in the market two for a penny. If one bought two pennies' worth he received an extra sparrow, making *five . . . for two pennies*. The penny (*asarion*) was a Roman copper coin; sixteen of them equalled in value a silver denarius which was worth about eighteen cents in American money. Each penny, therefore, was worth approximately one cent. For two cents one could buy four sparrows and get one thrown in free. It was this extra sparrow of which Jesus said, *And not one of them is forgotten before God*. His care for his creation is so great that this extra sparrow is noted by him.

*Even the hairs of your head are all numbered:* While modern medical and technological skill can compute the number of hairs on a given man's head at a given time, ancient man regarded that as an impossible task and put it in the same category as counting the stars in the sky or the grains of sand on the seashore. Jesus used the idea to illustrate God's careful concern for the least thing affecting his creation.

*You are of more value than many sparrows:* Jesus returned to his earlier illustration. If God is concerned about the tiny sparrow and notes its fate, how much greater must be his concern for man, who is of immeasurably greater value than the sparrow. Therefore, trust his loving care.

Verses 8–12: Jesus knew that difficult days faced his disciples. As they went out to witness for him they would face great danger. Addressing himself to that situation he again joined warning and encouragement.

*Verse 8: Everyone who acknowledges me:* In these words, Jesus placed responsibility directly upon men. To acknowledge Jesus before men means to admit his lordship in one's life, to accept Jesus as Lord. Such a person Jesus accepts as his own and acknowledges such acceptance and ownership in the presence of the angels of God. While this acknowledging before the angels is likely a reference to the anticipated judgment, it need not be limited to that. It is a temporal as well as an eternal reality.

*Verse 9: But he who denies me . . . will be denied:* Responsibility for one's actions also involves the negative side of judgment. The one who denies Jesus as Lord experiences Jesus' denying of him as a servant. The denying of Jesus' lordship is of this world—*before men;* Jesus' denial of man's servanthood is of the eternal world—*before the angels of God.* As in verse 8, while this denying anticipates the day of judgment, it is not limited to that.

*Before the angels of God:* The Jewish people looked upon the angels as a spiritual order of servants of God superior to the human order. They referred to the angels as the "higher family" and believed that God did nothing which he did not first discuss with them. In other teachings, Jesus spoke of the angels as agents of God in the final judgment separation of good and evil, God's people and Satan's people (Matt. 13:36–43). That idea is the backdrop for this teaching.

*Verse 10:* There were people in Jesus' day who not only denied him as Lord but also went beyond denial to reviling him. They charged him, for example, with breaking the law by healing on the sabbath. They charged him with leading the people astray by his example in ignoring many of the traditional religious laws and practices. There were some who went beyond that and charged that the power working in Jesus was not the power of the Spirit of God but the power of the "prince of demons"—Beelzebul (11:14–20; Matt. 12:22–32).

Jesus made a distinction between men's speaking *against the Son of man* and man's blaspheming *against the Holy Spirit*. To speak evil words against

Jesus as a man working among men was a serious charge, but it was an evil which could be forgiven. There are numerous examples in the New Testament of people who first opposed Jesus but later turned to accept him. But to blaspheme *against the Holy Spirit* was an evil of such character that forgiveness was not possible. In this setting in Luke, there is no indication of what constitutes blaspheming *against the Holy Spirit.* Elsewhere in Jesus' teaching, however, the sin is more specifically defined. See the discussion on Luke 11:14–20. In Matthew 12:22–32, Jesus said that to attribute to Satan the work of the Spirit of God was to sin beyond forgiveness. Since the work of the Spirit is to bring man to repentance and salvation, to reject his work is to reject the only way by which repentance and salvation may come. Such sin is not committed in ignorance. Nor is it committed inadvertently. It is so crystalized in its opposition to God that it calls even the unquestionable working of God's Spirit demonic. In such character there is nothing to which even the Spirit of God can appeal to produce repentance, forgiveness, and salvation.

*Verses 11–12:* Jesus' disciples were to find that this very Holy Spirit, whom some people were reviling, would be their aid in time of trouble.

*When they bring you before the synagogues . . . rulers . . . authorities:* This continues the persecution theme and the counsel not to fear men but to trust God (vv. 4–7). Jesus was experiencing growing opposition. He saw nothing ahead except an increase of that opposition which inevitably would engulf all those identified with him. The court of the local synagogue was the lowest Jewish court, but even it had authority to administer physical punishment. Later Paul reported that on five different occasions he had received the Jewish punishment of "forty lashes less one" (2 Cor. 11:24). Forty lashes was the maximum, but to be on the safe side, the Jews usually stopped at thirty–nine.

*Rulers and authorities* are a probable reference to courts higher than the synagogue and, hence, probably administering more severe punishment. It is not clear whether Jesus, at this point, was speaking only of Jewish courts or whether he was looking beyond that and preparing his disciples to face Roman courts as well. Both he and they were to experience both. From Luke's historical perspective both courts had become realities for Jesus and his disciples.

*Do not be anxious:* The word translated *anxious* means literally "distracted." They were not to panic at approaching danger or become so distracted that they became defenseless. They had good reason for fine defense: right was on their side. Help was available.

*How or what you are to answer:* The ancient manuscripts of Luke are divided on this reading. Some have "what you are to answer"—the content of their defense. Some have "how you shall answer"—the method of their defense. Some have both. This last reading has the best support and is most likely the original. Both questions lend themselves to distracting anxiety, "What shall I do? How shall I answer?"

*The Holy Spirit will teach you:* Rather than becoming distracted they were to face trial with full confidence that the Holy Spirit would help them.

*In that very hour:* The hour when they faced their accusers and were required to answer charges made against them. They were to prepare no lengthy defense, but to trust the Spirit's prompting them as they answered.

*What you ought to say:* More precisely "what it is necessary to say." The Holy Spirit's directions would prompt them to fit their defense to the particular charges which would be made. Their defense would be the true nature of their conduct and the reason for that conduct. In a later setting when Jesus spoke of his disciples' facing difficulties and of his prompting them in their defense, he said that their trial and defense would prove to be an opportunity for them to bear witness for him (Luke 21:12-19).

## 14. Warning Against Greed (12:13-21)

A listener requested that Jesus assist him in gaining a part of an inheritance which a brother was holding from him. The request was not unusual; the rabbis and lawyers served frequently in this way. Nor is the claim explained. It may have been a just claim, that the man's brother was fraudulently holding back a part of an inheritance. On the other hand it may be that the man did not have a rightful claim on the inheritance and that he was actually grasping for something that was not his. Jesus' refusal to become an arbiter in the case was no indication of whether or not the man had a just cause. He refused because there were those among the Jews properly appointed to serve in this capacity. Jesus was not so appointed and he had no intention of being turned from the one thing he *was* appointed to do, which outranked serving as a divider of material goods.

Verses 15-21: Jesus used the occasion to issue a warning about greed for material things. He illustrated his warning with the parable of the rich fool —a parable appearing only here in the New Testament, but in a much shorter version in the Coptic Gospel According to Thomas (Logion 63).

*Verse 15: Take heed, and beware of all covetousness:* Jesus warned his hearers—*the multitude* (v. 13)—against a preoccupation with material provisions for this life which leaves out more important matters related to God and one's spiritual well-being. *Covetousness* is a desire for material goods to the exclusion of that which is both right and appropriate. Paul associated covetousness with moral uncleanness (Eph. 4:19), insisting that it was not even to be mentioned as something fitting for Christian conduct (Eph. 5:3), and with idolatry (Col. 3:5)—to put desire for material things ahead of desire for spiritual things is to "worship" something other than God.

*Man's life does not consist in the abundance of his possessions:* The word for *life* is not the word for mere physical being; lower orders of animals have that. It is the word for life *(zōē)* on the higher plane of meaningful existence which is not made up of material things—riches, houses, lands, well-filled barns—but of "riches" in relationship to God (v. 21).

*Verses 16-20:* The parable of the rich fool illustrates the futility of trusting in material possessions for well being. A landowner produced such an abundant crop that his barns were inadequate. Planning carefully the number and size of the barns he needed to store his harvest, he built them, and gathered the harvest. On the very night that he completed his harvest, he congratulated himself on his abundant provision for *many years;* he could live in ease and merriment. But also on that same night he was required to give up a greater possession—his *soul*—and leave all the material possessions because they had no value for the life to which he was called.

The story graphically portrays effectiveness in labor and shrewdness in providing for the results of labor. By the standards with which men measure success, the man was successful. But the story also portrays graphically a lack of wisdom in maintaining a proper sense of values. To this man, *soul* was the total of man and it could be provided for in physical ways. To God, *soul* was the total of man, but it could not be provided for in physical ways alone. The first person pronouns "I" and "my" are used eleven times in the man's brief words, reflecting his entire self-centeredness which left God out of his planning and his hungry fellowmen out of his concern.

God had the last word in the man's experience. *Fool* means senseless, without mind, without reason. The man planned, but he planned without reason as his guide. Reason would have made it clear to him that he could not nourish his *soul* on food alone, and would have caused him to see that life is from God rather than from grain and gaiety.

The Gospel According to Thomas has the story in a greatly condensed and yet very dramatic form. Whereas in Luke the rich man was a farmer, in Thomas he was a man who invested his money in farming. The end was the same.

*Logion 63:*

Jesus said, there was a rich man who had much money. He said, "I will use my money in sowing, reaping, planting, and filling my barns with fruit so I will lack nothing."

In his heart this was what he thought and that night he died.

Whoever has ears to hear let him hear.

*Verse 21:* The conclusion in the Thomas account draws attention to the conclusion in Luke: In the manuscripts of Luke there are three different forms. The best manuscripts have the conclusion just as it appears in the RSV: *So is he who lays up treasure for himself and is not rich toward God.* Some manuscripts omit verse 21 entirely. The scribe may have omitted it because he regarded it as not original with Jesus but a conclusion added by a later hand, either Luke or the source from which Luke took the story. Still other manuscripts have verse 21 just as it is in the RSV and then add, "Having spoken these things, he said, 'Whoever has ears to hear let him hear.' " This is almost certainly an interpolation by a later hand and has the force of giving the story a double conclusion. The correct reading is the one which appears in our New Testament text. Its lesson is that to lay up material treasures out of self-interest and to fail to acquire spiritual riches of God is to lose all.

## 15. Trust in God as a Way of Life (12:22–34)

Having given to the multitude his warning about trusting in material goods for life, Jesus addressed *his disciples*—probably the Twelve—on trusting in God as a way of life.

*Verse 22: Do not be anxious:* Literally, "Stop being distracted." Very precisely it means to stop pulling one's self in two by allowing one's self to be tugged at by two opposite principles of life: "I can trust God to care for me" versus "I cannot trust God to care for me."

Jesus related the teaching mainly to two elements of physical life—food to sustain life, and clothing to cover the body. The word translated *life* is translated "soul" in the previous parable. It is more than animal life *(bios)*, but it is also something different from spirit *(pneuma)*. Perhaps the best way to think of it is one's total self *(psychē,* animated being).

*Verse 23* puts the four elements into proper perspective. *Life* is more important than the *food* which sustains it; the *body* is more important than the *clothing* which covers it. Jesus was arguing from the greater to the lesser. Any Jew would have granted that God gives both *life* and *body.* Jesus' argument was that if God gives the life and body, he can be trusted to give the sustaining food and covering clothing which are of lesser importance.

Verses 24–28 give two illustrations of God's provision.

*Verse 24: Consider the ravens:* Take careful knowledge of the ravens. Let them be man's teachers. They are not pulled in two by distracting anxiety about food. They employ the strength and the wisdom with which a benevolent Creator has endowed them to take out of his creation that which they need to sustain life. Since man is of *more value . . . than the birds,* he can trust God's provision for him, too.

*Verses 26–28: Consider the lilies:* Again, take careful knowledge of the flowers; let them be man's teachers. They gather sunlight and minerals out of the environment through their endowment by a benevolent Creator. The result is a covering which the richest of men—*Solomon in all his glory—* cannot duplicate. This is beautiful vegetation one day and fuel to cook man's food the next, but it is the object of God's provision. How much more can man trust God for covering (v. 28). It is a mark of little faith not to trust him.

*Verse 25:* Between these two illustrations is a saying whose meaning is disputed—*which of you by being anxious can add a cubit to his span of life?* Was Jesus saying that anxiety cannot make a man live longer or that it cannot make him grow taller? Because the idea of one's inability to grow taller by worrying because he is short is so absurd, it is rather commonly held that Jesus was speaking about the inability to prolong life by worry about losing it. This may be. Indeed, modern medical knowledge suggests that worry may shorten life rather than prolong it.

Jesus, however, sometimes used absurd and exaggerated illustrations. The Greek words for "camel" and "rope" differ only by one letter. (See discussion on 18:25.) Did Jesus speak of threading a needle with a rope or of pushing a camel through the eye of a needle? Both are impossible; one is a more natural illustration; the other is comically absurd and by that fact more dramatically effective! Did Jesus speak of getting a log out of a brother's eye or out of his spring? (See discussion on 6:41–42.) One is more natural; the other more exaggerated and hence comically absurd. Authorities are almost unanimous in holding that "camel" and "eye" are Jesus' use—the absurd rather than the natural.

This may be a similar case. Two words are important in seeking a solution. The first word, translated cubit, is used three times in the New Testament: of the distance of the fishing boat from the shore (John 21:8); of the measurement of the wall of the city (Rev. 21:17); and this passage with the exact parallel in Matthew 6:27.

The second word, translated *span of life* (or "stature" in the RSV margin), is used six times in the New Testament: of Sarah's length of life or age when she conceived Isaac (Heb. 11:11); being of age or full grown (John 9:21, 23); of stature—metaphorically of the full stature of Jesus Christ (Eph. 4:13); literally (Luke 2:52, 19:3); and this passage and the exact parallel in Matthew 6:27.

On the basis of this it seems that Jesus was using an exaggerated illustration; the very comical absurdity makes it more impressive. A small Jewish man—four feet six inches tall—intimidated by the towering Roman soldier —six feet tall plus his plumed helmet—worrying and worrying, wishing he were six feet tall! A cubit was the length of a man's forearm from the inner bend of the elbow to the end of his middle finger. But his anxiety did not add the desired eighteen inches.

*Verses 29–30:* In contrast to distracting anxiety as a way of life, Jesus recommended trust in God. Such trust did not rule out industry and work; the ravens and the lilies "worked." But it ruled out distraction. In verse 30 Jesus points to the *nations of the world* in their distracting pursuit of material necessities. These were the Gentiles, the non-Jews, the people who did not know the God known to Jesus and the Twelve. They did not know of a God who desired to provide for their needs. The Twelve did know of him; the way for them was the way of trust in him.

*Verse 31:* Jesus gave to the Twelve their proper alternative: *seek his kingdom.* The expression *his kingdom* has good support in the manuscripts of Luke. The better supported reading, however, is "God's kingdom." The first concern of God's people is God's kingdom—his rule, his reign in the individual heart and in the total society. The secondary matters of concern, food and clothing, Jesus said, *shall be yours as well.* They are important, but they are not first. First in importance is trust in God and commitment to him.

*Verse 32* in the RSV is placed in the paragraph with verses 33–34 rather than in the paragraph preceding it (vv. 22–32). The placement is a matter of editorial judgment. The verse is transitional in nature but appears to be essentially part of the thought of verse 31. Jesus counseled the Twelve to seek God's kingdom as their primary goal with the assurance that the secondary needs also would be theirs. Then he assured them that it was God's good pleasure to give them the thing they sought—his kingdom, that is, his reign in the hearts of men. Jesus addressed the assurance to the Twelve as his *little flock.* He was the Good Shepherd (John 10:11) who would lay down his life in order that his *little flock* might have God's kingdom.

*Verses 33–34* direct the attention of the Twelve to the pursuit of the true spiritual treasure and sustenance.

*Sell your possessions and give alms:* In another setting, Jesus counseled a ruler who asked the way of eternal life to sell his possessions, give the money to the poor, and come and follow Jesus who made no claim on material possessions. The man professed to have kept the law but still felt a lack of being right with God. Jesus' teaching showed him where he was lacking— he cherished his possessions more than being right with God (Luke 18:23). Something of that same spirit was still evident in the Twelve. Jesus' advice was that they give their material possessions to the needy and commit themselves totally to God's care and God's work for them.

*Provide yourselves with purses that do not grow old:* This is a metaphorical way of saying, "Find in God's care for you a provision superior to any provision of earthly treasures." Jesus on another occasion spoke of having from God a sustenance which was superior to earthly food or support (John 4:32–34). The Twelve, too, could know that support.

*Treasure in the heavens that does not fail:* In the Sermon on the Mount (Matt. 6:19–21) Jesus set in contrast earthly treasures and heavenly treasures. The same contrast is implied in this slightly different version. Earthly treasures *fail;* heavenly treasures do not. Earthly treasures may be stolen by thieves (money) or devoured by moths (costly fabrics); no thief or moth can touch the heavenly treasure. In this world, no treasure is secure; in heaven, every treasure is secure.

*Verse 34:* This is proverbial or axiomatic truth. One's *heart*—his total interest and controlling concern—will be right where his treasure is. The word translated *there* is very specific, meaning right there in that very spot. Earthly treasures have a way of coming to control or own their possessors. Interest and concern localize in them so that interest and concern in heavenly treasures become secondary. This does not necessarily have to be the case, but the likelihood is so great that strong warning of the danger is necessary —which Jesus gave.

### 16. A Caution to Watchfulness in Impending Crisis (12:35–59)

It is difficult to determine the purpose and meaning of these teachings at this place in Luke. The materials definitely relate to a time of impending crisis in the lives of Jesus' hearers. Exactly what was that impending crisis? To which of the groups mentioned in chapters 11–12 were these teachings addressed? Several alternatives may be established, but the evidence is not clearly on the side of any.

(1) In Luke's setting, were these teachings addressed to the Twelve in view of the days just ahead in Jerusalem? That was the impending crisis uppermost in Jesus' mind at the time. But some of the teachings do not fit the Twelve, and some of them seem to look beyond that impending crisis to a future one.

(2) Were they addressed to the Twelve in view of the crisis at the second coming of Christ and the judgment? Some appear to point to that event, but the Twelve had little if any background at this point for understanding such a reference; and, again, some of them do not fit the Twelve.

(3) Were they addressed to the "multitude" (v. 1) of hearers, and if so, in connection with which crisis, the one near at hand or the one in the future at the second coming? Jesus did address some of the teachings in this chapter directly to the multitude. They, however, would have had little background for understanding either of the two crises mentioned above. If the teachings were directed to them, the application must necessarily be a rather general one relating to responsibility to God who will judge.

(4) Were they addressed to the religious leaders—the scribes and Pharisees (11:15, 27–44) and the lawyers (11:45–52)—in view of the coming crisis in Jerusalem and their consistent missing of their responsibility under God by rejecting him? This fits more of the teachings than any other alternative. The big problem, however, is that most of these teachings are in

either Mark or Matthew and in entirely different settings from Luke's. (Compare Matt. 16:2–3; 5:25–26.)

The biggest difficulty of all is in the use made of the several parabolic stories. In slightly different form, Mark's parable of the porter (13:33–37) and Matthew's parables of the householder and the thief (24:43–44) and the waiting servants (24:45–51), are the same as Luke's parables of the waiting servants (vv. 35–38), the householder and the thief (vv. 39–40), and the faithful and the unfaithful servants (vv. 42–48). Mark and Matthew have these stories in the Mount of Olives teaching on Tuesday evening before Jesus' death, in which Jesus moved from speaking of the destruction of Jerusalem (Matthew, Mark, and Luke all have that) to speaking of the second coming and the judgment at the end of the world. They have all these parables applied to the second coming. Luke, on the other hand, omits all the teachings on the second coming and uses the parables here in this section when they were on their way to Jerusalem.

Only a very fragile case can be made for Jesus' having used the teachings twice with different applications. If he used them only once, which is the original setting? Does Luke have the original application with Matthew and Mark representing a later adaptation for a different purpose? Do Mark and Matthew have the original setting with Luke representing a reorientation of the teaching for a theological focus on Jesus' death and the ensuing fate of Jerusalem? Has the original setting and application by Jesus been lost or replaced by the early church with an application to its situation as it awaited the delayed second coming? Opinion is divided. Pursuit of the question requires a comparative study beyond the scope of this commentary.

For the purpose of this commentary, the materials of Luke alone will be used with only an occasional reference to the parallels. For the most part they will be treated from the viewpoint that they were addressed to the people in general but that the center of focus was on those who occupied the place of responsible leadership in the religion of Israel—the scribes, the Pharisees, the lawyers, and even the Twelve. The crisis might be any crisis which called them to a reckoning with God concerning their responsibility. It might be the immediate crisis in Jerusalem, but it might also have overtones reaching to the ultimate crisis of the second coming.

Verses 35–45 contain three parabolic illustrations of the relationships and responsibilities of masters and servants, on the theme of alertness to crisis and fidelity to responsibility in the face of crisis. Beyond that, specific application is very difficult. Whether or not a solution is at hand, the problems involved must be pointed out in the exposition of the text.

*Verses 35–38:* Jesus compared his hearers and their situation to a group of servants awaiting their master's return from a marriage feast. Such feasts were of very indefinite length. The master might return in the second night watch (9:00–12:00) or the third night watch (12:00–3:00). There was nothing to indicate that it might not even be later in the fourth night watch (3:00–6:00). Because of that uncertainty the servants were to have the house lighted and their long robes tied up about their waists so that they might serve their master's wish when he arrived.

For the Twelve, this story had definite overtones of a second coming teaching. For the church in Luke's day it had definite overtones of an explanation of a delayed second coming—whether the master returned early or late was not to be the concern of his servants. Their concern was to be only their preparation to receive him upon his return.

Such ready servants would be rewarded by their returning master. He would put aside the splendor of his position as lord; he would tie his robe up about his waist like a servant, have them take their places at the table like lords, and would serve them. Such was unheard of in the relationships of masters and servants as the world knew it. It was, however, one of Jesus' favorite concepts of his role as a servant.

To apply this to the Twelve and the second coming is easy, except for the fact that they had little foundation for the idea at this time. To apply it to the Twelve and the immediate crisis in Jerusalem is very difficult and strained. To apply it to the religious leaders or the people generally and to the second coming makes no sense. They had no foundation for that idea. To apply it to them in view of the impending crisis in Jerusalem is almost as difficult. Perhaps it is best understood as a general teaching on alertness to responsibility—a teaching which would be more meaningful to the Twelve and to the Christian community later as they related it to the second coming.

*Verses 39-40:* The idea of watchfulness is continued in the next story but in a different form. Here the watcher is a householder and the uncertain coming is that of a thief. Apparently in the process of watching and the thief's delay, the householder went to sleep—and then the thief came and plundered his house. How this parable could have had any specific meaning for the Twelve in relation to the coming crisis in Jerusalem is very obscure even in the explanations of those who so interpret it. They were not expecting the coming of the Son of Man. In their view he had already come and he was their Lord. It would have been equally as meaningless to the religious leaders in their role in those Jerusalem events, apart from further elaboration. Were they the "householders" and was Jesus the "thief" who was about to invade their territory and "plunder" their house? They were indeed not expecting the Son of Man to come as Jesus came, but it requires a rather far-fetched allegorical interpretation to find that here.

In Matthew 24:43-44 this parable is definitely applied to the second coming. That seems also to be the natural force of verse 40 in Luke's account —*You also must be ready; for the Son of man is coming at an hour you do not expect.* To the Twelve and the church later this could have been a meaningful reference to waiting and watching without giving up in weariness at the seeming delay. It would have been more meaningful to the Twelve later than at this time. The idea of Jesus' coming in judgment like the unexpected arrival of a thief was commonly held by the early Christians (1 Thess. 5:2; 2 Pet. 3:10; Rev. 3:3; 16:15). Whatever the difficulty of its place here when the Twelve had such little background for understanding it, the second coming must be the meaning of the teaching.

*Verse 41:* A bit uncertain as to the proper application of the illustration, Peter asked Jesus whether he meant the parable of the householder and the thief for the Twelve or for all the people present. Jesus did not answer the question with the directness of his conclusion to the parable of the porter in Mark 13:37: "And what I say to you I say to all: Watch." Instead, he gave another parable in which a wise and faithful servant was contrasted with an unwise and unfaithful servant in the performance of tasks assigned by the master.

*Verses 42–48:* The parable of the faithful and unfaithful servants permits application both to the Twelve and to all. The servants by their response to assigned tasks divide themselves into two classes: those who wisely and faithfully fulfill their tasks (v. 42–43) and those who foolishly exploit their assigned tasks in malconduct and malpractice (v. 45). The former are rewarded by the master (v. 43); the latter are punished by the master (v. 46). It is the type of parable which affords effective application in multiple situations. The Pharisees and scribes could see themselves as the servants, God as the absentee master, and the ultimate reckoning as the inevitable result of their response to their assigned tasks. The people generally could see a similar application to themselves in relation to God's requirement of a life of obedient service. The Twelve could understand themselves as the servants, and the responsibility for proclaiming the kingdom of God as the assigned task, with Christ as the master. At the time, his being an absentee master may have held no more meaning than their separation from him when he sent them out to witness (see 9:1–6 or 10:1–12). The reckoning could have called to mind their reporting to him at the end of a period of witnessing.

In the days which would follow his death, resurrection, and ascension, the parable would take on new meaning for them in light of the anticipated second coming. It was in that time that Luke incorporated this parable into his Gospel. To the waiting church the parable had one very clear meaning: every believer's responsibility to live and witness for Christ until his return. At that time he would reckon with men on the basis of how they had fulfilled their task. This has been the application of the parable through the history of the church. One labors under severe hardship to find another meaning in it. The wise and faithful servant, of verses 42–43, is the one who faithfully fulfills his task and, upon the Master's return, experiences blessing (v. 43) and further opportunity of service (v. 44). The foolish and unfaithful servant of verse 45, who abuses his task and lives as if no day of reckoning will come, will be punished at the unexpected return of the Master, and will have no place of further service with the faithful ones. While this story relates to *service,* not *salvation,* it must be remembered that the consistent teaching of the New Testament is that the ultimate test of genuine faith is the demonstration of that faith through a life of fidelity. Regardless of the "thief on the cross" (Luke 23:24) and the "saved so as by fire" (1 Cor. 3:15), the idea of a salvation which is not demonstrated in life is foreign to the spirit of the New Testament.

*Verses 47–48:* The parable appears to end with verse 46. Two additional "conclusions" or "applications," however, follow. Verses 47–48a contrast two servants who by their life do not fulfill their master's will. One of them (v. 47) knew what the master desired but boldly and deliberately did not do it. The other one (v. 48a) did not know what the master desired—perhaps as a lower servant he had received no explicit orders—and did not do it. Both deserved and received punishment, but their punishment varied according to their degree of guilt. The one who deliberately refused to do the master's will received a *severe beating* (v. 47). The one who ignorantly failed to do what the master willed received a *light beating* (v. 48a).

*Verse 48b* contains a general principle of responsibility, requirement, and retribution. It has been frequently understood as teaching degrees of reward and degrees of punishment (because of the preceding two illustrations). This represents a human sense of justice—among those to be rewarded, some clearly deserve greater reward than others, and among those to be punished, some clearly deserve greater punishment than others. We often tend to seek in the Scriptures specific answers to specific questions when the Scriptures contain, not specific answers, but general principles. If this passage is to be applied to final rewards and punishments, it must be on the basis of general principle. In application of that principle it may be well to include the idea of *capacity for* the bliss of heaven or the woe of hell. One may anticipate enjoying the bliss of heaven to the extent of his capacity to enjoy it, though he may lack the capacity of a Jeremiah or a Paul. In the Scriptures such matters as these are left in the wisdom and love and power of an infinite God. God, not finite man, will determine the ultimate issue.

Verses 49–53 continue the counsel of Jesus regarding crisis. The impending crisis appears definitely to relate to the events immediately facing Jesus and his followers—his arrest, death, resurrection, ascension, and the continuing witness of his followers in a world hostile to them as it was to him.

*Verse 49: I came to cast fire upon the earth: Fire* has been variously interpreted as meaning the Holy Spirit, the new religion which Jesus was introducing, or judgment. Jesus' presence meant the fire of God's judgment as it swept the world of men. This is reminiscent of the words of John the Baptizer concerning the one to come after him—"he will baptize you with the Holy Spirit and with fire" (Luke 3:16); "even now the axe is laid to the root of the tree; every tree that does not bear good fruit is cut down and thrown into the fire" (3:9); "the chaff he will burn with unquenchable fire" (3:17). That fire which had been smoldering through the period of his public ministry would flame up and engulf the world in his death and the subsequent events.

*Would that it were already kindled:* This was Jesus' attitude as he faced the inevitable cross in Jerusalem. He had "set his face to go to Jerusalem" (9:51) soon after the confession, his transfiguration, and his first statement of his coming death to the disciples (9:18–36). Mark 10:32 presents Jesus walking out ahead of the Twelve as if eager to get to Jerusalem, and the disciples, amazed at his eagerness to reach the place where death awaited him, following reluctantly and with fear. Because of its ultimate meaning, Jesus yearned for that agonizing and terrifying end.

*Verse 50:* The idea of verse 49 is repeated in another figure. Jesus' death was to be like a baptism (compare Mark 10:38)—a baptism of fire as a part of that judgment of God upon sin. He could not redeem sinful men without in some way entering the fiery judgment of God upon their sin. In his death he entered into and shared the direful consequence of man's sin.

*How I am constrained until it is accomplished:* In common usage as well as in other places in the New Testament (Acts 18:5; 2 Cor. 5:14; Phil. 1:23) the word translated *constrained* meant to be totally occupied with or absorbed in a thing. Jesus was totally occupied by or absorbed in the events which would climax God's redemptive purpose in him and for men. Nothing else mattered for him; this was the total of his being as he journeyed to the cross.

*Verse 51: Do you think that I have come to give peace on earth?* Where *peace on earth* was concerned, Jesus' coming was a paradox. On one hand, it did mean peace, just as the angels sang at his birth (2:14), peace between God and man, between men and men. On the other hand, however, it meant not peace but *division.* Although it is in another setting, Matthew has, "I have not come to bring peace, but a sword" (10:34). The Gospel According to Thomas combines all the ideas of the two passages in Matthew and Luke— "Men think perhaps that I have come to cast peace upon the world. They do not know that I have come to cast divisions upon the earth, fire, sword, war" (Logion 16).

*Verses 52–53:* All three Gospels have Jesus' explanation of the divisions as relating to the family. Even in the close-knit group of the family, people will divide over the question of relationship to Jesus. In a family of five, three (son, daughter-in-law, daughter) will take one side and two (father, mother) the other. Father will take one side and son the other. Mother will take one side and daughter the other. Mother-in-law will take one side and daughter-in-law the other. This has been the course of Christian history. No family ties are stronger than those united in Christ. No family cleavage is sharper than the division over Christ. Jesus on the cross would commit his mother to the care of a beloved friend (John 19:26–27) because "even his brothers did not believe in him" (John 7:5).

*Verses 54–56:* Addressed to the Pharisees and Sadducees in another setting (Matt. 16:1–4), this saying is addressed to *the multitudes* in this passage. In the Matthew setting, Jesus rebuked the Pharisees and Sadducees because they could read the weather signs but could not read spiritual signs to see in him God's true prophet like Jonah. In Luke, he rebuked the multitudes because they could read the weather signs but they could not read the spiritual signs to see what was ahead of him, of them, and the nation of Israel. There may be a connection between the fire and water (baptism) of verses 49–50 and the scorching wind (as fire) and the rain (as water) in verses 54–55. It is not pressed. All the "signs" pointed to his being the Redeemer and to the crisis which was coming in Jerusalem with Israel's rejection of him—a crisis which in the days ahead would catch them all up in fiery judgment as well as divisive decisions even in families. To him it was all clear. They were blind to it. *The present time* was a time of critical decision which they could not escape. To side with him was to side with God.

*Verses 57–59:* This saying appears strangely placed here. In Matthew 5:23–26, Jesus was teaching that wrong relationships with one's fellowmen interfere with true worship of God, so that there are spiritual as well as practical reasons for settling differences of opinion—even lawsuits—quickly and without the delay of appearing in court. In Luke, however, if the teaching has an application to the immediate situation, it must be a call for wisdom in settling difficulties with another in view of the crisis experiences just ahead. Settlement before a judge would involve both time and risk. The accuser would demand that a *magistrate* arrest the accused. The magistrate in turn would drag the reluctant accused before the *judge.* If the judge found him guilty, the accused would then be delivered to an *officer* who would put him in prison. This procedure required the time-consuming service of three extra persons—magistrate; judge; officer—when actually accuser and accused could

*judge . . . what was right* more quickly. The risk involved was that of imprisonment until the accuser had been paid all which the judge agreed was
rightly due him. It is beyond the nature of the Scripture and this setting to try
to apply this to the ideas of purgatory and hell. That was no part of Jesus'
meaning, nor was it a part of Luke's use. No one in that company—including
Jesus—had any concept of purgatory.

These words are a solid, commonsense sort of suggestion in any kind of
dispute. But what did Jesus mean by it in reference to the impending crisis?
No dogmatic answer can be given. It may have been another way of saying,
"The present is a time of crisis in which decisions of ultimate spiritual concern will be demanded of every person. Make haste to exercise your power
of critical judgment to clear up every other matter demanding decision. Thus
you will be able without impairment to face and make the supreme decision."

## 17. A Call to Repentance (13:1–5)

As indicated previously (9:51), it is impossible to determine the geographical setting of most of this large section of Luke. Jesus was on his way to
Jerusalem, but that journey included Galilee, a part of Samaria, Perea, and
Judea. A few touches in chapter 13 suggest Perea. This paragraph is one of
them. If Jesus' hearers grasped the idea that danger lay ahead in Jerusalem,
they might be reminded of other Galileans who had perished in Jerusalem (v.
1). That may have prompted their reporting to Jesus an event which he
seems already to have known. He used it and another tragedy as examples
stimulating thoughtful people to repentance facing the prospect of judgment.

*Verse 1:* An unnamed number of otherwise unidentified Galileans had
been making a sacrifice in Jerusalem. The Roman governor of Judea, Pontius
Pilate, had sent soldiers to slaughter the Galileans and commit sacrilege in
the Temple by mingling the blood of the worshipers with the blood of the
animals they were offering for sacrifice. There is no record of this event other
than Luke's account. During the ten years he served as governor, Pilate committed many known violent acts against the Jews. This may well have been
another of them. No reason for the act is indicated, a detail which would
have added nothing to the story and its use here.

*Some present:* This could have been some of the multitudes, or of the
Pharisees (as in v. 31), or of the Twelve who did not want to go to Jerusalem. They could have been people desiring by this report to stimulate Jesus
to lead a revolt against Rome and such atrocities. Since they are not identified, the likelihood is that they were from the multitudes who had caught
the element of danger and crisis in Jesus' teachings.

*At that very time:* The time element appears to be in relation to the last
sequence of teaching. Did Jesus, the Twelve, and other Galilean pilgrims face
in Jerusalem the danger and fate of those other Galileans? Jesus did not take
up the story from that viewpoint.

*Verse 2* suggests that Jesus detected a note of pious superiority in the
report: the Galileans met that fate because of some unknown wickedness,
but the present company of Galileans would not be in danger because they
were good men. He approached the report from a philosophical question
about evil—did those other Galileans perish because of excessive

wickedness and had other Galileans not perished (or would not perish) because they were not evil?

*Verse 3: I tell you, No:* Jesus' answer to the unspoken question was that physical tragedy is not the consequence of sin. Degrees of wickedness did not mean the tragic death of some Galileans and the safety of others. Jesus did not give them an opinion on the "why" of that mystery. He never engaged in such abstract conjecturing.

*But unless you repent you will all likewise perish:* Jesus focused attention on his hearers and their need to repent. He did not mean that they were in danger from Pilate and the Roman soldiers and that repentance from sin would lift that danger. He meant that, regardless of the fate of those Galileans or the reason for their death, Jesus' hearers would perish just as certainly unless they repented.

Some interpreters relate this to the crisis events just ahead. They hold that Jesus was calling upon the people to identify with him so they would not share the fate of the nation of Israel and her leaders in their rejecting him. It is difficult to see just how "repentance" could have effected that result. More likely, Jesus was looking to God's judgment on every man's sin and was calling them to repentance while there was time and opportunity. The days just ahead would be critical; they had no way of knowing what their fate would be; time might be short; repent while there was time and opportunity. This was the consistent pattern of Jesus, and it was particularly true of this period of his ministry in which he put more emphasis on sin than in any other period recorded in the synoptics.

*Verses 4–5:* To the tragedy reported by his hearers Jesus added another. In an otherwise unrecorded fall of a tower—likely a part of the city wall—near the pool of Siloam, eighteen people had been killed. Whether they were workers engaged in repairing the tower or merely a part of the city crowd is not indicated. Jesus used the accident to pose the same question as in verse 2 —were these eighteen killed and others not killed because of a relative degree of wickedness? Jesus again answered, *I tell you, No,* and again passed over the question of the reason for the tragedy to use it as a personal call to repentance on the part of his hearers: wickedness is certain, time and opportunity are uncertain, therefore repent.

## 18. The Parable of the Barren Fig Tree (13:6–9)

Matthew (21:18–22) and Mark (11:12–14, 20–24) record a miracle story of Jesus' blighting a fruitless fig tree. In Matthew, the disciples observed that the tree withered immediately, and they asked Jesus how he did it. In Mark, the disciples noted the following day that the tree had withered, and in amazement they called Jesus' attention to it. In both Matthew and Mark, Jesus used the event to teach a lesson on faith and prayer.

Many readers and interpreters have been uncomfortable with and even repulsed by this story of Jesus' killing a fig tree which was not his. There is nothing repulsive about Luke's parable. It is a very natural story. It is not in the province of this volume to explain the incident in Matthew and Mark. One might suggest, however, that it may have been originally a parable story which, in the process of transmission, came to be used as a miracle story. Or at least that the miracle was followed by the parable at a point when so much of Jesus' thinking was on Israel's failure to bear fruit for God and the inevitable removal of that responsibility for giving to another nation—the Gentiles.

The parable was of a man who found that for the last three years, a fig tree in his vineyard had produced no fruit. He spoke of his disappointment and ordered the caretaker of the vineyard to cut the tree down, since its only purpose in being there was to bear fruit. The caretaker, however, asked that the owner leave the tree one more year. He would dig the ground to let air to the roots and would fertilize it. If with that special care it bore fruit, it could be left; if not, then it could be cut down.

From other vineyard parables and allegories of Jesus (Matt. 20:1-15; 21:28-32, 33-46; John 15:1-11), this one has been understood as a parable of Israel's failure to carry out God's purpose for her and his decision to replace her as his fruit-bearer. All the others are set in the last week in Jerusalem; this one is set in the journey to Jerusalem. It is not feasible to try to allegorize the details of the parable—the *three years* (v. 7), the *vinedresser* (v. 7), the additional *year* (v. 8), the digging and fertilizing (v. 8), the *next year* (v. 9). These are natural details to dramatize the central teaching. Historically, God had revealed himself to Israel as a Redeeming God. He had called her to make him known to the other nations. Rather than doing that, they had called upon the other nations to become Jews in order to be worshipers of the one true God. In this narrow and exclusive approach, they had failed to produce fruit for God—to bring the Gentiles to know him in his work of redemption. Now, through Jesus and his interpretation of God as a God of mercy for Gentiles as well as Jews, God had given them one last opportunity. They were rejecting that. As a fruitless fig tree they were to be cut down and replaced by others who would bear fruit for him (Matt. 21:41-45).

## 19. Healing a Woman of Curvature of the Spine (13:10-17)

This miracle story is only in Luke. No setting is given other than a synagogue on a sabbath. As an event pointing up Israel's failure to carry out God's purpose—failure because justice had been replaced by meticulous and unmerciful legalism—it is kindred in spirit to the fruitless fig tree teaching.

*Verse 11: A woman . . . for eighteen years . . . bent over and could not fully straighten herself:* The expression *spirit of infirmity* described a condition in which the woman's spine was curved so she could not straighten up. The extent of her infirmity covering *eighteen years* indicated that her case was well known. She was a familiar figure to synagogue attendants.

*Verse 12: Woman, you are freed from your infirmity:* Jesus focused the attention of the woman on the fact that he was going to do something about her spinal condition. Specifically, he was going to "free" her of it. This expression and a subsequent one *(loosed from this bond,* v. 16) represent Jesus' view that the woman was enslaved by a physical malady and could experience well-being only when liberated from it.

*Verse 13: He laid his hands upon her:* In some cases of healing Jesus only spoke to the person. In other cases, he touched that part of the body which was to be healed: for instance, ears, tongue, eyes, arm. That practice would suggest that he put his hands on this woman's curved spine. This may have added to his words another stimulus to faith. The one through whom God's power was working had touched her. (Compare comments on Luke 8:43-48.) Her cure was immediate. The result was that she began to praise God for what Jesus had done.

*Verse 14:* It must be remembered that by the Jews' traditional laws, the practice of medicine or of healing in any way was illegal on the sabbath. The ruler of the synagogue was not unfeeling for the unfortunate woman, nor was he inclined to deny that Jesus had healed her. He was *indignant because Jesus had healed on the sabbath.* To forestall anyone else's coming forward to request healing, or even going out to bring sick people to be healed, he addressed the people, calling attention to the fact that there were six work days out of the seven and that if any desired healing he should return on one of those days and not share with Jesus in violating sabbath laws. His instruction indicated the religious leaders' priorities: first, sabbath laws; second, people's well-being.

*Verse 15: The Lord* was not a commonly used term for Jesus in the days of his earthly ministry. It was, however, commonly used in the day when Luke wrote, and it is a characteristic term in Luke's Gospel. Luke contrasts *the ruler of the synagogue* (v. 14) and *the Lord* (v. 15). Jesus' priorities were: first, human well-being; second, sabbath laws.

*You hypocrites:* Recall that this was a word from the stage. It was play-acting to charge that Jesus had done wrong by healing on the sabbath and to charge the people to come for healing on some other day rather than the sabbath. By such conduct this *ruler* and all others like him (even people who would obey the order and wait for another day?) indicated that they only pretended concern for the sabbath.

They would "work" on the sabbath by loosing an ox or an ass and leading it to a watering place. By so doing they showed more concern for bound and thirsty animals than they did for bound and suffering people. Concern for the animals was commendable, but it was wrong if it had priority over concern for suffering people.

*Verse 16:* Jesus called attention to the woman. She was *a daughter of Abraham.* If John, with his scorn for "the Jews," had included this story, one would feel that Jesus was using sarcasm in confronting the ruler. The woman as *a daughter of Abraham* was a person privileged above the Gentiles but below the ox and the ass!

*For eighteen years* she had been bound by Satan. The Jews traced all evil in one way or another to the presence and power of Satan in the world. Here was *a daughter of Abraham* victimized by Satan—enemy of man and God—for eighteen years. Why should she continue another day thus bound when God's power was present and working? Why not set her free from Satan's power by God's power, on God's day, and in God's house?

*Verse 17:* Jesus' logic was unanswerable. *All his adversaries were put to shame* when they saw their conduct and attitude in the clear light of Jesus' illustration and questions. The people rejoiced at all the things Jesus was doing. This is a pattern in Luke and in Acts—the success of Jesus and his cause versus the failure of his opposition.

## 20. Two Kingdom Parables—Mustard Seed and Leaven (13:18–21)

The kingdom parables follow the healing of the lame woman. Luke relates them logically to the people's reaction to Jesus' success in opposing the ruler of the synagogue.

*Verse 18: Therefore* is a connective particle relating these parables to the preceding event. How they are related is not made clear. The probable answer is that Jesus opposed the ruler of the synagogue—a leader in the religion of Israel—and was successful. That was a small matter, but it was a victory (v. 17a). The people rejoiced at *all the glorious things* that were being done by him (v. 17b). The kingdom is like that; it started as a small thing, but by one event and experience added to another it was a growing thing, and was destined to become a large thing.

The two parables belong together and must be treated together. Jesus did not mean that the kingdom of God is like a mustard seed or a bit of leaven. The point of comparison is not in the object but in the action. The kingdom of God is like what happens when a man plants a grain of mustard in a garden or a woman puts a bit of leaven in meal or flour. Natural touches beautify the details. It is *a man* who plants the seed but *a woman* who makes the bread. Exaggerated touches dramatize the result. The mustard plant be-comes a tree-size plant; the woman puts a bit of leaven in four and a half pecks of flour—an abnormal amount for family cooking!

*Verse 19: Grain of mustard seed:* Matthew (13:32) includes the com-ment that the mustard was the smallest of seeds but made the largest of shrubs. Some interpreters understand Matthew's reference to a "Jerusalem mustard," which had a very tiny seed but produced a plant taller than a man on horseback.

*The birds of the air made nests:* There is no allegorical significance to the birds or their nests. The detail is simply to point up the small-to-great nature of the kingdom of God.

*Verse 21: Leaven* is yeast. There is no reason to hold that the leaven represents evil. It is not a sound principle of interpretation to maintain that a symbol must always symbolize the same thing. In the New Testament, the lion is used as a symbol both for the devil (1 Pet. 5:8) and for Christ (Rev. 5:5). A symbol means what a writer or speaker intends for it to mean in the place where he uses it. Jesus was not emphasizing the idea that the yeast corrupted or changed the flour but only its relatively small size.

*Three measures of meal:* The word translated *meal* means a ground wheat or grain product—flour in American use. The word translated *measures* means a kitchen measure with a capacity of one and one-half pecks. Three of them, hence, would be four and one-half pecks.

*Till it was all leavened:* The bit of yeast, proportionately small, when placed in four and one-half pecks of flour would indeed be *hid*. But it would make its presence known by spreading until all the flour was affected by it.

Some interpreters find further significance in the two parables. They understand that the mustard plant's growth teaches the external spread of the kingdom in society, and the yeast's spread teaches the internal spread of the kingdom in the individual. This may be true in a secondary or derived sense. In Jesus' use, the lesson emphasized the small-to-great destiny of the kingdom of God in the world of men.

### 21. Teaching on the Road to Jerusalem (probably in Perea) (13:22–30)

The text identifies the setting of this passage only as some town on the road from Galilee to Judea. The opinion commonly held is that it was in Perea and perhaps two days out from Jerusalem. The threat of danger from Herod (v. 31) could represent either Galilee or Perea, since his tetrarchy included both. If Jesus used the expression *today and tomorrow, and the third day I finish my course* (v. 32) literally, the suggestion is that he would arrive in Jerusalem on the day after next. A further possibility is that he was near the place where John the Baptizer had encountered arrest and death at the hands of Herod. This would mean southern Perea.

*Verse 23:* The teaching was prompted by a question from some unidentified person. In general use the word translated *Lord* was a term of respect approximating "Sir." That use would indicate only some person in the crowd. In subsequent use by Jesus' followers it was a title of worship. This use is characteristic of Luke. In that case the questioner was most likely one of the Twelve. The question of the relative number of the saved and the unsaved might occupy the mind of any person of religious inclination; it was more naturally a question characterizing people interested in speculative argument on a religious theme—a scribe or a lawyer of the Pharisees. The conclusion of the teaching (vv. 27–30) and the reaction of the Pharisees (v. 31) suggest that most likely the questioner was one of that group.

*Will those who are saved be few?* The Jews considered themselves as the people of God—the saved—and all the rest of the world's people as the unsaved. Even within Israel there were those who made no effort to conform to the regulations and practices in the religion of God. Were some of that group "unsaved" so the number of the redeemed was even smaller? The questioner may have had in mind Jesus' insistent position that God's mercy was for all people—even Gentiles and Samaritans—and not just the Jews. The question was one to stimulate debate on an explosive issue.

Verses 24–30: Jesus' answer reflected his policy of not arguing on speculative religious questions. Again, he did not answer the question directly but counseled his questioner to make sure that he was one of the saved.

*Verse 24: Strive to enter by the narrow door:* In the Sermon on the Mount (Matt. 7:13–14), Jesus illustrates the application of his teaching to life by contrasting two gates and two roads. The broad gate and road lead to destruction and can be entered without effort. The narrow gate and road lead to life and have to be sought. The relation of another part of the Sermon to another part of this text (vv. 25b–27) indicates that the meaning here is the same. To *enter by the narrow door* means salvation, and requires personal interest, desire, and effort—*strive to enter.* This and verse 28b—*you yourself thrust out*—indicates that some of those hearing Jesus and debating this issue with him were not saved.

*Many . . . will seek to enter and will not be able:* The reference is to those who appeal for salvation on the basis of an acquaintance with Jesus (v. 26). That will not be enough.

*Verse 25: When once the householder has . . . shut the door:* The symbolism is that of a householder who has left his door open as an invitation for any who wish to enter. At the appropriate time—when the feast begins, probably—he closes the door. In the religious thought of Israel, the age of the Messiah was conceived of in terms of a messianic banquet when the Messiah and his people would enjoy table fellowship together (vv. 28-29). That is the symbolism here. Jesus as the householder leaves an open door of invitation for all who wish to enter, but the time will come when the door will be closed.

*You will begin . . . to knock . . . saying . . . 'Lord, open to us':* People who have not taken advantage of the open door request entrance when the door has been closed. Jesus' words were a warning that they should come while there was opportunity. It is a warning of continuing urgency.

*I do not know where you come from:* Those seeking entrance are strangers. The words, in effect, classify these Jews with alien Gentiles! It may be no more than a natural detail of the situation which Jesus was describing for the people. But it is possible that it was a rather subtle thrust at people who thought geographical location or racial identification played some role in the matter of who was to be saved and who was not. This is the sort of detail which was of great interest to Luke—"I cannot let you in until I know where you come from!"

*Verse 26: We ate and drank in your presence:* This identifies them as people with whom the householder had shared table fellowship. Surely he would know them and admit them. It must be recalled that Jesus accepted the hospitality and table fellowship of Pharisees.

*You taught in our streets:* They had not only shared table fellowship with him, they had also listened as he taught in their towns. Many of the Pharisees and Saducees heard him teach but rejected his teaching.

*Verse 27: I do not know where you come from; depart from me, all you workers of iniquity:* In other words, "I do not know where you are from, but I know what you are like; you are workers of iniquity." If they had not been workers of iniquity, they would have accepted the invitation while the door was open. The expression *workers of iniquity* has definite religious meaning. The noun *workers* characteristically refers to those "doing the works of the law," following carefully the demand of the law as a way of being right with God. *Iniquity* means more precisely "unrighteousness." The efforts to produce "righteousness" through conformity to the law had produced only "unrighteousness." A good example is Jesus' charge that in their meticulous concern to keep the law of God's ownership—tithing—they had missed the real principle of God's ownership of the total person, including spirit, disposition, and social attitudes demonstrated in mercy, justice, and love. (See exposition of 11:42.) Hence, *depart from me;* you lack the character for sharing the messianic banquet.

*Verses 28-29* graphically portray the messianic banquet—a symbol of the joys of the age in which the Messiah will rule. Sharing that fellowship are the great ones in Israel's history—Abraham, Isaac, Jacob, and the prophets. Sharing it, too, will be the non-Jews who have accepted the invitation; *men will come from east and west, and from north and south.* This refers to mankind beyond the nation of Israel.

*Sit at table in the kingdom of God:* A symbolic reference to the glorious fellowship to which the Jews looked in the messianic feast of the age of the Messiah. Jesus used it as a detail of his illustration. Those who had refused the open-door invitation would find the door closed to them. Their great distress at their loss is pictured in their weeping and grinding their teeth as they see others enjoying that fellowship.

*Verse 30* may be Jesus' conclusion to the scene, or it may be Luke's fitting commentary. Its rhetorical structure of chiasmos has caused some interpreters to regard it as a development too late for Jesus' time and, hence,

$$\begin{matrix} \text{last} & \diagdown \diagup & \text{first} \\ \text{first} & \diagup \diagdown & \text{last} \end{matrix}$$

Luke's addition. The application of that principle, however, would rule inauthentic many teachings of Jesus set in this pattern and otherwise regarded as genuine.

*Some are last who will be first:* This probably refers to Gentiles or Samaritans who, in the opinion of the Jews, would be at the bottom of any listing by rank. Those despised people would in some cases outrank the Jews.

*Some are first who will be last:* This probably refers to some Jews who in the final state would prove to be of lower rank than some of the despised Gentiles.

The two parts of the conclusion should not be understood as suggesting some order of rank in the consummation of God's kingdom or in heaven. They are means of pointing out how man's views are often erroneous in the matter of what constitutes right standing with God. Jesus' total answer to his questioner about the probable density of population in heaven included three ideas: (1) There will be some in heaven whom the Jews did not expect to be there—the Gentiles (v. 29); (2) there will not be some in heaven whom the Jews expected to be there—some of the Jews (vv. 26–27, 28b); (3) every person should strive to be one of those who will be there (v. 24).

## 22. Rejecting a Warning about Danger from Herod (13:31–35)

Some of the Pharisees warned Jesus to leave the region because of danger from Herod. Jesus rejected the warning and used the occasion to speak of his finishing his work, of Jerusalem's rejection of him, and of Jerusalem's subsequent fate.

*Verse 31: At that very hour:* These words relate this warning to the teaching immediately preceding. They suggest the idea that the Pharisees were displeased with Jesus' teaching that some of them would not be saved but some of the Gentiles would. They wanted him to get out of the region, as the villagers of Gadara had wanted him to leave their region after the healing of the possessed man and the destructive stampede of the swine (8:37).

*Herod wants to kill you:* This reference is to Herod Antipas who had killed John the Baptizer. This was in his territory—either Galilee or Perea, most probably southern Perea. There is no indication elsewhere that Herod Antipas desired to kill Jesus. There is evidence of his perplexity over the reports by some people that Jesus was John the Baptizer alive again (9:7–9). When he had an opportunity at a later time to improve his position with the Jews by passing judgment on Jesus, he refused to do so and sent Jesus back to Pilate for judgment and sentence (23:6–12). The warning by the Pharisees seems to have been a ruse to get Jesus to leave their territory.

*Verse 32: Go and tell that fox:* In rabbinic writings the fox was frequently used as a term for an unimportant person. This may have been Jesus' meaning. In his plans and purpose, Herod was of no significance. Jesus' point of comparison may have been the cunning of the fox. No foxy Herod could deter him in his work any more than the foxy Pharisees could. That he had no fear of the Pharisees had been often demonstrated. That he had no fear of Herod was demonstrated in such public defiance of his power or of any threat from him.

*Behold, I cast out demons . . . and the third day I finish my course:* This was Jesus' way of indicating that no man by plea (Pharisees) or threat (Herod) controlled his movement toward the completion of his appointed work. He was in control of his movement toward that goal. The Twelve had been unable to stop him; no other person, including an earthly king, could stop him. Casting out demons and performing cures were parts of his work which he understood to be means of validating his claim that the kingdom of God was present in him.

*Today and tomorrow, and the third day:* This may have a literal meaning —he would reach his destination day after next. The actual reaching of his goal—death and resurrection—was certainly more than three days away. *I finish my course* had a sort of double meaning—such as is found often in John. In one sense the *course* to which he had set himself was this journey to Jerusalem. In another sense it was the journey to death and resurrection. So the expression, *today and tomorrow, and the third day,* could also have a metaphorical reference—whatever time was needed to finish his course would be his; Herod could not prevent that.

*Verse 33: I must go on my way:* The word translated *must* is an impersonal verb frequently rendered "it is necessary." It refers to a necessity if a desired end is to be realized. So it was necessary for Jesus to press on to Jerusalem, not because of fear of Herod, nor was the desired end escape from him. The necessity was Jesus' redemptive mission, and the end to be realized was the cross.

*It cannot be that a prophet should perish away from Jerusalem:* While there is little actual record of prophets slain in Jerusalem, it was traditional for the Jews to think of Jerusalem as the scene of the martyrdom of prophets. (See exposition of 11:47–51.) That tradition Jesus used in this passage. It was cutting sarcasm. He could not be hurt until he reached Jerusalem. That was the place where they killed prophets. It was true that Herod had slain John the Baptizer at Machaerus east of the Dead Sea. But that was a very unfitting event. John should have been slain in Jerusalem where it was proper. Jesus would be slain there.

*Verses 34–35:* Matthew places Jesus' lament over the fate of Jerusalem on Tuesday afternoon of his last week in Jerusalem and as the closing part of his denunciation of the Temple leaders (23:37–39). It is a very dramatic and fitting setting. Luke's setting—if Jesus was indeed nearing Jerusalem at this time—is less dramatic but still plausible. There can be no doubt that his rejection by Jerusalem, the determination of the Jews to find a messiah who would lead a revolt against Rome, and the inevitable disastrous result of the destruction of Jerusalem weighed heavily on Jesus' mind. Even though the Pharisees could not "interpret the present time" (12:56), Jesus could.

*O Jerusalem, Jerusalem:* There is pathos in the address, and it is made more emphatic by the repetition of the name.

*Killing the prophets and stoning those who are sent to you:* One commentary states that Jerusalem "had a monopoly in murdering prophets."[1] Another states that "in no other place were so many prophets put to death."[2] Yet not one example is given. Hebrew history does not reveal them. This was a case of Jesus' using a commonly accepted but undemonstrated view of the people. One thing which makes Matthew's setting more fitting than Luke's is that it occurs the same day that Jesus told the parable about a householder whose tenants beat, stoned, and killed his messengers. The story applied to the Jewish nation in its rejection and abuse of God's messengers, which was about to be climaxed in the killing of Jesus (Matt. 21:33-43). The *stoning those who are sent to you* carries over into a very natural reference to Jesus in the lament over Jerusalem.

*How often would I have gathered your children together as a hen gathers her brood:* The synoptics contain no reference to frequent visits of Jesus to Jerusalem as they are suggested in the words *how often.* John, however, does refer to multiple visits, and to the conflicts and angers Jesus faced there. There were attempts to stone him in Jerusalem (John 7:19; 8:59; 11:8). As a loyal Jew he loved Jerusalem; he grieved to feel her rejection and to see her end.

*As a hen gathers her brood:* The word translated "hen" is a general one for a mother fowl. The picture is of a bird protecting her brood from danger, a familiar figure, not only from observance but from Jewish songs in which God was praised for giving the shelter of his wings to his people (Ps. 17:8; 61:4). Jesus had frequently longed to shelter Jerusalem from approaching danger, but she *would not* accept him. The words *would not*—literally "you have not wished it"—point up the element of personal choice. It was Jerusalem's choice to accept or reject his offer of God's mercy. She rejected it. He had wished it; Jerusalem had not.

*Behold, your house is forsaken:* "Look, is left to you your house!" is the literal translation. By their rejecting his offer they were taking their destiny into their own hands. God was leaving them to their choice and the inevitable result. In the Matthew 23:38 parallel there is good support for the addition of the word "desolate"—the usual translation of the word for desert or wasteland: "Look, your house is left to you a desert." This was not a specific reference to the Temple—as some interpreters hold. To the Jewish people, the Temple was God's house, not Jerusalem's house. The term *your house* refers to Jerusalem, or more properly to the nation of Israel. She had made her choice, and that meant the loss of everything she cherished: nation; Jerusalem; Temple. In Matthew the statement is followed immediately by discussion in chapter 24 of the destruction of Jerusalem by the Romans which came in A.D. 70.

*You will not see me until you say, "Blessed is he who comes in the name*

---

1. Charles R. Erdman, *The Gospel of Luke, An Exposition* (Philadelphia: Westminster Press, 1942), p. 136.

2. Lenski, op. cit., p. 951.

*of the Lord!"* These are difficult words to interpret in Matthew where they follow the triumphal entry into Jerusalem during which the people had said those words. They are less difficult in Luke's setting where the immediate reference is to Jesus' coming entry into Jerusalem for the last time. The double negative construction in Greek makes a very positive assertion; they definitely will not see him again until his coming to Jerusalem as one final offering of himself as God's Messiah. He had been there with such offering frequently and had been rejected. Not another offering would be made until that final one in which he would offer himself as the messianic Son of David king (19:28-40).

## 23. A Sabbath Healing in a Pharisee's House (14:1-6)

Jesus accepted the hospitality of any who invited him whether publican (5:29-32) or Pharisee (7:36). On this occasion the host was a Pharisee who was also a *ruler*—one of the officers of the local synagogue.

*Verse 1: They were watching him: They* is a reference to the Pharisees and lawyers who were present (v. 3). These were the strict interpreters and observers of all the Law, written as well as traditional. Not by the written but by their traditional laws, healing on the sabbath was illegal. While the host Pharisee and his friends welcomed Jesus to dine, they observed him carefully for any breach of the law.

*Verse 2: There was a man before him who had dropsy: Dropsy* identifies the man's malady as excessive water in his flesh. The expression *before him* indicates Jesus' confrontation with the man. Since no indication is given, it is idle to speculate whether the man came of his own volition hoping to be healed even though it was the sabbath, whether he was brought by the Pharisees as a possible way of trapping Jesus, or whether he was there merely as a friend or relative with no particular significance.

*Verse 3: Is it lawful to heal on the sabbath, or not?* By this question, Jesus put the matter immediately before them in a way which challenged them to answer. On a similar occasion he had challenged the scribes and Pharisees with a similar question that called for speculation on what constituted doing good or saving life (6:9). This was more pointed, focusing on healing on the sabbath.

*Verse 4: They were silent:* They would not answer his question. In the written Law of Moses prohibiting work on the sabbath, there was no specific definition of work. In the unwritten traditional laws which had been developed as the people undertook to interpret the written Law and define work, healing had been included in the things which were prohibited.

*He took him and healed him:* The word translated *took* literally means "took him on." Probably it meant only that Jesus accepted the task of healing the man even though it was the sabbath. The word might also be translated "take hold of," meaning that Jesus put his hands on the man or took the man's body in some way into his hands. In Luke's reporting, the method of healing was unimportant.

*And let him go:* This may mean that the man was not one of the guests but had come to Jesus anticipating healing. When Jesus had healed him, he dismissed him.

*Verse 5:* Jesus rebuked the Pharisees by showing two things: in emergency situations they performed more *work* on the sabbath than he did in healing; they showed more mercy for an animal in distress than they did for a sick man.

*An ass or an ox:* This is the reading chosen by the editors of the RSV and the KJV. The ASV editors follow the reading "a son or an ox." The ancient manuscripts of Luke are divided on the reading. No appeal can be made to the other Gospels since only Luke includes this event. In his account of the sabbath healing of the man with the withered hand, Matthew refers to helping a sheep out of a pit on the sabbath, but Mark and Luke do not refer to the sheep (Mark 3:1-6; Matt. 12:9-14; Luke 6:6-11).

The best manuscript evidence by far supports the reading "a son or an ox" here. This was probably the original and some later scribe changed it to "an ass or an ox" to make it agree with the reference in 13:15 to leading an ox or an ass to water on the sabbath. If Jesus said "an ass or an ox" on this occasion, he was rebuking the Pharisees because they would work to rescue a work animal which had fallen into the shaft leading down to a spring or well of water, but they would not permit a physician to work to heal a sick man on the sabbath. The argument is from the lesser (beast of burden) to the greater (man).

If Jesus said "a son or an ox" there is an added difference. They would help one of their children as they would help a beast of burden on the sabbath, but they were unconcerned about a needy fellowman and made laws to prohibit his being helped on the sabbath. The problem was one of a distorted sense of values—laws and institutions were to be served by men rather than to serve men.

*Verse 6: They could not reply to this:* The logic of Jesus' charge was clear. They did not even attempt to answer it.

## 24. A Parable on Humility (14:7-14)

The setting is the same dinner party as that of the last paragraph. When the healing incident had passed, the guests went about selecting their places at the table.

*Verse 7: He marked how they chose the places of honor:* The word translated *places of honor* is literally "the first couches" or "the chief couches." This was a formal dinner where the host and his guests reclined on couches about the table. The "head couches" would be those nearest to the host starting with the two immediately to his right and left. The more important a person was, the nearer he would be to the host.

*Verses 8-10:* The scramble for the head couches prompted a humorous parable from Jesus which is told from the viewpoint of *application*. Behind the application may have been a parable along this line:

A certain man gave a great feast and invited many guests. It came to pass that when all the guests were assembled, one guest, assured within himself of his importance, went quickly to the most honored position next to the couch where the host would recline. As the other guests were taking their positions, a second man, feeling honored simply to be included in those invited, stopped at the couch farthest from the host. When the host took his place and looked about the table, he instructed the man on the first couch to exchange places with the man on the last couch. In humiliation he did so.

Jesus' application instructed the guests to practice humility rather than pride. To be invited to a place of greater importance than one had chosen is most gratifying. Simply to share the table of the host is gratifying, whether or not one is offered a place of greater importance. But to be assigned to a place of lesser importance than the one selected results only in humiliation.

What was Jesus' reason for giving this teaching on this occasion? There must have been more than a social interest in who reclined in which position. The most likely application is to the immediately preceding event. By their interpretation of God's law, the Pharisees and lawyers had assumed the role of determining relative rank and importance when that was really the prerogative of God. They gave primary importance to an unfortunate animal which was at least partially responsible for its predicament; God gave primary importance to an unfortunate man who was the victim of disease. By Jesus' teaching and action, they had experienced humiliation. How much better it would have been if they had forgotten their pride in their role as interpreters and keepers of the law by requesting that Jesus heal the man even though it was the sabbath.

*Verse 11:* This conclusion universalizes the particular. Just as in the case of the two men in Jesus' story, the person who exalts himself to a high position will be humbled, but the person who humbles himself will be exalted to a high position. The form is that of paradox—the way down is up and the way up is down. Some interpreters hold that the conclusion was not a part of Jesus' teaching but was a later development which Luke added. Their argument is largely based upon the rhetorical structure of chiasmos which they regard as a development too late for Jesus' time:

exalts          humbled
humbles          exalted

The argument is not convincing since other sayings of Jesus in this form are unquestionably genuine.

*Verses 12–14* contain Jesus' recommendation to the host who had also observed the guests scrambling for places of rank. Jesus advised the host that in giving a dinner he not invite his friends, relatives, and rich neighbors (v. 12), but the poor, maimed, lame, and blind (v. 13). The first group would be those whom the host accepted as his own class of people—the ones with whom he naturally associated. The second group would be those who, if not actually spurned, would be ignored as people below the level of association with this important officer in the synagogue.

There was surface humor in Jesus' recommendation, but there was a deeper significance, too. To invite one's friends, relatives, and rich neighbors to a dinner is to see them scrambling and arguing over preferred position and imagined rank! *Lest . . . you be repaid* (v. 12) may indicate that inviting them results in return invitations so that the host becomes a guest scrambling for position according to his self-assumed rank! On the other hand, to invite the unfortunate ones of verse 13 is to serve those who do not scramble for position; indeed, many of them, because of their physical condition, would have to be helped to the table. Simply to be invited and to share the host's bounty would be exaltation for them. Nor could they repay the host by a return invitation (v. 14). But he would be repaid in a better way—he would receive a twofold blessing. He would be blessed by the sense of gratification from having helped those who really needed the food and by their blessing him for his bounty. He would be blessed too in the realization that he would *be repaid at the resurrection of the just*. This was Jesus' way of expressing the contrast between the temporal and the eternal. To give a dinner and to receive a return invitation is to experience only physical and temporal reward. To help the needy with no thought or even possibility of return is to experience spiritual and eternal reward. Compare Luke 18:22. Jesus did not mean that one should help others with the *motivation* of having heavenly rewards—"you can't take it with you, but you can send it on ahead," as popularly expressed. It was rather that the one naturally follows the other.

Attention must be given to the expression *the resurrection of the just* (v. 14). There was much division of opinion among the Jews on the idea of survival after death. Some people rejected any idea of survival either by immortality of the soul or by the resurrection of the body. Some believed that only the Jews would be raised from the dead, others that only the good Jews would be raised, still others that all men would be raised. From other instances in the teaching of Jesus it is clear that he believed in the resurrection of all—some to punishment and some to blessedness. *The resurrection of the just* means that only those share the experience of what Jesus called "the resurrection of life" (John 5:29) who have believed on him, in contrast to "the resurrection of judgment" for those who have not believed on him.

### 25. The Parable of the Great Feast (14:15–24)

The parable of the wedding feast for the son of a king (Matt. 22:1–14) is very similar to this one, and is part of Jesus' Temple teaching on the Tuesday before his death. The differences are so marked, however, that some interpreters regard them as separate parables. On the other hand the similarities are so great that it appears correct to identify the two and understand adaptations in different settings. The parable is also in the Gospel According to Thomas (Logion 64). The differences in the three accounts may indicate that all three had separate sources. If Thomas used a synoptic source, it appears to have been Luke. The rabbinical writings also contain a parable which, while different from this one, is more like Luke's account than any other parable of Jesus.

*Verse 15:* The parable was prompted by a table guest who said, *"Blessed is he who shall eat bread in the kingdom of God."* His reference was to the messianic banquet which the Jews anticipated as a part of the glorious age when the Messiah came to rule. Jesus' response showed how men refuse God's invitation to become a part of his kingdom here and now rather than in some distant future. In Jesus' view, God's kingdom had already come in his presence in the world, but people were rejecting him and thus rejecting the kingdom.

*Verses 16–17:* The parable tells of a man who sent out invitations to a great banquet. When the time for the banquet came, he sent messengers to announce that all was ready. The parable submits to some allegorical interpretation. There is no doubt that the man giving the banquet represents God. Probably the initial invitation embraces the preparatory announcement of God's redemptive purpose (or kingdom) as it was given through the prophets. The message that all was ready most likely brings the invitation up to date in the coming of Jesus to inaugurate the fulfillment of God's purpose—now was the acceptable time.

*Verses 18–20:* The excuses offered by the invited guests are clearly that, demonstrating that they did not want to accept. The excuses are ridiculous and humorous.

The first man begged off because he had bought a field and had to go to examine it. As a *great banquet* (v. 16), it took place at night. This man had apparently bought a field without examining it and was now going to examine it *at night!* The second man had likewise bought five yoke of oxen without examining them, and was now going to examine them *at night.* The third man had just married, and that ended his nights out. He had to stay at home!

The master was very angry when he heard the excuses. Obviously the guests had no real reason for refusing, but every reason for accepting so gracious an invitation. They just did not want to accept. Clearly they represent the people who were rejecting God's invitation to share his kingdom in association with Jesus. (Compare Matt. 22:1–14, with the king—God—giving a marriage feast for his son—Jesus—and seeing the invitation spurned.)

*Verses 21–23:* The man then sent his servant to invite others: *the poor and maimed and blind and lame.* These are the same unlikely recipients of an invitation to a great banquet whom Jesus had mentioned earlier to his host (v. 13). To make sure that the banquet hall was filled, the servant was told, *Go out to the highways and hedges, and compel people to come in.* The expression, *highways and hedges,* refers to the rural roads and fields which were divided by hedgerows serving as fences.

There was likely no particular significance distinguishing the town people (v. 21) and the country people (v. 23) invited. Together, however, they represent a different group from those who received the first invitation. Even in Matthew's account, and more particularly in Luke's, those who were first invited and refused represent the Jews. Those who were invited later represent the Gentiles. This was another of the many indications that God's mercy was for both Jews and Gentiles. It was not a matter of God's preference for one over the other, but rather of historical precedence. God made himself known to the Jews. They were naturally the first in opportunity to receive his grace. Paul's favorite expression for the idea was "to the Jew first, but also to the Greeks."

*Verse 24:* The statement, *none of those men who were invited shall taste my banquet,* does not mean that no Jews would experience God's mercy. It means that none of those who rejected the invitation would experience it. Acceptance of God's offer is the condition of sharing his mercy. It also means that God's purpose would not fail because some men refused his invitation. He proposed to bless with the favor of his kingdom those who accepted his invitation. And that blessing he bestowed—and bestows—whether those accepting were Jews or Gentiles.

## 26. Teaching on the Cost of Discipleship (14:25–35)

Jesus never made the terms for accepting his lordship easy. He challenged people to follow him recognizing the hardships involved.

*Verse 25: Great multitudes accompanied him.* There were many reasons for their following him: to hear his teaching; to see his miracles; to enjoy his routing the haughty Pharisees who oppressed them; to see if he was not indeed the Messiah who would bring them deliverance from Rome. He detected superficiality in many of those following him and he spoke to them of the demanding nature of discipleship.

*Verse 26: If any one . . . does not hate: Hate* is a very strong word. The Greek word had many meanings in Jesus' day—a harsh vindictive attitude toward another as an enemy; a constant fixed displeasure in a person or a thing; indifference to one person out of preference for another. Jesus' use in this instance can hardly be equated with any of these, though it is closest to the third. To be his disciple meant that not even those whom a man loves most on the human level—his own family—could come between him and his Lord. Compared to devotion to his Lord, every other devotion must be so secondary that it can be spoken of as hate or rejection.

*Even his own life:* The word *life* means the total of one's being. Even that was not to come between the disciple and his Lord. He was to give up his life rather than give up his Lord. This is graphically illustrated in the next verse.

*Verse 27: Whoever does not bear his own cross and come after me, cannot be my disciple:* This unquestionably means death rather than denial. The cross which the condemned man carried was the instrument of his death. In his speaking of his own death up to this point, Jesus had given no indication that it would be by crucifixion,[1] yet the people understood the carrying of a cross as a sign of death. The cross as a symbol of service (as it is used in Christian vocabulary today) was unknown at that time. It meant one thing only—death. Even that was not to deter one from following his Lord.

*Verses 28–32:* To emphasize this strong counsel of counting the cost of what it meant to follow him, Jesus used two parabolic illustrations. The first was a man planning to build a tower.

*To build a tower:* This was probably a tower in a vineyard, used for guarding the vineyard against men or animals who might damage it. It was a worthy goal.

*Count the cost:* A man wanting to build would wisely reckon what it would cost and whether he possessed the requirements. Beginning to build without being able to finish would shame him in the eyes of his neighbors. He lacked the capacity to carry through.

*What king . . . will not sit down first and take counsel:* In the second

---

1. The exact nature of his execution was not revealed until the third prediction of his death (Luke 18:32–34). In his parallel to that account, Matthew has the specific word "crucify" (Matt. 20:19).

parabolic illustration Jesus spoke of a king who was facing an encounter with another king. Wisely he counted the cost to see if he had the military forces to be able to defeat the enemy who had double his military strength —10,000 soldiers versus 20,000 soldiers. If he decided that the risk was too great and not worth the effort, he would give up and not engage in the battle at all.

*Verse 33:* These illustrations do not mean that Jesus discouraged anyone from following him. They mean that he wanted every man to understand clearly that following him meant taking the total risk. Count the cost; then take the total risk even if it means humiliation and total loss. One cannot be his disciple unless he is willing to renounce everything that would prevent total commitment to discipleship. Becoming Jesus' disciple means recognizing one's inabilities and the risk of humiliation and loss, but in spite of that renouncing everything except one thing—his lordship.

*Verses 34–35* appear to relate to this teaching on discipleship, but exactly how is not clear. Salt as a symbol for discipleship appears in three different settings and variations in the Gospels (Matt. 5:13; Mark 9:50; Luke 14: 34–35). In Mark, salt represents some quality of life (not explained) which makes possible one's living peacefully with others. In Matthew, salt represents service as a disciple and there is an inherent caution about the result of losing that power to serve. In Luke, salt represents readiness to renounce kin, comfortable living, and life itself for the sake of being Jesus' disciple. There is a genuine form of discipleship which is "salt"; it is good, and serves to preserve and make palatable. But there is a false form of discipleship which appears to be "salt," but it is not; hence, it is not "good" for seasoning nor for returning to build up the land as the lowest form of matter —manure. In Jesus' time there was a high tax on salt. This led to varying degrees of adulterating salt with sand mixtures. A mixture might be so much sand and so little salt that it had no seasoning or land-building power—it was discarded on the streets.

*He who has ears to hear, let him hear* appears often as a call to discernment in the application of a teaching. Let everyone with the power of spiritual discernment listen and apply the teaching. Count the cost of becoming a disciple of Jesus, take the total risk, renounce everything except his lordship. Thus one becomes "salt."

NOTE ON CHAPTER 15: Chapter 15 consists of three parables which Jesus told in response to a complaint by the Pharisees and scribes that he was admitting tax collectors and sinners to his teaching and was having table fellowship with them. There is nothing in the text to indicate a geographical setting. The parable of the lost sheep is in a different teaching setting in Matthew with a different application there (Matt. 18:11–14). Its location in Matthew cannot be used to attempt a location in Luke. The other two parables are only in Luke.

The purpose of the parables is clear—to teach God's loving concern for all people. They reflect Jesus' response to the criticism of the Pharisees and scribes. He associated with tax collectors and sinners because he represented a God who loved people like that. What the Pharisees and scribes regarded as being to his discredit, he regarded as being to his credit.

The three parables are ordered toward a climax. The lost sheep was one out of one hundred; the lost coin was one out of ten; the lost son was one out of two. The climax comes in the parable of the lost son, in the father's joy at the sinful son's return contrasted with the elder brother's complaint at the welcome extended to the returning sinner. It was the sort of complaint being registered by the Pharisees over Jesus' welcome to the tax collectors and sinners.

### 27. The Parable of the Lost Sheep (15:1–7)

*Verses 1–2* present the background. The Pharisees and scribes regarded *tax collectors and sinners* as social and religious outcasts. When Jesus received them and ate with them he outraged the Pharisees' sense of right.

Verses 3–7 present the parable and Jesus' application of it.

*Verse 4: What man of you:* The introductory question was addressed directly to the complaining Pharisees. In Matthew a similar introductory question—"What do you think?"—was addressed to the Twelve. In the Logion 107 version in the Gospel According to Thomas no question is used; the parable simply begins with "The kingdom is like a shepherd who had a hundred sheep." In Luke, the question asked the Pharisees for a decision; it was a call to think, to decide, to act.

*Having a hundred sheep, if he has lost one:* In the Matthew and Thomas versions, the sheep "strayed away." In Luke there is no emphasis on how the sheep became lost; it was simply lost and that lostness was the concern of the owner.

*Leave the ninety-nine in the wilderness:* This did not indicate unconcern. The ninety-nine were not left out in the open as the prey of wild animals. Shepherds had enclosures in the pastures, and the sheep were placed inside the enclosure at night. The shepherd left the ninety-nine securely in the fold when he went in search of the one. Indeed, most likely it was in counting them as they went through the narrow opening of the enclosure that he discovered that one was missing.

*Verses 5–6:* Having found the lost sheep, he carried it home *on his shoulders* and called in his fellow shepherds to share in his joy. In Matthew, he rejoiced over it more than over the ninety-nine. In the Thomas version he embraced the sheep and spoke to it of his love; he told it that he loved it more than he did the ninety-nine because it was the fattest sheep in the flock!

*Verse 7: There will be more joy in heaven:* apparently, the joy of God. (See comment on v. 10 closing the next parable.) The central meaning of all three parables is God's concern for the lost, and, hence, Jesus' accepting them for teaching and fellowship.

*Over one sinner who repents:* That is, over any one of the tax collectors and sinners. In heaven, God rejoiced to see them respond to Jesus.

*Than over ninety-nine righteous persons who need no repentance:* The Pharisees and scribes. To debate over whether or not they really were righteous is to miss the point of the story. They thought of themselves as righteous and the others as sinners. Jesus simply argued on the basis of their claim. In effect he was saying, "If you are righteous and these are sinners who are repenting, God rejoices more over one of them than over all of you, because he longs to see all men come to righteousness."

In this parable we have one of the finest illustrations of how the early Christians applied a parable to different settings and purposes. In Luke, the setting is the complaint of the Pharisees and Jesus' assurance that God loves every human being regardless of his sin, and wants all men to come to his care. In Matthew, the setting is one of pastoral concern in which Jesus shows the Twelve that God is concerned about the welfare of the most insignificant one in the worshiping community. Note the instance in Luke 18:15–17 in which the Twelve tried to prevent children from coming to Jesus. Jesus used the children to illustrate the nature of kingdom citizens just as he did in the passage which closes with the Father's concern for the children in Matthew 18:1–14. In Thomas, the setting is a Gnostic community of people who taught that God was concerned only about the one who has the *gnosis*—the special intellectual enlightenment for God. The "fattest" sheep in the flock represented that one out of a hundred who had the en-lightenment—God was only concerned about him. This was a deliberate change of the parable by the Gnostics (about A.D. 140 perhaps) to put the authority of Jesus behind their views. Jesus could never have used the parable in that way. This parable was used in still another second-century work—The Gospel of Truth. There the central purpose of the parable was so lost that concern for *persons* disappeared completely and only concern for *things* remained. The shepherd tired himself out even on the sabbath seeking the sheep because he wanted a perfect number of sheep—99 + 1, and not 100 − 1. Such use is a caution for keeping close to Jesus' purpose in the parables.

### 28. The Parable of the Lost Coin (15:8–10)

This parable has the same meaning as the previous one. It differs only in details.

*Verse 8: What woman, having ten silver coins:* The word translated *silver coins* is *drachma,* a coin worth about sixteen cents. Its buying power, however, was much higher than sixteen cents in American money today. Note that the proportion has changed from the previous parable; here it is one out of ten which was lost.

*Light a lamp . . . sweep the house . . . seek diligently:* The statement is in the form of a question whose construction indicates that the answer expected is affirmative: "She lights a lamp, sweeps the house, seeks diligently until she finds it, doesn't she?" Answer: "Yes, she does." The *lamp* was a small, shallow, dishlike container of oil with a wick. The poor light might not be sufficient for the dark floor, so the woman took a broom made of a handful of straw or stems and swept every dark corner of the floor. The concern is reflected in the grammatical construction which may be accurately translated "she keeps on seeking carefully."

The exact nature of the ten coins cannot be known. They may have been her entire household budget for an undetermined time. They may have been a part of her wedding dowry with symbolic value beyond their cash value. The dowry broken by the lost part was a bad omen regarding her marriage and her fidelity to her husband. Whatever it was, she had a compelling reason to search.

*Verses 9–10:* Her rejoicing was addressed to her friends and neighbors as was the shepherd's. Jesus' application was the same, but stated slightly differently.

*Joy before the angels of God* is apparently God's rejoicing in the presence of the angels, just as *joy in heaven* (v. 7) is God's rejoicing. While the comparison here is not so carefully made, the parable probably compares the nine coins to the Pharisees and the one lost-and-found coin to any lost person, even a tax collector or sinner. God rejoices over the recovery of every one of them.

### 29. The Parable of the Lost Son (15:11–32)

If this sublime story stood alone it might be called the parable of the elder brother or the parable of the waiting father. It has been called by both of these titles and many variations of them. Some have called it the parable of the two sons and have thought of it as a variation of Matthew's parable of the two sons and the vineyard (21:28–31). Because of its association in Luke 15 with the parables of the lost sheep and the lost coin, it seems more fitting to use the title—Parable of the Lost Son.

Here the proportion has been reduced from one out of one hundred to one out of two. Whatever the relative value of sheep to coins, there is dramatic significance in the reduction to one out of two when human beings are the point of comparison. In the parable the father clearly represents God; the sinning and returning son represents the tax collectors and sinners; the elder brother represents the Pharisees. The central teaching is God's concern for the sinners with whom Jesus was associating (the association about which the Pharisees were complaining). To put the experience of the so-called "prodigal son" into a framework of debate over whether it is possible for one to be saved and then lost and then saved again is to miss Jesus' point and to seek an interpretation against a background of theological debate foreign to the story. On that basis one might debate over the question as to whether or not the elder brother was a saved person. One at least hopes for a better attitude in saved persons!

Verses 11–13 present the father, his two sons—apparently his only children and heirs—the request of the younger son for an immediate division of the inheritance, the departure of the younger son, his squandering of his inheritance in debauchery. The details are a part of the total story and require little specific attention.

*Verse 12:* The fact that the father *divided his living between the two sons* suggests that there were only two. Jesus was contrasting people by putting them into two classes—younger-brother kind of people and elder-brother kind of people. From that viewpoint the brothers were like the two sons of the Matthew parable—one professed disobedience but repented and did the father's will; one professed obedience but never really did the father's will.

*Verse 13: Journey into a far country* was Jesus' way of speaking of the son's flight from the presence and influence of his father. It was a graphic way of agreeing that the tax collectors and sinners had gone away from the way of God.

*Squandered his property in loose living* was a necessary way of indicating why the son eventually returned. *Squandered* means literally to scatter everywhere. With careless abandon he showed no respect for what the father had given him. *Loose living* translates two words, literally "living loosely." The adverb appears only here in the New Testament. In a noun form it appears three times in the sense of "dissipation," "riotous living" (Eph. 5:18; Tit. 1:6; 1 Pet. 4:4). In literature outside of the New Testament it refers to debauched or profligate living. Jesus did not approve of the son's way of life; no more did he approve of the way of life of the sinners whom the Pharisees condemned. He saw them, however, as objects of God's concern; the Pharisees did not.

Verses 14–19 continue the account of the younger son and the degradation to which he came.

*Verse 14: Spent everything* indicates the end of the squandering of his property. Subsequently a *great famine arose* in that distant country to which he had gone. *He began to be in want* may indicate that not only was he without funds of his own but that he was also without friends who could help him. He was totally destitute.

*Verse 15: He . . . joined himself to one of the citizens of that country:* The implication of the *far country* (v. 13) is that he left his home country— Jewish—for Gentile country. This implication is made more explicit in the statement that he became a swineherd. It would be natural for a Gentile citizen to own swine, but most unnatural for a Jewish citizen.

*Verse 16:* That he was hungry enough to share the food of the detested swine which he kept for the citizen indicates the extremity of his degradation. The *pods* were the hornlike bean pods of the carob tree which contained not only seeds but a sweet gelatinous substance adding to the food value. In conditions of extreme want the very poor people of the Mediterranean world ate these pods, but they were not regarded as fitting human food; they were food for the beasts. That was Jesus' intent in the story. He showed how the young man had forsaken his family, how he had been forsaken by the friends of his more affluent days, and was even abandoned by the citizen for whom he worked—*no one gave him anything.* No one brought food fit for humans; he was forced to the practical extremity of sharing the food of the unclean swine—a most pitiable plight for a Jewish youth of high social and economic rank.

*Verse 17: When he came to himself:* At this moment of self-realization he considered who he was, what he had been, what he had become because of his own will and action, and what course he might take to remedy his present situation and assure for himself a better future. There is no indication that he blamed anyone except himself. His situation was totally one of his own making. How wrong it was for him to be there he expressed in his soliloquy.

*How many of my father's hired servants:* He did not speak of slaves; he himself was not a slave. He spoke of employees as he himself was an employee. But what a difference. The employers were a respected Jewish man versus a despised Gentile. The employees of the father were in the good Jewish country; the son was in a faraway Gentile country. The employees of his father had *bread enough and to spare*—the expression means "an abundance of bread"; he had no bread at all, and the food was inadequate for his needs—*I perish here with hunger.*

*Verse 18:* That self-realization was his first step back toward his father's house. His second step was the determination to act to remedy his condition. *I will arise:* He was leaving his low place down among the swine and was going up to a higher place. *Go to my Father:* He realized the advantage of the father's house and had confidence that his father would accept him. *I will say to him:* He was ready to make a full confession of his wrongdoing and to request help from one who could and would give it. *I have sinned* has been called the hardest statement any person can make. The word translated *sinned* means to miss the mark in aiming at a target. He had aimed at well-being and the good life, but he had completely missed it. That was his confession. *Against heaven:* He realized that there was a higher source of concern over his conduct than his father. *And before you* took due recognition of his offense to the love and concern of his human father. The order of the two, however, indicates the primary importance of his sin as being against God.

*Verse 19: I am no longer worthy to be called your son:* His plea was not based on his own worthiness. His previous actions had indicated that he had no worthiness. *Treat me* (literally, "make me") *as one of your hired servants:* His plea was based on the father's compassion. He had no right to ask the position of a son, but to share the home and provision of his father he was willing to accept the lower position of a hired servant. In this decision was registered the total of repentance, confession, faith, and the promise of a different life.

Verses 20–24 present the return of the son to the life of well-being in the father's house.

*Verse 20: He arose and came to his father:* In contrast to his careful gathering together of all his goods and his going into the far country, these words suggest a quick journey home. As if waiting and watching for the returning son, *his father saw him* while he was still some distance from the house. Moved with *compassion* for a son returning in such a pitiable state, the father *ran and embraced and kissed him.* His conduct indicates that the son's confidence in his father's acceptance was well founded. It also indicated that the father's desire to welcome his son back was far beyond anything the son had anticipated. He did not really know the father's compassion until he surrendered himself to his father's decision about him.

*Verse 21:* The confession is identical with the determination expressed in verses 18–19 with one exception. While in some manuscripts they are identical, in the ones which show the least evidence of alteration by copyists the last part is omitted—"treat me as one of your hired servants." That omission seems to be the accurate reading. The result is an impression that the father in his joy interrupted the confession before the son could request the status of a servant. No matter what he had done, he had returned in repentance and confession of his sin. The father had but one thing in mind for him—the position of one who was still his son even though he had been disobedient and wayward.

*Verse 22: Servants* is a different word from the one translated *hired servants* (vv. 17, 19). The latter means a day laborer or one who worked for wages. This word means a slave—one who was owned by the master and a permanent part of his household. These were ordered by the father to serve the son as they doubtless had served him before he went away. Instead of the garments soiled from his working with swine, the son received *the best robe*. The word translated *best* means first or finest in quality. It was the kind of garment fit for a son—not a swineherd. *A ring on his hand* was another indication of honored position and affluence. (Compare the idea of a fine robe and a finger ring in James 2:2.) *Shoes on his feet* may indicate that he had come home barefooted. It may, however, refer to the custom of discarding soiled sandals at the door and receiving fresh sandals for use in the house.

*Verse 23: The fatted calf:* A grain-fed calf, in contrast to just any calf in the pasture, was the kind kept for festive occasions when important company came. No more important company could be anticipated by the rejoicing father. This was an occasion of joy similar to but more meaningful than the finding of a sheep or a coin.

*Verse 24: This my son was dead, and is alive:* The primary meaning is that he had been considered as dead but was found to be alive. It is not likely that the words have a double meaning—spiritually dead but now spiritually alive. *Dead . . . alive* mean the same as *lost . . . found*. The son had been as one dead or as one lost to the father; now he was as one alive from the dead. That was the reason for the rejoicing.

Verses 25-32: The contrast between *this my son* (v. 24) and *his elder son* (v. 25) marks the transition from the father's joy in receiving the disobedient son to the elder brother's anger and frustration at his brother's reception. The background discussed above (vv. 1–2) appears to indicate clearly that the returning disobedient son represents the tax collectors and sinners, and the elder brother represents the Pharisees and scribes who murmured because Jesus accepted the sinner.

If that is the case, this third parable goes beyond the other two. They closed on the emphasis of joy in the finding of that which was lost comparable to God's joy in "finding" even a tax collector or a sinner because he was concerned for them and loved them. The first part of this third parable closes in the same way (v. 24). For that reason, the second part of the parable has been studied with the view that it may represent a later addition or even a separate parable. This view cannot be strongly supported. This second part gives the same balance to the parable that is found in Matthew's parable of the two sons. It also has the force of pointing the attention of the Pharisees and scribes to their own unbrotherly attitude and behavior as well as to the truth that in the Father's house there is room for both Pharisee and publican, both scribe and sinner.

*Verse 25:* The elder brother returned from working in the field. There is intentional contrast to the return of the younger brother from the life of the far country. The elder brother also *drew near to the house*. The festive sounds were unmistakable. *Music* translates a Greek word for instrumental music produced usually by several instruments. The word translated *dancing* means "choral music" and was used either for choral dancing or choral singing. If choral dancing is intended, it was most likely the type of group dancing by which a story is acted out. Jesus may well have meant to indicate that they were "acting out" the story of the younger son's experience in going away in splendor, returning in shame, and being received back by the happy father.

*Verses 26–27: He called one of the servants:* This is a third term for servant meaning a child who renders household service. He asked the meaning of the music and the child reported the return of the younger brother and the father's joy in receiving him *safe and sound*—that is "in good health."

*Verse 28:* The elder brother refused to enter the house, so the father came out to him as he had gone out to greet the younger brother. The father's action was the same toward both. He started exhorting—*entreating* —the elder brother to come in and share the joy. But there was no joy in the heart of the older brother. He had only anger that the father would receive the younger brother under the circumstances and with such expressions of joy.

*Verses 29–30:* He pointed with pride to his own record of faithful and obedient service, and reflected resentment that through those years the father had shown no appreciation; he had not even provided him a small goat for a dinner with his friends. But now he had butchered the fatted calf for the younger son. The grammatical construction of the expression, *this son of yours,* reflects scorn—"your son, *this one* who has eaten up your life in the company of harlots." Some interpreters suggest that the brother was only assuming such conduct for which there is no indication on the part of the younger son. That view overlooks the expression *loose living* (v. 13) which really means a life of dissolution or debauchery. The emphasis of Jesus' parable is that the elder brother was right in his appraisal of what the younger brother had done. His error was in leaving out the fact that the younger brother had come back to the father.

*Verses 31–32:* The father's words to his elder son reflect his affection for both sons. He did appreciate the fact that the elder son had not gone away; he assured the elder son that everything he had was his. That still left room for his joyful acceptance of the returning penitent son. He could love them both without injustice to either.

Matthew indicates that when the Pharisees heard Jesus' parables—including the two sons and the vineyard—"they perceived that he was speaking about them" (21:45). There is no indication in Luke's account of whether or not the Pharisees saw themselves in the figure of the elder brother. The application was so obvious in the situation that it is difficult to think that they missed it. But the parable must not be imprisoned in the first century and in religious or irreligious groups of that day. It must issue its warning against the unbrotherly attitude in every age, its assurance of God's compassion for sinners, and its counsel that only when the sinner returns to the Father's house does he really understand sonship to God.

NOTE ON CHAPTER 16: Chapter 16 continues the teaching of Jesus. There is no geographical or chronological setting anywhere in the text. The teachings could be from any part of his ministry. Some of them are in definite settings in Matthew. The larger amount of these teachings are only in Luke. The major theme of the teachings is stewardship but verses 16–18 do not relate to that theme and, indeed, have no definite relation to the other teachings in the chapter.

### 30. The Parable of the Shrewd Steward (16:1–13)

The parable of the shrewd steward was addressed to the Twelve (v. 1). It was overheard by the Pharisees (v. 14) who scoffed at the teaching because they loved money more than they loved God (vv. 13–14).

The central character in the parable is a steward who was charged with inefficiency in office and wasting the goods of the rich man he served. When called to give an account of his stewardship, he acted in a shrewd way to assure his future well-being. The result was that he was commended for his shrewdness in taking care of himself materially. Three separate conclusions or applications are made in verses 8b, 9, and 10–13.

*Verse 1: Steward:* The word means one whose duty is to order the affairs of his employer, to "rule the house" in its financial affairs. Someone reported to this steward's master that he was *wasting his goods.* The word rendered *wasting* is the same as the one used of the younger son in the last parable (15:13)—"scattering" or "squandering." There is no reflection of riotous living in the text, but that may be understood. The charge brought against him was lack of efficiency in the discharge of his master's *goods*— precisely, "the things over which he ruled."

*Verses 2–4:* When he was told that he would no longer be maintained in the office and that he had to make a final inventory of his master's goods, he was in an embarrassing dilemma. He was too weak to work manually for a living—*to dig*—and too proud *to beg.* Begging was a profession in Jesus' day, as in many parts of the Orient and Mediterranean world it still is. But the steward felt that it was below his station in life.

*Verse 5:* His actions have brought upon him the name "dishonest steward." He was dishonest. The story closes, however, with an emphasis, not on dishonesty but on shrewdness. He moved to put other people under obligation to him so when his stewardship was ended they would give him a place to live—whether out of appreciation for what he had done for them or out of fear of being reported is not indicated.

While his specific instructions are explained only in the case of two of his master's debtors, the expression, *summoning his master's debtors one by one*—literally "each one"—suggests that there were many and that he made his deal with each individually and without witnesses.

*Verse 6:* The first debtor owed the master *a hundred measures of oil.* The steward instructed him to change the record to indicate that he owed only *fifty* (v. 6). Each measure—a Hebrew liquid measure called a "bath"— contained about nine gallons. The *oil* was olive oil. The large amount—nine hundred gallons—indicates a trader rather than a renter.

*Verse 7:* The second debtor owed the master *a hundred measures of wheat.* Each *measure*—a Hebrew dry measure called a "kor"—contained about twelve bushels. Again, twelve hundred bushels suggests a trader, not a renter. This debtor was instructed to change the record to show that he owed only *eighty* kor (v. 7).

The steward "saved" one debtor half of what he owed and the second one-fifth of what he owed. How much he "saved" other debtors is not stated. This was a business venture in which the steward assured his future welfare by helping several retailers cheat a wholesaler with whom they traded. He made them *his* debtors so they would be influenced to help him.

*Verse 8* suggests that the wholesaler—*the master*—later learned what had happened and, probably taking it as an expensive joke played on him, *commended the dishonest steward for his prudence.* It is important that he did not commend the man for his dishonesty; he commended him for his shrewdness in getting out of a bad situation and turning it to his financial advantage.

This is a perplexing parable. It appears to put the approval of Jesus on bad business ethics. That does not follow if one takes the parable as a whole as the point of comparison. The first application (v. 8b) appears to be the way the master looked on the situation and commended a man for taking care of his material interests no matter what method it required. One can imagine the master saying of his former steward, "Now there was a man who knew how to take care of himself. As a man of the world, he knew what real values are and how to deal with the men of his own time. One of these 'sons of light' would never have known how to do that." To the master it was becomingly shrewd for his former steward to take care of his own material interest as the most important thing in life.

*Verse 9:* The second application was Jesus' application of the parable as a whole. His disciples were represented as *sons of light.* Jesus gave counsel to them about using material things (of secondary importance) to their spiritual advantage (of primary importance).

*I tell you:* The *I* here is the emphatic use of the subject pronoun, putting Jesus in contrast to the rich man. To the rich man the most important thing was to look out after his needs in this world, even if that involved dishonesty. But Jesus did not agree with that view. His counsel was to his disciples as *sons of light* in contrast to the dishonest steward as one of the *sons of this world.* He counseled his disciples to take a different approach to the matter of material goods, using them in such way as to further their spiritual advantage.

*Make friends for yourself by means of unrighteous mammon: Mammon* is spoken of as *unrighteous* because it is used as the opposite of God in a master-servant relationship (v. 13). It is used in the sense of money or material possessions. As such it summarizes the total of "worldliness" in the minds of the *sons of this world* of whom both the rich man and his dishonest steward were examples. They used it, but not to their ultimate good; it came to be their enemy, not their friend. Jesus counseled his disciples to use whatever material possessions they had in such a way as to produce total righteousness rather than total unrighteousness.

*So that when it fails:* The *it* refers to mammon. The construction indicates the indefinite future, literally, "whenever it leaves off." Material possessions are of this world's order. They have an end which will come at an uncertain time. While you have them, use them in such a way that when they have ended their use in this world, they continue working to your advantage.

*They may receive you into the eternal habitations:* The material possessions were used by the dishonest steward with such shrewdness that when his job stopped he still had a place to live. But it was only a temporal and material place of habitation. Jesus counseled his disciples in their use of material things to exercise the kind of shrewdness which would be of eternal value to them. It was another way of saying "lay up for yourselves treasures in heaven" (Matt. 6:20). In that same passage Matthew uses the God-versus-mammon teaching which Luke uses here (Luke 16:13; Matt. 6:24).

*Verses 10–13* constitute a sort of third application of the parable. It is more of a stewardship teaching drawn out of the principle which Jesus gave regarding the wise use of material possessions.

The *very little* of verse 10 refers to material things and the *much* refers to spiritual things. Faithfulness in the use of material possessions is followed correspondingly by faithfulness in the higher stewardship of spiritual things. By the same principle, dishonesty in the use of material possessions is followed correspondingly by dishonesty in the higher stewardship of spiritual things.

That principle is applied in verse 11 by way of a question. If anyone has not been faithful in dealing with material possessions, who will trust him with a higher stewardship, *the true riches* of spiritual things? To default at the point of material stewardship is to give no grounds for confidence that one will not default at the point of spiritual stewardship.

The argument is continued in verse 12. *That which is another's* was Jesus' way of saying that material possessions are not really ours. We hold them as stewards for God and we must anticipate reckoning with him for the way we have used them. *That which is your own* must correspond to the spiritual things of verses 10 and 11. What Jesus meant by the question, *who will give you that which is your own,* is not clear. Possibly the whole verse can be interpreted as a challenge to recognize that we must account for our use of material possessions given us in trust, but that no one here in this life will call us to account for our spiritual destiny, which is our own. "If you are unfaithful in your use of that for which you expect to give an account, how do you expect to be trusted with the use of that for which you do not expect to give an account?"

The final part of the teaching contrasts God and Mammon (personified) as two lords with men as their slaves. *No servant can serve two masters* means literally, "No servant can be a slave owned by two masters." The wealth of Luke's vocabulary is evident in the use of still another word for "servant"—a house servant. The importance is in the literal meaning of the verb, "to be the slave of." It is contrary to the very idea of being owned as a slave to think of being owned by and trying to serve two lords of opposite views and wills.

*Either he will hate the one and love the other:* The word *hate* here means to abhor or to be constantly displeased with. To *love* is to put highest value on and give first place in life to. If one assumes a situation in which a person is a slave of two masters opposite in character, the natural consequence is rejection of one and fidelity to the other.

*Or he will be devoted to the one and despise the other:* This is another instance of rhetorical arrangement of the four parts of a contrasting situation:

hate one —— love the other<br>
devoted to one >< despise the other.

To *be devoted to* is to maintain a face-to-face relationship with—honest and open. To *despise* is to look down on or think against one. *Hate* and *love* are emotional opposites. *Devoted* and *despise* are rational opposites. Together they present the impossibility of being owned by two lords.

*You cannot serve God and mammon:* This is an axiom stated as a conclusion and left as needing no support. *Mammon* is personified to represent the material as God represents the spiritual. Literally the axiom is "You cannot to God continually render service and also to Mammon." So Jesus instructed his disciples that they should understand the impossibility of being "owned" by God and at the same time being "owned" by money.

### 31. A Rebuke to the Insincere (16:14–18)

*Verse 14:* The Pharisees heard these teachings on stewardship which Jesus had addressed to the Twelve (v. 1). Luke describes the Pharisees as *lovers of money.* There is some support for this charge in Mark 7:9–13 and from a variant reading in Matthew 23:14. In the Mark passage Jesus charged the Pharisees with circumventing the Mosaic law of taking care of one's needy parents (Exod. 20:12, 21:17; Deut. 5:16; Lev. 20:9) by greedily holding their money and claiming that they had promised it to God. His meaning was that they had no intention of giving it to God; they were merely using a religious claim to support their greed. The Matthew passage, however, is not in the best manuscripts, so it can be used only in a qualified support of Luke's statement. In it Jesus charged the Pharisees with greed in that they devoured widows' houses and robbed the helpless to support their own greed.

Luke's statement that they were *lovers of money* is best supported in a general way by the unchallenged fact that the people regarded wealth as an indication of God's favor and the absence of wealth as an indication of God's disfavor. That idea was the background for another stewardship story in this chapter (vv. 19–31). Their love for money was also evident in that *they scoffed at him* when he warned his disciples of the danger of trying to love both God and money and to serve both God and money.

*Verse 15:* Jesus' rebuke was a general one related to inner attitudes. In the eyes of men, the Pharisees could make themselves appear very pious; this they did by their outward demonstration of devotion to God and his law. But *God knows your hearts.* God does not see as men see; while men look on outward appearances, God looks on the heart (1 Sam. 16:7). He knew what they were really like on the inside. In this context, the immediate implication was that they served, not God, but mammon (v. 13).

*What is exalted among men* is a general appraisal of the opinion of men of the world—*the sons of this world,* for example, of verse 8. The specific application was to the immediate subject of the love of money and its controlling interest. This was an acceptable thing in the opinion of men. The Pharisees approved it so they could justify—demonstrate—their piety before men and win their approval. But much of what is exalted by men as valuable and praiseworthy *is an abomination in the sight of God.* The word translated *abomination* means something displeasing or nauseating because of its stink. In Hebrew religious literature, both biblical and non-biblical, it was used of idol worship. That may be Jesus' suggestion here—that love of money is exalted by men but in the mind of God it is idol worship. Paul identified covetousness as idolatry (Eph. 5:5). On the other hand, Jesus may have been reminding them of the Old Testament prophets who insisted that burning animals on the Temple altar was only a stench in the nostrils of God when the sacrifice was made as an outward religious demonstration apart from genuine inner religious devotion.

*Verse 16* has a parallel in Matthew where Jesus appraised the work of John the Baptizer in relation to the attitudes and actions of men (11:12-13). In this setting Luke presents Jesus as using the saying to rebuke the insincerity of men and their continuing variance from the way of God. It is a very forceful use.

*The law and the prophets:* This is a technical reference to the total of the Hebrew religious system. The rabbis used it to refer to two major divisions of the Hebrew Scriptures—*the law* was the first five books also called "Moses" and *the prophets* were the writings of the prophets and the historical books related to the deeds of the prophets. What Jesus meant here was that the history of Israel was one of continual discrepancy from the way of God as it was set out in *the law* and by *the prophets.* From the first of his prophets—probably Moses—to the last of his prophets—John the Baptizer—men had desired their way rather than God's way.

*Since then the good news of the kingdom of God is preached:* John marked a point of transition. He stood at the end of the line of the old order and at the beginning of the line of the new order. In the old order the message proclaimed was that the messianic king was coming to inaugurate the kingdom of God—the Age of the Messiah. Beginning with John, the message proclaimed was that the Messiah had come and that his kingdom was present.

*Everyone enters it violently:* Matthew helps to clarify the meaning of this statement—"the kingdom of heaven has suffered violence, and men of violence take it by force" (11:13). Jesus meant that men in their attitudes and actions had not changed. They were still trying to force their way upon the kingdom. They would not accept Jesus' understanding of the kingdom. Their way was the way of violence and force in opposition to his way, just as in the time of the prophets they had rejected God's way and his messengers in preference for their way.

*Verse 17:* Jesus spoke with confidence that, in spite of what men did, God's way would be realized and that *the law* would accomplish its purpose. *The law* was more enduring than the world order—*heaven and earth.* Even though they seemed eternal, they were not; they would pass away (Matt. 5:18; Mark 13:31). The law, however, would not fail. The *dot* was a very minute part of a written word; it could be the corner of an angular letter or a tiny accent. From that use the term *dot* came to refer to something seemingly insignificant and yet having its purpose. So Jesus meant that in spite of men with their insincerity and opposition, every part of God's law would realize its purpose.

*Verse 18:* There is no obvious reason for the appearance in this setting of this brief statement about divorce. Perhaps Jesus used it as an example of the way men in their insincerity were treating the law. The statement is too brief for a comprehensive explanation of Jesus' teaching on divorce and remarriage. Such explanation would require detailed examination of his teachings elsewhere (Matt. 5:31-32; 19:9; Mark 10:11-12) along with Paul's interpretation of Jesus' teaching (1 Cor. 7:10-11).

The practice of divorce and remarriage had its background in Deuteronomy 24:1-4. By that law, a man who, after he had married, "found some indecency in her" was permitted to send her back to her father, but he was required to send also a written statement of his reason. The law was given to assure some sense of justice to the woman. In its original intent the term rendered "some indecency" in the RSV—"some uncleanness" in the KJV—probably referred to sexual impurity in infidelity to the marriage responsibility. In Jesus' time, the rabbis were divided on the meaning of the term. Some interpreted it as a reference to sexual infidelity. Others interpreted it very freely with the emphasis on the matter of her finding "no favor" in the eyes of her husband. This could be caused by an almost limitless number of trivial reasons—talking about her in-laws; burning the food; even being less attractive than some other woman. In any of these and many more cases, the husband could divorce his wife as long as he gave her the written statement of divorce. The result was a type of insincerity and injustice which Jesus rejected.

In the Luke passage there is simply the unqualified statement prohibiting both the marriage of a man after he has divorced his wife (v. 18a) and the marriage of the divorced woman to another man (v. 18b). Both are labeled *adultery,* which is sexual union with another when the previous marriage is still legally binding. Qualifications of this in other passages (such as the Matt., Mark, and 1 Cor. passages above) are outside the scope of this treatment in Luke. Also beyond our scope is the total approach to the problem of divorce in modern society in which each case is considered redemptively from the viewpoint of trying to salvage human worth in a grievous situation.

## 32. The Rich Man and the Beggar (16:19–31)

This is usually called the parable of the rich man and Lazarus, but it is not called a parable in the New Testament. It does not have the central idea of comparison characteristic of parables, nor does it have the form of a parable—introduction, analogy story, application. Its form is that of an example story for the purpose of illustration. It is not beyond reason that Jesus' hearers were acquainted with such a case of a rich man and a beggar who died at the same time.

The purpose of the story is related directly to the Pharisees and their love of money. The story contrasts two men in their material status in this life and in their destiny beyond this life. The point is that when the true situation is known, it is the poor man who has God's favor and the rich man who has God's disfavor. Their relative poverty and wealth is not emphasized as the reason for God's favor or disfavor; no reason is given. The story simply shows that the money-lovers were wrong in thinking that wealth per se means God's favor and the lack of wealth per se means God's disfavor. It must be recalled, too, that Jesus used this as a stewardship story, not as a teaching on the nature of heaven and hell. Whatever elements of man's ultimate destiny are present in the story are of secondary application.

*Verse 19: There was a rich man:* The text precisely has "a certain man was rich." The word indicates no one in particular, but has the force of "there was once a man who was rich." The hearers may or may not have known of such a person. No name is given; the name Dives which is sometimes used is derived from the Latin Bible and means "one who is rich."

*Purple . . . fine linen . . . feasted sumptuously every day:* The man had every material thing. *Purple* was a dye, but in the Bible it is always used of the purple cloth sought by the wealthy as an indication of their rank and frequently worn by royalty. *Fine linen* was the clothing of prominent and important people. *Feasted* is really the word for living in enjoyment and merriment. While the idea of food is not necessarily a part of the word, the entire setting implies a festive occasion daily. *Sumptuously* is an adverb more naturally related to the clothing than to the feasting, meaning "in splendor." For this rich man, every day was a banquet occasion. If there is any sense of evil in this it is only an implied one. Festive occasions are often occasions of evil, but not necessarily so. If there is apparent evil in the man's conduct it appears to be in his unawareness or his unfeeling attitude toward a starving sick man at his gate. That appealed to Luke.

*Verses 20-21: At his gate lay a poor man:* The construction in the Greek is identical with that of the phrase introducing the rich man—"a certain poor man named Lazarus lay at his gate." Lazarus—Hebrew Eleazar—was a very honored name among the Jews. It was the traditional name through which the Aaronic priesthood was traced and is the only name to be given to a character in any of Jesus' stories and parables. That fact and the reference to someone's being raised from the dead (v. 31) have influenced some interpreters to think of this as a variant of the John 11 account of Jesus' raising Lazarus of Bethany from the dead. The evidence is not strong and cannot be reviewed here. The status of this poor man was the very opposite of the rich man. He was *full of sores*—"covered with ulcerous boils" rather than purple and linen. He begged for the scraps, even tiny crumbs, which *fell from the rich man's table.* That was food for dogs, and dogs were his only companions and comfort. They came and relieved some of his misery by licking his sores as they would lick their own. The dogs showed more concern for the poor man than the rich man did.

*Verses 22-23* continue the contrast of the two men, rich man and beggar. Just as there could be no more dramatic contrast between two men in life (vv. 19-21), so there could be no more dramatic contrast of their status after death.

*The angels*—messengers of God—carried the poor man to be welcomed in the embrace of Abraham, father of the Jewish race. No better fate could have been desired by any Jew. The ancient man's concept of the universe is used in the contrast between the fate of the poor man and that of the rich man, who also died and was put down into the earth by men; his ultimate abode was *Hades,* "the unseen world." Generally in the New Testament the word means only the region of the dead. (See discussion on 10:15.) Only rarely does it mean the same thing as Gehenna—hell—as the place of punishment beyond this life. This is one of those rare instances. The poor man was finally in comfort in Abraham's bosom—heaven. The rich man was finally in torment in hell. Perhaps his seeing the once despised beggar now embraced by Abraham added to his own misery.

Verses 24–31 continue the contrast between the two by means of a conversation between Abraham and the rich man.

*Verse 24:* The rich man begged Abraham, addressing him as father—he, too, was descended from Abraham—to send Lazarus to his relief. Did he think he deserved some return for favoring Lazarus with the scraps from his table and the service of his dogs? He wanted Lazarus merely to dip the tip of his finger in water and to touch his parched tongue for relief in the flames of hell. Even while recalling that this is primarily a stewardship story and not a direct teaching on eternal punishment, the description of the man's plight is appalling.

*Verse 25:* Abraham told the rich man to remember the comfort he had once known and the anguish Lazarus had known; to consider now his own anguish but Lazarus's comfort. This was not to gloat over the man's misery; nor was it to indicate that their reversed status beyond death was the natural result of their status in life. It was just to make more vivid the truth that wealth here does not mean God's favor nor does poverty his disfavor. In the case of these two, the poor man had God's favor and the rich man his disfavor—though the reason for that is not explained.

*Verse 26: And besides all this* translates a phrase meaning literally "and in all these things." In the total circumstance of the differing destinies of the two men there was an impassable chasm between them. In this life they had been closely related in physical proximity but not in spiritual realities. Now they were far removed from one another by the very nature of those spiritual realities. There could be no communion by passing back and forth. Whatever the nature of the ultimate abode of the good and bad—heaven and hell—the matter of importance is not one of two places separated by an impassable chasm. It is a matter of two destinies so completely different that they have no community with one another.

*Verses 27–28:* The rich man finally showed some concern about people other than himself—his five brothers. If Lazarus could not be of service to him, he requested that he might be sent to warn the five brothers. The warning he anticipated would likely include a description of his condition and some instruction to the brothers as to how they might avoid sharing that destiny. The implication was that they shared the same kind of life which had been his and that they faced, therefore, the same fate.

*Verse 29:* Abraham answered that the five brothers had *Moses and the prophets* to instruct them. This was a customary way of referring to their Scriptures. The answer recalls Jesus' advice to the man who asked how he could attain eternal life; he called his attention to the way of God set out in the Scripture and summarized in the two tables of the law—the first, man's relationship to God, and the second, man's relationship to his fellow-man (Luke 18:18–25). The man and his brothers had had sufficient instruction concerning the trusteeship of life in relation to God and man. The rich man should have heeded what he knew; his brothers still could do so.

*Verse 30:* The rich man responded that the warning of one who had experienced death and returned from the dead would be a more compelling warning than that in the Scriptures. His brothers would heed that kind of warning; they would repent.

*Verse 31:* Abraham's final word was that people who would not heed the warning of the Scriptures would not be convinced of the right way to a blessed destiny even if one should return from the dead to warn them.

By this illustration Jesus showed the money-loving Pharisees that material status of wealth or poverty in this life is no index to standing with God. But there was surely a deeper current running below this surface in the mind of Jesus. Prominent in his mind in those days was his coming death and resurrection. The sad part was his realization that these leaders of the religion of Israel were so set in their rejection of him and of God's way in him that they would not repent even when he did arise from the dead. They did not believe on him and accept his way when he raised Lazarus of Bethany from the dead (John 11:45–53). They not only counseled as to how they could kill Jesus (John 11:53), but they planned to put Lazarus to death again because he was such an unanswerable argument for Jesus' power and authority from God (John 12:9–11). No more would they accept him in his own resurrection. Theirs was the sin of character crystallized in opposition to God.

### 33. Offending and Forgiving (17:1–4)

These verses have no specific setting in Luke. They are parallel to a much longer section which Matthew has as the final teaching of Jesus in Galilee before his setting out for Jerusalem (Matt. 18:1–22). In both Luke and Matthew, the teachings are addressed to the Twelve.

*Verse 1: Temptations to sin* is the rendering of one word meaning "stumbling blocks" or "offenses." It does not refer to temptations which would come to the Twelve to sin, but to the danger that they would "offend" or cause others to sin. Such occasions Jesus said were *sure to come.* He meant that they were inevitable in a society made up of imperfect people. The author of James—by early tradition the half brother of Jesus—said that the office of teacher was particularly marked by danger because of the many ways of offending others; the easiest way is in the teacher's use of the tongue (3:1–3).

*Woe to him by whom they come:* Even though they are inevitable in society, offenses are the responsibility of the offender. To be guilty of offending is a calamity.

*Verse 2:* As a specific area of offense, Jesus warned against offending *one of these little ones* by influencing him to stumble. In Matthew 18:1–22, *little ones* refers to the children whom Jesus was using as examples of the childlike nature of kingdom citizens. Probably the same is intended in this passage. Some interpreters, however, think that Luke has dropped the idea of children, and uses the term to refer to the spiritually immature of whatever age; the use would be similar to Paul's idea of Christians as "babes in Christ."

Whatever their identity, the warning to be on guard against offending them is cast in very strong language. It would be better to die than to be the reason of a little one's stumbling. A *millstone* was a round stone wheel used in grinding grain. Tied about the neck of a person cast into the sea it would guarantee a quick death—perhaps an ignominious death since the Jewish people regarded the sea as a symbol of evil. If it is a choice between death and causing one of the *little ones* to stumble in his spiritual journey, choose death.

*Verses 3–4:* Jesus turned from the idea of being an offender to the idea of being the one offended with the responsibility to forgive the offender.

*If your brother sins, rebuke him: Brother* is used in the sense of one's fellowman, not just a physical brother or even a spiritual brother. *Sins* naturally indicates "sins against you," that is, he is an offender where you are concerned. The offended was not to take the offense in silence. The word rendered *rebuke* is used elsewhere in the Gospels to mean "stop." He was to stop him in his offending action.

*If he repents, forgive him:* Even as you are arresting him in his action, you are to have the right attitude. You are to accept his repentance as genuine and forgive him. If you refuse to forgive, you could become the offender and he the offended. It is foreign to the spirit and intent of Jesus to ask, "But what if he does not repent? Can I not forgive him anyway?" The follower of Christ is not justified in holding a spirit of unforgiveness just because no apology is offered. That would put the responsibility for the Christian's attitude upon the offender; this Christ would never do. The true spirit of his teaching is clear in the next verse.

*Verse 4:* If a brother sins against you seven times in one day, but each time he turns to say "I repent," you must forgive. *Seven times* is an expression for the whole, the complete, the ultimate. In Matthew 18:21–22 Simon Peter asked Jesus if he should forgive his brother seven times. It was the custom to help a fellowman out of six difficulties, but that was regarded as the limit which exhausted responsibility. Jesus answered Peter, "I do not say to you seven times, but seventy times seven." He raised the perfect number as men considered it—seven—to a most perfect seventy times seven. He did not, of course, mean forgive him 490 times and then you are justified in not forgiving him. He was using the high multiple to mean that there is no limit to the responsibility to forgive.

## 34. Believing and Serving (17:5–10)

The two teachings in this section could be separate teachings. In the RSV, as in some other works, they are regarded as one saying. They will be so treated here—humble service growing out of faith.

*Verse 5: The apostles* is a rarely used term in the Gospels. Luke last used it in 9:10. Here it clearly means the Twelve. They may have sensed that to avoid offending others (vv. 1–2) and to exercise forgiveness (vv. 3–4) would make heavy demands. They asked Jesus to *increase* their faith—to "add to" their faith. It was a request for a practical quality of faith for facing practical problems.

Jesus responded by a figure in which he taught that a small quantity of faith put to use would accomplish unbelievable things. The same mustard seed figure and meaning are in Matthew 17:20 as an explanation of Jesus' healing a possessed boy when the disciples could not.

*Verse 6: If you had faith as a grain of mustard seed:* The idea is that of a very small thing which possesses the potential of great results—as in the parable of the grain of mustard (13:18–19).

*Sycamine tree:* This was a type of mulberry. There is no particular significance in the use of this rather than some other. It may have been the nearest large object which Jesus could use in comparison. In Matthew 17:20, Jesus spoke of moving a mountain from one place to another; they were at the foot of a mountain when he said it. In Matthew 21:21 Jesus explained the blighting of a fig tree on the basis of faith which could cause a mountain to be plucked up like a tree and cast into the sea. Here it is a mulberry tree which faith could cause to be *rooted up, and be planted in the sea.*

All of this imagery presents one very graphic lesson. Jesus was telling the Twelve to put into action what little faith they had. Without his adding to it, it was enough to accomplish tremendous and unbelievable things.

*Verses 7–10:* If this section belongs with the faith teaching of the last two verses, Jesus' meaning was that even when the Twelve used their little faith and accomplished those great things, they were to maintain the attitude of humility expressed in doing their assigned work. It is not a clear connection; nor is it a forced one; it is only a possible one.

In this example story, sometimes called the parable of the unprofitable servant, Jesus made each of the Twelve both the master (vv. 7–9) and the servant (v. 10) with the words *will any one of you.* If they were masters and had servants coming in from working in the fields, they would not invite the servants to sit down and eat (v. 7). Rather, any master would order the servant to prepare food for him, and only when the master had eaten could the servant eat (v. 8). That was what would be expected in any normal master-servant relationship. The master would not even bother to thank the servant for doing what it was his duty to do (v. 9). That, too, is normal; no one really expects to be thanked for doing what he is supposed to do.

The climax comes in verse 10, when Jesus turned the story to put the Twelve in the role of the servant. When they had done all they were supposed to do, they were not to be puffed up with pride and look for commendation. They were to be humble, recognizing that they had done their task; they were to expect no commendation. The illustration and its meaning serve as a practical lesson by example which may be applied in many different situations in life: church, home, business.

## 35. Healing Ten Lepers on the Border of Samaria and Galilee (17:11–19)

This miracle is only in Luke. It has no logical relation to the teachings which precede and follow it. It took place on the border between Galilee and Samaria as Jesus was on the road to Jerusalem. If Luke understood that the teachings which precede and follow it took place on the same occasion, Matthew's use of them in other settings is a part of the continuing question of the theological purpose of the placement of materials in both Matthew and Luke.

*Verse 11: Between Samaria and Galilee:* Reference to any map of Palestine in Jesus' time will suggest that this was the border extending from the river Jordan to the Mediterranean Sea separating Galilee on the north from Samaria on the south. Since the territory of Herod Antipas included Galilee (west of the Sea of Galilee) and Perea (east of the Jordan), the total territory of Galilee and Perea was sometimes referred to as "Galilee." If Luke used such a general reference here, the location could be some un-identified village on the road south toward Jerusalem and near the eastern bank of the Jordan. Jesus' instruction to the ten to report their condition "to the priests" is not necessarily an indication that it was near Jerusalem.

*Verse 12: Ten lepers . . . stood at a distance:* Because of the dread nature of this skin disease, lepers were socially ostracized. They did not approach other people, and if they did come near others they were to cry out, "Un-clean, unclean," as a warning for others not to approach them (Lev. 13:45). These lepers were on the outside of the village but near the road Jesus traveled.

*Verse 13: Jesus, Master, have mercy on us:* Their addressing Jesus by name suggests knowledge of his identity. This could have been by previous visit of Jesus to this village or by information given to them by others. *Master* is the word used only by Luke and only in reference to Jesus (see discussion on 8:24). The Greek means one who "stands over" others, that is, one of authority. Luke uses it sometimes in situations where Mark and Matthew use "teacher" or "rabbi."

*Have mercy on us:* The ten lepers asked for Jesus' merciful attention. The request was not expressly for healing. Probably that was what they meant and Jesus so understood it.

*Verse 14: Go and show yourselves to the priests:* On the surface this was a curt dismissal and a refusal to help them. In the history of Israel, leprosy was associated with sin and those who had it were under strict observation and treatment by the priests. Chapters 13–14 of Leviticus con-tain detailed instructions concerning the responsibility of lepers to put them-selves under the care of the priests, and the responsibilities of the priests in treating lepers and directing their sacrifices in case they were cured. In this case, Jesus appeared to dismiss the lepers by reminding them that their condition was to be supervised by priests, not by him. That, however, may not be the case.

On a previous occasion, in an unidentified town in Galilee, Jesus had healed a leper and followed the healing with instruction that he report to the priests and make the customary sacrifice (Luke 5:12–14; Matt. 8:1–4; Mark 1:40–45). Here he merely directed ten lepers to the priests. Does this indicate that the ten knew about the previous case and that their obedient response showed faith that in some way they would be cured under the priests' direction?

*And as they went they were cleansed:* The ten started on their way to show their condition to the priests. Whether Luke meant priests in Jerusalem or priests there in the village is not indicated. As they went they became aware of the fact that their leprosy had been cured.

*Verses 15–16: One of them . . . was a Samaritan:* One of the ten who were healed returned praising God. He prostrated himself before Jesus and thanked him for the healing. That one was a Samaritan. (On Samaritans, see discussion on 9:52–56; 10:33.) Samaritans and Jews mutually despised and avoided one another. The entire event suggests that the other nine lepers were Jews. In their physical misery and social and religious alienation from others, the ten had found a common bond.

*Verses 17–18: Where are the nine?* Jesus' response was the sort of thing which appealed to Luke. An outcast, despised *foreigner* became an example of appreciation because he returned to express his thanks while the nine Jews went on their way with no word of gratitude. It can be assumed that the nine continued on their way to the priests, showed the evidences of their cure, and made the traditional sacrifices. Jesus' question in verse 18, however, casts some doubt on their doing even that. The Samaritan may have gone to the priests later in order to be permitted to resume his place in society. Jesus used the Samaritan's return to show that gratitude sometimes comes from unanticipated sources but does not always come from anticipated sources.

*Verse 19: Rise and go your way; your faith has made you well:* While there is no verbal expression of faith related to the lepers' obeying Jesus' order in verse 14, there is an indication in this concluding statement of Jesus' that faith had been present and that it had made possible their cure. One, a Samaritan, was vocal in his thanksgiving and came to be for the succeeding centuries an example of the grace of gratitude. Nine merely "went their way."

## 36. The True Nature of the Kingdom of God (17:20–21)

This brief teaching of Jesus is only in Luke. There is a helpful and suggestive version of it in the Gospel According to Thomas (Logion 113). In Luke the Pharisees ask the question; in Thomas the disciples ask it. Jesus' answer in both contains the statement that the kingdom will not come with observable signs so that one may see it by responding to the suggestion, "Lo, here it is" or "there." The closing part of his answer reflects an interesting variation. In Luke it is, "the kingdom of God is in the midst of you"; in Thomas it is, "the kingdom of the Father is spread out over the earth and men do not see it." Also in Thomas Jesus said, "the kingdom is inside of you and it is outside of you" (Logion 3). Jesus' emphasis was on the internal and spiritual nature of the kingdom while the Pharisees were thinking in terms of an external and material manifestation of it. Their interest was not only in when the kingdom would come, but on visible signs and proofs that it had come.

Later Jesus told the parable of the pounds (Luke 19:11–27) because his listeners "supposed that the kingdom of God was to appear immediately." These hearers were those who had murmured that Jesus had "gone in to be the guest" of a sinner—Zacchaeus (19:7). All of this suggests the Pharisees as those who were supposing that the kingdom would appear immediately. That explains their question as to when the kingdom was to come in this passage. Their anticipation was the common one of the Jews of Jesus' day, the coming of the Messiah to usher in the messianic age by restoring Israel to a glorious place as a nation—a political, material kingdom more golden even than the days of David and Solomon.

*Verse 20: The kingdom of God is not coming with signs to be observed:*

In Jesus' view the kingdom of God was the spiritual rule of God in the hearts of his subjects. As such it could not be identified by the observable phenomena of material kingdoms—kings, thrones, armies, subjects, lands, etc. Its nature is such that one cannot point and say, "Look, here it is" or "Look, there it is over there."

*Verse 21: The kingdom of God is in the midst of you:* The optional translation in the RSV margin is "the kingdom of God is within you." The New American Standard Version has the same translation as the RSV both in the body of the text and in the margin. *The New English Bible* renders the term "among you" and in the margin lists several paraphrase interpretations —"within you"; "within your grasp"; "suddenly . . . will be among you."

The word translated *in the midst* or "within" is in the New Testament in only one other place; in Matthew 23:26 it refers to the inside of a cup or a dish. Whatever qualifications may be used of the kingdom of God in other teachings, one thing only can be derived from this Luke passage—Jesus' emphasis on the kingdom as internal and spiritual, not external and material.

### 37. The Day of the Son of Man (17:22–37)

This is a most difficult passage. The overall reference appears to be to the coming of the Son of Man—Christ—in judgment at the end of the age. Some small parts of it, however, are repeated in Luke 21 in reference to the destruction of Jerusalem (A.D. 70), and larger parts of it are in Matthew 24, also in reference to the destruction of Jerusalem. The entire complex cautions one against dogmatism in interpreting.

These teachings were addressed to the disciples (v. 22) rather than to the Pharisees (v. 20). Jesus taught the disciples that while the kingdom, because of its nature, could not be identified by visible, tangible manifestations, his coming in judgment could and would be so identifiable (vv. 34–37). Before that time should come, however, there would be other events: his death (v. 25), and days of difficulty which would make the disciples long for the end (v. 22).

*Verse 22* contains Jesus' warning to prepare the disciples for the difficult times they would experience before the end. The nature of those times is more clearly defined in Luke 21:10–19. The days would be filled with such difficulties that they would desire to see one of the *days of the Son of man—* the glorious time following his triumphant return in judgment to separate the good from the evil and to usher in the eternal order which would be days free of trouble, sorrow, or suffering. By contrast the days to follow his death would cause the disciples to experience suffering which would make them desire relief by his return.

*You will not see it:* This probably does not mean that Jesus told them they would not live to the time of his return in judgment. Since he did not know when that would be (Matt. 24:36; Mark 13:32), he did not likely tell them that it would be beyond their time. This statement meant simply that there would be no relief from their suffering; they could anticipate nothing less.

*Verse 23* reflects a natural condition in which rumors of relief multiply in times of difficulty, specifically rumors of Jesus' return. In Luke 21:8 (with parallels in Mark 13:5–6 and Matt. 24:4–5) these warnings are applied to claims of false messiahs in relation to the Jewish revolt and the destruction of

Jerusalem in A.D. 70. Such troublesome times produce rumors such as these: "Look; he has come over there" or "Look; he has come over here."

*Do not go, do not follow:* They were not to respond to such rumors in hope of finding that Jesus had indeed returned. The reason for the warning that the rumors and hopes were false is obvious in the next verse.

*Verse 24* makes it clear that the coming of the Son of Man will be self-evident. It will not be of such nature that one person must report it to another—he is over here in this place, or that place. As the lightning flashes in one place and lightens the sky from east to west and from north to south, so will his coming be self-evident, a matter which will require no reporting.

*Verse 25* was Jesus' reminder to the disciples that the next thing in order was not that glorious day of judgment and consummation. The next thing was his rejection and death in Jerusalem. That drew nearer daily as they approached Jerusalem. He wanted them to remember his previous predictions of his death and to associate that death with both their future difficulties and his future coming in total triumph.

*Verses 26–30* contain Jesus' teaching that his return will be dramatically sudden and that it will come when people are so engrossed in the affairs of everyday life that they have no consciousness of impending judgment. The illustrations of the days of Noah, the days of Lot, and the body and eagles (v. 37) has led to the popular view that Jesus was emphasizing the excessive wickedness to characterize the world near the end. While the presence of evil in the world right up to the time of the Lord's return is a consistent theme in the New Testament, it is doubtful that that was Jesus' major emphasis here. His emphasis was rather on that which is basic to the world's evil—man's being so engrossed in the material affairs and activities of life that he has no consciousness of God's impending judgment; it takes him with dramatic unexpectedness. Two major examples of judgment illustrate.

*Verses 26–27: As it was in the days of Noah:* God's judgment by the waters of the deluge served Jesus as a good illustration (Gen. 6:5–8; 7:6–24). It is true that the Genesis story attributes the deluge-judgment to excessive wickedness. Jesus, however, spoke not of that but of the way men, without regard to God's way or the danger of God's judgment, were engrossed in everyday activities: eating, drinking, getting married, making marriage arrangements for their daughters. Their life was so taken up in the ordinary that they gave no consideration to the requirement of God; they sensed no impending doom. Though every blow of Noah's hammer in building the ark should have been a warning, it was not. With startling suddenness judgment fell.

*Verses 28–30: Likewise as it was in the days of Lot: Likewise* puts the experience of the people in Lot's day (Gen. 18:20–33; 19:24–25) parallel to Noah's day, only here it was God's judgment through *fire.* The people of Sodom were engrossed in the affairs of everyday life: eating, drinking, buying, selling, planting, building. Of themselves, these activities were normal, as were those of the people of Noah's day. That was exactly Jesus' point of emphasis. They were doing the things natural to man's life in the home, in the business world, in society. But they were doing it in the absence of any consciousness of God's requirement or judgment. With startling suddenness judgment fell.

Jesus applied both illustrations to his coming—*so will it be in the days of the Son of man* (v. 26); *so will it be on the day when the Son of man is revealed* (v. 30). One might understand the reference to *the days* (plural) *of the Son of man* to apply to the way men conduct themselves prior to his return and *the day* (singular) *when the Son of man is revealed* to his coming at the end of "the days." That distinction is doubtful. The three sayings about *the Son of man* (vv. 24, 26, 30) most naturally refer to one thing—his coming in judgment.

*Verse 31* was Jesus' caution about the controlling concern for material possessions. It was a solemn warning about the futility of cherishing the things of this life in face of the nearing of the eternal order. *On the day when the Son of man is revealed* (v. 30), it will be futile to try to preserve material possessions in another part of one's house or out at the edge of the field where one is working. These have no part of that eternal order. Forget them and leave them as unnecessary.

*Verse 32* is a reminder of the tragic example of Lot's wife (Gen. 19:26). In the day of God's visitation of judgment she did not try to *go back* to retrieve possessions. She merely *looked back* to where they were and so lost both the past and the future. How much more serious is the frantic holding on to material and temporal things when the spiritual and eternal is dawning. Face the future with hands empty of the material.

*Verse 33* is a general teaching capable of application in many situations. Such use is clear in an analysis of the other places in which it appears in the Gospels. (See the previous exposition of Luke 9:24.) In the present passages it is a conclusion to the warning in verse 31 and the reminder in verse 32. It relates to the matter of priorities and a sense of values. One can lose the eternal and the spiritual by putting priority value on the temporal and physical. Lot's wife looking back is not to be understood as only curious to see what was happening in the city whose name has passed down through history as a name of shame. Her looking back symbolizes a longing for the life which had been hers in the city where her husband had been a judge. In seeking to gain one life she lost another, while Lot in losing one life gained another.

*Verses 34–35* revert to verse 30 and "the day when the Son of man is revealed." A popular interpretation relates this to the resurrection of dead believers, and the taking out of the world of living believers, leaving only the unbelievers in the world. It is a view forced upon this passage rather than derived from it, and it ignores the major emphasis of Jesus in the teaching. One thing only was Jesus' intent—his coming will mean judgment so discerning that it severs even those most closely associated. The separation will be based on their true character. As his presence in his first coming divided people into two classes (Luke 12:49–53), so his presence in his second coming will divide them.

*In that night* is a natural detail of Jesus' illustration. It can no more be used to suggest that the return will be at night than "on that day" (v. 31) can be used to suggest that it will be in the daytime. Such questioning is quibbling which misses the main point.

*Two men in one bed* does not necessarily mean two adult men. The Greek does not use the word for "men" here, only the numeral "two." That two

males are intended is clear in the masculine gender of the expressions *one
. . . and the other.* The reference may be to a man and his son, regardless
of age. The coming of the Son of Man will mean separation of the two men.
*One will be taken* in judgment. Since judgment is the sole emphasis in the
total passage this must be the meaning here. *The other* will be *left* to the
happy union with the returning Son of Man. Those who say that this refers
to the believer's being taken out of the world and the unbeliever's being
left in the world must reverse the illustration, which is then out of keeping
with the whole passage and not valid interpretation. Even in the two
illustrations of Noah and Lot it was the good who were left and the evil
who were by judgment taken out of the world.

Noah and Lot are representative of those who are *left,* that is, those who
do not fall under God's judgment. The people of Noah's day, the people of
Lot's day, and Lot's wife are representative of those who are *taken,* who
perish under God's judgment. The idea of separation in judgment related to
the Lord's return is a consistent pattern in the New Testament—the parable
of the tares (Matt. 13:24–30; 36–43); the parable of the net (Matt. 13:
47–50); the parable of the ten virgins (Matt. 25:1–13); the example story
of the sheep and the goats (Matt. 25:31–46). That is the most obvious
meaning of this passage.

*Two women grinding together* does not necessarily mean two adult
women. Again, the Greek uses the numeral two, followed by feminine
adjectives for *one . . . and the other.* The imagery is that of two women
at the household task of grinding grain, facing each other across the small
household millstone and turning the round flat stone. They could be mother
and daughter, mother and daughter-in-law, two sisters, or two female
servants. The important matter is that such close association will be struck
by separation. *One will be taken* in judgment; *the other left* for the union
with the returning Son of Man.

*Verse 36* in the KJV is an interpolation from Matthew 24:40. It obviously
belongs there, and its place is supported by all of the ancient manuscripts.
There is no manuscript authority for its presence in Luke before the sixth
century.

*Verse 37:* The disciples asked, *"Where, Lord?"* indicating that they did
not understand where this separation (vv. 34–35) was to take place.
Jesus answered with a proverb, *"Where the body is, there the eagles will
be gathered together."* In Matthew 24:28 this proverb applies to the false
reports of the Lord's return in connection with the destruction of Jerusalem.
The main verbal difference is that Matthew has "carcass," whereas Luke
has "body"—though RSV has "body" in both places. Both use the same
word for carnivorous birds in general. In Matthew it undoubtedly means
"vultures" in association with "carcass." Jerusalem would be like a rotten
carcass attacked by the Roman vultures.

To interpret the use of the proverb in Luke to refer to Jerusalem and
the Romans is erroneous. To understand *body* as a figure of the world as a
rotten carcass is to miss the distinction between Matthew's word and Luke's
word. It also puts one in the difficult position of finding some corresponding
meaning for the "eagles"—angels or the Lord himself. The most obvious

meaning of the proverb is the same as the proverb of the lightning flashing (v. 24). In fact, Matthew has both proverbs in the same verse though it leaves his understanding of the lightning proverb in doubt, because it is difficult to understand it in parallel to his application of the carcass and vultures proverb. Luke's use of them in parallel to the coming of the Son of Man is clearly drawn. Both refer to the self-evident nature of the coming. It will be as self-evident as the lightning flashing in one part of the sky but visible in every other part. It will be as self-evident as the presence of a body where eagles are gathered. The answer was not given geographically— the separation will be at some particular place. It was given logically—when it takes place it will be self-evident and unquestionable. No one will need to inform another as to what is taking place.

## 38. An Unjust Judge and a Just God (18:1–8)

*Verse 1:* Luke indicates that Jesus' purpose in this parable was to encourage his disciples. In his predictions of the difficult experiences they faced in the future (17:22), he had given them cause for discouragement. It must be recalled, too, that from his first prediction of his death (9:22–24) the Twelve had lived under a cloud of gloom and perplexity. They were nearing Jerusalem where death awaited him. He gave them this parable that they might see the importance of prayer and faith in opposition to losing heart in prolonged difficulty.

The parable has been named "the parable of the importunate widow" and "the parable of the unjust judge." The major emphasis is on the unjust judge who did not want to respond to needy petition in contrast to the just God who eagerly responds to petitions. The more appropriate title, therefore, is "the parable of the unjust judge."

*Verse 2: A judge who neither feared God nor regarded man:* This characterization justified Jesus' reference to the man as an *unrighteous judge* (v. 6), one who lacked an accurate sense of justice. The point of comparison in the parable is a judge without concern for man, versus a God who does have concern for man.

*Verse 3: A widow in that city:* She was a citizen of his town and, hence, one for whose welfare he was responsible as a judge.

*Who kept coming to him:* She recognized him as the right one to deal with her case. Because she felt the importance of her case, she found it necessary to go to the judge repeatedly to seek a just settlement.

*Vindicate me against my adversary:* Although her adversary is not identified and the nature of her grievance is not described, one safely assumes that it was some form of oppression in which someone was taking advantage of her defenseless widowhood. The place of widows as needy people is very prominent in the New Testament and there are more references to them in Luke than in any other book. The woman's adversary may have been some important person known to the judge. On another occasion, Jesus rebuked the Pharisees for taking advantage of their position of leadership in the community by devouring widows' houses (Luke 20:47).

*Verses 4–6:* After continuous refusal to make a decision in the case (v. 4), the judge finally decided to settle the woman's grievance. His thought

process may be paraphrased as follows: "I will not do it because I have fear
for God or concern for man—I have neither—but I will do it to get rid of
her continuous nagging" (vv. 4–5). Literally, he said, *because this widow
bothers me, I will vindicate her, or she will wear me out by her continual
coming.* Undue stress on that part of the parable has led to the view that
Jesus was teaching that persistent prayer will get from God that which he is
reluctant to give. The same meaning has been found in the similar parable
of the needy friend (Luke 11:14–36). This view overlooks the major point
of the parables—which is one of contrast (vv. 7–8)—and in so doing
misinterprets them. If a man can get from a friend what the friend does not
desire to give (11:14–36), and if a woman can get an unjust judge to do what
he does not want to do (18:1–8), *how much more* can one be encouraged
that he will receive from a God who delights to give (11:14–36) and who
is just (18:7–8) that for which he asks. The central teaching is not that
man can, by repeated prayer, break down the will of God. It is rather
that man can be encouraged in prayer by the realization that he prays to a
just God who desires to give and to do that which his child needs.

*Verse 7: Will not God vindicate his elect who call for relief?: Vindicate*
means to render justice in a given situation, "to do the just thing." The
emphatic construction of the question anticipates a strong affirmative answer:
"Yes; he most certainly will." He will see that justice is done in that their
troubles will not be without his undergirding presence and help. *Elect*
means literally "chosen ones." In the Gospels and the Epistles of Paul and
Peter it is a synonym for believers or Christians. God will hear their cry
in their distress and will help them.

*Will he delay long over them?:* The construction of this question leaves
the answer open without anticipating either a "No" or a "Yes." It raises
the question, "Will a just God delay an answer the way an unjust judge
does?"

*Verse 8* gives Jesus' answer to his own question: *he will vindicate them
speedily.* God will do the just thing, the right thing, by his people quickly
or without delay. Because he is a just God, he will do the right thing without
being begged. That is what Jesus meant to be the reason for his disciples'
not losing heart (v. 1).

*Nevertheless, when the Son of man comes, will he find faith on earth?*
The source of this question which closes the passage is a matter of divided
opinion. Was it a part of Jesus' saying, or was it Luke's comment as he
wrote a long time afterward? If Jesus said it, it represents some feeling of
pessimism or near despair as to whether or not his people in days of trouble
will pray or will lose heart ("faint," in KJV, v. 1). Even at the time, with
the difficulties he had predicted for this visit to Jerusalem, the Twelve were
showing more evidence of losing heart than of praying.

If the question is Luke's conclusion rather than Jesus', it reflects an appraisal of the attitudes and reactions in his own day—probably around A.D.
80—as some Christians under pressures of the world and disappointed in the
delay of the Lord's return were losing heart rather than praying.

Whether it was Jesus' question or Luke's question, it is relevant in every
age and to every individual. Just how courageous is any follower of Christ
in the face of difficulty and danger? Who betrays, as did Judas? Who denies,

as did Peter? Who runs away, as did nine of the Twelve? Who goes all the way to the cross, as did only one of them—the beloved disciple of John's Gospel?

### 39. The Parable of the Pharisee and the Publican (18:9–14)

Verses 9–14 contain another parable on the theme of prayer which relates it to the preceding parable. It closes with a lesson on humility which relates it to the paragraph which follows.

*Verse 9:* This parable was addressed *to some who trusted in themselves that they were righteous and despised others.* That is a clear reference to the Pharisees. *In themselves,* by their own efforts at obedience to the law of Moses, they considered themselves *righteous* or upright, meeting God's standard for conduct. In their self-righteous pride they despised all others who did not share that righteousness. They believed that they had God's approval and all other men his disapproval.

*Verse 10: Two men . . . one a Pharisee and the other a tax collector:* Two men who mutually regarded one another as opposites were the characters in Jesus' parable. *Pharisees* identified a religionist of the most strict sort. *Tax collector* ("publican" in KJV) identified a religionless man in the eyes of his contemporaries. (See discussion on 5:27.) As a Jew who had taken a Roman office to collect taxes from the Jews and for the Romans, he was loathed as a traitor to the nation and religion of his people. The tax collector would accept the Pharisee's appraisal of him as a religionless man and would agree that the Pharisee was his opposite.

*Went up into the temple to pray:* Both men possessed an inner motivation for prayer—communion with God. *The temple* was the heart of the Jewish religion and culture and one of the most magnificent buildings in the Roman world. Even if these two men were residents of Jerusalem, a visit for such a purpose would be awe-inspiring. If Jesus thought of them as pilgrims in the city for one of the rare visits, the Temple experience would be packed with emotion.

*Verse 11: The Pharisee stood and prayed:* Standing was one of many specified postures for prayer in the Jewish religion, so the man's posture itself was not blameworthy. On another occasion, however, Jesus charged with hypocrisy men who stood to pray with the motivation that others would see them praying in that position and be impressed (Matt. 6:5). Jesus did not regard such action as genuine prayer. There may have been something of that intended in his reference to this Pharisee as standing to pray.

*With himself* is an expression meaning precisely "facing himself." He looked himself straight in the face as he addressed God. It is a suggestive expression: in his consciousness of uprightness by his own power, he was his own "god" and was worshiping his own "creator." It was a monologue of self-praise; it was not prayer—communion with God.

*God, I thank thee:* He used the correct words for prayer. Thanks to God, properly considered, means thanks for what God has done for the one praying. This man was thanking God, not for what God had done for him, but for what the man had done for himself.

*That I am not like other men:* This was a general appraisal of himself in comparison to others. He was different; he was righteous—in his own opinion. The general appraisal is broken down into particular categories in the words that follow.

*Extortioners* were those who robbed others by exorbitant interest on loans. They sometimes required such valuable securities for loans that they could never be redeemed. The Greek word has the root meaning of grasping or rapacious and is the basis of the English word "harpy." In Greek mythology the Harpies were foul half-human and half-bird creatures which snatched men's souls from them. Fittingly the word came to mean extortioners. This Pharisee took pride in his freedom from that sin. He did not cheat in business.

*Unjust:* literally, "not upright." It refers to one who is not trustworthy, who never does the right thing. This Pharisee regarded himself as free from that sin. He was trustworthy.

*Adulterers:* those who have sexual relations with other than their own wives, and are unfaithful to their marriage responsibilities. This man was not guilty of that sin. In his own opinion he had not violated the seventh commandment on adultery (Exod. 20:14), as he had not violated the ninth commandment on trustworthiness (Exod. 20:16), nor the eighth commandment on stealing (Exod. 20:15).

*Or even like this tax collector:* From praising himself for freedom from three of the vicious sins prohibited in the Ten Commandments, the Pharisee turned to praise himself that he was not like the tax collector who had entered the Temple at the same time. The reference may be to tax collectors in general as traitors to their nation. The construction, however, is so emphatic—"this particular tax collector"—as to give the impression that as the Pharisee had been praying he had also been observing the struggle of the tax collector to give expression to his confession of his sins (v. 13). The Pharisee thanked God that he had no sin to confess.

*Verse 12: I fast twice a week:* Two days between sabbaths he abstained from food. This was going far beyond both God's requirement of observing the Day of Atonement as one day of fasting in the year (Lev. 16:29; 23:27), and the traditional four days out of the year which the Jews had established in their history. He practiced private fasting far beyond any expected requirement. On another occasion Jesus had rebuked fasting as a means of impressing others with one's piety (Matt. 6:16–18).

*I give tithes of all that I get* was another indication of his going beyond the prescribed regulations in the Jewish religion. He tithed even those things which the rabbis excluded from the tithing responsibility. (See exposition of Luke 11:42.)

Within themselves all the above practices were desirable. One who observed them with right motivation was to be commended. Wherein, then, was this Pharisee's failure? In his pride and self-righteousness he was guilty of the sin most displeasing to God—the sin of self-sufficiency which recognizes no need of God's power. He was conscious of no lack, but he lacked the most meaningful quality of the upright life—a sense of unworthiness and need which casts one upon God in trust for his merciful help.

*Verse 13: But the tax collector, standing afar off:* The adversative conjunction *but* prepares the reader for contrast between the two men. *Standing afar off* introduces the contrast. It suggests that he stood off to one side away from others, away from the Pharisees. His was an experience strictly between himself and God, as it would have been if he had been in his private room with the door fast shut, as Jesus had taught (Matt. 6:6).

*Would not even lift up his eyes to heaven:* Precisely rendered, the statement is that "he did not wish" to do so. With face downcast and a sense of unworthiness to look up to God he stood.

*Beat his breast* is an indication of his emotional distress. It was a practice customarily used to express agony. The impression is that the man could not utter the words within him. As if to force them out physically he *beat his breast* until the words came out.

*God, be merciful to me a sinner:* In these words was all the pent-up misery of a man conscious of his sin and his need of God. He began as the Pharisee began—*God*—but beyond that their words can only be contrasted. His prayer was everything the Pharisee's was not. The word translated *merciful* is not the usual New Testament word for mercy in the sense of having pity and helping. It is rather the word for the expiation of sin or for being reconciled to another by the removal of the sin which alienates them —"expiate my sin and be no longer alienated from me because of it."

*A sinner:* The Greek actually says "the sinner." It may be a conscious contrast with the Pharisee in the sense of "He is righteous and needs no expiation of sin; I am the sinner; I do need expiation." More likely, however, Jesus' emphasis was that this burdened confessor felt that he was *the* sinner of all sinners, the greatest of sinners. From the viewpoint of the Old Testament prophets, this was the prayer of a contrite heart which is pleasing to God.

*Verse 14:* The two men returned to their homes, but the tax collector went as a changed man, *justified,* right with God in the forgiveness of his confessed sins. In classic use, *justified* meant acquitted of the charges or pronounced not guilty. In the New Testament, the word took on a more vital significance in the sense of sins forgiven and character renewed on the basis of confession and faith. While that use is usually associated with Paul (particularly in Rom. 3:21–31), it fits the use in this parable. The permanence of his condition is emphasized in the grammatical construction—"a man in a justified state of being" is a good rendering of the term. He went to the Temple conscious of his sin; he went back to his home conscious of the well-being of forgiveness and new life.

*Rather than the other:* The Pharisee also went *down to his house,* but with no change in his life. He went to the Temple filled with pride in his worthiness through his own efforts and unaware of the fact that such pride is itself sin. He went through the form of prayer but it was more a matter of talking to himself about his piety than a matter of talking to God about his need. He went back to his home an unchanged man, no better for the experience, still a sinner.

There is something a bit terrifying about the parable—the prospect it places before the reader today. There is within every person that which makes it possible for him to do the same thing the Pharisee did. He can go to the place of worship and go through the forms of worship and still go home the same person he was. He has been through the form but not the function of worship. Nothing has happened; nothing is changed.

*For every one who exalts himself will be humbled, but he who humbles himself will be exalted:* This conclusion may be the words of Jesus on this occasion or they may be a proverb of Jesus from some other occasion which Luke applied to this parable. The same proverb is used in other places in the New Testament. (There is a hint of it in Matt. 18:4. In Matt. 23:12 it has only grammatical differences from this Luke 18:14 form. In the Luke 14:11 parallel to Matt. 23:12, the form is identical to Luke 18:14. In 1 Pet. 5:6, it appears in a different verbal form but it is the same proverb.)

Whether it is Jesus' conclusion or Luke's it is a very fitting one. The form is that of chiasmos; exalts-humbled versus humbles-exalted. The force is that of paradox: the way up is down but the way down is up. This is a classic example of wisdom literature in the New Testament.

## 40. Little Children and Kingdom Children (18:15–17)

These verses continue the theme of humility. As Jesus had used the tax collector to teach humility, he also used little children. (The parallels, with some verbal differences, are Matt. 19:13–15 and Mark 10:13–16.) A similar teaching is in Matthew 18:1–4 in answer to the disciples' question about who is greatest in the kingdom of heaven. That is the setting in which Matthew uses Jesus' parable of the lost sheep (18:10–14) to illustrate God's concern for little children. Jesus' concern for them was demonstrated in this passage in Luke by his receiving little children and using them as object lessons when the disciples were trying to keep them away from him.

*Verse 15: They were bringing even infants to him:* In many paintings of this scene, mothers are the ones who are bringing the children. This is a normal assumption. Actually, those who brought them are identified only as *they.* No pronoun is used to indicate gender; the subject is in the verb. *Infants* is used only in Luke's account. The word was used of unborn and very young babies. Paul uses it of Timothy who had received religious instruction from babyhood (2 Tim. 3:15). Luke uses it of the embryo in Elizabeth's womb (Luke 2:41–44). He also uses it in Acts 7:19 regarding Pharaoh's slaughter of the Jewish babies during the bondage in Egypt. Matthew and Mark use a different word, which Luke also uses in verse 16, meaning very young children in contrast to a related word for older children or youths. From all of this, it appears that babies in arms as well as other young children, both boys and girls, were brought to Jesus.

*That he might touch them:* Matthew says the mothers wanted Jesus to "lay his hands on" the children "and pray," which he did. Mark concludes the incident with the statement that Jesus "took them in his arms and blessed them, laying his hands upon them." The desire of the mothers was that their little ones might have the "God bless you" of the kind of person they knew Jesus to be.

*The disciples . . . rebuked them: Rebuke* here means to intimidate. The disciples tried to prevent the mothers and children from getting to Jesus. Their motivation was doubtless to protect Jesus from such small matters in order that he might not be distracted from more important ministries. Their motivation was good; their sense of values was in error.

*Verse 16: Let the children come . . . do not hinder them:* The positive and negative commands reflect Jesus' sense of values. He did not regard the children's coming as an interference with other matters, but welcomed them. He knew their importance to God, and desired for them every possible spiritual or religious advantage. Mark says that Jesus "was indignant" with the disciples for trying to keep the children away from him.

*For to such belongs the kingdom of God:* The Greek word translated *such* means kind or quality—of people of their nature. The RSV translation *to such belongs* is more interpretation than translation. The verb does not mean *belong;* it is the simple verb for being. Literally, the expression is "for of such ones as these is the kingdom of God." The emphasis is on their nature, not on what they possess.

*Verse 17* makes clear Jesus' meaning. One cannot enter the kingdom of God unless he possesses the childlike nature. On another occasion the disciples had asked Jesus who was greatest in the kingdom. His answer was that to enter the kingdom one must "turn" from seeking greatness and like a little child be a receiver. And only "the one who humbles himself like this child" is the greatest in the kingdom (Matt. 18:3–4).

In all these related passages on children, the emphasis is on the quality of childlike humility. "Kingdom children" are those who possess the humility of "little children" in contrast to the grasping-for-greatness of adults.

### 41. The Rich Ruler and the Way to Eternal Life (18:18–30)

From the viewpoint of teaching, this passage is closely related to the two preceding ones. It emphasizes the same qualities of kingdom citizens— self-abasement, humility, the consciousness of one's littleness in contrast to a consciousness of greatness. The ones who have no consciousness of merit by piety (the publican), or greatness (the little children), or wealth (those who have no riches) are the ones who enter the kingdom of God. The parallel passages are Mark 10:17–31, Matthew 19:16–30.

*Verse 18: Ruler:* one of the officers in the local synagogue. Since the town is not identified, no more of his official position can be known. It is clear that he was a *very rich man* (v. 23), and Matthew states that he was a "young man"—a word for one in his middle twenties. All these details indicate a man of prominence in his community.

*Asked him:* Luke gives no more than the factual inquiry. Mark states that Jesus was on his way out of town when the man came running to kneel before him in making his inquiry. This suggests genuine sincerity on his part rather than the interpretation sometimes given that he was another self-complacent Pharisee. His manner in asking and Jesus' manner in responding do not warrant the charge of complacency; the young man was sincerely interested in Jesus' view of how one might have eternal life.

*Good Teacher:* He addressed Jesus as a teacher of the religion of Israel. It was a religion which began with the first principle of God in relationship to man, and the good life which grows out of that relationship. *Good* meant morally good when applied to persons and beneficially good when applied to things or actions. Luke here follows Mark's *Good Teacher,* but Matthew changed the Markan reading to "Teacher, what good deed must I do?" This change is in line with Matthew's interest in the Jew's religion of good works. Mark and Luke appear to have the original wording. The young man recognized Jesus as a *Good Teacher* whose opinion would be valuable.

*What shall I do to inherit eternal life?* The young man recognized that "life" consists of more than "being"; there is more to life than mere physical existence. The word rendered *life* is the one consistently used in the New Testament for the transcendent life which consists of a right relationship with God. It is a major concept in Jesus' teaching contained in the Gospel of John. It is also magnified by Paul. It occurs less frequently in the synoptic Gospels, but its meaning is the same.

*Eternal* has both temporal and qualitative significance. In Jesus' use, *eternal life* means a quality of life in relationship with God which begins in this world and continues forever; it is not even interrupted by the physical dissolution of the death of the body. It is as eternal as God is eternal— without end of being. In Jesus' view, those who have, by faith, committed themselves to God have already entered into that life which never ends.

Was this what the young ruler meant by the term *eternal life?* If so, the assumption is almost unavoidable that he had heard Jesus in some discussion of the theme. While that is possible, it does not appear to be probable. Most likely the young man was thinking in terms of the best kind of life for here and now—the highest good attainable by man in response to God. Whether he thought in terms of life beyond death, of resurrection—or of resurrection of good people only, as some Jews believed —is not clear. It is clear that in his answer Jesus challenged the young man to a demanding kind of life in this world—one so demanding that the youth sadly declined to attempt it (v. 23), and "went away sorrowful" (Mark 10:22; Matt. 19:22).

*Verse 19: Why do you call me good? No one is good but God alone:* In Jesus' mind absolute moral goodness was a characteristic to be named of God only. His seeming to turn the word away from himself was no reflection of consciousness of sin on his part; it was rather a genuine indication that there was in him the very self-abasement and humility which he upheld as necessary traits of kingdom citizens. In his incarnation he did not welcome the attribute *good* as he understood that it belonged only to God. His question was a word of caution: "Be careful how you use the word 'good'; it fits God only."

It has been suggested that this young ruler was recognizing Jesus as "a teacher come from God" (like Nicodemus, the older ruler, in John 3:2, 4). If Jesus so understood it, he may have sensed that the young ruler was hoping to receive eternal life from him. In that case, Jesus' answer called his attention to the fact that only God could give eternal life and only God could dictate the way to obtain eternal life; whatever Jesus could give would come from God.

*Verse 20:* Traditionally in the history of Israel, the way to the life well-pleasing to God was the way of obedience to the commandments of God— the Ten Commandments of Moses' two tablets of stone. To these laws for life Jesus pointed the young ruler's attention—*you know the commandments.* Implicit in Jesus' answer is the meaning that to obey these commandments is to have eternal life. In Matthew's account that is made explicit, "If you would enter life, keep the commandments." This was good Jewish religious thinking.

According to Luke, Jesus quoted five of the Ten Commandments in this order: the seventh, *Do not commit adultery;* the sixth, *Do not kill;* the eighth, *Do not steal;* the ninth, *Do not bear false witness;* the fifth, *Honor your father and mother.* While the order differs from that in Exodus 20:12–16 and Deuteronomy 5:16–20, this quotation includes all of the "second table"—man in relation to his fellowman—except the tenth, "Do not covet." Mark has a different order from Luke but the same commandments with the addition of the tenth in his "Do not defraud." Matthew also has a different order from Luke but the same commandments, and then adds (from Lev. 19:18), "You shall love your neighbor as yourself."

This freedom of the Gospel writers in reporting Jesus' words indicates that they are not simply reporting. They are reporting event and interpreting meaning at the same time. Jesus did include love for neighbor as a law which ranked at the level of love for God (Matt. 22:39). Matthew legitimately uses it in this event too. While Mark alone includes the tenth commandment in Jesus' quotation, Luke has it clearly in the background of Jesus' words in verse 22. (See discussion below.)

*Verse 21:* Jesus quoted these commandments because they were the easiest by which man might measure his conduct. The first four of the Ten Commandments are of such subjective nature that one might not feel competent to judge whether or not he had obeyed them. It is easier, however, to know whether one has in physical action killed, or stolen, or lied, or committed adultery. Reviewing his experience the young ruler boldly affirmed, "All these I have observed from my youth." He felt perfectly secure in his conduct, but he still sensed a lack; he did not have that *eternal life* which he desired; he sought the way to have it.

*Verse 22:* In his response, Jesus led the young ruler to see that not even a sincere effort at obedience to the law could give him life. All the law could do was point him to his need and reflect his inability to keep it. The young man's downfall was in relation to the tenth command, "You shall not covet."

*One thing you still lack:* The young man's failure was not at the point of outward effort to obey the commandments of God. It was rather at the point of inner understanding of the true purpose of the commandments. Jesus taught that God's real purpose for the commandments was not just regulation of outward conduct—physical killing, or sexual impurity, or dishonest action. It was rather to regulate the inner disposition which, unchecked, led to the /physical act of sin. So he said that the disposition of anger came under the law prohibiting killing; the desire for adultery came under the law prohibiting the act of adultery; the wish to deceive in giving testimony came under the law prohibiting lying (Matt. 5:21–48).

Paul found in his experience that the tenth commandment summarized all the others. "You shall not covet" meant that he was not even to want to do what was prohibited in the law. The desire to do what the commandments prohibited was the evidence to him that something was wrong between him and the God who gave the commandments (Rom. 7:7–12).

*Sell all that you have and distribute to the poor:* This was Jesus' way of showing the young man exactly where his lack was. In outward action he did injury to no one—he did not kill, steal, defile, lie, dishonor. But in inner disposition he had no real concern for the welfare of others; he had no compassion for them in their need; love was absent. Both Paul and James used the law of love for one's fellowman as the summation of all the other laws—those prohibiting murder, theft, lying (Rom. 13:9; James 2:11). James called the law of love for one's neighbor "the royal law" (2:8), the law for king's sons. Matthew rightly understood that Jesus' enumeration of the commandments had to include this law. At that point lay the young ruler's failure; outwardly he kept the commandments, but inwardly he did not love his neighbor.

*You will have treasure in heaven:* This idea of using earthly possessions to store up treasure in heaven occurs often in Jesus' teaching. (See the discussion on Luke 12:33–34, and 16:13.) Jesus believed that heaven will be richer for one who has used earthly riches in good stewardship to God and compassion for needy people.

*Come, follow me:* Jesus invited the young man to follow him in total rejection of self-interest, leaving his wealth and position and giving himself to God in humble service to suffering humanity. In doing that the young ruler would find that *eternal life* for which he yearned but which he lacked. The price was high but it was small in comparison to what it could buy.

*Verse 23:* For that young man, the price was too high. When he learned from Jesus just what it would cost if he was to secure that sense of fulfillment in having eternal life, *he became sad.* Other translations capture the intensive expression better—"he became exceeding sorrowful" (KJV). Mark has "his countenance fell, and he went away sorrowful" (10:22). The reason for his sorrow was that he knew he was not to possess eternal life. *He was very rich* meant that he was not willing to give his riches up to others —although they needed it greatly—or to give himself in self-denial and humble service to God. In a manner of speaking, he did not have great possessions; the great possessions had him.

*Verse 24:* As the young man went sadly away, Jesus commented on how difficult it is for the rich to enter the kingdom of God. *How hard* is the rendering of an expression meaning "how very difficult." The remaining part of the sentence is not a denial that they do enter; it is not a matter of impossibility, but of extreme difficulty.

*Verse 25:* Just how very difficult it is—seemingly impossible—Jesus illustrated in one of his most striking hyperboles: *it is easier for a camel to go through the eye of a needle than for a rich man to enter the kingdom of God.*

The camel was the biggest animal commonly known in Palestine. The eye of a needle was the smallest hole commonly known. The ludicrous picture of trying to drive or lead a camel through such a hole made the figure dramatic and unforgettable. The absurdity of the figure has led to many efforts to make it a more natural one. In his commentary on Luke, Cyril of Alexandria (died A.D. 444) substituted the word "rope" for "camel" —it is easier to thread a needle with a rope than to get a rich man into the kingdom. (In Greek there is only one letter's difference—*kamelos,* camel vs.

*kamilos,* rope.) The word for rope does appear in some of the ancient Byzantine texts of Luke, but not in any Greek texts. Some of the late manuscripts may have been influenced by Cyril's use.

Much later, around the fifteenth century, the popular view arose that there was a low gate through the wall of the city of Jerusalem that was called the "needle's eye gate." A camel could get through it, but first he had to get down on his knees and have his pack removed; then he could squeeze through. Delightful allegory is immediately apparent in the need for the rich man to get down on his knees in humility and give up his rich burden so he can squeeze through! Historically, the view has no validity. In reputable works on the ancient city of Jerusalem, one searches in vain for reference to such a gate.

Theologically both of these efforts at a more natural understanding of Jesus' figure—rope or gate—miss his entire point. The very exaggeration of the "entrance" to the absurdity of a camel's going through a needle's eye emphasizes the idea of the impossible where human action is concerned. The Babylonian Talmud includes a rabbinical saying that not even in a dream does a man see an elephant going through a needle's eye! Elephants were a common sight in Babylon, but in Palestine the camel was a more natural figure for the proverb. In the Koran, Muhammad predicted that those who rejected his message would not enter Paradise until a camel passes through the eye of a needle! The impossible was the point in all three of these proverbial sayings.

*Verses 26–27* reveal that Jesus was using this figure of the impossible in order that he might show it *is* possible for a rich man to enter the kingdom.

*Those who heard:* Matthew identifies these hearers as "the disciples." The reference is apparently to the Twelve. They are definitely the ones involved in the discussion which follows Peter's question in verse 28.

*Then who can be saved?* Their response was one of amazement (Matt. 19:25; Mark 10:26). The common view was that wealth indicated God's favor. (See discussion on Luke 16:14, 19–31.) Here they understood Jesus to mean that it is not possible for a rich man to enter the kingdom—as impossible as for a camel to pass through a needle's eye. Their wonder was, "If a rich man cannot enter the kingdom, who can? *Who can be saved?*" Some fifth-century and later manuscripts of Mark 10:24 have Jesus saying, "how hard it is for those who trust in riches to enter into the kingdom of God," but the older manuscripts do not have the qualifier, "those who trust in riches." It is probably the attempt of a late scribe to show that the difficulty is not in having riches but in trusting in them as the way into the kingdom.

*What is impossible with men is possible with God:* This was the climax toward which Jesus moved. By the power of men it is impossible for any man to enter the kingdom, rich or poor, Jew or Gentile. But by the power of God it is possible for every man to enter the kingdom—even the poor, rich, Jew, Gentile. The account moves from law to grace. It is impossible for any man to enter the kingdom through his own efforts in trying to keep the law, but it is possible for every man to enter through God's redemptive grace. This is a thoroughly worked out concept of Paul in his sermons in

Acts and in his Epistles—particularly Galatians, Romans, and Ephesians. However, the concept cannot be attributed in Luke to Paul's influence. The concept is also in Mark and Matthew, and its foundation is in Jesus' interpretation of God, man, law, sin, and salvation.

Verses 28–30: In these verses the discussion returns to the theme of giving up one's possessions and following Jesus in service to humanity. The rich young ruler did not meet that test. He held on to his goods and went away from Jesus. Peter, so often the spokesman for the Twelve, reminded Jesus that he and the others had done what the rich man had refused to do.

*Verse 28: Lo:* This little word is most meaningful in the New Testament. It is the imperative form of the verb "to look" or "to see," and it is always followed by something dramatic: "Look! the Lamb of God" (John 1:29); "Look! I am making everything new" (Rev. 21:5, author's translation). Here the dramatic thing which follows is that which the Twelve have done: "Look! We have left all our things and followed you" (author's translation).

*We have left our homes:* The *we* is emphatic—*we* in contrast to the rich young ruler who had departed. *Our homes* is the translation of an expression meaning precisely "all the things which belong to us." The RSV rendering *homes* is due to Jesus' emphasis in the next verse on leaving one's home and loved ones to serve him. In the Matthew and Mark parallels the word is simply "everything." When Jesus called Peter, Andrew, James, and John, they left their nets, goats, father, and fellow workers to follow. Matthew had left his tax business to follow. They had, indeed, done what the young man had failed to do.

In Peter's statement there was an implied question, or at least an invitation for Jesus to apply his teaching to their experience. In Matthew the implied question is stated explicitly, "What then shall we have?" or, very literally, "What do we get out of it?" In the background of Peter's question there is the suggestion of a question as to whether or not it was worth it. They had left homes, friends, business; they were on the way to Jerusalem where he told them they would face danger, mistreatment, rejection. What were they to realize out of it all? Was the goal worth the giving?

*Verse 29:* Jesus assured them that their gain was greater than what they had given up, both in this age and also in the age to come. The one who has left *house . . . wife . . . brothers . . . parents . . . children, for the sake of the kingdom of God* does not lose. The word translated *for the sake of* means "because of" or "on account of." It was because of what the kingdom of God was and what it meant to them and their people that they had given up all their things to follow him.

*Verse 30: Who will not receive manifold more: Receive* translates a word meaning "get in return for what is given up." *Manifold* means "many times more" than what has been given up. Luke simplifies Mark's wording here which is "a hundred times" applied to every object given up—a hundred houses, a hundred brothers, a hundred sisters, a hundred mothers, a hundred children! The exaggerated number is impressive—you gave up a home—you have a hundred homes; you gave up a brother—you have a hundred brothers! Countless followers of Jesus through the centuries of Christian history have found that this is true.

But the return is not for this age only; it is for the age to come. *In this time* is a simplification of Mark's "now in this time." Matthew has no temporal reference though one is implied. *In the age to come* meant, in Jewish religious thought, the future glorious age of the Messiah. *Eternal life* was what the rich young ruler desired, but not enough to meet God's terms for it. The disciples had met those terms; it was theirs and would be theirs in the age beyond this age of material concerns and possessions. Together, the two expressed total gain; one does not really "give up" things and life. He gains them for this world and the next.

### 42. The Third Passion Prediction (18:31–34)

In Mark's account of the preceding incident, Jesus says that along with gaining a hundredfold of everything they had given up, the disciples would have "persecutions." Luke omits the persecution reference, but he includes at this point the third of Jesus' teaching concerning the fate which awaited him in Jerusalem.

*Verse 31* was addressed only to the Twelve. Jesus took them apart from all the others for this instruction. *We are going up to Jerusalem* suggests that they were nearing the end of the much interrupted journey they had started (9:51) soon after his first (9:22) and second (9:44–45) instructions concerning his death. Although several months had intervened since that first occasion, the Twelve proved to be no more willing to accept it or able to understand it.

*Everything that is written . . . by the prophets:* In 13:33–34, Jesus had referred to the commonly held tradition that Jerusalem was the place where God's prophets were slain. From the time of his baptism he had identified himself with the Suffering Servant of Isaiah. He saw Israel as an entire people suffering in God's redemptive purpose but narrowing down to one person, in whose suffering that redemptive purpose would have its realization; he understood that he was that person. Just what writings he had in mind here is not indicated, but one can guess their identity from his known use elsewhere of suffering passages from Deuteronomy, Isaiah, and the Psalms.

*Will be accomplished:* The verb means "to bring to an end" and the construction means that in his suffering all of the prophecies would be brought to the end to which they looked. The verb is used in Jesus' last expression from the cross in John 19:30, "It is finished," meaning that God's redemptive work through the ages had been brought to the end toward which it moved.

*Verse 32a:* This is Jesus' first explicit statement that his death would be at the hands of Gentiles—the Romans. In the previous passages (Luke 9:22; Mark 8:31–33; Matt. 16:21 and Luke 9:43–44; Mark 9:30–32; Matt. 17:22–23), he had spoken of his death in Jerusalem, but the only agents mentioned were the Jews—elders, scribes, chief priests. Death at their hands would have been by stoning. This was also the first time, according to Matthew, that Jesus explicitly names the method of his death—crucifixion (20:19). For the first time Jesus' previous discussion about taking up the cross and following him—the cross as a symbol of identification with him— could really be meaningful.

*He will be delivered* naturally suggests that someone would be the agent. Although the verb is the one used later for Judas's identification of Jesus to the arresting officers (22:48, *betray*), that was not likely his meaning on this occasion. It was the Jewish authorities who ultimately *delivered* him to the Romans.

*To the Gentiles*: The Jews did not have the authority to carry out capital punishment (John 18:31). If they had stoned Jesus to death, it would have been a case of mob violence. For his death to be legal, it had to be carried out by the Roman authorities.

*Verses 32b–33:* The verbs used in these verses forecast Jesus' mistreatment in his trial and death, and all of these actions appear at different places in his trial and execution. Some interpreters have thought that the details of spitting, scourging, crucifying indicate the evangelists' handling or shaping of Jesus' prediction in the light of what actually happened later. This is not necessarily true. Roman crucifixions were common in Jesus' day. He had doubtless seen them and he knew their revolting details. Too, some of his words recall passages from his favorite Suffering Servant section of Isaiah. The materials for his prediction were in his knowledge and the events were to be expected.

*Mocked* may be understood by reading Luke 23:35–43 (with Mark 15:29–32; Matt. 27:39–44). The people made a game of mocking him at his inability to save himself from the cross when he had promised to save others.

*Shamefully treated* may be understood by reading the treatment of the Jewish authorities when they voted him worthy of death and then heaped their scorn upon him by blindfolding him, striking him, and challenging him to guess who had struck him (Mark 14:65; Matt. 26:67–68; Luke 22:63–65). It may also be understood by reading the description of the Roman soldiers playing a game of "King of the Jews" with him by dressing him in a royal robe, making for him a crown of thorns, giving him a weed as a scepter, and bowing their knees in mock obeisance as they addressed him, "Hail, King of the Jews!" (Mark 15:16–19; Matt. 27:27–30; John 19:2–3).

*Spit upon* recalls Isaiah 50:6, "I hid not my face from shame and spitting." Both the Jewish authorities and the Roman soldiers spat on him (Matt. 26:67; 27:30; Mark 15:19).

*Scourge* also recalls Isaiah 50:6, "I gave my back to the smiters." Matthew, Mark, Luke, and John all refer to his being struck by the Jewish authorities and the Roman soldiers. Pilate also had Jesus scourged by the whips of the Roman soldiers. He seemed to hope that such gruelling punishment—which sometimes killed the prisoner—would satisfy the Jewish authorities and they would not insist on his death (John 19:4–5).

*Kill him:* Luke makes no explicit reference to the means of death. Matthew explicitly has "crucify" (20:19). Since the Roman method of execution was crucifixion, the Twelve doubtless anticipated this in Jesus' statement that the "Gentiles" would kill him (v. 32).

*On the third day he will rise* repeats his prediction on the two former occasions of his speaking of his death. In each case, without exception, when he spoke of his death he spoke of his resurrection on the third day. This

becomes an important part of subsequent events in that when he was crucified, the Twelve did not anticipate his resurrection and were slow to believe
it and to be convinced of it.

*Verse 34:* The reaction of the Twelve to Jesus' words followed the pattern
of the two former occasions. At the first announcement they resisted it and,
under Peter's leadership, argued against it (Mark 8:32-33; Matt. 16:22-23).
On the second occasion, they were greatly distressed (Matt. 17:22); they
did not understand; it was as if understanding were concealed from them,
and they were afraid to ask about it (Luke 9:45).

On this third occasion, Matthew and Mark record no reaction of the
Twelve. Luke, however, repeats the previous reaction: *they understood none
of these things.* They were aware of no reason for Jesus' execution by the
Romans. He had done nothing that would warrant crucifixion. They were
fully aware of his conflict with the Jewish authorities, but that warranted
only being severely rebuked by the authorities or perhaps even banned from
fellowship for not keeping the sabbath laws—not death. Besides all that,
they believed he was the Messiah and there was no place in their thinking
for the death of the Messiah.

*This saying was hidden from them:* It was not *hidden* in that Jesus did
not want them to understand. It was *hidden* because of their reluctance to
accept it and because there was nothing in their experience to help them to
understand the reference to being raised from the dead. They had seen him
"raise" the daughter of Jairus when she had been dead only a few minutes
and the son of the widow at Nain when he had been dead for a few hours.
But who was to raise him three days after his death? Luke's final statement
summarizes their perplexity; they simply *did not grasp what was said.*

### 43. Healing a Blind Man near Jericho (18:35-43)

Frequent references indicate Luke's interest in Jesus' coming to the end
of his journey to Jerusalem (17:1; 18:31; 19:11, 28, 41). Here are recorded
two events near the end of the journey—the healing of a blind man and the
salvation of a publican (19:1-10). They took place in Jericho which was
only a few miles from Jerusalem. The parallel accounts are Matthew 20:29-
34, Mark 10:46-52.

*Verse 35: As he drew near to Jericho:* Mark and Matthew indicate that
this healing incident took place as Jesus left Jericho. The difference of detail
is unimportant. Those seeking exact harmony of accounts have conjectured
that the event took place between the Old Testament city of Jericho and the
New Testament city of Jericho about one mile south of the old city. If
harmony is required, that is as good an explanation as any.

*A blind man was sitting by the roadside begging:* Matthew has two blind
men; Mark has one blind man and gives his name, Bartimaeus; Mark also
has the detail that the blind man was a beggar. Many people were going to
Jerusalem for Passover. This was the only road of importance. The blind
man was in a strategic place for begging alms from religious people.

*Verse 36: Hearing a multitude going by:* That was not unusual. He was
there because that was where the crowds would be. There was something

about the conduct of that particular multitude which caused him to sense
something unusual or different. No indication is given of what it was. Probably it was the excited voices of those who always gathered about Jesus to
hear his teaching or just to see him.

*Verse 37: Jesus of Nazareth is passing by:* Frequent references in the
Gospels indicate the spreading fame of Jesus as a healer and teacher. The
man may have heard of Jesus, or the people may have given him a more
detailed report than is recorded in the Gospels. He was convinced that Jesus
could help him.

*Verse 38: Jesus, Son of David, have mercy on me: Jesus* was a very common name. *Son of David* was a messianic title. There is nothing to indicate
that the man had knowledge of Jesus' relationship to David by physical
descent. The implication is that those who told the blind man what was
happening told him also that Jesus was regarded as the anticipated Messiah.

*Verses 39–41:* When people tried to prevent his calling out to stop Jesus,
the beggar cried out all the more for this *Son of David* to have mercy on
him. Attracted by the call for help, Jesus asked that the man be brought to
him. Even his final journey to Jerusalem and the cross he would interrupt
at the call for mercy. Pointedly he asked, *"What do you want me to do for
you?"* Was the man wanting Jesus to give him money? Or did he wish something more than that? This was another instance of Jesus' calling forth the
response of faith from a person desiring healing.

*Lord, let me receive my sight:* The answer was also pointed. He asked
no money; others could give that. He asked what he believed only this one
could give—his sight. If he had that, he would not have to beg. The man's
precise statement was "Lord, that I may see again."

*Verse 42:* Jesus responded just as precisely, "See again" or *receive your
sight.* Matthew says that Jesus was moved with compassion at the request.
Here was a man reduced to begging because he could not see to earn. He
called for Jesus' merciful help because he believed Jesus could give him sight.
Jesus related the healing to the man's faith: *your faith has made you well.*
The grammatical construction means permanent healing. There would be
no return of darkness for this man.

*Verse 43:* The healing was instantaneous. The man joined the company
of those who were following Jesus, expressing his praise to God. There are
theological overtones in this story which are more commonly associated with
John's Gospel. Jesus' word translated *has made you well* (v. 42) literally
means, "has saved you." The word is used in the New Testament for salvation from physical danger, from imprisonment, from sickness, and from
sin. There is a suggestion that this man not only was "saved" from physical
blindness but also from "spiritual blindness." Hence, his following Jesus
with his doxology to God. All who witnessed the event joined in a community
of praise to God for what he had done through Jesus of Nazareth, Son of
David.

## 44. The Salvation of Zacchaeus in Jericho (19:1–10)

*Verses 1–2:* The RSV omits some of the drama in Luke's opening words,

"Lo! a man named Zacchaeus . . . *he* was a head tax collector . . . *he* was rich!" (author's translation). The emphasis on the man, his importance, and his wealth, is beyond the ordinary. As *chief tax collector,* Zacchaeus had a number of tax collectors working under his supervision. Jericho was a very wealthy center. It was famous for its balsam gardens which had once been Anthony's gift to Cleopatra and had been redeemed later by Herod the Great, who desired their great revenue for himself. The place of toll would be at some point on the road where the heavy trade from the palm groves and balsam gardens could be taxed. Through his work for the Romans Zacchaeus had come to be a very wealthy Jew.

*Verses 3–4:* Zacchaeus was big in wealth but little in stature. Unable to see Jesus because of the crowd, he ran ahead of the procession until he came to a sycamore tree which he climbed in order to see over the crowd. His pride of position in the city was secondary to his desire to see the teacher from Nazareth. This *sycamore* tree was variously called sycamore-fig or fig-mulberry and is still found in Palestine. Its leaves and the white patches on trunk and branches from peeling bark make it resemble the American sycamore. However, its branches frequently spread out from the trunk at a much lower point, making it easy to climb and affording a good perch for this publican. The fruit of the tree is similar to small figs, but they grow in clusters right out of the large branches rather than on smaller twigs. In no other way does it resemble the fig tree and in no way at all does it resemble the tree commonly known as mulberry.

*Verses 5–7:* Probably to Zacchaeus's surprise Jesus called him by name, asked that he descend from the tree, and informed him that he desired to be his house guest for the day. Had Jesus known Zacchaeus before? Did someone indentify the rich tax collector in his unusual perch for Jesus? The text gives no clue. In the synoptics, there is none of the emphasis in John on Jesus' remarkable intuitive knowledge of men. Details of how Jesus knew Zacchaeus is not a part of Luke's story.

*I must stay at your house today:* This was the heart of Luke's interest. Zacchaeus as a Jew collecting taxes for Rome was, in the eyes of the other Jews, an outcast and traitor to his people. To enter his house would be for them as repelling an idea as to enter the house of a Gentile. But Jesus did not wait for Zacchaeus's invitation. Zacchaeus, knowing how people felt about him, probably would not have considered inviting a good Jew to be his guest.

*Received him with joy:* Zacchaeus's joy in welcoming Jesus into his home was stimulated not only by Jesus' willingness to ignore the social bans imposed by the Jews, but also by the opportunity of a visit with this well-known rabbi. The healing of the blind beggar on the edge of the town may have intensified his interest in Jesus.

*They all murmured:* The reaction of the crowd accompanying Jesus was not one of joy. They were offended that Jesus would go *to be guest of a man who is a sinner* (v. 7). To be a guest at a meal was the most intimate fellowship they knew. They regarded such fellowship with a social and religious outcast as unthinkable.

*Verse 8:* All that took place during Jesus' visit in Zacchaeus's home is not indicated. What teaching did Jesus give? What instructions on the way of salvation and life were discussed? The Scripture is silent. Whatever it was, whatever the total background of Zacchaeus's relationship to Jesus, the result was positive. Zacchaeus's announcement indicated that.

*Zacchaeus stood* most naturally suggests that he arose from his place at the dinner table. His standing indicates a spirit of determination—resolution for action.

*Half of my goods I give to the poor:* Giving to the needy was a common indication of piety. To give half of his possessions meant a tremendous gift; he was known to be a wealthy man. This was an expression of generosity similar to a king's saying "half of my kingdom." Whether literal or hyperbole it indicated remarkable generosity.

*If I have defrauded any one of anything:* The grammatical construction is one which ordinarily affirms the condition and more precisely translated would be, "Since I have defrauded." The nature of the tax collector's office was conducive to fraud. The officer paid an agreed amount for the privilege of collecting taxes. All he collected over that amount was his profit. Only a scrupulously honest man would collect merely a fair amount. Exorbitant overcharges were expected. Few Jews who became agents of the Romans would likely have been scrupulously honest. Doubtless Zacchaeus had amassed his wealth by fraud.

*I restore it fourfold:* From a practical viewpoint it would likely have been impossible for Zacchaeus to determine all the cases of fraud and the amount involved in each. Such careful records were not likely kept. There may have been some outstanding cases where such determination could be made and fourfold restitution could be made. It is more likely that Zacchaeus meant that by giving half of his wealth to the poor, he would be balancing the scales by four to one repayment for fraud, even though all the individuals defrauded might not receive back four to one. In doing this, Zacchaeus was going beyond the requirement of the law which made a distinction between fraud and theft. In the case of fraud, the individual was required to return the part illegally gained and add to it one-fifth of the amount (Lev. 6:5; Num. 5:6). In the case of theft, the individual, when apprehended, was required to repay either four to one or five to one for what he had stolen (Exod. 22:1; 33:15). Zacchaeus took the viewpoint that his fraudulent dealings were all to be regarded as theft and he would restore on that basis.

In his action was reflected the attitude of confession of sin and the desire to make amends for his sin. All of this may have been a part of Jesus' discussion with him, the Twelve, and any others present. He did not offer his restitution as penance to gain divine favor but with the spontaneous gratitude of one who has come to know the joy of confession and the sense of well-being in the commitment of himself to God's way. It was not labeled faith, but it had all the marks of genuine faith—the desire to do something for others in response to what Jesus had done for him.

*Verse 9:* The statement is that Jesus said all the next words *to him,* that is, Zacchaeus. Because of the grammatical construction, however, it is more natural to understand the first phrase as addressed directly to Zacchaeus and the second as an aside to the others present. To Zacchaeus: *Today salvation has come to this house.* To the others: *since he also is a son of Abraham.*

*Today salvation has come:* Zacchaeus had come out of his old life of sin and into a new life of obedience to God. *Has come* could be more precisely translated "has come to be." *Today* emphasizes the present reality. That which had not been before had now actually come to be—salvation. In the New Testament the spiritual experience of salvation is described in different places with different emphases. Sometimes the emphasis is on the beginning of salvation; sometimes it is on the continuing process; sometimes it is on the ultimate consummation of God's purpose for the individual. In this case, it was the first of these three.

*To this house* may be rendered "in this house." If *house* is used in the literal sense, salvation had come to make its home in Zacchaeus's house as Jesus had come to make his home there. In Jesus' case, it was his home for a day. In the case of salvation, it was a permanent home. On the other hand, *house* may be used in the sense of "family." If this is the use, it means that salvation had come to the family, making its beginning with the father.

*Since he also is a son of Abraham:* While it may be understood otherwise, the construction of this statement most naturally indicates that Jesus addressed it to those present—the Twelve. Some of them may have been uncomfortable in the home of so notorious a sinner as Zacchaeus appears to have been. Jesus' words called their attention to the fact that Zacchaeus, too, was descended from Abraham and was the object of God's favor. God rejoiced at his repentance; so should all those present. It was the sort of situation in which Peter would later ask concerning Cornelius and his believing family, "Can anyone forbid water for baptizing these people who have received the Holy Spirit?" (Acts 10:47).

The term *son of Abraham* in Paul's use had a metaphorical meaning. It meant one who was a spiritual son of Abraham because he had exercised the kind of faith in God which characterized Abraham. If the past tense had been used here—"since he also *was* a son of Abraham"—one might think that this was a Paulinism added by Luke to explain Jesus' words, "Today salvation has come to this house"; Zacchaeus the Jew (physically descended from Abraham) was now really by faith "a son of Abraham." The verb form, however, is present tense, not past. So the total saying appears to have been Jesus' saying—in part to Zacchaeus; in part to the others.

*Verse 10:* This conclusion to the event gives Jesus' understanding of his purpose for being in the world. *Son of man* is the term discussed previously as the title which Jesus seemed to prefer for himself (5:24; 9:22). The role of seeking and saving the lost recalls Jesus' parables of the lost sheep and the lost coin (15:3-10), in which he explained to the Pharisees why he associated with sinners.

The role of seeking and saving the lost, both in chapter 15 and here in chapter 19, recalls God's words to the shepherds (spiritual leaders) of Israel, "I will seek the lost, and I will bring back the strayed" (Ezek. 34:16). Even though Zacchaeus was a Jew—a son of Abraham—he was as lost as the Gentiles who knew not God. Jesus had come to seek and to save just such lost ones.

## 45. The Parable of the Pounds (19:11–27)

This parable and the parable of the talents (Matt. 25:14–30) are very similar in much of their structure, but greatly different in detail. Interpreters are divided on whether they are separate parables or whether they represent two versions of an original parable which stood behind them—versions shaped by Matthew and Luke (or by their sources) for theological purposes. Some regard them as examples of a parable which Jesus may have directed originally to the Jews but which has been restructured in the two forms appearing in the New Testament and applied to Jesus' followers in relationship to the coming of the Son of Man (Christ) at the end of the age.

As they appear in the New Testament, Luke's parable of the pounds was given in the house of Zacchaeus in Jericho before Jesus arrived in Jerusalem; it was addressed to all those who were present—the Twelve, Zacchaeus and his family, perhaps others. Matthew's parable of the talents was given on the Mount of Olives, to the Twelve, late on Tuesday afternoon after Jesus' arrival in Jerusalem on Sunday. In the pounds, a nobleman went into a far country to receive a kingdom. In the talents, a man went on a journey to another country. In the pounds, ten servants received the same amount—one pound—totaling about twenty dollars. In the talents, three servants received a varying number of talents totaling about seventeen hundred dollars; one received five, one received two, and the third received one, and stress is put on the distribution according to the ability of each one. In the pounds, only the first three servants rendered an account when the nobleman returned as a king. In the talents, all three servants rendered an account. In the pounds, the faithful servants were rewarded by being put in authority over ten and five cities corresponding to their gaining ten and five pounds in trading. In the talents, the two faithful servants had doubled their money (one returned an additional five talents and one an additional two), and they were commended by their master and told that they would be set "over many things." In both parables, the unused pound and the unused talent were taken from the unfaithful servant and given to the servants who had ten pounds and ten talents respectively. In the pounds, no additional punishment was assigned to the unfaithful servant. In the talents, the unfaithful servant was not only deprived of his money but was also cast into the outer darkness where there is weeping and gnashing of teeth. In the pounds, there was a group of citizens who rebelled against the absentee king and were slain when the king returned. In the talents, there was no such group.

If these were indeed separate parables told by Jesus on separate occasions, there is no great problem. If, however, they represent two later versions of an original parable, fascinating areas of investigation regarding the nature and setting of the original parable are open. Such investigation, however, is beyond the nature and scope of this commentary.

*Verse 11:* This verse gives Jesus' reasons for telling this parable to this particular group and in this particular setting. The two reasons given are related: the nearness of his entry into Jerusalem, and the view of his hearers regarding the immediate appearance of the kingdom of God. The thrust of the parable is a warning. Jesus did not actually pursue the idea of the immediate appearance of the kingdom of God—either their concept of it or his own—but rather, the idea of the coming of the Son of Man. His emphasis was on the responsibility of his followers in the interim between his going away and his return. This emphasis was of great interest to Luke, who wrote at a time when the delay of the Lord's return was a disturbing factor in the minds of the Christians.

*As they heard these things:* What they had heard in Jesus' use of the messianic term "Son of man" (v. 10), encouraged them to expect the kingdom of God to appear immediately. The fact of Jesus' going to Jerusalem encouraged them in their hope that he would inaugurate that kingdom. Salvation (v. 10) means "deliverance," and the Messiah was expected to be a "deliverer." The deliverance Zacchaeus had experienced was spiritual deliverance from sin. But they were more interested in the deliverance they expected from the Messiah, who would liberate them from Rome, make them a free nation, and give them the messianic kingdom. Jesus' followers, including the Twelve, hoped that in Jerusalem he would announce himself as the Son of Man–Son of David king. Their idea of the kingdom of God was still political and material. The Twelve traveled to Jerusalem torn between fear for what might happen and hope for what could happen. The immediacy of the coming of the kingdom was in their minds. James and John were even scheming for the places of honor at Jesus' right and left when he became King. Their requests were made as the group neared Jericho (Mark 10:35–45; Matt. 20:20–28). A few more hours—a few more miles —Jerusalem the capitol—would he set up the kingdom?

There in Jericho, before they went on up to Jerusalem, Jesus told this parable to dull their expectation that the kingdom was to come immediately. His view of the nature of the kingdom differed from theirs. But he wanted them to understand that its consummation in the coming of the Son of Man was to be preceded by a time of service in which the loyalties of all men would be tested by their response to his absentee lordship and their responsible trusteeship. The parable contains much allegorical detail.

*Verse 12: A nobleman* means one of high or royal birth. The reference is unquestionably to Jesus himself, and it may refer to his physical descent from the royal line of David. The *far country* refers to heaven, and the going refers to Jesus' ascension. *To receive kingly power* can be more exactly translated as "to receive a kingdom." The meaning is that Jesus entered upon his reign as king in the kingdom of God at his death, resurrection, and ascension. This concept appears frequently in Acts and Hebrews. It was a detail which was more meaningful to Jesus' followers after the event than before. It is doubtful if the active voice of the verb should be stressed— "to take up his kingship"—in contrast to the idea of God's giving it to him. Some interpreters regard as important the view that he took it up himself because he had earned the right to do so. The *return* is Jesus' coming back to earth to bring to finality God's purpose with men in the world. This is consistent New Testament eschatology.

*Verse 13:* The number *ten* represented for the Jews the idea of the full number; all the nobleman's servants received responsibility, and each one received the same responsibility. This meant that all were equally responsible for what they did with their trust. The *pound* was a Greek monetary unit (*mina*) with a value of about twenty dollars. Its buying power, however, was immeasurably greater than the buying power of twenty dollars today. It was a trusteeship large enough to occupy the total work time of a trader.

*Trade with these* is literally "be engaged in a business occupation with these pounds." No particular business was assigned. There was room for variety depending on individual interests—one might trade in foods, another in clothing, and another in livestock. This element of freedom to choose was important and will be discussed further in the comments on the unfaithful servant in verses 20–24.

*Till I come* means simply, "Be engaged in your trust until I return." No time was set for the nobleman's return; it might be soon, it might be long. Indeed, the idea of setting up and carrying on a business operation naturally suggests a period of some length. That, too, was of particular interest in the time in which Luke wrote. The Lord's return seemed to be delayed beyond all anticipation of his earliest disciples, and some were beginning to grow discouraged. There are reflections of this in the Epistle of James and in 2 Peter. Jesus' emphasis was on the idea that however long it would be before the return, the servants were to be engaged in their assigned responsibility.

The servants unquestionably stand for Jesus' followers who receive responsible trusteeship while in the world. They are responsible to Jesus, the absentee king. The *pounds* represent that trusteeship whose exact nature is not defined. In such an allegorical parable, the pound may be interpreted variously as a life to live, a work to do, a word to proclaim, etc. When addressed to men in general it most naturally suggests the use of one's life in obedient service to God. When addressed to such a group as the Twelve (or Christ's ministers in the years following), it most naturally suggests faithful proclamation of his teachings on salvation and life. In either case, the responsible trusteeship is a continuing one—for the life of the servant or until the king returns.

*Verse 14* is almost like an intruder. It breaks the continuity of the story which is resumed in verse 15. The rebellious citizens do not appear again until verse 27. Verses 14 and 27 seem to reflect an earlier occasion when Jesus used the parable in a different form and addressed it to the Jews who were rejecting him. Its use in this parable, which is addressed largely to the Twelve, indicates the continuing rejection of Jesus' lordship even after his death and resurrection. With the part about the unfaithful servant, it bears out Jesus' view of his coming as a time of judgment on the unfaithful and disobedient as well as blessing upon the faithful and obedient.

*His citizens hated him:* The rebellious Jews were under Jesus' lordly rule but they were in hostile rebellion. That hostility is a part of the record of all four Gospels. Here, Jesus reflected its continuance; they would (and did) not change even when he conquered death and returned to the Father. The tense of the verb *hated* indicates continuous action. They hated him when he was in the world; they continued to hate him after he went away.

*Sent an embassy after him:* This appears to be only a detail which was necessary for carrying the story forward, but it is a dramatic detail. It was as if they were so hostile that they sent a special embassy to heaven to inform God of their rejection of Jesus' lordship! Some interpreters understand it more literally. They interpret this *embassy* as the martyrs of the early church, beginning with Stephen. Every Christian who was killed by the Jews became a part of that embassy to inform heaven, "The Jews are still in rebellion against Jesus as king."

*We do not want this man: Want* means wish or will. They were expressing their will in opposition to God's will—the old story of sin. *This man* is the translation of a demonstrative pronoun meaning "this one." In Luke's other book, the Acts of the Apostles, the pronoun is used by the Jews who refused even to pronounce the name of Jesus (Acts 5:28). There was contempt in their use of this word rather than his name.

*To reign over us:* "To be king over us." They desired a messianic king who would give them a kingdom. But they refused the kind of kingdom Jesus offered them and they refused him as king.

*Verse 15:* Here Jesus resumes the main progress of the parable. The nobleman, having received his kingdom, returned from the far country. As a king he called for a reckoning with his servants. *When he returned* is a clear reference to the *parousia* as it was called by the early Christians. The Greek word means "being present with," in contrast to being away. From the middle of the second century, Christians have used the term "second coming" in the same sense in which the first-century Christians used "the presence." The expression "second coming" is not in the New Testament. The nearest thing to it is the expression in Hebrews 9:28, "Christ . . . will appear a second time. . . . " The earliest known use of the phrase was by Justin Martyr (about A.D. 160) who used it to refer to the coming of Christ at the end of the world in contrast to his coming at his birth. The teaching regarding such a coming at the end of the world is a prominent part of the New Testament. Justin's term "second coming" has come to be the most common way of referring to the doctrine.

*Having received his kingly power:* This emphasizes that Jesus received his kingdom when he went away (ascended); his rule started then. He returned in his kingly role. In Matthew 25:31–46 Jesus spoke of the return of the Son of Man as a king (v. 34), which is the idea here.

*Verses 16–19* contain the reckoning with the first two servants. Both had used their pounds as their master had instructed them. Both were rewarded by receiving an assignment of administrative authority in proportion to their previous productivity.

The first servant returned to his master ten additional pounds. He had profited ten to one. He was commended: *Well done, good servant!* Because he had proved faithful in the one thing committed to his trust, he was rewarded by being given administrative authority over ten cities. The nature of this administrative authority is not explained. Does it mean that he was elevated from a merchant to a ruler? Or does it mean that he was given a ten-city territory in which to continue his trading as a merchant? Such detail probably goes beyond the purpose of the parable. The purpose was to contrast faithfulness and unfaithfulness to a trust. It is better to leave it at that.

The second servant returned to his master five additional pounds. He had profited five to one and in proportion to his productivity he received administrative authority over five cities. The absence of the *Well done* indicates no displeasure of the master for the second servant. The fact that he was rewarded in exactly the same way as the first one indicates equal pleasure. Two things stand out as continuing lessons in these examples. One: every person who faithfully carries out the Lord's purpose according to the ability which he has will receive the returning Lord's *Well done, good servant!* Two: the returning Lord will have further work for his servants; heaven will not be an eternity of inactivity! The nature of that work may be left to his wisdom.

*Verses 20-24* contain the shameful record of a third servant. He returned to the master the pound which he had received. He had not squandered it but had kept it carefully wrapped so that even corrosion could not harm it. The tragedy of the servant was that he had done nothing. The master had trusted him. But he had trusted neither his ability to use the money profitably nor the master's character and conduct. He had not taken the venture of faithful action in obedience to the trust.

His excuse was that he feared—did not trust—the master. He regarded the master as a *severe man.* The word translated *severe* is the parent word for the English "austere." It means to be strict and exacting in either a favorable or an unfavorable sense. Such exacting nature intimidated the servant. Distrusting his own ability, he feared the result of trying and failing, and therefore did not try. He regarded the master as a dishonest man. *You take up what you did not lay down* means to steal furtively. In the marketplace someone would put money or merchandise on the table. While he was looking away, another would take it up, steal it. *You reap what you did not sow:* you harvest another man's grain field for yourself. Even today in some parts of Palestine families move into tents in their grainfields as they begin to ripen, lest others harvest them at night. In summary, the servant charged the master with being a hard taskmaster and a dishonest man.

The master's response was a charge that the servant was himself a *wicked servant.* The word translated *wicked* is one commonly used for evil or sin with the basic meaning of "grasping" or acting totally in self-interest. The servant's very words against his master indicated his own grasping, self-interested nature. The master had shown trust and generosity in assigning the trust. The servant had shown distrust and selfishness in refusing to use the trust.

*You knew that I was a severe man . . . .* ? Some interpeters have a problem with this verse. In the parable, the nobleman-king must refer to Jesus. The problem is in Jesus' comparing himself with a thief. The reader should observe that Jesus did not compare himself to a hard taskmaster and thief. That was the servant's charge. Jesus answered the servant by taking him at his word. If the servant thought that about the master, he should have turned the money over to another who would have used it profitably for the master (v. 23). The reader should recall that in the ancient world no punctuation marks were used in writing. Their use in the New Testament reflects the translator's interpretation of the construction and its meaning. The RSV (and many other versions) rightly understands this as a question rather than an agreement. It is the form of reasoning which, for the purpose of argument, assumes the opponent's position to be true and argues from that position—"if you knew that I was that kind of man, why did you not let some other servant use my money?" (author's paraphrase). If that had been done this pound would have brought profit as those of the first two servants.

*Verse 24* indicates the outcome of the unfaithful servant's action. His pound was taken from him. This meant that he had forfeited his opportunity to serve the master. He had proved unfaithful in his trust; he received no further trust. Note the strong contrast to the proportionately greater trust given to the first two servants. In this case, no other punishment was indicated; it was punishment enough that the master had no further use for him.

An added feature of the idea of reward for faithful service is the master's order to give the pound to the first servant who had proved the most able of the three. Trust upon trust was his. Detailed allegorical application to the second coming is of doubtful use here. One thing is central and certain —blessing and further responsibility for the faithful; punishment and deprivation of all responsibility for the unfaithful. Let the time of waiting be a time of working.

*Verse 25* represents the natural response of men. To those present when the king gave the order, it seemed unfair to give the pound to the servant who already had ten pounds. Their attitude was, "He has all that he can manage!" The verse is a clear introduction to the conclusion of the part about the servants. Some interpreters have regarded verse 25 as not an original part of the text but an interpolation to make verse 26 reasonable. The verse is not in some of the ancient manuscripts of Luke. Cyril did not use it in his fifth-century commentary. However, it is in the oldest and best of the manuscripts.

*Verse 26* is a repeated wisdom saying in the teaching of Jesus with varying applications in his parables and parabolic sayings (Mark 4:25; Matt. 13:12; Luke 8:18). Except for necessary grammatical differences, the saying here is identical with Luke's use in 8:18, with one major exception. The phrase "what he seems to have" is omitted here. It would have been unnatural in this verse. What Jesus said paralleled exactly what had taken place. The faithful servant had ten pounds (great responsibility) but he received more. The unfaithful servant had one pound but it was taken from him. In the mind of Jesus this was right and wise. It proves to be true in life. The one who works at his assigned responsibility finds other areas of work opening before him. The one who does not work at his assigned responsibility loses the opportunity to do even that. A twentieth-century slogan on the wall of a great industrial plant reads, "The long arm of opportunity reaches out to lay hold of the man who is able to take on greater responsibility." So it does in the Lord's work.

*Verse 27* resumes the story of the citizens who rebelled against the king's rule. The king ordered that they be seized and executed in his presence. They were called *citizens* in verse 14. By their hostile rebellion they have become *enemies* in verse 27. They had every opportunity to accept him as king; they refused and by so doing proved themselves enemies. In the imagery of oriental custom the king's enemies were destroyed in his very presence. This appears harsh treatment when in the total imagery of the parable, Jesus was the king. As indicated earlier (see comment on v. 14), these enemy-citizens represent the Jews who rejected Jesus as king. Their fate is in all likelihood a reference to the destruction of Jerusalem in A.D. 70 and the slaughter of the Jews. The early Christians interpreted that event as judgment upon the Jews for rejecting Jesus. Jesus himself used that destruction as a descriptive symbol of judgment upon the world at the second coming (Mark 13; Matt. 24–25).

# V. THE MINISTRY OF THE UNIVERSAL SAVIOR IN JERUSALEM
## (19:28–23:56)

Jesus' journey to Jerusalem after the announcement of his coming death was a major interest in the theology of Luke. The first indication of that journey was the 9:51 statement that "he set his face to go to Jerusalem." Although he moved about in different parts of Galilee, Samaria, Perea, and Judea before he reached Jerusalem, it was all under the shadow of that meaningful journey. The journey was more "theological" than "geographical" for Luke. It reached its geographical end when Jesus rode into the city on a donkey (19:28–44). It reached its theological end when he ascended from the Mount of Olives (24:51). Or—has it yet reached its theological end?

The exposition of this section will be organized by the activity of Jesus on the days of the week beginning with his triumphal entry (Sunday) and culminating with his resurrection (the following Sunday). The use of the days of the week makes it easier for the reader to understand the movements and why they came to their tragic climax on Friday. One cannot make this division of activities by using only one Gospel. It requires comparison of all four to follow the sequence.

## 1. Sunday—a Day of Triumph (19:28–44)

### (1) Entering Jerusalem as the messianic king (19:28–40)

The day for Jesus' triumphal entry has been identified as Sunday by the reference in John 12:1 to the supper in Bethany "six days before Passover" and the statement in John 12:12 that the triumphal entry was the next day. If Friday of Jesus' death was Passover Day, the supper was the Saturday before and the triumphal entry the Sunday before. This identification has been challenged by some interpreters, however. The people's waving branches from the palm trees to welcome Jesus to Jerusalem has given the name "Palm" to this Sunday. Mark (11:8) and Matthew (21:8) mention the use of branches from the trees; John (12:13) designates them palm branches. It was a day of rejoicing for all who followed Jesus.

*Verse 28: When he had said this* refers to Jesus' teaching to correct the erroneous views of his hearers (v. 11). Some time soon after that, they left Jericho and went on *up to Jerusalem.* In the New Testament the expression *up to* is always used of the approach to Jerusalem. Geographically, this was certainly due to the high elevation (2,500 feet) of the city in the hills of Judea bordering the low plains. At times the impression is that the pride of the people in the city of Jerusalem gave an almost metaphorically spiritual air to their "going up to Jerusalem" for the holy weeks.

Verses 29–36 give the details of what was obviously a very careful plan of Jesus as to the manner in which he would enter the city.

*Verse 29:* In Mark and Luke, the village names "Bethphage" and "Bethany" are joined in that order; Matthew names only Bethany; John names neither in relation to this event. From Mark's and Luke's accounts the assumption is that they were very close together, with Bethphage a bit east and reached first as they journeyed from Jericho to Jerusalem. Bethphage is not mentioned elsewhere in the New Testament and all the efforts to locate it exactly by study of frequent references to it in ancient Jewish and Christian writings leave only uncertainty. Bethany is well known from Jesus' visits, and it continues as a village at the same location today—across or around the Mount of Olives from Jerusalem.

*Verse 30:* Jesus sent two of his disciples (unidentified) *into the village opposite.* If the third-century writer Origen is correct, Bethphage and Bethany were separated only by a ravine. If that is so, it would seem that they were in Bethphage and Jesus waited while the two went into Bethany to bring the colt on which he would ride into Jerusalem.

*On which no one has ever yet sat:* Both Mark and Luke include this detail. Some interpreters see a religious significance in this—it was fitting that in announcing something entirely new, the coming of the messianic king of Israel, a young, never-ridden animal should be used. That may be correct. It is also possible that it was the way they would identify the animal among others, as in Matthew 21:2 they were to identify it because it would be with its mother.

*Verses 31–34:* The answer, *The Lord has need of it,* was given as if it were a "password." Since Matthew, Mark, and Luke seem to have Jesus making this entry immediately upon his arrival from Galilee, readers of these Gospels alone have sensed some supernatural knowledge of Jesus in knowing that there would be such a colt and that the owners would respond in that way. A reading of John with its indication of Jesus' considerable activity in the area of Jerusalem and Bethany before he actually made the entry minimizes the idea that there was anything involved other than prearrangement. Jesus knew how he was going to make his entry; he arranged in advance with friends in Bethany and sent two of the Twelve known to those friends to get the colt. It was all a part of a careful plan for his significant use of the little donkey.

*Verses 35–37:* The two disciples may have been Peter and John, who were also sent into Jerusalem on the following Thursday to prepare for the Passover Supper (22:8). They used their own outer robes to make a sort of saddle for Jesus. As they proceeded on toward Jerusalem, those who accompanied Jesus began to use their own robes to line the path on which he rode. Sensing the significance of what Jesus was doing, the disciples' excitement mounted. It was caught by the entire multitude of pilgrims who were entering Jerusalem for Passover. As Jesus started the descent from the Mount of Olives to cross the brook Kidron and go up the hill to the Temple, the multitudes began their shouts of rejoicing. According to John 12:12, it was at this point that the people began to break off and wave leaves from the palm trees. That was a symbol of rejoicing ordinarily used in the celebration of the Feast of Tabernacles.

*Verse 38:* To grasp the significance of all of this, it is necessary to note all four Gospel accounts (see Matt. 21:1–9; Mark 11:1–10; John 12:12–18). Matthew indicates that Jesus' riding of the ass was a fulfillment of prophecy, and he combines fragments of Isaiah 62:11 and Zechariah 9:9 to make the "quotation" (in 21:5)—it is not an exact quotation of either. The important matter is that it is to the "daughter of Zion" (Jerusalem) that the "king" comes "humble and riding on an ass." The Zechariah passage includes words omitted in the Matthew passage: "your king comes to you; triumphant and victorious . . . ." In addition to this, note the words of the praising people as they are in the different Gospels:

Mark 11:9–10:

Hosanna! Blessed is he who comes in the name of the Lord!

Blessed is the kingdom of our father David that is coming!

Hosanna in the highest!

Matthew 21:9:

Hosanna to the Son of David!

Blessed is he who comes in the name of the Lord!

Hosanna in the highest!

Luke 19:38:

Blessed is the King who comes in the name of the Lord!

Peace in heaven and glory in the highest!

John 12:15:

Fear not, daughter of Zion; behold your king is coming, sitting on an ass's colt!

This volume is not the place for an exposition of all these passages—not even a comparative study of the different versions of the people's praise. It is important, however, to note that in each one the central emphasis is that Jesus was entering Jerusalem as a king and that it was as a Son of David king. One historical precedent for Jesus' method and purpose is overlooked by practically all interpreters of this event. When Solomon was inaugurated as king succeeding his father David, he rode David's favorite mule. He went first to the spring of Gihon, part of the brook Kidron which separated the Mount of Olives from the mountain on which Jerusalem was built. After he was anointed as king he rode on into Jerusalem on the mule supplied by his father (1 Kings 1:32–40). Again in Jesus' entry, a Son of David was coming to Jerusalem as king; he rode an even humbler beast of burden, but it was borrowed from his friends.

The people sensed the significance of what Jesus was doing. Many had wanted him to assume the role of the Messiah who would bring them deliverance. In his symbolic action they understood that he was announcing publicly that he was offering himself as the Son of David king—the Messiah. That accounted for their welcome. *Loud voice* indicates that they were shouting their words of praise to God. Specifically, they shouted their praise *for all the mighty works that they had seen,* the miracles. It was anticipated that the messianic age would be marked by miracles done by the Messiah. Jesus had used that expectation in pointing out to John the Baptizer that he was doing what the Messiah was expected to do (see Luke 7:18–23). The people were convinced that Jesus was the Messiah and praised God for the evidences they had witnessed.

*Blessed is the King:* They associated his riding the ass with the previously noted Scriptures. He came to be king after the royal line of David. Once again the line of David and Solomon was to be restored. Once again they would be a nation. That was their hope.

*Who comes in the name of the Lord:* The Greek term is literally "the Coming One." It was a messianic term and as such identified Jesus with the anticipated Messiah. *In the name of the Lord* means as the Lord's authorized representative.

*Peace in heaven:* Traditionally, Solomon's reign was thought of as a period of peace in contrast to the war years of David. The messianic age was also thought of as a time of peace. The emphasis in this word of praise was on *peace in heaven*—God at peace with men and blessing them through his Messiah.

*Glory in the highest:* This was a shout of praise to the glorious God and his heavenly purpose for his people. All of that purpose was to be realized through his messianic king.

*Verses 39–40:* The Pharisees present in the company of people going to Jerusalem were displeased at the seemingly uncontrolled enthusiasm of the disciples. Indeed, it seemed that the whole world had become Jesus' disciples (John 12:19). They understood that the people were identifying Jesus as the Messiah, an identification they did not make. They regarded Jesus as a law-breaker, and no doubt called the praise of the people blasphemy. *Teacher, rebuke your disciples,* was their reaction. The word rendered *rebuke* is the one used regularly for silencing or stopping turbulent action, as the winds and waves of the sea (8:24).

He did not rebuke his disciples. He answered the Pharisees' request with the statement that on that particular day, if his people did not proclaim him as Messiah, *the very stones would cry out.* That day was so momentous that if men did not recognize it, the hard rocks of God's creation would become vocal and praise him. In his answer there was rebuke, not for his disciples but for the Pharisees. He charged them with being harder and less sensitive than the rocks.

There was one element in Jesus' choice of this method of announcing himself as the Son of David king which the people missed. By riding the gentle ass rather than the horse of a military conqueror, he was proclaiming that he came as a peaceful Messiah rather than as a revolutionary one. Solomon had come to Jerusalem as a peaceful king. Jesus was coming as a peaceful king. A king's messenger riding a horse meant war; a king's messenger riding an ass meant peace. Even the Twelve did not grasp all the significance of his action until after his resurrection (John 12:16). There are evidences that right up to the point of Jesus' arrest at least some of the Twelve hoped he would lead a revolution against Rome.

### (2) Weeping over the city (19:41–44)

This triumphal procession was interrupted by a scene of sadness. When Jesus came into full view of the city, he stopped to look at it. From the Mount of Olives the view of Jerusalem across the Kidron valley is one great panorama. (Today the most prominent structure is the Moslem mosque, the Dome of the Rock, built on the location where the Temple stood.) John's Gospel mentions frequent visits of Jesus to Jerusalem in which he went to the Temple and which were marked by controversy between Jesus and the religious authorities who disagreed with his teaching and practices. The synoptics, however, do not mention any ministry of Jesus in Jerusalem until this last week of his life. Luke contains reference to Jesus having been in the village of Bethany (10:38-41), but there is no explicit reference to his having been in Jerusalem after his visit to the Temple as a boy of twelve. There is intentional drama in Luke's use of this incident. Jesus would offer himself as Jerusalem's king. He would be rejected. Before the week was over, everything that the sacrificial system of the Temple pointed toward would be fulfilled in his redemptive death. Israel's rejection of him was a part of her determination for a revolutionary deliverer who would free her from Rome. She would not stop until that futile revolution brought her destruction in A.D. 70. That was inevitable in her collision course. And it brought Jesus to tears.

*Verse 42: Would that even today you knew the things that make for peace:* Israel had a veritable passion for freedom and peace. Through the exodus she had become a nation born in freedom. No nation has been so zealous for freedom and peace. Few nations have known so little of both. Jesus spoke of real *peace.* There was a higher peace than the political peace which Israel sought—the peace that comes only from God. *The things that make for peace* in that sense are recognition of God's purpose and commitment to it. Men and nations have known that kind of peace even in periods of suppression and suffering at the hands of tyrants. Jesus desired that kind of peace for Israel.

That does not mean that Jesus approved the cruel domination of Rome or sympathized with it. But he knew that the ambition and revolutionary planning of the Jews could meet only frustration which resulted in destruction. He knew that God's way for him was not the way of a military conqueror, such as Judas Maccabaeus, who was successful in leading Israel to victorious rebellion against Greek domination. Jesus knew he could lead her to higher peace with God. But it would require her acceptance of him and that she would not give. She would have a revolutionary messiah or no messiah, and it would mean her ruin.

*Verses 43-44* point to the coming of the Romans in culmination of the Jewish wars of A.D. 66-70. To *cast up a bank* means to raise a bulwark in siege of the city. To *hem you in on every side* refers to surrounding the city in such a way that there could be no escape. Under starvation and attack, Jerusalem would fall to the armies of the Roman general, Titus, who would himself come to be Emperor of Rome.

*Dash you to the ground* reflects the cruelty which struck down and trampled underfoot both adults and children. So complete would be the destruction that the very buildings would be razed to the ground to make the place uninhabitable. The extent of this is reflected in the words, *they will not leave one stone upon another.* This same expression appears again in Jesus' specific reference to the destruction of the Temple (21:6; Mark 13:2; Matt. 24:2).

*Because you did not know the time of your visitation:* The word translated *visitation* means "to look upon" someone, either in blessing or in punishment. In this passage it has the force of a "day of opportunity." In Jesus' presence and offering of himself as Messiah, God was "looking in on" them; he was offering them an opportunity for acceptance which would mean blessing. Their rejection could mean only judgment, and that judgment would come as a result of their own rebellion.

## 2. Monday—a Day of Authority (19:45-48)

### (1) The cleansing of the Temple (19:45-46)

The cleansing of the Temple is placed on Monday according to Mark, who indicates a sequence of days where Luke has none. According to Mark (11:11-15), when Jesus entered Jerusalem on Sunday, he went to the Temple; while he was there he observed all that was going on; then he went back out of the city to Bethany for the night. On the next day he went from Bethany back into the city. On the way in he blighted a barren fig tree, and when he arrived at the Temple he cleansed it of its merchants. Then on the next day (Tuesday) the fig tree was found to have died. Luke does not have this miracle of the fig tree; he has a parable of the fig tree later (21:29-33).

Matthew (21:12-22) has both the miracle of the fig tree and the cleansing of the Temple, but he has them in the reverse of Mark's order. He has the cleansing of the Temple at 21:12-13, seemingly on the afternoon of the triumphal entry (Sunday), and the blighting of the fig tree on the next morning (Monday) at 21:18-22. He also has the immediate withering of the tree (v. 19) and Jesus' use of it in a lesson on prayer and faith, whereas Mark has that on Tuesday. John is of no help at this point because he uses the cleansing of the Temple for a theological purpose in 2:13-22 and omits it from his materials of this week. Out of consideration of all these differences, different conclusions can be drawn. Mark's order is followed in the present exposition because it is the least complicated and the most natural.

Two matters of importance stand out in this event: What Jesus did; what he meant by it. What he did is rather simply indicated. Why he did it and what he intended by it constitute the more difficult area in exposition.

*Verse 45: He began to drive out those who sold:* The other Gospels indicate what was being sold. Since it was Passover, the people who came from distant places would need animals for sacrifice. Pigeons are named by Mark and Matthew. John (2:14) includes oxen and sheep in addition. The animals had to be without sickness or blemish of any kind. To take such perfect animals on a journey of many days and miles and arrive with them still perfect would be most difficult. So some of the officers of the Temple were providing perfect animals for the travelers' sacrifices. The other Gospels also indicate that the Temple officers were "selling" money—exchanging Judean coins with no images on them so the people from outside Judea could pay their Temple tax acceptably. Coins with the image of the emperor (or any other person) could not be used in paying the Temple tax. All of that appears on the surface to have been a convenient service rendered. Jesus' words, however, indicate that there was much more involved.

*Verse 46: My house shall be a house of prayer:* This is a phrase from Isaiah 56:7. The total passage (Isa. 56:1–7) is addressed to all true worshipers in the Temple, and the emphasis is on Gentiles who came to join themselves to the worship of the God of Israel. The passage closes with the phrase "for all peoples." It is interesting that Mark includes the phrase but Luke, who shows such interest in the Gentiles, omits it. The entire passage from Isaiah suggests that the officers had taken over those outer parts of the Temple into which the Gentiles were permitted to come in their seeking to know about the God of the Jews. The Gentiles were thus driven out from even these fringe areas, and deprived of the privilege of seeking God in his house.

*You have made it a den of robbers:* This is a quote from Jeremiah 7:11 and is a part of Jeremiah's famous Temple sermon. Jeremiah accused the people of stealing from one another, cheating one another, and other sins. When they were about to be apprehended in their evil, they would take refuge in the Temple and say, "We are safe!" Jeremiah said that there was no safety for them, and that their presence in the Temple made it a dwelling place of robbers. Jesus' application of the quotation to the merchants reflects exorbitant prices for the animals sold and exorbitant rates of exchange on the money. They were depriving the Gentiles of a place to seek after God; they were also exploiting their own people in dishonest business traffic in the name of religious service and in the house of God.

Subsequent events reflect a further significance in Jesus' action. What he did amounted to assuming authority to determine the use which was to be made of the Temple. In John's account, Jesus used the riddle of his body and the "New Temple" of God in the world; they would destroy it as the heathen had destroyed the ancient Temple in Jerusalem but in three days it would be raised again. In all of this, some have understood that Jesus' action in cleansing the Temple was to stop the flow of animals to the altar because he felt that there was no further need for the Temple—in him God had a new dwelling place and place of sacrifice in the world. That theological understanding is less clearly associated with the synoptic account. In the synoptics there is no indication that Jesus would have objected to the honest sale of animals for sacrifice and exchange of money for tax payment in other places and under conditions which did not deprive men of a place of worship. He assumed authority to indicate that his Father's house was not to be misused.

### (2) Beginning a week of teaching (19:47–48)

This brief section is a summary statement introducing the conditions under which Jesus carried on his teaching following the Temple event. He continued to teach in the very porches from which he had driven the merchants. That was the customary place for rabbinical teaching. He did so in spite of opposition from the Temple officers.

*Verse 47: The chief priests . . . scribes . . . principal men:* These were the leaders of the religion in Jerusalem. They jealously guarded their right to conduct the sacrifices and services of the Temple. They saw Jesus as a threat because of his popularity with the people—a popularity demonstrated at his entry into the city. The *chief priests* opposed him because he was assuming authority over their special area—the Temple. The *scribes* opposed him because he did not agree with their interpretation of the law. The *principal men* opposed him because they feared his potential as a popular revolutionist. The people were seeking just that type of leader.

*They sought to destroy him:* In the synoptic Gospels, it was Jesus' assumption of authority, to the apparent delight of the people, that occasioned the leaders' determination to destroy him. They looked upon him as a dangerous man. They had been unable to defeat him in logic; they turned to force and violence.

*Verse 48: They did not find anything they could do:* They were frustrated in all their planning. The source of their frustration was his popularity with the people who *hung upon his words.* The common people welcomed Jesus' teaching. They felt that in him they had found their leader. Opposition from the authorities would have met immediate danger from the people. When the authorities finally worked out their plan for arresting Jesus, it was done in the absence of the multitude (22:6), and by the time the multitude learned what was going on, Jesus was in the hands of the Roman governor.

### 3. Tuesday—a Day of Controversy and Teaching (20:1–22:6)

Luke gives no definite identification of this day which he introduces with the simple expression, "One day" (v. 1). If the Tuesday identification is correct, it is due to Mark's expression "in the morning" referring to the cleansing of the Temple the day before (Mark 11:20; the controversy report begins in v. 27).

#### (1) The controversy with the Sanhedrin over authority (20:1–19)

*Verse 1:* The Sanhedrin was the Jewish supreme court in authority over all religious matters. The name is used in this commentary as a comprehensive term for *the chief priests and the scribes and the elders* who were the rulers responsible for regulating all matters of doctrine and practice in the religious life of the Jews.

*Verse 2: What authority:* The leaders questioned the nature of Jesus' authority to perform his deeds. When used with a noun—as it is in this instance—the word translated *what* means "what kind." They could have had several alternatives in mind. Was his authority prophetic or messianic? Was he claiming to be a prophet and as such ruling out sacrifice as essential? His action in cleansing the Temple could have suggested that. Was he claiming to be the Messiah? His triumphal entry could have suggested that. By Jesus' counter-question in verse 4, it appears that he understood a simple alternative between human and divine. Was his authority from men or from God?

*These things* refers to all that Jesus had done since coming to Jerusalem— the entry as a Son of David king; the cleansing of the Temple; his healing blind and lame people in the Temple (Matt. 21:14). By what kind of authority was he acting?

*Who . . . gave you this authority?* By this they challenged the source of his authority. If he answered that his authority was from a human source, they could counter that they alone had authority in the Temple and they certainly had not given authority to him. If he answered that his authority was from God, they would demand that he give them unquestionable evidence. Indeed, they knew that he claimed authority from God. They hoped to embarrass and discredit him in the minds of the people who stood between them and their desire to destroy him.

*Verses 3–4:* Jesus countered by asking them a question on authority. He took what he understood to be the alternative they had in mind—divine or human—and substituted John the Baptizer in place of himself—*Was the baptism of John from heaven or from men?* John had been the son of a priest, but he claimed no authority from the priests. In fact, he had nothing to do with the Temple and its priestly cult. He had come, not in the role of a priest, but of a prophet—one who spoke under the direct motivation of God. Was his authority from God or from men?

*Verses 5–6:* In their discussion as they sought a satisfactory answer, the leaders found that either answer they gave would hurt their own position. If they answered, "John's authority to baptize men in view of God's coming king and kingdom was from God," Jesus would ask, "Then why did you not believe that John's message concerning the coming king was true?" That would defeat their cause because it would force them to admit that Jesus, for whom John was the forerunner, was the Messiah.

On the other hand, if they answered, "John's authority was from men," they feared that the people would stone them for speaking blasphemy. The people were certain that John had been sent by God. Denial of that would have been blasphemy against God who had sent him.

*Verses 7–8:* They found themselves impaled on the two horns of the dilemma they had set for Jesus. They could not answer without putting themselves into an impossible position. They sought to get out safely by answering *that they did not know whence it was.* They were unwilling to say that it was from God; they were afraid to say that it was from man. Jesus responded that since they would not answer his question, he would not answer theirs. He then proceeded to relate the very discerning parable of the wicked tenants which, to their discomfort, they easily applied to themselves.

*Verses 9–16:* The parable of the wicked tenants was doubtless built on the song of the vineyard in Isaiah 5:1–7. The passage in Isaiah is not a parable but an allegorical poem or song in which Israel is portrayed as God's vineyard, but one that bore only the grapes of oppression and bloodshed instead of justice and righteousness. Reading the poem in Isaiah and then this parable makes it clear that the parable was framed out of the material of the poem.

The parable is included in the synoptic Gospels (Mark 12:1–9; Matt. 21:33–41), and also in the Gospel According to Thomas (Logion 65). While latest in written form, Thomas's version is the shortest. Next in length is Mark's version; if verse 5 in Mark's version is omitted it has the exact order of Thomas. Basically, the structure is the same in all four accounts. Only Luke's version is considered in the following exposition. The parable requires allegorical interpretation. Some of the details, however, cannot be identified with exactitude.

*Verse 9: A man planted a vineyard:* The *man* clearly represents God and the *vineyard* represents Israel. (See Isa. 5:7: "the vineyard of the Lord of hosts is the house of Israel.")

*Let it out to tenants:* The *tenants* who were to care for the vineyard were the leaders of the religion of Israel. Jesus' hearers recognized that he referred to them (v. 19) and were enraged. They were, of course, the contemporary successors to all the leaders before them.

*Verses 10–12:* The *servants* represent God's messengers sent to Israel at different periods of her history. No more definite identification can be made. It is doubtful if there is particular significance in the fact that three were sent or if identification is possible through the punishment they received. The number three suggests completeness. Mark 12:5 and Matthew 21:36 refer to other servants (plural) besides the three which they have in common with Luke. The idea is similar to Stephen's charge against the Sanhedrin in his defense: "you always resist the Holy Spirit. As your fathers did, so do you" (Acts 7:51).

*Verse 13:* The climax in all the Gospel accounts comes in the owner's sending his son. All three stress that this was his only son, and Mark and Luke have *beloved son.* This *beloved son* represents Jesus who had been sent as God's final and supreme representative to plead God's cause with the religious leaders of Israel.

*Verses 14–15a:* In oriental custom, the coming of the only son suggests that the owner had died and that the heir had come to claim his inheritance. The tenants resolved to kill the heir, thus removing the last obstacle to their complete control of the vineyard. *They cast him out of the vineyard and killed him* is symbolic of Jesus' death outside the city limits, a matter theologically important to the early Jewish Christians (Heb. 13:11–13). To Jesus it did appear that the leaders of Israel recognized him as the only thing standing between them and their goals. They had to destroy him.

*Verses 15b–16:* Having finished the parable, Jesus posed a question as to what the owner of a vineyard would do in such a situation. In Matthew's account, the priests and scribes answered the question. In Mark's and Luke's accounts, Jesus answered his own question. Except for verbal differences the answers are the same—*He will come and destroy those tenants, and give the vineyard to others.* Jesus envisioned two things: the end of the nation of Israel as God's fruit-bearers; the giving of that responsibility to other fruit-bearers, the Gentiles. The destruction of the tenants was another reflection of the impending doom of Jerusalem and the Temple. The response of his hearers at such a prospect was an expression of awe, "God forbid!" This customary rendering of the Greek term is not really a translation. The expression means, "May it never come to pass." They understood the point he was making, and were horrified and enraged.

*Verse 17:* To his teaching that he was the rejected son in the parable, Jesus added that he was the rejected stone of Psalm 118:22 and Isaiah 8:14–15. Psalm 118 was a song of worship in celebration of the construction of the Temple. In the stories which the people told in recounting the building of Solomon's Temple, a legend had grown up. When the workmen were building the Temple they had one stone of an unusual shape. (The stones were all pre-cut in the quarry.) It was hard to fit it into the structure, so they cast it aside. When they came down to the finishing of the Temple, however, they needed a stone of an unusual shape. In searching about, they found the rejected stone, and it was an exact fit. It was the most important stone in the structure. Psalm 118 recounts the story.

Jesus applied the psalm to himself. He was the stone which did not fit. The chief priests and elders were the builders who were rejecting him. But once again the rejected stone would become the most important of all the stones. 1 Peter 2:4–8 contains another application of this stone motif in reference to Jesus as the foundation and believers as living stones built upon him.

*Verse 18:* All of this is allegory, applying Old Testament language to Jesus, as is the use of Isaiah 8:14–15. For Isaiah God was the stone over which both Israel and Judah would stumble, fall, and be broken. He was like a stone used in a trap for small animals. When tripped, the snare would fall upon the animal and destroy it. God's judgment on Judah and Israel was to be like that in those days culminating in their downfall and captivity.

Jesus applied this to himself—he was the stone in the path of men—including the leaders of Israel—who were rushing toward their self-determined goals. They would stumble over him and be broken to pieces. This was judgment by Jesus in the passive sense—men stumble over him to their ruin. Judgment by Jesus in the active sense is in the second part of the quotation. When he comes to men in judgment, it will be with the crushing force of a falling snare.

Some interpreters doubt that this could have had meaning for Jesus' hearers at this time. They think his hearers had no background for understanding the saying until after his death. They question that Jesus even spoke these things and suggest that they are the work of the early Christian interpreters of the significance of Jesus' death and Israel's rejection. Others think that Jesus spoke the parable and the rejected-stone quotation, but that the early Christian interpreters added allegorical details to the parable and also added the application from Isaiah.

When other features of the week are included in the whole, these objections are minimized. The total of Jesus' claims, the hostility of the Jewish leaders, their plotting to kill Jesus, Israel's history of suffering when she had rejected God's previous messengers—all these supply adequate background for making Jesus' teaching meaningful to them at that very time. They understood enough—*he told this parable against them*—that they desired to arrest him on the spot, but they were prevented by their fear of reaction from the people.

### (2) The controversy with Pharisees and Herodians about taxes (20:20–26)

Unable to seize Jesus, the rulers *sent spies* to try to trap him into saying something which they could use to prejudice the people against him. Mark 12:13 identifies the spies as Pharisees and Herodians.

*Verse 20: They watched* means that they waited for an opportunity. The word "him" is not in the Greek text. The word translated *spies* means people "hired to lie in wait." Whether or not these men were paid by the rulers, they were serving in the truest sense of spies.

*Who pretended to be sincere:* The word translated *sincere* is the word for righteous. These Pharisees came pretending to have a genuine problem as to whether or not an upright and loyal Jew should pay the Roman tax. The Herodians, who came with them according to Mark, were a nonreligious political party. They supported the political claims of the Herod family and really desired the overthrow of the Romans and the restoration of the rule to the Herod line. They feigned loyalty to the Romans, however, because the Romans did give support to the Herod line. If Jesus spoke some word *against* the Roman tax, the Herodians would be acceptable witnesses to report it to the Roman officials. The Jewish rulers would have grounds for having Jesus arrested by the Romans (v. 20), thus avoiding trouble with the people. If he spoke some word *for* the tax, the religious leaders could use it to prejudice the people against him. They could charge that he was supporting Rome. Their plan was carefully laid to trap Jesus no matter how he answered.

*Verse 21:* Here was their clever foundation for their question. It was designed to deceive him as to their motives and throw him off guard. Luke correctly used the word *pretending* (v. 20) which was the word for a stage actor—wearing a mask to represent one character but actually beneath the mask was an entirely different character.

*We know that you speak and teach rightly:* They affirmed their confidence in the honesty of Jesus' speech and the correctness of his teaching. Since there is no previous record of his contact with the Herodians, Jesus may have accepted their affirmation. He knew enough from previous confrontation with the Pharisees, however, to know that they were not sincere but up to some trick.

*Show no partiality:* He could possibly have accepted this statement as sincere from either group. They may have meant partiality in general. Or they may have meant partiality where the Jews and Romans were concerned; that is, in the conflict over taxes, Jesus had given no evidence of being on one side or the other.

*Truly teach the way of God:* Jesus had taken no part in partisan politics but had confined his teaching to the religious area, pressing upon men their responsibility where God's way of life was concerned. Stressing Jesus' non-involvement in politics was a wily approach and crafty practice at its worst, laying the groundwork for the trap.

*Verse 22:* Their trap was in the form of a question. *Is it lawful for us to give tribute to Caesar, or not?* Mark (12:14) and Matthew (22:17) use the word for the individual personal "head" tax which was particularly distasteful to the Jews because they felt that it degraded them to personal bondage to Rome. Luke used the more general word for a tax paid by one nation to another. It was distasteful but not personally degrading.

*To Caesar:* All the tax money was his as the emperor of the Roman nation. To the Jews it was like paying tribute to a heathen god. Was it fitting and proper *(lawful)* for upright worshipers of God to pay tribute money to a Roman who, by the Roman senate, was voted divine and the proper object of worship? How could a good Jew answer any way but negatively? Jesus found a way. He understood their *craftiness.* Mark has "hypocrisy" here, and Matthew has "wickedness," to contrast with their feigned righteousness. He answered in a way which defeated their purpose.

*Verse 24:* Jesus asked for a *coin,* which was a *denarius,* used for paying the distateful "head" tax. Its value was about twenty cents, but in buying power it was about a day's wage. Perhaps more significantly it was the daily wage for the Roman soldiers stationed in Judea to keep the peace. Every time a Jew paid the tax he was helping to support his tormentors. This small silver coin bore the image of the emperor who was ruling when it was minted, or of some member of the emperor's family. It always bore the emperor's name and title. In the account of this in the Gospel According to Thomas (Logion 100) Jesus himself produced a gold coin which, like silver, could be minted only by the emperor. The senate could authorize copper money, but only the emperor could authorize silver and gold money. When Jesus asked *whose likeness and inscription* was on the coin, there was one obvious and apparently innocent answer—*Caesar's*. By that answer, they opened the way for Jesus to frustrate their purpose.

*Verse 25:* With the slight exception of an introductory word in Matthew and Luke, all three synoptic Gospels have the identical answer—*render to Caesar the things that are Caesar's and to God the things that are God's*. In the Gospel According to Thomas there is a third line:

> Give to Caesar Caesar's things;
> Give to God God's things;
> Give to me my things.

The verb translated *render* means "give back in full payment that which is due." In many business records of that day which have been discovered, the word is used in exactly the same sense in which a merchant today stamps a bill "paid in full."

*The things that are Caesar's:* In Roman monetary philosophy, coins minted under the authority of an emperor were regarded as his possession but let out for the use of the people. When the Jew returned one of the coins in paying his tax, he was returning to Caesar that which belonged to Caesar. But there was a deeper meaning in what Jesus said. He called his Jewish questioners to consider the fact that they enjoyed certain privileges from the Roman government, such as roads, water systems, sewer systems, protection from robbers, protection from enemy nations on their borders, and the very convenience of using coins in trade in contrast to the bartering which would be involved without it—trade an ox for a sheep and get two pigeons and a sparrow in change!

The principle involved in Jesus' answer was valid then and now. Whatever the form of government, there are privileges involved in being a part of the governed society. But privilege always involves responsibility. The responsible man in the governed society must anticipate meeting his obligations with integrity in the areas of taxes, obedience to the law, and participation in the government to the extent of his ability and opportunity. Paul (Rom. 13) and Peter (1 Pet. 2:11–17) argued for this same responsibility. The ramifications of the principle are both complex and endless and related to the nature of the government. That does not invalidate the principle nor the responsibility of the privileged person.

*To God the things that are God's:* Jesus called attention to the fact that his hearers also had responsibilities to God because of privileges extended to them. As the likeness of Caesar was stamped on the coins, the likeness of God was stamped on man. That was a part of Hebrew theology growing

out of their concept of God as Creator. As a man carries out his responsibilities to the state so he must carry out his responsibilities to God. Man
must render to Caesar that which is Caesar's, but he must never render
to Caesar that which is God's. The order in Jesus' imperative is climactic—
the higher loyalty is to God, but neither can be rightfully omitted. Since the
higher relationship is the divine, it is the responsibility of the spiritual man
to be something of a conscience for the state. As such he must be alert to
point out those areas in which the state is in danger of encroaching on the
prerogative of God. Caesar must never attempt to supplant God.

In the Thomas account of this saying, the third line is intriguing—"Give
to me my things." This saying fits exactly the situation of Jesus in relation
to the Pharisees. They would be quick to render to God the loyalty due
him. They would, with some reluctance, even render to Caesar the loyalty
due him. But they were so set in their opposition to Jesus that they would
render no loyalty to him as God's messenger. Because it fits so perfectly,
it has the ring of a genuine saying. If it was an authentic saying of Jesus
on that occasion, the synoptic writers did not know of it; it is too good
to have been omitted.

*Verse 26:* Luke emphasizes two results of the bit of dialogue: One, the
opposition failed in its purpose to trap Jesus. He said nothing which they
could use against him to discredit him before the Roman authorities (v. 20)
or the people (v. 26). Two, they marveled silently at his answer. It was
cleverly framed. But more than that it contained such evident truth and
wisdom that there was no logic to answer it. Matthew (22:22) says that
"they left him and went away." The reference is to the Pharisees. They
dropped the question.

## (3) The controversy with Sadducees about the resurrection (20:27–40)

The Sadducees came to Jesus with a doctrinal question—the nature of the
resurrection or of survival after death. *The Sadducees* constituted a religious
party which was in opposition to the Pharisees in many areas of faith and
practice. When the Pharisees failed in their controversy with Jesus, the
Sadducees stepped in to try. Whereas the Pharisees were most influential
in the synagogues, the Sadducees were most influential in the Temple. Their
opposition to Jesus was meaningful. They hoped to lure him into some
doctrinal views which could be used against him.

*Verse 27: Who say that there is no resurrection:* The Pharisees believed
in a resurrection which was so physical that they anticipated the begetting
of children in the resurrection life. The Sadducees denied the doctrine of the
resurrection and any survival after death. They believed that death brought an
end to being and were in frequent controversy with the Pharisees on the
subject.

*Verses 28–33:* Their question was prefaced by a clever story of seven
brothers who had been married in turn to the same woman according to the
Mosaic law of levirate marriage (Deut. 25:5–10). By this law, if a man died
childless, his brother was to marry the widow and rear children by her.
The first son born to them would be the son of the dead brother; all other
children would be their own. In this way, the son born under levirate marriage
would keep the family line of the dead man from dying out.

In the Sadducees' very exaggerated story built on that custom, seven brothers in succession married the same woman and each one of them died without having a child by her (v. 31). Afterward the woman also died (v. 32). Their question, "Which one of the seven brothers will have this woman as his wife in the resurrection?" was framed to reduce the matter to the absurd—almost the comical. They assumed that Jesus believed in the same kind of resurrection as the Pharisees. If one believed in that kind of resurrection, one in which there would be the physical union of marriage and the begetting of children, their question was exceedingly difficult. One can assume that they had frequently confused the Pharisees with it.

Verses 34–40 contain Jesus' answer and its result. He pointed out their error along three lines; only two are in Luke's account. They had erred in their consideration of the resurrection because: they left out the power of God (only in Mark 12:24 and Matt. 22:29); they did not understand the nature of the resurrection; they did not know the teaching of the Scriptures.

*Verse 34: The sons of this age marry:* Marriage is a part of the physical order of the kind of life for this kind of world. It is a life of physical relationships and physical functions including the begetting of children to keep the life line alive. This was accepted Hebrew religious thought. It went back to the doctrine of creation in Genesis. To have children was considered to be a sign of God's blessing, and not to have children was considered to be a sign of God's displeasure.

*Verse 35:* The future and eternal age which will succeed this one is of a different nature. It will not be an age in which physical functions will be a part.

*Those who are accounted worthy to attain to that age and to the resurrection:* This is a poetic way of referring to the life of resurrection in the eternal age. It does not reflect the view that only some people would be raised and others would not. Elsewhere Jesus spoke of the resurrection of all—both good and evil (John 5:28–29). Paul believed that all will be raised (Acts 24:15), but he could also speak of his own hope to "attain the resurrection from the dead" (Phil. 3:11). In Jesus' answer to the Sadducees in the other Gospel accounts, the matter is more simply stated— "in the resurrection" (Matt. 22:30); "when they rise from the dead" (Mark 12:25). That is all that is meant in Luke's more poetic expression.

*Neither marry nor are given in marriage:* To *marry* refers to a man's taking a wife. To be *given in marriage* refers to a daughter's being given in marriage by her father. The two expressions together cover the entire practice of marriage. Marriage would not be a part of the life of the eternal age.

*Verse 36: For they cannot die any more:* Marriage and death are both physical functions and are possibilities in the age of the physical. But the eternal age will not be an age of the physical. Therefore, physical functions will be no part of it. No man will need to marry a woman because his brother has died and the family line must be perpetuated. There will be no death; there will be no marriage; there will be no begetting of children.

*Because they are equal to angels:* Mark and Matthew have "as angels in heaven." Luke has a word which is used nowhere else in the New Testament, a compound word made by joining together the noun "angels" and an adjective meaning "equal to" or "like unto." In the eternal men are *equal to* or "like" angels, in that by nature they will not be physical nor will they be subject to death. The emphasis is on a higher order of life than that which is known at the human, physical level. This passage may have resulted in the idea that in heaven people will become angels. That is not a biblical idea. It is not the teaching here.

*Sons of God, being sons of the resurrection:* Luke has the expression *sons of the resurrection* where Mark and Matthew have the expression "in heaven." The term *sons of God* is not unusual. As in this age and at the physical level there is a son-father relationship, so in the eternal age (heaven) there is a son-Father relationship at the spiritual level. The term *sons of the resurrection* is, however, a very unusual expression. It is best understood in apposition to *sons of God*—the two meaning the same thing. They are "resurrection sons" rather than "physical sons" or "this world sons." The entire line of relationship involved in physical life, marriage, sex, reproduction of children, is a necessary part of this world of the death of parents and the succession of children. It will be no part of the life of the eternal age.

*Verses 37–38:* The second error of the Sadducees was that they accepted as authoritative only the books of Moses—a technical reference to the first five books of the Jewish Scriptures commonly called the Pentateuch. They did not find any idea of survival after death—life after death—in those books. They granted that life after death was taught in the other two parts of the Scriptures—the Prophets and the Holy Writings. Even the doctrine of the resurrection was taught in Daniel 12:2. But they did not accept those books as authoritative Scripture. In contrast, the Pharisees accepted all three sections as authoritative.

*That the dead are raised, even Moses showed:* Here Jesus went to that section of the Hebrew Scriptures (Old Testament in Christian terms) which the Sadducees did accept as authoritative (Exod. 3:6) and pointed out a passage affirming life after death. The Sadducees had cited a passage from another part of their accepted Scriptures (Deut. 25:5) but had misinterpreted it. Jesus selected this passage from Exodus and correctly interpreted it.

*In the passage about the bush:* The reference is to the account of Moses at the bush in which a fire burned without burning the bush. A voice told him that he should remove his sandals because the ground was holy, and then the speaker identified himself as God.

*Where he calls the Lord the God of Abraham and the God of Isaac and the God of Jacob:* Actually it was not Moses who called God by that name. Moses reported what God said, "I am the God of your father, the God of Abraham, the God of Isaac, and the God of Jacob."

*Now he is not God of the dead, but of the living:* The God worshiped by Israel was the God of creation, of life, of living people. Their neighbor nations had a god of death and decay, but not they. Jesus' argument was that since God is the God of living people and not dead people, when he said he was the God of Abraham, Isaac, and Jacob, he meant that in some form they were still alive even though physically they had died hundreds of years before. It was reasonable and exceedingly discerning of the implications of the Scriptures.

*For all live to him:* In relationship to God these patriarchs had a meaningful existence even beyond death. Jesus says that this is true of others, too. Death does not bring an end to meaningful existence in relation to God. Paul wrote that not even death makes any essential difference between a believer and God.

*Verse 39:* Some of the *scribes* (the official interpreters of the Scriptures) answered, *"Teacher, you have spoken well."* Immediately they discerned the wisdom and accuracy of Jesus' understanding of that name of God. Apart from life after death, God would ultimately become the God of the dead, of corpses. His statement refuted all their thinking about God.

Could they have responded that he had not proved "resurrection of bodies" but only "life after death"? No. They rejected both life after death and the resurrection of the body as a total concept. If they were convinced of life after death in any form, they would not stumble at the idea of resurrection as Jesus had explained it—a life transcending the physical and mortal. Too, for the eternal God with whom there is no past, present, and future, but only one eternal now, the resurrection of men is an accomplished fact even though it becomes reality for men "at the last day" in Jesus' teaching—at the return of the Lord in Paul's terminology.

*Verse 40:* As the rulers had been silenced, as the Pharisees and Herodians had been silenced, so the Sadducees had been silenced. *They no longer dared to ask him any question.*

### (4) The controversy with Pharisees about the Messiah (20:41–44)

The main theme in all of the discussions between Jesus and his antagonists was Jesus' claim that he was the Messiah. That was the significance of the challenge to his authority in verses 1–8, the challenge to his loyalty to Israel in verses 20–22, and the challenge to his competence as an interpreter of the Scripture in verses 27–33. When he had silenced their objections by giving unanswerable responses in every instance, they ceased their challenging. He then challenged them with a question which cut across all three of those areas. It related to the nature of the Messiah, and in answering it they would have to reveal their own loyalties to that which was central in the religious life of Israel and their discernment of the real implications of the Scripture.

*Verses 41–43: How can they say that the Christ is David's son?* The Greek word translated *Christ* is the equivalent of the Hebrew word Messiah which means "the anointed one," the deliverer whom God had promised and for whom the Jews fervently hoped. It was standard messianic expectation that the Messiah would be descended from the royal line of David. Jesus challenged them to consider the implications of that in relation to a statement from David himself, from Psalm 110:1:

> The Lord said to my Lord
> Sit at my right hand.
> till I make thy enemies a stool for thy feet.

The remainder of the psalm emphasizes the rule of this "Lord" from Zion—Jerusalem—as a priest after the order of Melchizedek. The argument in Hebrews 7:1–28 for the authentic and eternal priesthood of the risen Christ is based on this psalm. Even though Jesus came from the tribe of Judah rather than the priestly tribe of Levi, he was an authentic priest after a different order—that of Melchizedek—which was eternal, standing outside of temporal order, since it was not derived from ancestors nor was it passed on to descendants.

In Jesus' use of the same psalm, he was emphasizing the eternal nature of the Messiah and his rule by appointment from the eternal God.

*The Lord* is a translation of the Hebrew name for God which is frequently referred to as the "tetragrammon," or "four-letter." It was a name so sacred that the Hebrew people would not pronounce it lest they violate the commandment about taking the name of God in vain. The approximate English consonants for the name are the letters Y, H, W, H. When Hebrew scholars added vowels to the original Scriptures which used only consonants, the four-letter name became *Yahweh.* Even then it was not pronounced; some other term for God or the word for the place where God dwells (heaven) would be substituted.

*My Lord* is a translation of another Hebrew name for God, *Adonai.* It was a name which the Jews were permitted to pronounce and was many times substituted for *Yahweh.* In the Greek translation of the Hebrew Scriptures—the Septuagint—the same word was used to translate both of these Hebrew words—the word, *kurios,* which meant "lord." The result is an English construction which is perplexing because the sentence seems to suggest a distinction but the words give no clue to it. In the Hebrew text of the psalm the distinction is clear: *Yahweh,* the eternal and covenant-making God, spoke to *Adonai,* the one whom he had appointed as the priestly-king to rule, that is, his anointed one.

The Hebrew construction translated into Greek and then into the English *The Lord said* literally means "the whispered communication of *Yahweh.*" The idea is the revelation of a mystery. The mystery revealed is the anointing of his Ruler to *sit at his right hand,* the place of honor and authority. The meaning in the psalm is that *Yahweh* (God) had given *Adonai* (his anointed one) the place of authority as his Ruler-Priest.

*Till I make thy enemies a stool for thy feet:* The expression *stool for thy feet* means a pedestal on which to stand or to rest one's feet while sitting. This is oriental imagery used of a conqueror; his enemies had been so subdued that they were crushed down to the status of a footrest. While it is not an appealing figure for modern Christians who do not like to think of Christ as such a crushing despotic ruler, it was for ancient man a meaningful symbol of absolute victory over every foe. Paul spoke of Christ's conquering every foe, including man's last enemy to be conquered—death.

*Verse 44:* Having quoted the commonly accepted reference to the Messiah, Jesus returned to his question of verse 41. This time it contained two parts: How can the Messiah be both David's Lord and David's son? How could David refer to his own son as his Lord? The only answer is that the Messiah would be both human and divine. He would be *David's son* because of his physical descent from the line of David; he would be *David's Lord* because *Yahweh,* the eternal covenant-making God, had designated him *Adonai,* deity itself.

Luke gives no indication of the response made to Jesus' question. Matthew indicates that no one was able to give a word of answer to Jesus' question (22:46). They could not answer without admitting that the Messiah would be divine. They granted that he would be human—descended from David—but not that he would be divine. Jesus held that the Messiah would be both human and divine. Indeed he held that that was true in his own case—Son of David—Son of God. To have answered his question would have been to grant that the Messiah was the kind of person Jesus claimed to be. They would not grant that.

### (5) Denouncing the scribes and Pharisees for hypocrisy (20:45–47)

*Verse 45:* Jesus warned the people to beware of the scribes. Matthew definitely relates this to the preceding event—"then Jesus spoke" (23:1). Mark and Luke do not so definitely relate it to that event, but their introductions permit such relation. His warning was given *to his disciples* (the Twelve), but *in the hearing of all the people.* It was specifically given to the Twelve because they were to be in the position of being "leaders" of the people in matters of religion. That was the position of the scribes whom Jesus felt were unsafe leaders by their example and practice.

*Verse 46: Beware of the scribes:* Matthew's account includes the Pharisees in this warning. The meaning may be that Jesus' warning was against the scribes who were of the Pharisee party, and not of all scribes. On a previous occasion, Jesus had directed some of these same charges against the Pharisees (11:43).

*Long robes* were indications of men of importance—men who were not engaged in menial tasks requiring physical labor. As scholars and teachers they felt above such labor. Matthew's account refers to their making their robes longer by enlarging the borders which identified them as pious men (23:5). They wore the outward garb of the pious, but beneath them was the heart of the impious.

*Love salutations in the market places:* The reference was not to a simple and sincere greeting. It was to the long, elaborate, and ingratiating greeting commonly called today "bowing and scraping." Matthew added that they insisted on being addressed "Rabbi." A simple "Mr." would have been below their rank! Respect for one's position is honorable and constructive, but improperly motivated or exaggerated it can become the kind of grasping for recognition which is dishonorable and destructive. Jesus did not desire this for ministers who followed him in God's redemptive ministry.

*The best seats in the synagogue:* These were the seats near the one who was leading the service. Such seats put them in view of all the people so their presence and honorable position would be noted. It also made them available to lend their wisdom to any discussion which might arise. A beloved former theological professor put this into modern dress by referring to it as "sitting on the platform at the convention!"

*The places of honor at feasts:* At a festive table the places of honor were near the host. These places indicated rank approximating that of the host. Jesus had once given a parable on the theme of choosing for one's self a seat of honor and then suffering the embarrassment of being sent by the host to a lower ranking seat. (See previous exposition of 11:43 and 14:7–11.)

*Verse 47:* The practices pointed out in verse 46 relate to grasping pride in one's position in society. Jesus then turned to a more grievous expression of one's self-importance. *Who devour widows' houses* means that by oppression of defenseless widows the scribes used their position to rob. This is a part of the neglect of "justice and love" which Jesus had charged against the Pharisees in the earlier passage (11:42). It recalls God's complaint against those in Israel of old "who join house to house, who add field to field" (Isa. 5:8). An exaggerated sense of one's own importance leads to a depreciating sense of the importance of others. The next step from that is conscienceless robbery by exploitation of the unfortunate. It was not a vice limited to Pharisees nor to the first century.

*For a pretense make long prayers:* The Pharisees lengthened their prayers, not for the sake of communing with God, but for the sake of impressing men with the amount of time they prayed. Such is not prayer, only play-acting at praying. Long prayers on the day and in the place of worship do not really impress men that one is religious if, in the days that follow, one's demeanor in business and society is that of grasping pride and heartless exploitation.

*They will receive greater condemnation:* A consistent theme in the Scriptures is that of judgment in proportion to one's sin. Position of leadership in the religious community exploited for personal aggrandisement of position and profit is a sin which by its nature involves heavy punishment. (See exposition of 12:41–48 about punishment in proportion to knowledge and guilt.)

### (6) Commending the pauper widow (21:1–4)

The story of the "widow's mite" has captured the appreciation of millions. Her example has been used as an encouragement for sacrificial giving. Unfortunately, it has also been used as an excuse by many who have claimed to give "the widow's mite" when their circumstances and gift did not warrant the claim.

*Verse 1: He looked up and saw:* The impression is that this was an isolated event which Jesus observed almost by accident. Mark's account, however, indicates that Jesus had deliberately taken a position near the place of giving where he watched the procession of givers for some time. Luke's reference, therefore, is to one instance in which a group of worshipers made their gifts.

*The rich* is a plural form—rich people. Mark adds the detail that there were "many" of them.

*Putting their gifts into the treasury:* According to the Talmud there were thirteen treasure boxes in the Temple, located in the Court of the Women which was also accessible to men—hence, all could get to them. Each box had a trumpetlike opening into which the money was thrown. The coins would run around and around as they went down, thus calling attention to the gift. The practice was humorously referred to as "sounding a trumpet" when one gave and it may have been what Jesus referred to in Matthew 6:2. Some think so; others think he referred to a fanfare of trumpets which sometimes preceded a wealthy man on his way to make a gift. Jesus recognized neither as worship.

Into the treasure boxes the people cast their Temple tax as well as other gifts for the support of the Temple and the priesthood. Each trumpet opening was marked by a Hebrew letter and the people may have been able to designate the purpose of their gift by the choice of the box. At Passover great crowds were always present. Many of them came to Jerusalem only this one time in the year. Many others came only on rare occasions, not annually. Such a condition was conducive to much and generous giving.

*Verse 2: He saw a poor widow:* Out of all who had made their gifts on that day, Jesus noted this one. Mark has "one poor widow" in contrast to his "many" rich men. Luke has "a certain widow, a needy one." There is no indication of how this was known, whether by previous acquaintance in the Bethany-Jerusalem area or by her very appearance. The emphasis is on her own needy condition—her destitution with no man to provide for her. The story is most dramatic following Jesus' charge that the religious leaders exploited widows in their greed (20:47).

*Two copper coins:* This was the *lepta*—the word means "tiny." The coin was very small and its value was very small. One was worth about one-eighth of a cent. The woman's gift was approximately one-fourth of a cent.

*Verse 3: Truly I tell you:* The words were addressed to the Twelve. He said nothing to the woman.

*This poor widow:* The order of the words is emphatic and graphic in expression—"this widow herself, this poor one."

*Has put in more than all of them:* This appears to be a misrepresentation of fact. The others had given large sums of money. She had given only one-fourth of a cent. The Twelve listened probably with amazement at such an appraisal. It was a strange evaluation of money for any Jewish businessman or tax collector, and such they had been.

*Verse 4: They all contributed out of their abundance:* All the others who had been observed as they gave their large gifts had given a part of their wealth, but they had plenty which they had not given. The word rendered *abundance* means "overflow." Their personal treasure boxes were overflowing even after they had given.

*She out of her poverty put in all the living she had:* The word translated *poverty* means deficiency and makes a strong contrast with the *abundance*. While for the rich there remained an overflow of supply, there remained for the widow nothing; she had put into the treasure box in the house of God *all the living that she had*.

She came to the Temple with a fourth of a cent in her hands but with gratitude in her heart. She left the Temple with nothing in her hands but with the joy of having given all in her heart. Jesus did not encourage her— she walked by faith. He did not reward her—reward she already had. He did not commend her—her commendation was a good conscience. He did use her as an example of one who loved to the extent that she gave her absolute all. It was his last act in the Temple. He went out to do the same thing—to give his absolute all.

### (7) Teaching about judgment on Jerusalem and the world (21:5–36)

As they went out from the Temple, the Twelve called Jesus' attention to its beauty. He responded that the time was coming when it would be destroyed. Then as they went on to Bethany for the night, he stopped on the Mount of Olives to speak more fully of that coming catastrophe. The Lukan account has its parallel in Mark 13 and Matthew 24–25.

This is one of the most difficult passages in the synoptic Gospels. It is easier to interpret one of the accounts than the three of them together. Some parts simply defy clear interpretation. At such points caution is in order and dogmatic certainty is out of order. For the present purpose, the exposition must be limited to Luke's account. In fairness to the reader of these accounts, however, a brief preliminary comparison is essential.

Putting the three Gospel accounts together, the following pattern is developed: *One,* as Jesus and the Twelve left the Temple, they called his attention to its beauty. He answered with the prediction that the Temple was going to be destroyed. *Two,* silenced by that prediction, the Twelve waited until they had descended the hill, crossed the Kidron, walked up the steep ascent of the Mount of Olives, and stopped to rest before going on. Then the inner four (Peter, Andrew, James, and John—Mark 13:3) asked Jesus for an explanation—when that event would be and what would be the signs by which its coming and the coming of the end of the age could be detected (Matt. 24:3). *Three,* Jesus divided their question into two parts. First, he spoke of the coming destruction, enlarging it to include, not just the Temple, but the entire city of Jerusalem. Second, he spoke of the end of the age with the coming of the Son of Man in judgment.

Jesus cautioned them emphatically that the two events were not the same. The destruction of Jerusalem would be first (it came in A.D. 70). Its turmoil of judgment on the wicked city would be an illustration of the second—the turmoil of judgment on the wicked world at the coming of the Son of Man. In Luke (v. 25), there is no more exact relation of the two than that sequence. In Mark 13:24 the relation stated is that the coming of the Son of Man will be "in those days" but "after that tribulation"—after the destruction of Jerusalem. Matthew 24:29 has the expression "immediately after the tribulation of those days."

The word "immediately" intensifies the problem. Because the coming of the Son of Man did not take place *immediately* after the destruction of Jerusalem, some interpreters have felt the necessity of extending all of the prediction to the end of the world, with the view that before the coming of Christ there will be a restoration of ancient Jerusalem with its Temple, sacrifice, priesthood, and conflict with a restored Rome, once again, the supreme antidivine world power. The approach requires highly subjective interpretation of other passages of Scripture—both Old and New Testaments —and results in a tremendous burden to be carried by the one word "immediately."

A major difficulty in interpreting the entire section of teachings in the three Gospels is that Luke's dominating interest and emphasis is not on the *time* of the coming of the Son of Man, but on the *time of waiting* before that coming and the responsibility of Christ's Spirit-empowered witnesses in that interim. Luke does not reject the doctrine of the second coming, but neither does he emphasize it as do Mark, Matthew, Peter, and Paul. His minimizing the coming of the Son of Man (vv. 25-33) was due in part to his theological purpose of writing in a day when many Christians were perplexed about the delay of that coming.

This *theological purpose* presents an approach to the nature of history— a philosophy of history—which is very different from that of Mark and

Matthew. Mark and Matthew reflect the idea of a "closed end" for history. Note Mark 13:24-26: "But in those days, after that tribulation [i.e., the destruction of Jerusalem in vv. 14-23], the sun will be darkened . . . then they will see the Son of man coming in clouds with great power and glory." Note Matthew 24:29-30, "Immediately after the tribulation of those days [i.e., the destruction of Jerusalem in vv. 15-28] the sun will be darkened . . . then will appear the sign of the Son of man in heaven." These passages suggest a rather tight view of history with its close association with the coming of the Son of Man immediately after the destruction of Jerusalem.

In Luke, however, history is left with an open end while God works out his redemptive purpose. The end will be marked by the coming of the Son of Man after the period of waiting in which Jesus' followers engage faithfully in witnessing to all men. God's redemptive history is viewed in three stages: the *time of Israel,* with the law pointing to sin and the prophets pointing to the sinbearer, the promised Redeemer; the *time of Jesus,* with his fulfillment of God's promise to send the Redeemer; the *time of waiting,* with the church witnessing of the Redeemer until his coming in consummation of God's redemptive purpose at the end of the age. It is this third period which dominates Luke's use of this section of Jesus' teaching as well as his second volume, the Book of Acts.

Luke wrote at a time when Jerusalem had been destroyed and even that took place forty years after Jesus went away. Other years had passed—ten or more most likely—and still Jesus had not returned. His return seemed to be delayed far beyond anyone's anticipation. How was this to be interpreted? Did it mean that Jesus was not going to return? Definitely not. The Gospel of Luke retains Jesus' teaching of his return, even in a form which seems to anticipate an early return (vv. 25-36). In the Book of Acts, that return is reaffirmed in the very first chapter (1:6-11). Jesus indicated at that last appearance that the disciples were not to know times and seasons which the Father had fixed by his own authority; that they were to anticipate the receiving of the power of the Holy Spirit; and that, having received that power, they were to be his witnesses to the end of the earth (vv. 7-8). While they watched, he ascended; and then the divine messengers renewed the promise of his return (vv. 10-11). They waited for the power; it came at Pentecost; they began their witness. That witness included the coming of Christ whom heaven had received "until the time for establishing all that God spoke by the mouth of his holy prophets from old" (Acts 3:21). He would come to bring an end to history. Only God knew when that coming would be. In the time of waiting, they were not to be idle. They were to give themselves to witnessing to all men. That faith which marked their response to the "delayed coming" has marked the response of the church through the ages and marks it now—we wait, and while we wait we witness.

Another major difficulty in interpreting the entire section is that in Mark and Matthew, where both events are definitely included and the second emphasized, it is exceedingly difficult to identify exact transitions where Jesus ceased speaking about the destruction of Jerusalem and started to speak about the end of the world. The interpreter of all three Gospels must wrestle with these problems. Exposition of all three is not the prerogative of this volume on Luke. Therefore, the exposition to follow will be from the viewpoint of Luke's account only.

*Verse 5:* As they left the Temple, the disciples called Jesus' attention to the beauty of its structure. From both Jewish and Gentile historians it is clear that this Temple which had been restored by Herod was one of the most elaborate and beautiful structures in the Roman world.

*How it was adorned with noble stones and offerings:* The *noble stones* refers to the marble structure. Some of the pillars were forty feet high. Besides the regular stone work, there were special highly engraved and ornamented stones which were donations of wealthy and devout worshipers. The *offerings* may have referred to these votive stones as well as to great amounts of gold used as ornamental overlay. Worked into the entrance to the Temple was a huge gold grapevine with tremendous bunches of grapes, symbolizing Israel as God's fruit-bearing vine. The grapevine was a national symbol of Israel and was a part of its military coat of arms. Jesus' beautiful allegory of the vine and the branches (John 15) referred to this. In his view, the Old Israel had failed to bear fruit; he as the *genuine* vine was sending the disciples out as branches to bear fruit. The probable setting for that discourse was the Temple on the way from the Last Supper to the Garden of Gethsemane.

*Verse 6:* Jesus responded to the disciples' admiring wonder at the Temple structure by saying that all of it was destined to destruction. He repeated a part of what he had said in his weeping over the city at the triumphal entry (19:41–44). It was that previous prediction which likely prompted the disciples' expression of wonder. They could not envision such destruction and were silenced by the repetition of his prediction.

*Verse 7:* The accounts of Mark and Matthew place the disciples' request for further enlightenment and Jesus' response to their request on the Mount of Olives. They were going to Bethany which was at the foot of the Mount of Olives on the opposite side from Jerusalem. One could take a longer road around the mountain or he could take the road up, across, and down the other side. It was this road which they traveled, reversing the way of the triumphal entry on the preceding Sunday. There was a rest stop at the brow of the mountain where pilgrims leaving the city could stop to take a last look at the holy city with its Temple dominating the landscape.

There they stopped. The Twelve (led by Peter and his three associates) asked, *When will this be, and what will be the sign when this is about to take place?* Note Luke's omission of the question (in Matt. 24:3) about his coming and the end of the world. They were looking directly west. The late afternoon sun made the city stand out in profile. Most noticeable of all was the profile of the Temple of white marble and gold. The view must have been breathtakingly beautiful. In that setting Jesus spoke of the coming catastrophe.

His words fit so exactly many of the details of what happened in that destruction that some interpreters reject them as prediction on Jesus' part and attribute them to later history reported in the form of a prediction. Others accept his prediction but think that many of the details were added later after they had happened. There is no compelling reason for rejecting

Jesus' foresight in these events. Apart from the question of revelation, there is the plain fact of his sensitivity to the growing rebellion and the determination of the Jews for a revolution against Rome. One who knew the history of Jerusalem, the Temple, and the Jews at the hands of Sargon, Sennacherib, Nebuchadnezzar, and Antiochus Epiphanes could certainly discern the inevitability of the crushing armies of Rome. Whether or not Jesus knew the *time* of Jerusalem's end—he appeared to anticipate its coming in the lifetime of some of his hearers—he knew the *certainty* of that end, and the *nature* of that end. As matters were developing, to anticipate revolt and defeat in a matter of a very few years would have been most reasonable.

*Verses 8–9:* Jesus warned the Twelve that in the difficult times which were coming, there would be many rumors that he had returned. They were not to be deceived because those events did not mean the end. In such times devout people would be looking for "messiahs." They would be anticipating God's intervention to deliver them from the enemy.

Many false messiahs would arise pretending to be the Lord's authorized representative; *in my name* means "as my representative" or "in my stead." These false messiahs would proclaim, *I am he.* The pronoun *he* is not in the text. The text has just the emphatic *"I am,"* in the sense of "I am the deliverer for whom you are looking."

Many false reports would be raised, claiming *"The time is at hand!"* "The time has come." As the Twelve were not to be *led astray* by the claims of false messiahs, they were not to *go after* (follow) those who were reporting that the end had come.

Nor were they to *be terrified* when they heard of wars and tumultuous disturbances taking place. These were an inevitable result of man in conflict with man and nation with nation. Before the end of which Jesus spoke came about, there would be many disturbances due to man's compulsion for fighting to obtain what he desired.

*But the end will not be at once:* The adverb translated *at once* means "immediately," and it is in the emphatic first place in the phrase—"but not immediately the end." There would be many events taking place before that end.

*Verse 10* contains references to wars between nations. *Verse 11* contains references to calamities in nature—earthquakes, famines, pestilences, solar and lunar eclipses, meteors flashing through the sky. Through history there have been men who have tended to panic at all such things and to interpret them as "signs" that the end is near. Jesus saw them as inevitable in the kind of world in which men live. He warned his disciples not to panic at such reports.

In verses 12–19 Jesus focused the attention of the Twelve on the difficult experiences they would face personally in the years ahead. Some of this language was used earlier by Matthew regarding synagogue persecutions when Jesus sent out the Twelve (10:16–23). Luke did not use it there. He uses it here regarding the years after Jesus' death.

*Verse 12:* As Jesus' witnesses, they would face persecutions which might cause faint hearts to panic. They would be seized and dragged to trial in the *synagogues* and before *kings and governors.* This represented their persecution by the Jews as well as their being tried in Roman courts. The record of some of these persecutions and trials is in the Book of Acts. *For my name's sake* means that they would face these troubles because they were proclaiming him as Savior. An example of this was Peter's proclaiming to the Jewish court that "there is no other name under heaven given among men by which we must be saved" (Acts 4:12).

*Verses 13–15* contain Jesus' counsel as to how they were to meet those trials. They were to regard them as an opportunity *to bear testimony*. They were to settle in their minds that they would not prepare speeches for defense and have them ready (v. 14). He promised that he himself (the emphatic *I*) would give them *a mouth*—utterance or expression. He would also give them *wisdom*—the ability to make the right choice of what to say and how to conduct themselves. This utterance (words) and wisdom (thoughts) would be such that their accusers would not *be able to withstand or contradict*. Examples of this, too, may be examined in Acts 3:12–26; 4:8–12, 19–21; 6:10; 7:1–53.

*Verses 16–17* contain the warning that they would face persecution even in their own families—betrayal by parents, brothers, kinsmen, and friends. In his mind there may have lurked the sad realization that his own brothers did not believe in him (John 7:5) and that one of his friends (Judas) was to betray him.

*Some of you they will put to death:* The fact that they would have words and wisdom to defend themselves beyond contradiction (v. 15) would not guarantee release for all of them. Hostility for them would outweigh reason and would result in death for some. Earlier he had predicted a martyr's death for James and John (Mark 10:39). Later he would predict a martyr's death for Peter (John 21:18–19).

*You will be hated by all for my name's sake:* Some of them would find that hatred for what the name "Jesus of Nazareth" came to mean in Jewish religious circles would be stronger than the ties of kinship and friendship. Only the martyrdom of James is related in the New Testament (Acts 12:1–2). Early Christian sources of varying reliability relate martyrdom for all of the apostles. Some of the accounts are doubtless essentially true. Some are highly questionable. But even here Jesus spoke of martyrdom only for *some* of them.

*Verses 18–19* contain words of assurance which appear to be contradictory to what is contained in verse 16. There he said that some of the Twelve would be put to death. Here he is reported to have said that *not a hair of your head will perish* (v. 18) and *you will gain your lives* (v. 19). He did not say that not a hair of the head of *some of them* would perish nor that *some of them* would gain their lives. He spoke these verses to all. There is no easy resolution of the seeming contradiction.

One view is that the two sentences of assurance in verses 18 and 19 have been lifted out of other contexts and placed here without noting that they form a contradiction. That would represent a very careless arrangement of materials. Luke's arrangement of materials is not characterized by such carelessness. The place of the two verses in this text is secure. There are no manuscripts which omit them. Unsatisfactory as the explanation is, the presence of these verses in those other contexts must be noted.

Verse 18, in a slightly different verbal form, is in Luke 12:7. Jesus used it in encouraging his followers not to fear men, because he said that God took such careful notice of them that the very hairs of their heads were numbered. Matthew 10:30 has the Luke 12:7 form of the saying in another setting—Jesus' assurance to the Twelve when sending them out. It is also used in Acts 27:34 in Paul's encouraging the passengers who were facing shipwreck. All of them probably go back to 1 Samuel 14:45, referring to Jonathan's safety in the hands of King Saul.

Verse 19, again in slightly different verbal form, is a part of Matthew's account of Jesus' sending out the Twelve with the assurance of danger in persecution but also with the assurance that "he who endures to the end will be saved"—that is, by their waiting out the persecution "to the end" they would not die but would survive the persecution.

Another view of the meaning of these two verses proceeds along the lines of paradox. By that understanding Jesus was assuring them that even though they experienced death (v. 16), they would not be beyond God's care. If he had such watchful concern for them in this life that every hair was numbered, they could certainly know that he would care for their welfare in the next life (v. 18). Verse 19 is interpreted in a similar way. Even though they experienced death (v. 16), by their loyalty to him they would gain their *lives,* understood as souls in the sense of the essential person. Luke 9:23–26 is cited as clarification—one may lose his "physical life" but gain his "real life."

This interpretation regards the passage as the sort of teaching in which the rabbis delighted and which they called a *Mashal*—a riddle or a proverb. The *Mashal* teaching would be given, and the hearers would be left to seek out the meaning of the riddle so as to understand the teaching. While it was a valid method and Jesus used it—for example, the Temple riddle in John 2:19–22—it seems inappropriate in such a setting as this. If, however, that is not the correct approach, the meaning remains uncertain.

Verses 20–24: Having warned them against false reports of the end, and having spoken of the days of persecution and danger that lay ahead, Jesus came specifically to the point of the destruction which he mentioned earlier (v. 6). The destruction was enlarged to include the city as well as the Temple.

*Verse 20:* The *sign* they had requested by which they would know when the destruction was coming would be the sight of *Jerusalem surrounded by armies.* When they saw that, they would know that her *desolation* was near— her complete destruction. All of this he had indicated in 19:42–44. The only thing he adds here is the *sign*—the camps of the armies encircling Jerusalem.

*Verse 21:* When that time came, Jerusalem would be a place to flee rather than to enter for shelter. All the people of Judea—not just the city— should flee to the hills to hide from the enemy. Those who were inside the city should go out and seek safety. Those who were outside the city should not go in to seek shelter or possessions. History indicates that when the Romans approached, the Jews generally took the very opposite action. Those inside the city stayed. Those out in the country thought they would be safer within the walls. The result was murder on an almost inconceivable scale. A large company of the Christians fled Jerusalem as the war developed and established a new center at Pella, east of the Jordan.

*Verse 22: These are days of vengeance:* The destruction was judgment on the Jews for their rebellion against God and his total purpose for them. The early Christians interpreted it as a fate due to their rejection of Jesus as the Messiah. *To fulfil all that is written* is probably a reference to the words of the ancient prophets concerning the destruction of Jerusalem under the Babylonians and other ancient enemies. Those things had been fulfilled in the past, but a greater and more meaningful fulfillment was envisioned in the coming renewal of atrocities under the Romans.

*Verse 23:* Expectant mothers, *those who are with child,* and mothers with nursing infants, *those who give suck,* would have an unusually difficult time in the kind of travel necessary to escape to the hills. The *distress . . . upon the earth* and *wrath upon this people* refers to the conduct of the Romans. The revolution started in A.D. 66; Jerusalem fell in A.D. 70. In those years the Romans worked their wrath by ravaging the land, destroying the cities, and slaughtering the Jews. Josephus, the Roman-bred Jewish historian, devoted five chapters to the destruction of Jerusalem. Much of what the Gospels contain as prediction, he confirms as history.

*Verse 24:* Some were put to death—*by the edge of the sword.* Others were deported as captives. Ancient stone carvings of the event still decorate memorial structures in Rome—Jewish captives in a triumphal procession celebrating Titus's destruction of Jerusalem and victory in the war of the rebellion in A.D. 66–70. The city of Jerusalem was trampled under the feet of the Romans *until the times of the Gentiles* were fulfilled. They had their time in Jerusalem—their full opportunity for devastation. When those times were ended, all was in ruin. The buildings were razed. The gold and marble were carried away as plunder. The once mighty, rich, proud city of David with its unrivalled House of God was a mountain of rubble.

Verses 25–36 constitute the disputed section of this chapter. It has been noted previously (v. 7) that Luke does not have the question about the coming of Christ and the end of the age (Matt. 24:3). He has only the question as to when the destruction of the Temple would be and what would be the sign by which they could discern its nearness. The problem, then, is, does Luke's passage relate only to the destruction of Jerusalem, or does it also include teaching on the second coming at the end of the age? If he includes the second coming, what part of his text relates to the destruction of Jerusalem and what part refers to the second coming? Several approaches have been made.

*One:* Some interpreters understand that Luke has omitted the coming of the Son of Man at the end of the age and has reframed the material in such a way that references to the Son of Man in verses 27 and 36 are elaborate expressions of the idea that he came in judgment on Jerusalem in A.D. 70. This view might be completely satisfying were it not for the fact that some parts seem so definitely to refer to the coming at the end of the age (vv. 27, 31, 36). Too, the language of verses 25–26 more naturally fits the end of the age than the end of a city.

*Two:* Some interpreters understand that both the destruction of Jerusalem in A.D. 70 and the coming of the Son of Man at the end of the age are in this passage. Rather than being clearly separated, however, they are so fused together that it is difficult to determine with certainty which part refers to which event. Note these verses which appear to refer to the second coming: Verse 27, *then they will see the Son of man coming in a cloud with power and great glory.* Verse 31, *know that the kingdom of God is near.* Verse 36, *praying that you may have strength to escape all these things that will take place, and to stand before the Son of man.*

Embedded in these verses, however, are those indications that whatever was under discussion was anticipated in the lifetime of Jesus' hearers. Note verse 28, *Now when these things begin to take place, look up and raise your heads, because your redemption is drawing near.* This was addressed to the Twelve. Note verse 32, *this generation will not pass away till all has taken place.* Note verse 34, *take heed to yourselves,* and verse 36, *watch at all times, praying that you may have strength to escape all these things that will take place, and to stand before the Son of man.* These verses are in the section which seems to refer to the second coming, but they also seem to mean that Jesus anticipated that coming in the lifetime of some of his hearers. Interpreters hesitate to say that Jesus anticipated something which did not take place. It appears to them to reflect on his deity.

Some of these interpreters regard this as a confusion which was the work of Luke or that existed in the source he used. They do not regard the sayings as having been spoken by Jesus in this form. They understand that Jesus spoke of the two events, but the early church was responsible for the confusion of his sayings.

Some of these interpreters, on the other hand, think that Jesus spoke the words just as they are. The solution, in their opinion, is to identify the parts which refer to the destruction of Jerusalem (which as Jesus anticipated came in the lifetime of some of the Twelve), and those parts which refer to the second coming at the end of the age. They relate none of the passages anticipating fulfillment within the lifetime of Jesus' hearers to the second coming. By that approach:

Verses 25–26 relate to the second coming.
Verses 27–28 relate to the destruction of Jerusalem.
Verses 29–30 relate to the second coming.
Verses 31–32 relate to the destruction of Jerusalem.
Verse 33 relates to the second coming.
Verse 34 relates to the destruction of Jerusalem.
Verse 35 relates to the second coming.

Verse 36 again relates to the destruction of Jerusalem. Some even divide verse 36 into three parts: "watch at all times" refers to both events; "praying that you may have strength to escape" refers to the destruction of Jerusalem; "stand before the Son of man" refers to the second coming. Such fragmentation is almost inconceivable. Its only recommendation is that it eliminates the question of Jesus' anticipating the second coming in the lifetime of some of the Twelve.

*Three:* Some interpreters understand that Jesus did anticipate the second coming in the lifetime of some of the Twelve. Between his going away and his return there would be a time of waiting and witnessing under persecution. Within that time of waiting would be the revolt of the Jews against Rome with the devastating war and the destruction of Jerusalem. Then on beyond that would be the second coming.

Jesus stated that he did not know when the end would be. "But of that day or that hour no one knows, not even the angels in heaven, nor the Son, but only the Father" (Mark 13:32). The words "nor the Son" are not in many of the ancient manuscripts of Matthew 24:36, but they are unquestionably authentic in Mark.

The Jewish people believed that the angels were superior to men in knowledge. They called the angels "the higher family" and believed that God did nothing which he did not first talk over with them. One ancient rabbi interpreted Isaiah 63:4 as meaning that the one exception to that was the time of God's final reckoning with and judgment on men. Jesus said that no man on earth, including the Son, knew when the end would be; that in heaven the angels did not know, and only the Father knew. Jesus' words regarding the time of the end cannot be interpreted without taking that statement seriously; he simply did not know when it would be. The time of the end was hidden even from him; the Father reserved that for his knowledge alone. (See also Acts 1:7.) From that viewpoint the following exposition results.

*Verse 24:* This language is of the category called "apocalyptic," a type of symbolic language by which a message was revealed or unveiled. The word means a revealing and the noun form—apocalypse—means a revelation. It was a very popular type of literature among the Hebrew people of the ancient time. (For examples see Isa. 13:9–10; Ezek. 32:7–8; Joel 2:1–2, 10–11, 30–31; Amos 8:9; Zeph. 1:14–16.) Many religious books of this type were written by contemporaries of Jesus, and some were very popular in Galilee. When he used this way of referring to his coming, Jesus was using a method which was very familiar to his disciples.

*Verses 25–26: Signs in sun and moon and stars* (v. 25) and *the powers of the heavens* being shaken (v. 26) refer to disturbances in the celestial realm. The *roaring of the sea and the waves* (v. 25) refers to disturbances in the earthly realm—tidal waves related to the disturbances in the course of sun, moon, and stars. *Distress of nations in perplexity* (v. 25) and *men fainting with fear and with foreboding* (v. 26) refer to disturbances in the human realm as men observe the complete dissolution of the material universe.

Some interpreters understand these events to be literal as the material creation and the temporal order are replaced by the eternal order and the "new heaven" and the "new earth" of that eternal order (Rev. 21:1). It is certain that the material world is not of such nature as to last forever. It is doomed to end. In other places in the Scriptures other language is used to depict that end, for example, "But the day of the Lord will come like a thief, and then the heavens will pass away with a loud noise, and the elements will be dissolved with fire, and the earth and the works that are upon it will be burned up. . . . But . . . we wait for new heavens and a new earth in which righteousness dwells" (2 Pet. 3:10, 13).

Other interpreters understand these references to a disturbed universe—sky, earth, and man—to be a symbolic way of expressing the consummation of God's purpose for this creation. The giving way of the old temporal order to the new eternal order will be in every way a world-shaking event. In view of the total of biblical language this appears to be the more fitting interpretation. That consummation is to be at the coming of the Son of Man.

*Verse 27:* The exalted language depicting the Messiah's second coming is in dramatic contrast to that of his first coming. Once he came to the world as a baby born in a stable, cradled in a manger, and destined for humiliation and suffering. A second time he will come in power and glory.

*Then they will see the Son of man coming: Then* relates to the disturbances of men in the realization that their world is breaking up. As they behold that, they see the Son of Man coming. The weak gives way to the strong; the temporal to the eternal. *Son of man* was Jesus' favorite reference to himself. As it had embraced the concept of suffering and humiliation in the days of his flesh, so it embraces the concept of exaltation and glory in his eternal state. In the Hebrew use (Ps.; Dan.; 1 Enoch) the term involved exaltation through humiliation. Jesus came to exaltation through humiliation. It was a fitting title.

*Coming in a cloud:* The expression could be translated "on a cloud" and some interpreters so understand it—as if a cloud were the medium of his descent to the earth as it had been the means of his ascent from the earth. Clouds were spoken of poetically as the chariots of God (Ps. 104:3). The passage must also be considered in relation to Acts 1:9 and other New Testament references associating clouds with his coming (1 Thess. 4: 17; Rev. 1:7). The idea of the total is that as his going away was veiled by the clouds in mystery, so his coming back will be unveiled by the clouds in mystery. Both ideas are appropriate.

*With power and great glory: Power* is an indication of his conquering the entire hostile material order. He comes with power to dissolve the material world and constitute a new one. He comes with power over rebellious men and to establish his eternal lordship. Once men rebelled, rejected and crucified him; then every knee shall bend and every tongue shall confess, "Jesus Christ is Lord" (Phil. 2:11).

*Glory* is another contrast word. Luke alone has the story of Jesus' birth in a stable because there was no room in the inn. There was no glory in that. But Luke alone has also the announcement by the heavenly host who sang "glory" at his birth. From the human viewpoint there was no glory in a Roman crucifixion, though Jesus extended the idea of the glory of the Father even to the cross (John 12:23; 17:1). But in this scene of the coming of the Son of Man there is *glory.* The word, used so many ways in the Scriptures, probably includes all the fullness of the incarnate, crucified, risen, and glorified Christ.

*Verse 28:* This is a word of encouragement to the Twelve. They were not to panic or despair but were to know that the events predicted would mean for them not bad but good.

*These things* refers certainly to the breaking up of the temporal creation and order and the establishing of the eternal order with the glorious coming of the Son of Man (vv. 25-27). Some interpreters understand *these things* to include also the destruction of Jerusalem, and perhaps even the disturbing conditions of verses 8-17—war, false rumors of the end, earthquakes, pestilence, persecution, death of some of the Twelve.

*Begin to take place:* From the moment it was clear that the consummation of God's purpose was drawing to its climax and that the eternal order was

dawning, the disciples should *look up and raise your heads.* The beginning
of the events of verses 25–27 would be a time of encouragement for Jesus'
witnesses. They were not to be discouraged with a feeling of depression.
They were to raise up their downcast heads, and lift up their faces no longer
sad, but joyful in expectation.

*Because your redemption is drawing near:* The word translated *redemption*
means deliverance. The ending of the temporal order and the beginning of
the eternal order meant deliverance from all the turmoil of a world hostile
to God and to the people of God. It meant deliverance from hostility,
suffering, persecution, danger, and the threat of death. All of that which
characterized the material and temporal order as they knew it would be
ended. The new eternal and spiritual order would have no place for the old.
One of the most dramatic expressions of this concept is in Revelation 21:5
in the words of the eternal God on his throne, "Behold, I make all things
new"—a new creation into which the things of the old creation (Rev. 21:4)
can never intrude. That indeed will be *redemption.*

Verses 29–33 continue the words of encouragement to look up with the
parable of the budding fig tree. It is doubtful that there is a relation between
this parable and the miracle of the fruitless fig tree associated with Jesus'
teaching on prayer and faith (Mark 11:12–25; Matt. 21:18–22). Luke did
not include that miracle. Mark and Matthew, however, included both the
miracle and the parable (Mark 13:28–32; Matt. 24:32–36). There is no
reference to fruitlessness in either of the three accounts of the parable. It
is not valid interpretation to relate the two fig tree passages, to allegorize the
parable to mean that the fig tree represents the Jews and the other trees
represent the other nations, and conclude that the parable teaches that the
fruitless nation of Israel will once again bud and grow and bear fruit in
the end of time. That is imposing preconceived ideas upon the Scriptures, not
drawing meaning out of the Scriptures.

*Verse 29:* Jesus' encouragement in verse 28 was directed to the *beginning*
of all the things of verses 25–27. For that reason, he cited *the fig tree, and
all the trees,* in that order. The fig tree begins the process of budding and
leafing out earlier than most of the other trees. That puts the stress on
the *beginning* of encouragement.

*Verse 30: As soon as they come out in leaf:* When all the trees complete
their leafing out, one knows for certain and without having to be told by
someone else that *the summer is already near.* Summer follows spring;
spring is fully present when the last tree has its leaves. But one knows that
spring is in process and summer is next just as soon as the first tree begins
to bud and to leaf. Hence, as the first evidence of budding begins with the
fig tree, men begin to rejoice that the hard winter is passing and a new
season is coming. So for the Twelve, encouragement and the lifting up of
faces were to begin when they observed the beginning of the coming of the
new order.

*Verse 31:* Here Jesus applies his parable to his disciples. *These things*
does not refer to the budding and leafing of the trees; that was the example,
this is the application. *These things* in this verse has the same reference
as *these things* in verse 28. Specifically it refers to the breaking up of the old
order and the beginning of the new—when the disciples saw that beginning

they would *know that the kingdom of God is near.* In the Scriptures, the kingdom of God primarily means the rule of God—his reign as king in the heart of every one of his subjects. In different places in the New Testament this reign is emphasized from different viewpoints. Sometimes the emphasis is on the *beginning,* the inauguration of the kingdom. For example, Jesus' statement, "But if it is by the finger of God that I cast out demons, then the kingdom of God has come upon you" (Luke 11:20). His miracles were an evidence that the kingdom of God had broken into their history. Sometimes the emphasis is on the development, the *progressive growth* of the kingdom. An example is the parable of the mustard seed in which the kingdom is presented in process of growth from a tiny beginning to a tremendous ending (Luke 13:18–19). Here in Luke 21:31 the emphasis is on the *consummation* of the kingdom. That toward which the redemptive purpose of God moves will realize its consummation in the coming of Christ to terminate the temporal order and establish the eternal order. The beginning of the events of verses 25–27 would encourage the disciples to know that the consummation was near. To raise the question as to how long "spring" lasts before "summer" comes, is to attempt to answer by allegory a question which Jesus gave no indication of intending as a part of his teaching.

*Verse 32:* If this statement occurred in the section of the teaching which relates specifically and clearly to the destruction of Jerusalem (vv. 20–24), it would give a minimum of difficulty to interpreters. That destruction came within the lifetime of some of the Twelve—John, for example. But that is not the case. The statement is in that part of the teaching which certainly in Mark and Matthew and more naturally in Luke refers to the coming of the Son of Man at the end of the age. If one accepts the view that Jesus anticipated his return in the lifetime of some of his hearers, there is no problem. Unwillingness to take seriously Jesus' own statement in Mark 13:32 and reluctance to accept even that limitation on his knowledge has led many interpreters to seek some interpretation other than the obvious one—that Jesus anticipated that the end would come not long after the destruction of Jerusalem. To accept that is no reflection on his deity; it is a recognition of the reality of his incarnation with the self-limitation which he took upon himself in becoming man (Phil. 2:5–11). The time of the end was not revealed even to those whom God inspired to speak and write of it. Paul anticipated that it would come while he was living, but it did not. That does not invalidate the certainty of its coming at a time reserved for the knowledge of God alone. The same is true in the case of the incarnate Son of God.

The key in the attempts to interpret this verse so as to avoid such expectation on the part of Jesus is the word *generation.* Some interpret it to mean the Jews as a race. So they understand Jesus to mean that even though Jerusalem was destroyed and the nation dispersed, there will still be Jews in the world when Christ returns. Others interpret it to mean hostile Jews—that when Christ returns there will still be Jews hostile to him as the Messiah. Others understand it to refer to believing Jews such as the Twelve—Christian Jews. Some interpret it to mean Christians without regard to race—that in spite of all the persecution and effort to destroy Christians and Christianity, they will survive and will be in the world at the Lord's return.

All of these approaches are strained and forced. The word *generation* meant in Jesus' day what it commonly means now—the sum total of those born and living at relatively the same time, those who are contemporaries. That was Jesus' application of the word to the uniform mass of humanity which he confronted in his teaching and work (Matt. 11:16; 12:41, 45; Luke 7:31; 11:29–32; 17:25, and many others). Jesus anticipated that all of those contemporary with him and his listeners would not pass away before his return; some would still be living.

*Verse 33* is a solemn affirmation of the truth of his teaching. It is a general saying which is used in other places. He did not say "these words" in reference to this specific and immediate teaching. His reference was to the total of his teaching in a life that was nearing its end. *Heaven and earth* refers to the temporal creation, the world as men know it. It *will pass away;* its nature is one of impermanence. But Jesus' *words,* his teachings, are of a permanent and eternal nature. Their truth abides. That truth would survive the devastation of ruined cities, persecuted and slaughtered people, upheavals in the world of nature and of men. And when all of that has been ended, his truth remains.

*Verses 34–35:* Jesus then returned the attention of the Twelve to a consideration of their conduct in the time of waiting before his return. *Take heed to yourselves* means literally "have care with reference to yourselves." In all their witness and work in the interest of others, they were not to forget to keep a constant check on their own attitudes and conduct.

*Lest your hearts be weighed down:* This is a negative warning. The warning will be stated positively in verse 36. *Weighed down* means overloaded or overburdened with the result that they could not perform effectively.

*Dissipation . . . drunkenness . . . cares of this life:* These were the things which might overburden the heart of a servant to make effective service impossible. *Dissipation* is the translation of a word which means the dizziness or staggering which accompanies *drunkenness*—loss of control of physical actions because of the control of intoxicants. The language recalls some of Jesus' parables in which servants give way to reveling while their master is away. This is no indication that any of the Twelve had an alcoholic problem! Jesus was using strong language to indicate what happens when a man under pressure surrenders to physical impulses. History is replete with tragic illustrations of men—even ministers—who, under pressure, have surrendered to physical impulses including intoxicants.

*Cares of this life* refers to earthly affairs. *Cares* means distractions, specifically those things which pull a person into pieces. *Life* translates a word for which English has no exact synonym. It is the word for life in the world of nature—bird, beast, or human—from which English has the word "biology," the study of life at the natural level. As Jesus used the word here, it meant about what we mean by the everyday affairs of life—food, clothes, shelter, social life. The distracting anxieties of even these elemental needs have a way of assuming an exaggerated importance which can limit effective service to God.

*That day* is the day of the Lord's return in consummation of God's purpose. *Suddenly like a snare* is a graphic way of expressing the unexpected—as a bird or an animal approaches a lure that appears to be so important, but finds itself trapped by a snare. *That day* will assuredly come. It will come upon *all who dwell* in the earth. Obviously when that day comes all the people of the world will be affected by it. Jesus' reference appears to be more limited than that. The word translated *dwell* means to sit at ease. So the apparent reference is to all those sitting at ease and with no expectation of his return. His return will surprise them as a tripped snare surprises the unwary bird. The ominous tone of the saying is a warning of penalty or loss in being so surprised by *that day*. The loss is not defined. Probably it is the opposite of standing before the Son of Man (v. 36).

*Verse 36:* This is the positive side of the negative warning in verses 34–35. *Watch* means to be alert. It recalls the language of many of Jesus' parables which conclude with the imperative to *watch*. Several of them are in the Matthew 25 parallel. As used in those parables it did not mean that Jesus' disciples were (or are) to spend the time of waiting in looking to see his coming, but rather that they were to be active at the assigned task, anticipating his return at whatever time it might be.

*Praying* recalls Jesus' counsel to watch (Matt. 26:38) and pray (Luke 22:40) with him when he began the hours of waiting and praying in Gethsemane as he faced the cross on the next day. Working at the assigned task (watching) must be joined to conscious openness to and communion with God (praying) for every servant of Christ in every age.

They were to pray for *strength to escape* the trying events which they faced. The word for *strength* means "sufficiency." Pray that you will have the sufficiency needed for coming through those trying experiences. *To escape* does not mean "to avoid" but to come through them victoriously.

*To stand before the Son of man:* Luke concludes the Mount of Olives discourse with this powerful incentive and goal. *To stand* is often used in the Scriptures in the sense of standing in judgment—to face God and to give account of what one has done with the trusteeship of life (Matt. 27:11; Acts 26:6; Rom. 14:4; Col. 4:12). That is the meaning here. *To stand before the Son of man* means to meet him in his return without shame or fear of rebuke. They could do that only on the condition that in the time of waiting they had not succumbed to the pressures and cares of this life (v. 34), but had faithfully performed their assigned task in prayerful consciousness of its supreme importance.

### (8) Summary statement of Jesus' activity during the week (21:37–38)

Beginning early in the mornings that week, Jesus spent the days in the Temple engaged in teaching. He spent the nights *on the mount called Olivet*. This does not necessarily mean that they camped out. Matthew 21:17 has the only exact reference to a night's lodging. It was Sunday night and it was in the village of Bethany which was on the eastern slope of the Mount of Olives. The fact that on Thursday night Judas knew he could lead the arresting officers to Jesus in the Garden of Gethsemane on the western slope of the Mount may indicate that Jesus and the Twelve did spend some of the nights in that garden.

Chapter 22 opens with a reference to the approaching Passover, the plans of the Jewish rulers to put Jesus to death, and Judas Iscariot's agreement to make the identification necessary for a legal arrest (vv. 1–6). Luke has no clear indication of the time of Judas's meeting with the rulers to make the arrangements. In Mark 14:1 and Matthew 26:2, Judas's going to make the arrangement is specifically related to Jesus' rebuking the disciples at a Tuesday night dinner when they complained at the waste of money involved in Mary's anointing Jesus' feet. John 12:4 indicates that it was Judas who had led in the complaint and whom Jesus had rebuked. John places the dinner on Saturday night before the triumphal entry. Mark and Matthew place it on Tuesday night after that entry. Their time for it more naturally fits the details of the week. By that placing of the dinner, Judas's initial arrangements with the authorities could have been either later on Tuesday night or some time on Wednesday.

### (9) A reference to Jesus' approaching death (22:1–2)

*Verse 1:* Both *Unleavened* and *Passover* were used as names for this ancient and meaningful week. *Unleavened* refers to the use of bread without yeast which commemorated the hurried condition under which the original Passover was observed; there was no time for the preparation of yeast bread. In the practice over the years, all leaven was put out of the house during the eight days of the festival. A children's game developed in which the mother concealed a bit of leavened bread somewhere in the house. The rest of the family searched until it was found, and in so doing assured themselves that no leaven was in the house. Luke's word means only "unleavened things"; the word "bread" in the English translations is for clarity for those who are not acquainted with the custom of the feast.

*Passover* was the original name for the week, derived from the night the Hebrew slaves began the exodus from Egypt when the death angel passed over all the homes marked by the blood of the lamb eaten earlier in the supper.

*Drew near* indicates only that they were drawing closer to the culmination of the events of Jesus' arrest, trial, and death. Mark 14:1 and Matthew 26:2 indicate that it was two days away, hence, Tuesday evening before the Passover Supper on Thursday evening.

*Verse 2: The chief priests and the scribes* (Matt. 26:3 includes the elders) identifies this as the Sanhedrin. The Sanhedrin was the Jewish supreme court in all matters of religion. The Romans allowed them to continue to exercise jurisdiction over some civil matters also. They were not permitted to exercise capital punishment.

*How to put him to death:* The word *how* is important. They had already determined to do that. Their remaining problem was *how* to bring it about. *They feared the people* is the explanation of their perplexity. The people were around Jesus from early in the morning until night (21:38). The Sanhedrin was afraid to try to arrest him under those circumstances. Matthew (26:4–5) indicates their subtlety in deciding to arrest him after the week was over when the people would be leaving the city. Luke's expression *to put him to death* literally means "to put him away" and was used for assassination. They were planning to do it legally, but to the early Christians it was an act of murder (Acts 2:23).

### (10) Judas's preparation for the betrayal (22:3–6)

The Sanhedrin received help from an unexpected source—one of Jesus' own disciples, *Judas called Iscariot*. Readers of Luke alone have no preparation for this treachery. There has been nothing whatever to point the finger at one of the Twelve. Details from the other Gospels, however, point to at least some of the factors involved, particularly the supper at Bethany honoring Jesus. During the supper Jesus was lavishly anointed with a highly scented and very expensive oil. Judas (John 12:4) led others of the disciples (Mark 14:4; Matt. 26:8–9) in complaining at the waste. Jesus rebuked Judas (John 12:7–8) as well as the others (Mark 14:6–9; Matt. 26:10–13). Immediately after that, Judas went out and made his initial contact with the Sanhedrin (Mark 14:10; Matt. 26:14–15).

*Verse 3: Satan entered into Judas:* This was no case of demon possession like the demon possession stories in the Gospels. This meant that Judas became the tool of Satan to bring about the arrest and death of Jesus. It was no sudden possession. Apart from his being stung by Jesus' words of rebuke over the anointing, John (6:70–71; 13:2, 27) indicates that there was development in Judas's thinking about the betrayal and his deciding to carry it out. What he did could hardly have been motivated solely by the incident at the supper. John 12:6 indicates that, when all the events were over, it was found that Judas had been a thief all along, and that as treasurer of the group he had regularly stolen from the common bag. The uncertainty of the derivation of the name *Iscariot* has caused some interpreters to conclude that Judas was one of the Zealots—the political party plotting the revolution against Rome. The Roman word for the Zealots was "sicarius." The difficulty of the Jews in pronouncing the word could easily result in "scarioth." There is a hint of this in some ancient manuscripts of Luke which do have *Skarioth*. Judas could have been trying to force Jesus into the position of fighting, with the result that the revolution would start that week in Jerusalem. If so, he failed, and when he saw that his act was leading to Jesus' death, he took his own life (Matt. 27:3–10).

*Verse 4:* Whatever his reasons, Judas went to the Sanhedrin—securing a hearing through the Temple guard, *captains*—and offered to betray Jesus. The word translated *betray* means "give over." It refers to the formal identification by which Jesus could be legally arrested. It also includes the matter of when and how that would be done.

*Verse 5:* The Sanhedrin was delighted. They would not have to wait until the feast was over with the possibility that Jesus himself might get away before they could carry out their plan to arrest him (Matt. 26:4–5). They sealed their bargain with a payment of money. Luke names no amount; Matthew (26:15–16) has "thirty pieces of silver," which in Zechariah 11:12–14 was a sum paid in relation to the breaking of a brotherhood covenant between Judah and Israel. In Exodus 21:32 it was the compensation for a slave who had been gored to death by an ox. It is frequently said that Jesus was sold for the price of a slave. That may have been Matthew's interest, since the Exodus reference was a part of the Passover-exodus experience of Israel. This reference is rather remote however. It is much more likely that his words reflect the "blood money" concept of the early Christians (Matt. 27:6–10; Acts 1:19). Actually Matthew made a very strange "quotation" of Jeremiah, which is really a mixture of Zechariah 11: 12–13 and Jeremiah 32:6–15; 18:2–3. Zechariah has the thirty pieces of silver; Jeremiah has seventeen shekels of silver—the two cannot be equated. Jeremiah has the reference to a potter's house. Matthew combines the Jeremiah "potter" reference and the Zechariah "thirty pieces of silver" reference without distinguishing between them.

*Verse 6:* The agreement was that Judas would alert them to a time and place for arresting Jesus *in the absence of the multitude.* They did not want a riot to mar Passover.

#### 4. Wednesday—a Day of Rest in Preparation for Passover (no record in N.T.)

There is no record in the New Testament of Jesus' activities on Wednesday; perhaps it was a day of rest.

#### 5. Thursday—a Day of Joy and Sorrow (22:7–54a)

#### (1) The preparation for the Passover Supper (22:7–13)

Verses 7–13: These verses contain the record of the preparation for eating the Passover Supper after sunset on Thursday night. The preparations started on Thursday morning.

*Verse 7: The day of Unleavened Bread:* This was Nisan 14th in the Jewish calendar, Thursday morning by our calendar week.

*On which the passover lamb had to be sacrificed:* A lamb without sickness or blemish would be presented at the Temple and slaughtered under the authority of the priests. There would be a lamb for every family group of ten or more. In Jerusalem, without their families, Jesus and the Twelve observed the feast as a close-knit family group.

*Verse 8:* Because of the crowds, only two men were permitted to take the lamb to the Temple for the sacrifice. Jesus commissioned Peter and John to make all the preparations including the sacrificing of the lamb.

*Go and prepare the passover for us:* The preparation would include roasting the lamb, preparing the room, and providing the other foods. In the development of the feast it had come to be a banquet rather than the simple meal of the exodus. It included the essential loaves of unleavened bread, containers of red wine, bitter herbs, and the roasted lamb, all of which had symbolic meaning in the meal. But other foods were customarily added: fish, vegetables, and fruit.

*Verses 9–12:* In answer to the question by Peter and John as to the location for observing the meal, Jesus did not give street directions. His instructions reflected an air of secrecy as if he did not wish the location known by anyone else until he led the remaining ten to the supper.

When they entered the city they would encounter *a man carrying a jar of water* (v. 10). Since that was woman's work, such a man would be easy to identify. If, however, it was a young man, his carrying a jar of water would not be so unusual as to provoke undue attention. They were not to address the man, but to follow him to his destination. There they were to identify themselves to the householder and say that *The Teacher* wanted him to show them the *guest room* where he was to eat the Passover with his disciples (v. 11). Some interpreters explain this as divine insight on the part of Jesus. Others explain it as a part of a prearranged plan. That is much more likely. He was eager to have this last Passover with the Twelve. He knew, too, that the Sanhedrin was plotting to arrest him. He had sensed Judas's activities. He planned carefully so that he would not be interrupted before the feast. After that, he would be ready when they came for him.

*Verse 12* indicates that Jesus knew the nature of the room. Guest rooms were frequently built on flat rooftops and reached by an outside stair. Jesus said they would be conducted to *a large upper room furnished.* The word *furnished* is used in the New Testament only here and in the parallel in Mark 14:15. In other ancient writings it is used for either a room with a tiled floor or a room with table, couches, and rugs for reclining and eating. From the details of this supper, it is clear that the room was furnished with table and reclining couches. Whether or not it had a tiled floor is unimportant except that it would be a touch of elegance and some indication of the status of these unidentified friends of Jesus.

*Verse 13:* The two spent the day in carrying out Jesus' instructions. When sunset came, all was ready.

### (2) Observing the Passover Supper (22:14–18)

The activities of Jesus from sunset until he went out to the Garden of Gethsemane included the Passover Supper, the institution of a new memorial supper of bread and wine, and several brief teaching passages. Many seeming "gaps" in the evening are filled in by the other three Gospels, but they cannot be included in this exposition of Luke's account.

*Verse 14: When the hour came:* The meal itself was eaten on the Jewish day Nisan 15th. This meant after sunset on Thursday. Specifically, their new day began with the appearance of the first star.

*He sat at table:* The verb indicates that they reclined at the table rather than sat upright. This was a formal meal, and they observed formal meals Roman style. The table was low and about it were couches stretching out from the table. The guests reclined on these couches, supported themselves on the left elbow and forearm, and used the right hand in eating. Some of the events in John's account almost require that the tables were arranged either in a horse-shoe shape or as three sides of a rectangle. The absence of those events (Jesus' washing the disciples' feet and Peter's remonstrance; Jesus' word about his betrayal with the signaling of Peter to John; Jesus' giving the morsel to Judas but in such way that the disciples did not know why Judas left the room before the supper was over) from the synoptics leaves the shape of the table unimportant.

*Verse 15:* Jesus spoke of his earnest desire to eat this Passover with the Twelve before his death. John's Gospel records other Passovers when Jesus and the Twelve were in Jerusalem of which there is no mention in the synoptics. So there is no indication in the words that Jesus desired the experience one more time before his death. It is rather that this was to him a very significant Passover—his last. In the original Passover there had been no significance of redemption from sin in the killing of the lamb. In the years that passed, the Hebrew people interpreted the exodus deliverance as a redemption—redemption from slavery to freedom. Jesus appeared to think of his own death during Passover as a Passover sacrifice which would mean redemption from sin and the deliverance from the bondage of death. That appears to be a part of the theology of John's Gospel.

*Verse 16:* This was Jesus' stated reason for desiring to eat this Passover with them.

*I shall not eat it:* Some manuscripts have "I shall not eat it again." The reading has good support. The better support, though still far from certain, is for the reading *I shall not eat it.* If the reading "eat it again" is correct, the emphasis is on the fact that this was his last time to share the meaningful experience with them; he cherished that opportunity.

On the other hand, if the reading *I shall not eat it* is correct, the meaning is uncertain. If the phrase *eat it* refers to observing the entire week— as it was so frequently used by the Jews—the meaning could simply be that before the week was over he would have died as a Passover sacrifice. If that was not the meaning he could have been referring to his heaviness of heart. Although he had desired earnestly to share this meal with them, he would not now eat as they ate. He could not do so because it would be singularly inappropriate for him to eat the lamb when indeed he was the Lamb and by his own sacrifice the angel of death would pass over them.

*Until it is fulfilled in the kingdom of God:* The Jews looked to the age of the Messiah as a time that would be inaugurated by a great messianic feast—a time of rejoicing in the fulfillment of all of God's purpose. That appears to be Jesus' reference here. He would not share this with them again in this life. The next time he shared the Passover with them would be in that glorious time of the complete consummation of the kingdom of God—when that which was foreshadowed in all earthly Passovers, and Atonements, and Tabernacles, had realized its purpose and the perfect reign of God was reality.

Before taking up the detailed interpretation of verses 17–18, it is necessary to observe the way verses 17–20 present a major problem in the interpretation of the Gospels. John does not include the institution of the Lord's Supper. He includes Jesus' teaching about eating his flesh and drinking his blood in chapter 6 in relation to the bread of life discourse following the miracle of the multiplication of the loaves and fishes. Mark, Matthew, and Luke do include the institution of the Lord's Supper. The similarities of their accounts on the one hand, and the differences of their accounts on the other, constitute the problem. For clarity of exposition, it is necessary to include at this point the total of verses 17–20 and to put in brackets the part which the RSV has in a footnote.

[17]And he took a cup, and when he had given thanks he said, "Take this, and divide it among yourselves; [18]for I tell you that from now on I shall not drink of the fruit of the vine until the kingdom of God comes." [19]And he took bread, and when he had given thanks he broke

it and gave it to them, saying, "This is my body [which is given for you. Do this in remembrance of me. ²⁰And likewise the cup after supper, saying, "This cup which is poured out for you is the new covenant in my blood.] ²¹But behold the hand of him who betrays me . . . ."

The part in brackets is omitted by the RSV translators and editors because it does not appear in some of the early manuscripts of Luke. Omitting it avoids the problem of Luke's appearing to have two cups—one before and one after the bread—when all other accounts in the New Testament (Mark 14:22–25; Matt. 26:26–29; 1 Cor. 11:23–26) have one cup only following the bread. However, it leaves the problem of Luke's putting the cup before the bread, thus reversing the order of the other accounts. Therefore, omitting it solves only half of the problem—or, perhaps, less than half.

Do the variant readings of the ancient manuscripts warrant the omission? On the basis of comparison of the manuscripts the answer clearly is "No." The only major Greek source which omits it is the sixth-century manuscript, Bezae. In addition, one Syriac and some old Latin copies omit it. All the early and best sources contain it. It is in the very earliest, the early third-century Bodmer papyri. It is in the following early manuscripts: Sinaiticus (4th century); Alexandrinus (5th century); Vaticanus (4th century); Ephraemi (5th century); Freer (5th century); and other very good eighth- and ninth-century sources. All the weight of evidence favors its being an authentic part of Luke's account.

What is gained by omitting it? Eliminating the confusion of having two cups. But the problem remains of the reversal of the order by putting the cup before the bread.

What is lost by omitting it? If all which follows *This is my body* in verse 19 is omitted, Luke's account will have left out all linking of the cup to the words of Jesus setting forth the significance of death on these occasions: Caesarea Philippi (9:22–25); the second time in Galilee (9:43–45); the third time while on the road to Jerusalem (18:31–34); the request of James and John (Mark 10:35–40; Matt. 20:21–23); the anointing in Bethany (Mark 14:3–9; Matt. 26:6–13; John 12:2–8). That was the predominant theme of the months from the confession at Caesarea Philippi to the arrival in Jerusalem. In addition, to omit the section leaves out any linking whatever of the cup to the redemptive significance of his death. That removes the Lord's Supper completely from its significance in the other Gospel records, in Paul's interpretation (1 Cor. 11:23–26), and in the understanding and practice of the early church. The price is too big to pay in an effort to eliminate only one part of a problem.

The following exposition assumes that the entire passage (vv. 14–20) is authentic, that there were two cups in the original account by Luke, that in his recounting and interpreting the significance of all the events of the evening, he used the last cup of the Passover Supper and the cup of the Lord's Supper to link the old supper with the new, the old covenant with the new. The problems which this raises with respect to Mark and Matthew will be noted.

*Verses 17–18:* These verses continue the statement of Jesus in verse 16 that although he had desired to eat that Passover with them, he would not do so. Mark's and Matthew's "as they were eating" is a reference to the group participation in the ancient supper. By Luke's account, the Twelve were eating but Jesus was not.

*He took a cup and gave thanks:* Mark and Matthew state that he first took bread and "blessed" it and then took a cup and "gave thanks" for it. Note that difference. Luke has that he took a cup and "gave thanks" for it, that he took bread and "gave thanks" for it, and then in verse 20 He has *likewise the cup* by which he meant that he "gave thanks" as in the case of the bread.

There is a difference in the Greek words translated *took* in the different passages. Mark and Matthew use a verb meaning "to take up *(lambanō),"* as if Jesus took up a loaf of bread from the table and told the others to take up a loaf of bread from the table; then he took up a cup from the table and passed it to them. Luke, on the other hand, uses two different words. *He took,* used of the first cup, is a word for receiving from another *(dechomai).* The suggestion is that another at the table was urging him to partake of the supper when he had said that he would not. He "received the cup" from that one, gave the thanks which a Jewish father customarily gave for different parts of and at different times in the supper, put it back on the table, and said, "You take this up and divide it among yourselves for I tell you that from now on I shall not drink of the fruit of the vine until the kingdom of God comes." He continued the abstention from eating the supper which he had stated when the meal began and for the same reason (v. 16). During the course of the Passover Supper, several cups were used and each time there was a prayer of thanks. Sometimes there were four and sometimes five. This was the last one in that Passover Supper. In verse 19 with reference to the bread, Luke uses the same word used by Mark and Matthew; he took *(lambanō)* the bread from the table. The *likewise* in verse 20 with reference to the second cup indicates the same verb. The validity of the distinction between the two verbs in the total passage is open to challenge, but so are many details of interpretation of the three accounts from other viewpoints.

One of the objections to the above view is that Mark and Matthew have Jesus' statement about not drinking the fruit of the vine in relation to the cup of the Lord's Supper following the bread. Luke does not have it with that cup (his second), but with the earlier cup, relating it to Jesus' statement about not eating the Passover Supper. In weighing that difference as evidence, the interpreter must note other differences in the order of events on that evening. Some of the most notable are these: Mark and Matthew put Jesus' statement that one of the Twelve would betray him before the Lord's Supper; Luke puts it after. Mark and Matthew have Jesus' words about Peter's denial after they had left the room and while they were on the way to the garden; Luke has it before they left the room. Luke includes a section regarding a dispute among the Twelve as to which one would be greatest. It follows Jesus' statement about his betrayal by one of them and their questioning among themselves as to which one it was. That dispute is not in Mark and Matthew, but a large part of it is identical with their section on James's and John's request for the positions of honor at

Jesus' right and left which they locate in the territory of Jericho as they approached Jerusalem. All of this indicates the impossibility of being dogmatic about the order of events on that last evening.

### (3) Instituting the Memorial Supper (22:19-23)

*Verses 19–20* (including the part omitted in RSV) definitely relate to the institution of the Lord's Supper. Those who omit verse 20 do so in the belief that it was not an original part of Luke but was added by some very early copyist in a clumsy attempt to bring Luke's order of the bread and the cup into line with Mark, Matthew, and 1 Corinthians. In one way the task of the interpreter is simpler if that part is omitted. In that case, Luke contains no interpretation of the meaning of either the cup (v. 17) or the bread (v. 19). The reader might assume some symbolic meaning of the bread in Jesus' saying, "This is my body," but apart from an acquaintance with the other accounts including the bread of life passage in John 6, it would be only assumption. The reader would also have no basis for understanding any symbolism in the cup of verse 17; there would be only Jesus' indication that he was not drinking the cup.

To include verse 20 necessitates interpretation of the apparent inner meaning beneath the outward rite of the eating of the bread and the drinking from the cup. The *bread* was a flat sheet of the unleavened bread used in the Passover Supper, about the size of a large pancake, but not, of course, of the same texture, since it was without yeast. The words *when he had given thanks* dramatically reveal the attitude of Jesus toward his death. In giving thanks for the bread, which in a moment he would be speaking of as his body to be given in sacrifice, he was thanking God for his sacrificial death. The words of his prayer of thanksgiving are not reported by any of the writers. It is logical to assume that they indicated the way in which his death was a sacrifice for sin. The unknown words of the prayer prepared them for his next act and words.

*He broke it:* Some interpreters relate this to the words, "which is given for you," and find in the broken bread a symbol of his body which was to be "broken" on the cross the next day. The view perplexes even some of those who so understand it, because the bones of the Passover lamb were never broken; John saw particular meaning in the fact that Pilate's soldiers did not break Jesus' legs, though they broke the legs of the robbers who were executed with him (John 19:31–33). This seemingly unnecessarily cruel practice had the purpose of hastening and assuring death before the bodies were taken from the cross and thrown on the garbage disposal heap in the Valley of Hinnom. Jesus had already died so his legs were not broken.

To interpret the broken bread as a reference to the method of Jesus' death misses the main idea. Between friends or family members, or a host and his guests, the breaking of bread symbolized an experience in sharing. Eating the broken bread indicated the disciples' sharing with him in his redemptive sacrifice. His body was the one loaf by which they all shared in God's mighty act of redemption. The breaking of the one loaf symbolized that. It is a meaning which is difficult to perceive in the general practice today of multiple trays of tiny fragments with never a view

of the one loaf broken. Our practicality, which has solved the time problem of observing the rite in a congregation of hundreds of people, has made
us miss the meaning so clear to that first little band who shared the loaf.

*He gave it to them:* The method of that act was unimportant. He may
have broken off a part for each one. He may have passed the two halves
of the broken loaf down the table in both directions so that each one broke
off and ate a part and passed the remainder to the next man. The important part was that *he gave it*—in his death he was giving himself to them
for their redemption.

*This is my body:* The loaf of bread was not literally his body. His body
was still there at the table and before their eyes. Exactly how he was giving them his body in giving them the loaf was left in mystery. Some have
understood a miraculous transformation of the bread into the actual body
of Jesus. Others have understood that in some way his body was really
present in the element although the element remained bread. Sensing the
failure of either of these concepts to express the meaning of the mystery,
others have preferred to express the concept as symbol—the broken and
shared bread was a symbol or picture of the individual's sharing in the
experience of Christ's redemptive act. Along with its seeming advantage
over the other two views, there is a calculated risk of looking upon the
act as so merely symbolic that it loses its real meaning of a shared experience of redemption.

*Which is given for you:* The tense of the verb indicates a process in
action—"which is being given." Jesus' entire incarnation was redemptive,
and its end was drawing near. The nearer the end came, the more meaningful his redemptive sufferings became. They would reach their ultimate
significance in the cry, "It is finished" (John 19:30). *For you* is the translation of a prepositional phrase meaning "in your behalf." It is a part of
those New Testament passages which support the idea of the vicarious
nature of Jesus' death. Although the concept has been often abused by
exaggerations which go beyond New Testament meaning, there can be no
denial of the fact that in some way which is beyond finite man's wisdom
and concealed in the wisdom of God, the death of Jesus was substitutionary
for sinful men—in man's place.

*Verse 20* shares some of the terminology of 1 Corinthians 11:25 and
also of Mark 14:24 and Matthew 26:28. That fact is part of the reason
for some interpreters' rejecting it as authentic, even though it is in the
oldest manuscripts of Luke. The two features which it has in common with
the 1 Corinthians passage but in distinction from Mark and Matthew are
the statements, "after supper" and "new covenant," with the stress on the
idea of *new* covenant.

*Likewise the cup:* Likewise refers to the taking up of the bread and the
giving of thanks for it. Again, the content of the thanksgiving prayer was
not given, but no doubt he related the cup to his death and thanked the
Father for it. *The cup* by metonymy stands for what it contained, the red
wine which was used in the Passover Supper. It was customarily diluted
with water, but it still had the red color which made its suggestion of blood
natural. To institute the new memorial, Jesus used two ready and natural
foods from the Passover table: the brownish white bread suggestive of

flesh, and the red wine suggestive of blood. The idea that this was unfermented grape juice cannot be defended. The drink used in the Passover Supper was wine. They had no way of preserving fresh grape juice from harvest time to the next April, and fresh grapes could not be produced that early.

*After supper* distinguishes this "cup" from all the other "cups" which had been passed ceremonially in the course of the Passover Supper. It was Luke's way of making clear that this eating of bread and drinking of wine was not a part of the Passover Supper which had ended. This rite of eating and drinking pointed, not back to a distant past with its sacrifice, but to the future, a future so immediate that it was the next day. It pointed to a sacrifice which would fulfill all that had been foreshadowed in all those previous Passovers and sacrifices in Israel.

*This cup is the new covenant in my blood* (following the word order of the Greek text rather than that of the RSV): The demonstrative pronoun *this* distinguishes the cup from the one in verse 17 probably, and from all the cups of the Passover Supper certainly. It was different in meaning from all of them.

*The new covenant* is the unchallenged reading in Luke and 1 Corinthians. Some manuscripts of Mark and Matthew also have the word "new" but the best ones have only the word "covenant." The ancient covenant of God had been ratified by the sacrifice of blood (see Exod. 24:8; Lev. 4:18–20; Zech. 9:11). In Jeremiah 31:31–33 God had promised to provide a *new covenant* unlike the old covenant. The writer of the Epistle to the Hebrews interpreted the death of Jesus as the sacrifice whose blood ratified a *new covenant* which was gracious and sin-forgiving (Heb. 10: 14–18). He was following the interpretation of his death which Jesus made on the night before that death.

*In my blood:* The *new covenant* by which sin would be graciously forgiven was to be ratified by Jesus' sacrifice. He held the cup in his hands and looked at the red liquid it contained. He saw it, not as wine—*the fruit of the vine* (v. 18)—but as his own blood which on the next day would be poured out on an altar built in the form of a cross. He lifted up his voice in thanksgiving for that cup, because by it the *new covenant* between God and men would be secured. There in that scene of thanksgiving was supreme drama.

*Which is poured out for you: For you* repeats the construction of referring to the bread as his body (v. 19). In that same mysterious way which surpasses human wisdom, the blood of Jesus of Nazareth sacrificed on a Roman cross was substitutionary for the sins of men. *Which is poured out* can be translated "which is in the process of being poured out." The pouring out of his blood from the wounds by thorns, and nails, and a sword, was as much a reality that night as if they had already pierced his body.

Thus with the two cups (v. 17, Passover, and v. 20, Lord's Supper) Jesus linked the old order with the new. As the sacrifice of the ancient Passover lamb had created Israel as a people for God's redemptive witness, so Jesus' sacrifice of himself as the Lamb of God was creating a new Israel as a people for God's redemptive witness.

*Verses 21–23:* In that moment so highly charged with emotion, Jesus made the startling announcement that one of the Twelve would betray him. All four of the Gospels have this announcement, though they vary in the details of just when it came in the events of the evening and its wording. Luke has the simplest form of the four.

*Verse 21: The hand of him who betrays me is with me on the table:* This was not a means by which they were to identify the betrayer. All four Gospels indicate that no one identified Judas as the betrayer at that time. Matthew (26:31) has simply, "one of you will betray me." Mark adds to that "one who is eating with me" (14:18). John also has, "one of you will betray me" and then later, in response to a question from the beloved disciple, adds Jesus' words, "It is he to whom I shall give this morsel when I have dipped it" (13:21, 26). All of these four records stress the tragedy of the nearness of the betrayer to Jesus. They broke bread at the same table (Mark and Luke). That spoke of the social nearness of friends. He was near enough to be reached by Jesus in handing him a choice bit of food (John). That spoke of the very physical nearness at the table. All of that was a part of the unexpectedness of the act and, hence, its startling effect on the group.

*Verse 22:* In these words Jesus combined the mystery of the twofold aspect of his death. *As it has been determined* refers to the redemptive purpose of God. All that God had promised from the first indication of man's sin and need of a Savior (Gen. 3:15), and all of his mighty acts of redemption from the call of Abraham, through the exodus under Moses, and the institution of the sacrificial system of the Tabernacle and the Temple—his death was a part of that which had been *determined,* that is, planned. In his sermon at Pentecost (Acts 2:23), Peter spoke of the mystery of the two aspects of Jesus' death. From man's motivation it was brutal murder at the hands of lawless men. From God's motivation, however, it was encompassed in the infinite foreknowledge of God and it was part of the divine plan of redemption. God can turn tragedy into triumph. Observe this in the next paragraph.

*But woe to that man by whom he is betrayed* refers to the instrumentality of wicked men in bringing Jesus to his death. Peter spoke of that, too, in his words, "you crucified and killed by the hands of lawless men" (Acts 2:23). The death of Jesus of Nazareth was encompassed in the redemptive plan from God's viewpoint; it was an act of betrayal and murder from man's viewpoint. The *woe* pointed particularly to Judas, because he had of his own will given himself over as the tool of Satan to accomplish that evil purpose. Whatever the ultimate forces working the complex events of Jesus' death, Judas was responsible for his choice and his action. Part of that *woe* may be seen in the gruesome details of his suicide (Matt. 27:3–10; Acts 1:18, 19). The revulsion of the early Christians may be seen in the statement of Peter, "Now this man bought a field with the reward of his wickedness . . . the field was called . . . Field of Blood." John 13:30 indicates that Judas left the room at the end of the betrayal discussion. The synoptics have no reference to his leaving.

*Verse 23:* Luke omits most of the reaction of the Twelve which is contained in the other Gospels in varying forms. He includes only the fact that

Jesus' startling announcement provoked a discussion in which the Twelve were asking one another about opinions as to the identity of the betrayer. No one of them seemed to suspect another.

### (4) The dialogue around the table (22:24–38)

Verses 24–27: According to Luke 9:46–48, the argument concerning who was greatest among the Twelve had first arisen after the inability of some of the group to heal a possessed boy. That was several months before this occasion in Jerusalem. Matthew (20:20–28) and Mark (10: 35–41) report a similar argument over greatness while the Twelve were in Jericho on the way to Jerusalem, but they do not include this Lukan argument in the upper room on the night of the Lord's Supper. Much of Jesus' teaching in that Jericho argument, however, is in Luke's account of the upper room argument. The same service idea in Jesus' teaching in this passage in Luke is in his teaching in John 13:12–20 in connection with his washing the feet of the disciples—a detail of that night included only in John.

*Verse 24: A dispute also arose among them:* These words convey an air of tragedy—in the very shadow of Jesus' cross, his followers were arguing over position and relative greatness. Luke's placing of the argument relates it to their questioning one another as to which one would betray him. The one who betrayed him would be regarded as least, and *woe to that man* (v. 22). In contrast, which one of them would *be regarded as the greatest?*

*Verses 25–26:* In these verses Jesus contrasted the concept of greatness in the Gentile world with the concept of greatness which he desired in his followers.

*The kings of the Gentiles exercise lordship over them:* All of his hearers knew the relation of a Roman ruler to his subjects. *Exercise lordship* expressed that relationship. The vast gap which separated the ruler from the subject was itself an indication of their concept of what made a ruler great. Greatness was in direct proportion to the number of people who served him. Even though the rulers were called *benefactors* in benevolent rule, they were still reckoned great according to the loftiness of their position over the subjects.

*But not so with you:* Among Jesus' followers there was to be a different standard for greatness. One would not be reckoned great according to the number of people who served him, but according to the number of people whom he served. (See Mark 10:44 and Matt. 20:27: "whoever would be first among you must be your slave.")

*Let the greatest among you become as the youngest:* This refers specifically to the Jewish family practice of the preeminence of the oldest son. In the descending scale of rank among many sons, the youngest would be regarded as the least and the one most naturally pressed into service for the others. Jesus said that the one counted greatest among his followers would be the one assuming the role of the youngest son serving all the others. Correspondingly he said that the one regarded as the leader would be the one who was serving the others.

*Verse 27:* In these words, Jesus changed his illustration to that of one sitting at the table versus the one serving those at the table. By all human reckoning the one sitting at a table and being served would be regarded as greater than the one who was serving. Jesus' own example, however, reversed that concept. He was their leader but he was serving them. That statement relates this teaching to John's account of Jesus' serving the Twelve by washing their feet—a service traditionally rendered by the lowest servant on the staff of house servants. In his interpretation of that action, Jesus taught them the lesson that there is no necessary service which is too humble for one of his followers to perform for another. In the Mark and Matthew accounts previously cited, he said that as the Master he was in the world to serve others and that service extended to his death for them.

*Verses 28–30* point to a time of honor for those who had been with him through all of his suffering. As the Father had appointed the Son a kingdom in which he would be the honored Ruler, so Jesus said he was appointing them to a share in that rule.

*That you may eat and drink at my table in my kingdom:* This hardly refers to literal physical eating and drinking. The words are symbolic in the imagery of a great festive banquet in which Christ would be honored as king and these, his friends who had continued with him through all the hardships involved in discipleship, would share that table and honor. It was the imagery again of the messianic feast to inaugurate the messianic age in Jewish expectation. They would share it with him.

*Sit on thrones judging the twelve tribes of Israel:* This, too, is likely not literal in its meaning. Some interpreters, however, do understand it as literal, that Christ's rule will be from a restored Jerusalem and his government will be one in which the twelve apostles will rule over the twelve tribes of Israel in Palestine and they in turn over the non-Jews throughout the world.

Jesus' words indicate the sharing of his followers in the glory of his eternal rule as king. The saying means no more necessarily than their passing judgment on their fellow Jews in their acceptance of Jesus as the messianic king and the other Jews' rejection of him. The teaching is directly related to the preceding one in verses 26–27. He was appointing them to the role of servants in this life, and to the role of greatness in sharing his glory in the eternal life.

Verses 31–34 single out Simon Peter from all the others. This, too, continues the thought of greatness and service. Simon was likely singled out because of the position he held among the Twelve. In every listing of the Twelve in the New Testament, he is named first. On almost every occasion in which a spokesman for the group was needed, he was that spokesman. From their own evaluations the Twelve would probably nominate him as the answer to the question, "Who will be greatest."

*Verse 31: Simon, Simon, behold, Satan demanded to have you:* Preferred position always makes one most vulnerable to attack. Satan is always alert to the most effective way of accomplishing his purpose. To get a great one like Simon into his grasp and to use him as he was using Judas would be real victory. *Demanded* implies that Satan desired the opportunity of testing Simon Peter. It recalls his request to test Job to prove whether or not he was as loyal to God as he professed to be. *To have you* points to the rugged and impetuous nature of Simon. Such a nature often combines strong and weak characteristics. Simon was most vulnerable to attack. Jesus' own concern for him was reflected in the solicitude of the double address, *Simon, Simon.*

*That he might sift you like wheat:* The figure comes from the threshing floor. The head and stalk of wheat were beaten and trampled. Then that finer broken mass was placed in small quantities in a sieve. By the violent shaking of the sieve, the straw was tested for any wheat content in it. As the wind blew the chaff away, the valuable wheat emerged from the violent shaking. The hours just ahead were going to be trying ones for all the disciples. Peter above all the others was going to be shaken and sifted by the Satanic violence of those hours.

*Verse 32* shifts from the disturbing thought of Satan's testing to the assuring thought of Jesus' praying. Few assurances give greater encouragement to one undergoing great trials than the word of a trusted friend, *I have prayed for you.* When those violent hours came, Simon could remember Jesus' words and be strengthened in the realization that his Lord prayed for him.

*That your faith may not fail:* Jesus refers to the faith reflected in Peter's confession of confidence that Jesus was the Christ of God. The next few hours would bring experiences capable of shaking the faith of even a strong man. Jesus would be arrested and condemned by his own people; he would be tried by a pagan judge, and executed as if he were the lowest criminal in the land. Could Simon witness that and still confess, "You are the Christ, the Son of the living God"? Jesus prayed that he would.

*When you have turned again:* These words embrace both failure and recovery. Simon would waver, but the Lord was fully certain that he would turn again to that same confidence in Christ and in himself as the servant of Christ.

*Strengthen your brethren* voices confidence in that recovery. In the events that followed, Peter first ran for safety when danger came, then he denied that he was even acquainted with Jesus. Afterwards he wept bitterly in the realization of what he had done. But he was the one who assumed leadership of the group following the Lord's ascension. He was also the one who braved the rage of the Sanhedrin in his preaching at Pentecost and in the struggle of the young church to overcome the hostility of the Jews to all those who identified themselves with the Christ.

*Verses 33–34:* When Simon Peter professed his bravery, Jesus cautioned him against an overconfidence which would be dashed by inner weakness. Simon professed that he was ready to share whatever fate was before Jesus—*prison and . . . death.* He doubtless thought that he was. He was very certain of himself and his bravery in the face of danger.

*I tell you, Peter:* Jesus' response was a solemn affirmation, *I tell you;* "That is what you say; this is what I say." The contrast in Jesus' use of the name *Simon, Simon* in verse 31 and his use of the nickname *Peter* in this verse is forceful. He used the given personal name in tender concern for his friend. When it came to the matter of Simon's facing the danger ahead, Jesus shifted to the nickname, *Peter,* the "Rock." When the "Rock" really faced imprisonment and death because of his relationship to Jesus, that rocky disposition would dissolve into sand.

*The cock will not crow this day, until you three times deny that you know me:* All four Gospels have this exchange between Jesus and Peter, but they put it at different places in the events of that evening and with different details. In some accounts, Jesus predicted that Peter would deny him three times in relation to the cock's crowing twice. The reader needs to view all four accounts for an understanding of the total account. Luke's account gives no indication of Peter's response to Jesus' prediction. It does give three denials, the crowing of the cock, and Peter's bitter grief at his cowardice (vv. 54–62).

Verses 35–38 contain a brief exchange between Jesus and the disciples as the last event before they left the room to go to the garden at the foot of the Mount of Olives. No other Gospel has this event. There is a possible link between it and the account of Simon Peter's use of a sword when the officers came to arrest Jesus a few hours later.

*Verse 35: When I sent you out with no purse or bag or sandals, did you lack anything?* This question refers to Jesus' sending them as his representatives to proclaim the kingdom of God in Galilee (Luke 10:4; Matt. 10:9). At that time he told them that their only essential equipment was the clothes they wore, the message they were to proclaim, and his commission to proclaim it. They were to take nothing extra, and they would live in the homes where they served. Now he asked them if they had found need of anything other than those essentials. They answered, *Nothing,* they had needed only those simple essentials.

*Verse 36,* on the surface, appears to indicate a change in the direction of Jesus' orders. Some interpreters understand that Jesus was in reality counseling that after his death, when they went forth to witness, they were to arm themselves for protection. The total passage must be examined to determine whether or not that was the case.

*But now* refers to this time of crisis as they, with him, faced the immediate situation in which he had, by his triumphal entry, announced himself publicly as the Messiah of prophecy (Isa. 62:11; Zech. 9:9). That had set the fires of revolutionary hope burning in the hearts of hundreds if not thousands of oppressed Jews who were in Jerusalem for Passover. Some of the Twelve were of the Zealot movement plotting the revolution— Simon the Zealot definitely, and others probably. What was to be their response to and understanding of the way of the kingdom of God *now* in contrast to their proclamation of it months before when he had sent them out? That was the question which they faced and had to answer that night. Would they side with the militant revolutionaries to try to force that kind of messiahship upon him? Or would they side with him in his view that the Messiah of prophecy was a Messiah of peace and that that inevitably resulted in violent treatment and suffering at the hands of wicked men?

*Let him who has a purse take it . . . let him who has no sword . . . buy one:* If this was indeed an imperative from Jesus, he meant that the former way had failed; now they must turn to the revolutionary way which involved supplying themselves with *purse . . . bag* and a *sword,* even if they had to sell their outer robes to buy them. It serves no real purpose to hold that Jesus was not counseling them to join the revolution but only to provide for their physical needs and protection for escaping the danger of the next few hours and days. At no other place did Jesus ever bid his disciples to put personal comfort and safety first or to preserve it at the cost of using a sword.

The passage seems much more to fit the outlook of Jesus if his statement is understood as irony—gentle irony, but none the less irony. He was reminding them that *formerly* they had found his way adequate, but *now* they were ready to abandon that way and devote their energies to physical provisions for avoiding danger to themselves or even for joining the revolutionaries to bring about a messianic kingdom. To paraphrase his words, "Once you found my way to be completely adequate, but now, forget that; sell your clothes to buy a sword; join the Zealots; establish the kingdom of Israel."

*Verse 37* reassured them of what was coming to him. By joining the Zealots they could not spare Jesus the suffering which was coming to him.

*This scripture must be fulfilled in me:* The word translated *must* is an impersonal verb pointing to an absolute necessity if a desired end should be realized. The desired end was the completing of the mighty work of God for the redemption of men. In order for that to be realized, it was absolutely necessary for Jesus to experience the sufferings and death which were just ahead of him. The emphasis is the same as that which he had voiced in the words of verse 22, "For the Son of man goes as it has been determined." The Scripture he quoted was a part of Isaiah's portrayal of the Suffering Servant—"And he was numbered with transgressors" (Isa. 53:12).

In Old Testament prophetic thought, the total nation of Israel was God's suffering servant to bring to reality his redemptive purpose. All their suffering in being formed into a nation was included. The concept of Israel's suffering as God's servant narrows down in prophetic thought to one tribe within Israel—the tribe of Judah. That was particularly emphasized after the Babylonian exile. In Jesus' identification of himself as the Suffering Servant of Isaiah, the concept narrows down to *one person* within the tribe of Judah out of the total of Israel—Jesus himself. From his understanding and from the perspective of the cross as an accomplished event in history, Christians have no difficulty in seeing Jesus in Isaiah 53 as the crucified Suffering Servant of God *reckoned with transgressors*. The Jewish religious authorities condemned him as a transgressor of the law. Compelled by political pressure from the Jews, the Roman authorities executed him as a transgressor and crucified him between two lawbreakers.

The early Christians understood that this suffering as a part of God's redemptive work extended on to the total body of believers as the New Israel. The concept has been illustrated by the figure of an hour-glass. The total of the Old Israel as the suffering servant narrowed down to the tribe of Judah and then to one person in the tribe of Judah—Jesus. From him the suffering servant broadens out again to the Twelve as the smaller nucleus and then on to the total of the New Israel, the church. All share in his suffering and carry out God's redemptive witness.

*Verse 38* indicates that the disciples failed to detect the irony in Jesus' saying about buying a sword. They responded, "Look, Lord, here are two swords." Two of them already had swords; the others could go buy swords and they would all be ready to do their part! There is an air of excitement in the words "Look, Lord!"

It has been of interest to readers and interpreters of this scene and the arrests scene later in the garden, that some of the Twelve were armed with swords. That they should be armed is completely foreign to the expressed attitude of Jesus. The usual explanation is that the disciples had sensed danger for themselves and Jesus and that two of them had secretly armed themselves for protection. That is rejected by some interpreters as being too unlikely. It would be rare for any Jew to be carrying a sword, especially during a holy week.

Some interpreters stress the word *here*. They understand that Jesus' disciples were not armed but that two swords belonging to the host were hanging on the wall of the room, and Jesus and his disciples borrowed them as they left. But it would also be rare that swords would be hanging in a guest room or banquet hall rather than near the owner for his use!

Another view is that these were not actually swords. The word translated *swords* is the one regularly used for short sword, but it is also the word for a butcher knife—a knife for slaughtering animals and cutting them into pieces. The words is used in the Septuagint for Abraham's knife which he carried in preparation for the sacrifice of Isaac (Gen. 22:6, 10). Peter and John had slaughtered and prepared the lamb for the Passover Supper. The knives they had used were probably still there in the room, and could serve effectively as short swords! That appears to be the most probable of all the suggested theories for the presence of the two "swords."

*It is enough* was Jesus' response. If he had really told them to secure swords, and if they had understood him correctly and so called his attention to their already being partially armed, his answer must have meant "That is all you will need." Two swords may have been all they would need on that night, but Jesus' answer would not fit the need suggested above—that he meant for them in the future to go armed as they went out in missionary witness. The entire matter is so out of character that it seems unlikely that Jesus spoke literally. It seems much more likely that he had spoken in irony, but they understood him literally and thought he was now ready for them to join the Zealot movement. They eagerly responded that they were already partly armed, even though it was only with two long kinves used in the Passover sacrifice. Jesus' response was a curt dismissal of the entire matter. He did not say, "They are enought," referring to the two swords or knives. The verb is singular and the predicate adjective is in the emphatic first position—literally, "Enough it is," or "Enough of this matter!" With that, he dismissed the matter and they left the room. He had entered the upper room with heaviness of spirit (vv. 14–16); he left it with the same heaviness.

### (5) The agony and prayer in Gethsemane (22:39–46)

Although Luke's account is shorter and differs in some details, it is essentially the same as the account in Mark 14:26, 32–42 and Matthew 26:30, 36–40.

*Verse 39:* Jesus led his disciples from the upper room to the Mount of Olives. The particular place at the foot of the Mount of Olives and just across the Kidron brook was a garden named Gethsemane (Mark 14:32; Matt. 26:36; John 18:1).

Luke alone has one important detail in his report that Jesus went to that place *as was his custom.* Luke had previously noted that during the week Jesus went from the Temple each night "and lodged on the mount called Olivet" (21:37–38). Both statements indicate how Judas knew where to find him when the crowds would not be present.

How far the house of the upper room was from the garden and just where it was located in Jerusalem are details revealed in none of the accounts. How much time was consumed between the Lord's Supper and the garden experience is not clear. John 14–17 is a large section of teaching and activity between Jesus' dialogue with Peter about the denial (in the upper room) and the arrival in the garden. Chapter 14 most naturally fits the upper room setting, and chapters 15–17 most naturally fit a Temple setting on the way from the room to the garden. The synoptics have none of this material. Mark and Matthew place Jesus' dialogue with Peter about his denial after they had left the room and before they reached the garden. Luke and John place it in the room before they left for the garden. To account for all of these activities including the Passover Supper and the Lord's Supper, it is necessary to understand that their arrival at the garden was very late, near midnight if not after.

*Verse 40:* Jesus counseled the disciples, *Pray that you may not enter into temptation*—the temptation to lose faith in his being the Christ as they had confessed before they started the journey to Jerusalem (9:20). He had told them at that time that he was a Christ who would suffer and die (9:22), and had repeated that teaching several times in the intervening months. Now that suffering was only a few hours away. What he would experience would tempt even the strongest faith to question whether or not he was indeed the Christ. They were to pray for faith to undergird them at the time of that temptation.

*Verse 41:* Jesus went on beyond them *about a stone's throw* and knelt and prayed. His prayer was different from theirs. He had no doubt about his being the Christ. His concern was how his redemptive role as the Christ was to be realized—the same point of his prayer in those wilderness days following his baptism.

*Verse 42:* The exact words of the prayer differ in Mark and Matthew. Matthew states that Jesus prayed three times and that his words the third time were the same as the second. All of these accounts indicate that Jesus spent a long season of prayer in the garden, and that the central thrust of it was his death in relation to the Father's will.

*Father, if thou art willing:* These opening words indicate Jesus' keeping himself completely within the center of the Father's will. In the New Testament there are two Greek verbs which are rendered in English by the verb "to will." One of them means basically "to desire" or "to wish," the other "to plan" or "to counsel." Where the infinite God is concerned the two ultimately come to be the same. What God desires to do he carries out in his planning; what God plans to do, he desires to carry out. It is significant that whereas Mark and Matthew use the word for "wish" or "desire,"

Luke uses the word for "plan," and the grammatical construction is that of reasoning by concession—assuming or granting a condition—"Father, if it can be in your plan." If there was any other way by which God's redemptive plan could be effective, Jesus prayed for that way rather than the way of the "cup" which he saw before him.

*Remove this cup from me: This cup* refers to his death, recalling his words from earlier in the evening. He had looked into the cup and had seen its red liquid as his own blood (v. 20). At that time he had thanked God for that cup because of what it meant for the redemption of man's sin. Now in the garden he was a few hours nearer its reality. In a manner of speaking, he was holding that cup in his hands again, looking at its red contents, seeing it poured out on that cross-shaped altar and asking, "Is there any other way? If there is any other way, carry this cup on beyond and away from me" (author's paraphrase). The serenity of Socrates drinking voluntarily the poison required of him by the rulers of Athens has been compared with Jesus' anguish in facing the cross—to Jesus' discredit. The comparison is not a valid one. There was a tremendous difference in the physical aspects alone. Socrates drank the poison in private while surrounded by friends. The death was relatively easy. Jesus was going to the most humiliating and excruciating death-agony that could be devised by Rome—one so degrading it was not permitted for Roman citizens. Along with that was the spiritual agony of dying with the sin of the world focused upon him, as if he were the greatest sinner in the world, forsaken by his disciples, and in that last agony feeling that even God had left him to endure it alone. He shrank not merely from physical death, but from *that kind* of death and under *those conditions.*

*Nevertheless not my will, but thine, be done: Nevertheless* is an adversative particle. It looks to the matter from an opposite stance—"if there is no other way"—and expresses the Son's complete submission to the will or plan of the Father. Here the noun for *will* is based on the verb used in Mark and Matthew. The stress is on the Father's *will* ("wish" or "desire"), what he planned in Jesus' redemptive death. The verb translated *be done* means to come about, and the tense is present continuous action—"let not that which is pleasing to me but that which is pleasing to thee be coming to pass." There was no other way that an all-wise God could plan or that an all-powerful God could provide redemption for sin. The cup was the only way.

Verses 43–44 are not in the best of the ancient manuscripts of Luke. They are, however, in some good manuscripts. They occur also in some inferior manuscripts of Matthew (after 26:39). They definitely do not belong in Matthew. They are in no other Gospels. The only possibly authentic place for them is at this location in Luke.

*Verse 43: There appeared to him an angel from heaven:* This recalls the reports in Mark 1:13 and Matthew 4:11 that angels came and ministered to Jesus at the conclusion of the wilderness temptation, following his baptism. Luke has no indication that the appearance of the angel here was witnessed by anyone except Jesus. It was a matter of *strengthening him* as even then the death suffering was upon him. From this garden experience until the anguished cry of victory, "It is finished," there would be one continuing agony.

*Verse 44* cites the continuing praying of Jesus beyond the petition of verse 42. The petition of verse 42 indicates the nature of all his praying in the garden.

*In an agony he prayed more earnestly:* The ministry of the angel had given him strength but it had not brought an end to the agony which he experienced. The word translated *agony* is derived from the verb meaning "to be in great anxiety," and is closely related to other verb and noun forms meaning "to struggle," "to engage in a fight," "to strain every nerve." That which Jesus experienced cannot be captured in human language; it can only be represented feebly by that language.

*His sweat became like great drops of blood: Great drops* translates one Greek word from which the English "thrombosis" is derived, and means literally "a thickening." One Greek authority[1] gives the English equivalent as "a small amount of (flowing) blood, clot of blood." Another gives the English equivalent as "a large thick drop."[2]

It is of interest that our only source for this account is Luke, a medical doctor. Interpreters are divided on its meaning. Some understand it to be literal. Comparisons are made with medical reports of cases in which the tissues of a person under undue emotional stress appeared to break down with the result that blood comes out of the broken tissue. They understand that Jesus actually lost blood through the pores of his skin. Some have even suggested that the "cup" about which he was praying was this emotional and physical stress—he was praying that he would not die before he got to the cross. Such an interpretation appears to this interpreter as conjecture without foundation in this Scripture.

Some understand this as a figure of speech to emphasize that tremendous emotional stress under which Jesus prayed. The word translated *like,* when used in comparisons, means "as if." In the agony of prayer, even on a cold night, Jesus burst out in sweat. It was "as if" the death agony of the cross was upon him and his blood was already being shed before he experienced the thorns and the nails. This view seems more likely. If it had been literal blood coming from his skin, the figure would more naturally have been reversed—"his blood like great drops of sweat." That was not Luke's account; his report was, "sweat *as if* great drops of blood."

*Verse 45:* Jesus finished praying and returned to the place where he had left the disciples to pray. They were not praying but were *sleeping for sorrow.* Once before on the mountain of his transfiguration they had slept while he prayed about his death. (See exposition of 9:32.) Now again, wearied by the long day, burdened by his words regarding his death, they were unable to bear up in prayer for their own strength in the testing hours just ahead. While praying, they had gone to sleep and had left him alone in his prayer facing his own testing hours.

*Verse 46:* Jesus rebuked the disciples for their weakness in going to sleep. Luke does not include the last part of the event as it is reported in Mark and Matthew. His conclusion parallels Jesus' rebuke of the disciples following

---

1. W. F. Arndt and F. W. Gingrich, *A Greek-English Lexicon of the New Testament* (Chicago: The University of Chicago Press, 1957), p. 364.

2. J. H. Thayer, *A Greek-English Lexicon of the New Testament* (New York: The American Book Company, 1889), p. 292.

the first prayer in Mark and Matthew. The omission of the second and third parts also omits the difficult words of Jesus in Mark 14:41-42 and Matthew 26:45-46.

*Why do you sleep?* is a simple question. In its setting there is a suggestion of wonder on the part of Jesus that anyone could sleep when he had been told of the testing events just ahead. He repeated his counsel of verse 40 to pray so that they would not be tempted to lose faith that he was the Christ. It was no time for weak men to sleep; it was a time for strong men to pray.

### (6) The betrayal and arrest (22:47–54a)

*Verse 47: While he was still speaking* to the disciples about praying in the face of trouble, the arresting group arrived. *A crowd* had come to seize him, consisting of Judas, some of the chief priests and elders (the Sanhedrin representatives), and some of the Temple police. *Crowd* here does not mean the great company of people who had come to Jesus for his daytime preaching in the Temple (21:38). The Sanhedrin had planned carefully to arrest Jesus when that crowd was not around. Those people had observed the Passover Supper, and then had retired for the night. Only Jesus, his disciples, and the hostile Jewish authorities made up this phase of the drama.

*Judas, one of the twelve, was leading them:* One can imagine the scornful tone in which this story was told and retold in those years of oral reporting before it was reduced to writing. Every term is like an epithet.

*The man called Judas:* A most honored name in Israel's history, the name of the royal tribe and the country, but a name of scorn when applied to that man.

*One of the twelve:* There is tragedy in the phrase; one chosen, appointed to a responsible association with Jesus and the others, one who had worked in that company three or more years, was now the traitor.

*Was leading them:* He was out in front leading the arresting officers to the place he knew Jesus and the others would be. He had shared that place with them on other nights as they reviewed experiences in the Temple and in the service of God.

*He drew near to Jesus to kiss him:* Luke's tense indicates prolonged kissing. Mark and Matthew have a compound form indicating repeated kissing. The kiss was the salutation of warm and cordial friends bestowed on the cheek or the forehead. The Temple police did not likely know Jesus. In the moonlit shadows of the garden, Judas kissed Jesus several times so the officers could identify the one they were to arrest out of the group.

*Verse 48: Judas, would you betray the Son of man with a kiss?* The word order is emphatic—*"with a kiss are you betraying . . . ?"* Simply to have pointed him out and to have said, "That is the one" would have served. It was treachery added to treachery to use the symbol of friendship or respect (pupil for teacher).

*Verse 49: Those who were about him* meant the eleven disciples who had remained with him. They had formed a circle around him when the others had arrived but had allowed Judas to approach because they still had not identified him as the betrayer. Not until it was all over did they share their perplexity and their opinions as to why Judas had left the room during the Passover Supper. Not one of the reasons they had thought of related to the possibility that he was the betrayer (John 13:28–29).

*When the eleven saw what would follow:* When Judas made his identification and Jesus' words revealed to the eleven that this was his betrayal for arrest, they desired to prevent it. They asked, *Lord, shall we strike with the sword?* Whatever it was they had in the upper room (v. 38)—swords or butcher knives—they were ready to use them.

*Verses 50–51: One of them struck the slave of the high priest and cut off his right ear:* According to John 18:10, that *one* was Peter and the slave was named Malchus. All four Gospels report the incident of the slave's ear. Only Luke reports that Jesus healed the man with a touch of his hand.

Matthew, John, and Luke all contain Jesus' command that there was to be no resistance and no use of the sword. In the other Gospels there is a more detailed account including the fact that God's way was not the way of fighting, else God would have sent a legion (6,000) of fighting angels for each of the loyal Twelve—Jesus and the eleven! (Matt. 26:52–53). Luke has only the simple command, *No more of this.* He was going to conquer and rule the world, not by a sword, but by a cross. Moral power can neither be killed nor created by the sword.

*Verses 52–53:* In these verses, Jesus addressed himself to the arresting group—*chief priests . . . captains of the temple . . . elders.* The chief priests and the elders were from two of the groups which made up the Sanhedrin. The *captains of the temple* were the Temple guard for the purpose of maintaining peace and order in the Temple area.

He asked if they had come out as if they were to arrest a robber who had to be subdued by force. He reminded them that they could have arrested him in the Temple any day that week. They had not done so. What they did not know was that if they had arrested him in the midst of the people in the Temple, he would have submitted without resistance. He would no more have permitted violence by the people than he had by his disciples. His entry into Jerusalem on the donkey had meant that he came in peace and not in force and violence.

*Verses 53–54a: But this is your hour, and the power of darkness:* These words have the tone of something from the Gospel of John, but Luke alone has them. There is a mystic air of theological meaning in them.

*This is your hour* is a simple reference to the fact that they had chosen this hour instead of one of the hours when he was teaching in the Temple. Beneath that simplicity lurks the impression that he was putting "this hour," which was their hour of triumph and his of defeat, in contrast to a future "hour" which would be his hour of triumph and theirs of defeat. If the saying were in John with its abundance of double meaning sayings, one would be almost certain that there was a double meaning intended.

*And the power of darkness:* This intensifies the impression of a deeper meaning in the first clause. They had selected the hour of darkness to apprehend him and to bring his work to an end. It was an appropriate selection because the darkness typified the nature of their deed. Darkness—a symbol of evil—characterized the cities of the ancient world. In their unlighted condition, darkness was the cover for all manner of evil and moral chaos.

Light was good; darkness was evil. So it was with the action of the Sanhedrin in stopping him. The very authority by which they acted was characterized by darkness—evil. They had rejected the true light from God. At that, seeming to sense the spiritual meaning hidden in his words, *they seized him and led him away* and the power of darkness took over.

### 6. Friday—a Day of Trial and Death (22:54b–23:56a)

The events beginning at this point are placed on Friday for two reasons. One, the Passover Supper had started at sunset; all the other events of that evening must surely have extended to midnight and beyond. Two, the second phase of Jesus' hearing came after sunrise on Friday morning (v. 66). That must place this phase in the high priest's house (v. 54) and the related event of Peter's denial in the hours of darkness before dawn.

From the accounts of all four of the Gospels, it appears that there were six phases in the trial of Jesus. Three were in Jewish settings and three were in Roman settings. One, John alone states that when Jesus was arrested he was first taken to Annas, who had been high priest before his son-in-law, Caiaphas, took office (18:12–24). Two, all four Gospels report the hearing before Caiaphas, to whom, according to John, Annas sent Jesus (Mark 14:53–65; Matt. 26:57–68; Luke 22:54–65; John 18:24). This was the first official hearing since Annas had no authority—though the Jews still preferred him to Caiaphas. Three, the synoptic Gospels report a second hearing by the Sanhedrin after dawn (Mark 15:1; Matt. 27:1; Luke 22:66–71). Four, all four Gospels report the hearing before Pilate (Mark 15:1–5; Matt. 27:2, 11–14; Luke 23:1–5; John 18:28–38). Five, Luke alone reports that the hearing before Pilate was interrupted by Pilate's sending Jesus to be tried before Herod Antipas (23:6–12). Six, after the interruption indicated by Luke, the trial was resumed under Pilate. That last phase is in all four Gospels (Mark 15:6–15; Matt. 27:15–26; Luke 23:13–25; John 18:39–19:16). These are all noted here for the convenience of the reader in studying the total. Each Gospel includes many differing details and events.

### (1) Peter's denial (22:54b–62)

Peter's denial took place in the outer court of the high priest's house where the trial was being held (v. 54a). The high priest was Caiaphas; the Sanhedrin had been assembled. Probably they had been alerted for such a meeting before the arresting party was dispatched. This was an official council hearing (Mark 14:53–54; Matt. 26:57–59).

*Verse 55: When they had kindled a fire: They* refers to the Temple police who had arrested Jesus. *Kindled a fire* has no particular significance except that it reminds the reader that Jerusalem is on a high mountain elevation, it was the middle of April, and in the hours before dawn it was cold. *In the middle of the courtyard* refers to the outer part of the wall-enclosed place where the Sanhedrin had assembled for the trial. They, with Jesus and probably a limited number of the Temple police, were in the inner court. The others were in an outer court separated from it by a wall about chest high. The high priest's house was a part of the total Temple structure.

*Peter sat among them:* When Jesus was seized, the disciples fled (Mark

14:50; Matt. 26:56). Peter had followed at a distance (v. 54) and, having been admitted to the courtyard by another disciple who was acquainted with the servants in the high priest's house (John 8:15–16), he had taken a seat among the Temple guard about the fire. That is all simply a necessary part of the narrative. There is nothing essentially theological in it—though many who abhor the idea of allegorical interpretation have preached good sermons on "Warming at the Enemy's Fire"!

*Verses 56–57:* Peter was first accosted by a maid-servant. She saw him by the light of the fire and said, *This man also was with him.* It is unlikely that she had been in the arresting party in the garden. John 18:17 reports that she had questioned Peter when she had admitted him at the door upon the recommendation of another of Jesus' disciples. He had denied that he was a follower of Jesus. Luke reports that she examined him in the light of the fire and made the charge that he was one of Jesus' associates. Peter denied the charge with the words, *Woman, I do not know him.* The word translated *know* means precisely, "I have never become acquainted with him." Peter should have spent less time sleeping in the garden and more time praying for strength to resist temptation. The temptation was already confronting him and he was already showing inadequacy.

*Verse 58:* Peter was accosted a second time a bit later by the charge, *You also are one of them.* The identity of this second accuser is not clear. Mark 14:69 has that it was the same maid-servant as before. Matthew 26:71 has that it was "another maid." Luke has *some one else,* using a masculine pronoun meaning "a different one, a man"—probably he meant a male servant. John 18:25 has "they" masculine plural. Whoever the accuser was, Peter's response was a repetition of his denial, *Man, I am not.*

*Verse 59:* He was accosted the third time about one hour later. *Still another* indicates no identity except that it was another man. In the case of this third charge, John 18:26 indicates that it was a male servant of the high priest and that he was a kinsman of Malchus whose ear Peter had cut off in the garden. This time the charge was made very insistently. *Certainly* is literally "of a truth"; it indicates that there could be no mistake. The main reason for the insistence was *he is a Galilean.* The Greek text includes the word "also"—"for he also is a Galilean." Matthew 26:73 has the interesting detail that Peter's Galilean accent had given him away. Luke has Peter's answer, *Man, I do not know what you are saying.* He professed to know nothing about the whole content of the charge. Other Gospels report that he took an oath that he did not even know Jesus.

Why were these people so interested in Peter's identity as one of Jesus' followers? Why was Peter so interested in concealing that fact? The reason is related to the practice in that day. On other occasions when someone had claimed to be a messiah, he had proved to be a revolutionist. When he had been put to death, his followers had been sought, arrested, and put to death as a means of stopping the movement. The people were surprised to find this associate of Jesus not in hiding, but there in the very grasp of the officers. Peter wanted to be near Jesus, but he did not want to risk an identification that would endanger his own life. His bragging that he would die for Jesus had been just that—bragging—which now was proving to be false bravery.

*Verse 60:* When Peter had made that boast earlier on that night (v. 33), Jesus had predicted that Peter would deny him three times before the cock crowed to announce the approaching dawn (v. 34). While Peter was still speaking his third denial, he heard a cock crowing.

*Verse 61: And the Lord turned and looked at Peter:* Jesus may have looked at him across the wall separating two parts of the courtyard. He may have been on his way out of the place of the hearing and on the way to the place he would be held until after dawn. How they saw one another is a minor detail. The conditions under which they saw one another were important. By the timely crowing of the cock, Peter was reminded of his boasting and of Jesus' prediction. It revealed to him his own weakness. That was enough to cause shame. Was it enough to cause bitter weeping? It should be noted that the beating of Jesus which Luke has next (vv. 63–65) is related in Mark and Matthew before Peter's denial. It is clear from all that the trial of Jesus and the denials by Peter were taking place relatively simultaneously. If the beating and other mistreatment did take place before at least that third denial and the crowing of the cock, Jesus was a sad sight to look upon when Peter saw him. Read the details of Mark 14:65, Matthew 26:67–68, and Luke 22:63–64, and try to imagine how Jesus looked.

*Verse 62:* Remembering Jesus' words and seeing Jesus' condition was too much for Simon the Rock. *He went out and wept bitterly.* This means that he left the place of Jesus' trial and his own denial. How he got out is for the Gospel account an unimportant detail. *Wept* is the strong word for sobbing with disappointment. *Bitterly* does not qualify the physical action involved in the weeping—that is in the word itself—so much as it refers to the contrition of spirit which prompted the weeping. Peter was a man broken in humility and grief over his betrayal. The fall of a strong man is tragedy; the recovery of that strong man is triumph. The role of Simon Peter in the life of the witnessing believers after Jesus' resurrection and particularly beginning at Pentecost demonstrates how genuine his recovery was. It was triumph, and Peter was equipped to strengthen his brethren as Jesus had commanded him (v. 31).

## (2) The preliminary hearing before Caiaphas (22:63–65)

Luke reports none of the action in this first hearing which is in Mark and Matthew—witnesses, charges, demand for Jesus' own confession, and finally the vote that Jesus deserved to die—only the outcome. Luke's report of the outcome parallels the accounts of Mark and Matthew.

*Verses 63–65: The men who were holding him:* This may have meant only the Temple police. Mark and Matthew appear to include the chief priests and other members of the Sanhedrin in the shameful conduct. It is shocking to read of such conduct by the highest religious court in the land. It must be recalled that they regarded such treatment as a necessary part of the punishment deserved by one judged worthy of death. Such treatment showed the enormity of his crime and warned others against similar guilt.

*Mocked:* They scoffed at him for his actions and claims which had brought him to this sad state. *Beat him* indicates physical violence in addition to the mocking ridicule. There is no indication of beating with clubs. The buffeting was with palms and fists, suggesting a game. This prisoner was regarded by many as "the prophet . . . from Nazareth in Galilee" (Matt. 21:11). So they blindfolded him, rained blows upon him, and challenged him, *"Prophesy! Who is it that struck you?"* It was a child's game, but for him and them it was no game. With this treatment, accompanied by their *reviling him*—speaking evil things against him—the court recessed until after dawn.

### (3) The formal hearing before the Sanhedrin (22:66–71)

*Verse 66: When day came* means that it was after sunrise. This was related to the custom of the Sanhedrin. When a man was pronounced guilty on one day, it was the custom to have a second vote on the next day. This was a move to assure justice. After a night of sleep and, hence, a period of reconsidering the evidence, a second vote was taken on the chance that the verdict might be changed. Because of the pressure of time and the urgency of having Jesus executed before the sabbath started at sunset, the council waited the few hours of darkness after the first vote (Matt. 26:66) and then, on that technicality, after sunrise assembled for the second vote. It was a legal formality. There was little likelihood that any of them had "slept over the matter," and there was no likelihood that the decision would be reversed.

*Verse 67:* Jesus was led before the assembled council (v. 66) and commanded, *"If you are the Christ, tell us."* They were seeking an answer by which they could charge him before the Roman court and secure execution. The *Christ* in Greek is the same as the *Messiah* in Hebrew. It means the anointed deliverer from God. It could easily be explained to the Romans that it meant one who was a national deliverer and, hence, one who was a revolutionist against Rome. It was the one charge by which they were certain they could secure his execution. It had meaning for the Romans, who would not be concerned over matters of Jewish religion and laws.

*Verses 67–69:* Jesus' answer reflected the futility of his position. If he answered that he was the Messiah (the Christ), they would not believe him. That had been demonstrated at his announcement in his triumphal entry. On the other hand, if he asked them about his qualifications for being the Messiah, they would not answer. That had been demonstrated on Tuesday when he had challenged them with the question about whose son the Messiah would be (20:41–44).

He dropped their word—Messiah, or Christ—and used his favorite term for himself, Son of Man. He said, *But from now on the Son of man shall be seated at the right hand of the power of God.* That presented the idea of a much higher state of exaltation than their idea of the Messiah. It implied his being raised far above their paltry power, rule, and position, and seated at the powerful right hand of God. That meant the most honored, authoritative, and powerful position in the entire rule of God. *From now on* meant from the very time of their fulfillment of their purpose with him. That purpose was death and he was even then in its clutches. But out of his death would come exaltation to honor and power with the eternal God.

*Verse 70:* They did not comprehend all of his meaning. They probably thought that he expected God to intervene and rescue him from their grasp and establish him as an exalted ruler. To sit at the right hand of a human father was to be recognized as his honored son and heir. *They all said* implies a group understanding of the implications of his words. In chorus they asked, *Are you the Son of God, then?* Their meaning may be more readily understood by translating their question in the word order of Luke's text, *"You, then, yourself are the Son of God?"* The emphasis is on the pronoun. To them it was beyond belief that one they believed to be a lawbreaker could be possessed of deity. To make the claim of verse 69 could mean only that he claimed to be the Son of God. This, to the court, meant blasphemy and it was justification for execution.

*You say that I am:* literally, *"You,* you are saying that I am." The idiomatic expression means, "You yourselves are saying that I am what I really am." His meaning was that he did not have to say that he was the Son of God; they were saying it and speaking the truth in saying it.

*Verse 71* concludes this second hearing. The verdict was the same as in the first one. What further testimony did they need? The word translated *testimony* is the word for "witness." They needed no further witness against him. They had his own confession from his own lips. He had confessed that he was the Son of God and in so doing he had blasphemed God. In the ancient days, he would have been stoned to death. Under the Roman law, the council would have to leave his execution to the Romans. The Romans did not employ stoning; they had their own form of cruelty.

### (4) The hearing before Pilate (23:1–5)

This section contains the account of the Sanhedrin's committing Jesus to Pilate and their insistence on his guilt.

*Verse 1: The whole company of them* means that the entire council of seventy or seventy-two—the exact number is uncertain—plus the Temple guard, moved from their assembly hall in the Temple area to the government hall of Pilate.

*Pilate*—his full name was Pontius Pilate—was the Roman governor or judge. When Archelaus, son of Herod the Great, was deposed and banished to Gaul because of extreme cruelty in ruling the Jews (A.D. 6), the Romans took the rule of Judea from the Herod family and put it into the hands of a series of men who are variously referred to as judge, governor, or proconsul. Pilate was the governor from A.D. 26–36. The early Jewish writers Philo and Josephus report much of evil practice of Pilate in his treatment of the Jews. Early Christian writings not included in the New Testament present him as an evil ruler. Apart from references to his part in the events of Jesus' death, there is only one other New Testament reference to him— the slaughter of the Galilean worshipers (Luke 13:1–5). Outside the New Testament there is no record of that incident.

In later writings, there is a great deal of legendary material about his being removed from office as a Roman governor, his activities in central Europe, and death by suicide during the rule of the Emperor Caligula (A.D. 37–41). None of that is certain. Some historians have felt that he must have been a good ruler to have lasted ten years in Judea in a time when Jewish hostility to Rome was white hot. Some Christian groups have held to his ultimate conversion to the Christian faith. Both Pilate and his wife, who warned him about his involvement in the trial of Jesus (Matt. 27:19), have been canonized by the Coptic church. In reality, there is not enough information about him to make a valid judgment of the kind of man he was. From the New Testament accounts, he appears to have been a discerning judge, who concluded that Jesus was not worthy of death, tried in several ways to avoid having to sentence him to death, but finally yielded under political pressure and permitted the execution of a man whom he knew to be innocent.

*Verse 2* contains the only charge which the Sanhedrin placed against Jesus when they turned him over to Herod. In Luke's account the charge is totally a political one. Charges with religious overtones and dialogue with religious overtones between Jesus and Pilate are in the other Gospels.

*We found this man perverting our nation:* That was as close to a religious charge as they lodged. *Perverting* means leading astray in teaching or practice. *Our nation* refers to the Jews. They did not mention his leading the Jews astray in areas of religious matters. That was their real concern, but they knew it would have no standing in a Roman court. The Romans had no concern about how the Jews observed the sabbath or the food laws, or how they interpreted the Torah. So even the charge that Jesus was perverting the nation received a political association in the next two parts.

*Forbidding us to give tribute to Caesar:* That was a serious charge in the Roman court. If Jesus had been leading the Jews astray by forbidding them to pay the Roman tax, he was guilty of a crime against Rome—rebellion, resistance, or the next step, revolution. It was a false charge. On Tuesday of that week, when asked whether or not it was lawful to pay the Roman tax, Jesus had essentially answered that it was. He had argued the case so convincingly that those who had challenged him were silenced by the wisdom he spoke (20:20–26). Now they used an outright falsehood in charging him.

*Saying that he himself is Christ a king:* That charge was true, but not in the way in which they wanted Pilate to understand it. It was a charge of treason against the ruling Emperor Tiberius, a charge that Jesus was claiming to be a rival king. *Christ* means anointed one, and in Jewish theology it meant the Messiah who would deliver the Jews and reign in the messianic age.

Of the three charges, the first one—leading the Jews astray—was only partly true. From the Sanhedrin's view of the correct way of observing religious laws and institutions, Jesus' practice and teaching was leading the people astray; but from his viewpoint he was leading them into a new and more meaningful practice. The charge was really a value judgment. But even that charge was not clarified for Pilate and was left as a political one by association with the next one. The second charge—forbidding tribute to Caesar—was completely false. He had taught the very opposite. The third charge—that he claimed to be a king—was a half truth which they twisted out of Jesus' meaning in his triumphal entry as the Son of David king. They made it appear to be an act of treason against the emperor.

*Verse 3* contains a brief summary question by Pilate and answer by Jesus. The other Gospels fill in the details of Pilate's questioning Jesus on whether or not he was a king and, if so, the nature of his kingdom (John 18:33–38 in particular). In Luke's account there is only the question, *"Are you the*

*King of the Jews?"* The word *Christ,* equivalent of the Hebrew "Messiah," would have meant "Ruler of the Jews" to a Roman.

Jesus answered, *You have said so.* The Greek expression means precisely, "You yourself are speaking." There is much discussion as to the likely Aramaic expression which would be rendered by this Greek expression. It is assumed that Jesus spoke in the common language of the Jews—Aramaic. The conclusion—although sometimes a challenged one—is that Jesus meant, "Yes," or "You have said it because it is true."

*Verse 4:* Pilate reported to the Sanhedrin, *"I find no crime in this man."* The expression *no crime* means no cause for punishment, or no guilt. That response has influenced some interpreters to understand that Jesus' answer to Pilate (v. 3) means "No." By that understanding, Jesus said in paraphrase, "You are saying that; I am not." It would mean that he was not claiming to be the king of the Jews; he was not claiming to be Israel's ruler. Pilate accepted his word and announced his conclusion to the Sanhedrin.

Other interpreters understand that Jesus meant "Yes," but that Pilate satisfied himself by questioning Jesus about the nature of his kingship and kingdom. He understood that Jesus was not claiming to be the kind of king who was a rival to Caesar. That, of course, is the case in John's account (18:33–38), but there is no record of it in the synoptics. Of the two views, the second appears to be the correct one.

*Verse 5:* The Sanhedrin was not satisfied to leave the matter with that conclusion which meant that Jesus would be set free. The other Gospels include other details of their continuing demand. Luke says only that they were *urgent*—the basic meaning of the word and the tense used means, "they kept on insisting." They insisted by renewing the charge that Jesus was a troublemaker: *He stirs up the people, teaching throughout all Judea, from Galilee even to this place.*

*Stirs up* is a word for excitement. The people who saw Jesus at work and heard him teach were filled with excitement. Some were excited over the fresh note of authority in his teaching. Others were excited because of his power in working miracles. Many were excited with the hope that he would become their deliverer from the bondage of Rome.

*Throughout all Judea* embraces all the area of Jesus' influence and teaching in the south country. Very little of it before this last week is recorded in Luke; none of it before this week is in Mark and Matthew; John has great sections of Jesus' teaching in Judea.

*From Galilee even to this place:* His ministry had its beginning in Galilee but had extended from there to Jerusalem—*to this place.* All in between Galilee and Jerusalem he had taught and worked. He had a major ministry in Perea and he had some ministry in Samaria. He had deliberately avoided exciting the wrong kind of messianic expectation in the people. The synoptics are very clear on that even to the point of the much discussed "Messianic Secret" motif—deliberate efforts to conceal and play down his being the Messiah. The Sanhedrin, false as its intent was, was correct in one thing— he had excited the people. And this Passover week the entire city of Jerusalem had reached a peak of excitement.

Pilate, however, had rightly judged Jesus to be innocent of treason against Rome or of any other crime warranting death. He did not want to order the execution which the Sanhedrin was demanding (John 18:7). In the next two hours Pilate tried three ways of avoiding a sentence of execution. First, he tried to avoid it by sending Jesus to be tried by Herod (vv. 6–12). Second, he had Jesus scourged by the Roman soldiers in hopes that the Sanhedrin would accept that as sufficient punishment (vv. 13–16). Third, when that failed, he tried by using the custom of releasing a prominent Jewish prisoner to help carry out the Passover theme of freedom from bondage (vv. 18–23).

### (5) The hearing before Herod Antipas (23:6–12)

Verses 6–12 report an interruption in the hearing before Pilate. Only Luke has this incident. It was Pilate's first effort to avoid sentencing Jesus. When he heard that Jesus had started his work in Galilee (v. 5), he asked if Jesus was a Galilean. From every viewpoint except his birth in Bethlehem, Jesus was. He had lived from childhood to manhood in Nazareth. When his hometown rejected him and tried to stone him to death for claiming to be the Suffering Servant of Isaiah, he moved to Capernaum and made that his operating base until he went to Jerusalem for Passover.

*Verse 7: He belonged to Herod's jurisdiction:* Because he lived in Galilee he could be tried legally by the ruler of Galilee even though he was charged in Jerusalem. *He sent him over* is a legal term—literally, "sent him up"—for remanding a prisoner for trial. Even though he had already pronounced Jesus not guilty, Pilate was trying to shift legal responsibility to Herod.

*Herod:* Herod Antipas was one of the sons of Herod the Great. When the Herod family was deposed, the Romans had placed Judea under the system of governors discussed above under verse 1. The rest of the territory was divided among four of Herod's sons. Herod Antipas received Galilee and Perea. His official title was "tetrarch"—ruler of one-fourth—but the Jews commonly referred to him as a king. He had married his brother Philip's wife, Herodias, in an adulterous union and had beheaded John the Baptist for preaching against that relationship (Mark 6:17–28). When he had heard of Jesus' work, in his superstitious fear he thought that John had come back to life (Luke 9:7–9; Mark 6:14). Jesus once had shown his lack of fear of Herod Antipas by calling him a fox and by refusing to stop working in his territory (Luke 13:31–32).

Herod was only part Jew and from all indications not a pious one. He was, however, in Jerusalem that Passover week and furnished what seemed to be an excellent opportunity for Pilate to avoid a distasteful act.

*Verse 8:* Herod *was very glad* to see Jesus. The word *glad* means pleased or gratified. No doubt he was pleased that Pilate had recognized his authority—the word translated *jurisdiction* in verse 7. He was pleased that Pilate had sent the Galilean to him, but he was too "foxy" to fall into the trap. He was pleased for another reason. Since he had first heard of Jesus' work (9:7–9), he had wanted to see him. His desire had no relation to Jesus as a teacher of religion. He was interested in the reports of the miracles Jesus worked and hoped *to see some sign done by him.* The word for *sign* is the one regularly used in John for Jesus' miracles, but it is rarely used in the synoptics. In John it means that the miracles were more than just wondrous events. They were "signs" in that they pointed beyond the acts themselves to a greater spiritual truth—that the one doing them was the Christ. That was not Herod's interest. He simply wanted to see this man he had heard about do the same kind of magical feats as the court jesters used to entertain his retinue.

*Verse 9:* Herod questioned Jesus at length. The scene presents no impression of a court hearing. The questioning was likely focused on the area of Herod's interest—Jesus' miracles. Jesus refused to answer. He would enter into no discussion of his work with one whose only interest was magic. Jesus was no trickster and he would not discuss his work in that sort of atmosphere.

*Verse 10:* Members from the Sanhedrin had gone with those who took Jesus from Pilate to Herod. They hoped to get a more favorable judgment from Herod than from Pilate. Even as a part Jew, Herod should know more than Pilate about the serious nature of their charges that Jesus was leading the Jews astray (v. 2). Herod, however, had no interest in the charge and felt no threat from it. They kept on *vehemently accusing* Jesus. The word translated *vehemently* means a vigorous, strenuous charge. They tried to make a trial out of what Herod desired to be a court show.

*Verse 11:* When Herod realized that his hopes for seeing Jesus perform some of the feats for which he was famous would not be fulfilled, he had no further use for him. The soldiers who were a part of Herod's traveling retinue joined their king in treating Jesus with contempt and mockery. They scoffed at him as one who had a reputation as a wonder-worker but could provide no evidence to prove it. Herod had no intention of becoming involved in the legal problem facing Pilate. To him it was not worth the bother.

He and his soldiers hit on a plan for playing a joke on the Roman governor. It had likely come out in the Sanhedrin's accusations that, in claiming to be a king, Jesus was charged with treason against Rome. Therefore, they dressed Jesus in *gorgeous apparel* and *sent him back* to Pilate. The word translated *gorgeous* means "shining." It was no ordinary robe that they "threw around" him. It was one which indicated an illustrious person of great importance—a king, for example. No indication is given of a worded message to accompany their dramatized one. One can almost hear a mocking, "Here is your king; go on and try him." The expression translated *sent him back to Pilate* is the same legal term ("sent him up") used in Pilate's sending him to Herod. Pilate had said to Herod, "You should decide this case." Herod had answered "Oh, no; you go on and decide it."

*Verse 12* is a sad commentary on the nature of man. Luke states that before that time the Roman ruler in Judea and the Jewish ruler in Galilee had been hostile to one another. No reason for the hostility is given. Speculation is fruitless. In their neighbor territories and with their different cultural backgrounds, the hostility could have been for multiplied reasons. The sad part is that Pilate accepted the practical joke for what it was, recognized that Herod was deferring authority to him, and the two became friends. Friends are lost (Jesus and Judas) and gained (Pilate and Herod) in strange turns of human events.

### (6) The hearing before Pilate—sentenced to die (23:13–25)

Pilate tried a second time to avoid sentencing Jesus to death. He knew the Sanhedrin would not settle for Jesus' release without punishment. He hoped that they would settle for less than the death penalty.

He reassembled the Sanhedrin (v. 13), and reviewed their charges in bringing Jesus to him for trial (v. 14a). He reminded them that in his examining of Jesus he had found him innocent of all the crimes they had charged against him (v. 14b). Furthermore, he pointed out that the Jewish ruler of Jesus' home country, Herod, had also found him innocent and pointed, as proof, to Herod's having sent Jesus back (v. 15a). He was doubtless stretching greatly the implication of Herod's act. Then he stated that since neither Roman nor Jewish court had found Jesus guilty of any crime deserving death (v. 15b), he was going to *chastise* Jesus and release him (v. 16).

*Verse 16: Chastise* is the word for disciplinary beating. John 19:1 has the word for scourge. The Roman scourging was done with leather whips having pieces of sharp stone, metal, and bone tied into their three thongs. Descriptions of the act are gruesome, including details of torn flesh even to the rupture of the abdominal wall and exposure of internal organs. It was such severe punishment that prisoners sometimes died under it. Luke does not report the actual scourging. John does with the detail that when it was over, having been done inside the palace, Pilate took Jesus out to the Sanhedrin and showed the results of the scourging with the words, "Behold, the man." It was an appeal to them to let that be sufficient punishment. The only result was an intensification of their desire for his death, and they set up their cry, "Crucify, crucify!"

Verses 18–22 contain Pilate's third and last effort to avoid the sentence of death. *Verse 17* is omitted from the RSV text because it is not in the best manuscripts of Luke. Evidently it was not in Luke's original account but was inserted by a later copyist who borrowed it from Mark 15:6 as a clarifying introduction to Luke's account. It introduces the custom of releasing a prominent Jewish prisoner at Passover to help carry out the historic theme of the week—freedom from bondage. The origin of the custom is uncertain. It can be traced with fair assurance back to the rule of the Maccabees family in the period between the Old Testament and the New Testament. Just how it was usually carried out is also uncertain. In Jesus' case, Pilate named the two outstanding Jewish prisoners in Jerusalem that week and asked the Sanhedrin to choose one for release, thereby choosing the other for execution. All four Gospels record the event and their varying contribution of details clarify the whole (Mark 15:6–15; Matt. 27:15–26; Luke 23:18–23; John 18:39–40).

Jesus was one of the two. He was a prisoner charged with treason and a dangerous threat as a possible revolutionist. He had been examined by Pilate and pronounced innocent.

*Verses 18–19:* Barabbas was the other of the two. He was a prisoner who had already been found guilty of leading an attempt at revolution—*insurrection . . . in the city*—which had resulted in the crime of murder. He was awaiting execution.

When Pilate gave the Sanhedrin, along with the others who by this time had joined them, the opportunity to choose the one who would be released, they chose Barabbas. Some of the ancient manuscripts of Matthew (not the best ones) have a reading indicating that the first name of Barabbas was also "Jesus" (27:16). So when Pilate put the choice to the Sanhedrin he asked if they wished him to release "Jesus who is called Barabbas or Jesus who is called Christ" (Matt. 26:17). The reading is attractive but it is very unlikely that it is genuine. It represents the interpretation of some copyist who had a flair for the dramatic—and it is dramatic.

*Verses 20–21:* When Pilate put the question a second time, *desiring to release Jesus,* the question was, according to Matthew 27:22, "What then shall I do to the Jesus who is called Christ?" Pilate's efforts were sincere. He must have thought that the Sanhedrin—the highest court of the Jews—would drop prejudice and make a choice based on justice. That was not the case. They answered his question by setting up a chant, *Crucify, crucify him!* The Greek text has the measured cadence of the chant of a mob. Transliterated into English syllables it is:

Stau-rou, stau-rou-au-ton!

Stau-rou, stau-rou-au-ton!

Even in the English words the cadence of a chant is present:

Cru-ci-fy, cru-ci-fy-him!

Cru-ci-fy, cru-ci-fy-him!

That was the most dreadful "one-two—one-two-three-four" beat ever to sound in the ears of men.

*Verse 22:* Pilate would not leave it at that. He interrupted to ask, *Why, what evil has he done?* He repeated his words of verses 14 and 16, volunteering that even though he had found Jesus innocent of any crime deserving death, he would have him scourged again and then release him. It was to no avail.

*Verse 23:* They set up again their insistent chant, demanding that Jesus be crucified, this time with even louder cries. There are volumes of meaning in Luke's simple assertion, *And their voices prevailed.*

*Verse 24:* Pilate ordered that Jesus should be executed in compliance with their demand. Luke does not have their final charge that if he released Jesus who was claiming to be a king, he himself would be disloyal to the emperor (John 19:12). He would not risk his own position even at the cost of seeing an innocent man executed.

*Verse 25:* Pilate released the justly convicted Barabbas from prison as they had chosen and delivered Jesus *up to their will.* The Sanhedrin's will for him was the cross, but it had to be carried out by the Romans. From the New Testament accounts, there can be no absolving the Sanhedrin of responsibility in the death of Jesus. That has been frequently attempted. The most recent attempt has held that relatively only a few Jews desired the death of Jesus and that in the last analysis only one was responsible—the high priest, Caiaphas; the responsibility is placed on the Romans and the reason for Jesus' execution was the Roman fear of his threat as a potential revolutionist. That disposition of the matter is too naïve to fit the total situation. The Jews were guilty, and the Romans were guilty, and behind their agency in that dark deed is the fact that the whole mass of rebellious sinful humanity was and is guilty of a meaningful share of responsibility for his

death. It was *our* sins in the most comprehensive sense which nailed Jesus
to the cross.

### (7) Crucified and buried (23:26–56a)

Verses 26–49 embrace Luke's total account of the action from the time
Pilate sentenced Jesus to die and turned over to a company of Roman soldiers the responsibility for carrying out the sentence (v. 25), until Jesus
was dead (v. 49). Of the four Gospels, Luke has the shortest and simplest
account, particularly of the crucifixion itself. He has some meaningful details
which are not in the other accounts.

Verses 26–31 record the going from Pilate's judgment hall to the place
of crucifixion outside the city.

*Verse 26: As they led him away:* In Luke the reference is simply to their
leading Jesus away from the judgment hall. Matthew 27:32 has the compound verb form "as they were marching out," meaning their procession out
of the city. John 19:20 notes that the place of crucifixion was outside the
city. To the writer of the Epistle to the Hebrews, Jesus' death outside the
city had theological significance in parallel to the ancient Jewish practice
of disposing of the unused portion of sacrificial animals outside the camp
(Heb. 13:10–13). By an allegorical application he appealed to his Jewish
readers to go "outside the camp"—to leave their old Jewish sacrificial system and to identify with the new one in Jesus Christ whose sacrifice was
the fulfillment of the old.

*They seized one Simon of Cyrene: Cyrene* in North Africa was one of
the important centers of the dispersed Jewish people and culture. *Simon* was
a very common Hebrew name. This man was a Jew who lived in North
Africa. There is not one breath of the unfortunate tradition that he was a
Negro and that the Roman soldiers exploited him because of his color. As
a racial and social barrier in that day, the color of one's skin had no significance. Mark identifies this Simon to his Roman readers as the father of
Alexander and Rufus (15:21). Paul sent greetings to a Rufus and his
mother in Rome (Rom. 16:13). He described Rufus as "eminent in the
Lord," and his mother as dear to Paul as his own mother. The identification
of the Rufus in Paul's letter to Rome and the Rufus in Mark's Gospel for
Rome is not certain; neither is it nebulous.

*Coming in from the country:* Simon was coming into Jerusalem and met
the soldiers and Jesus as they were going out. He may have been traveling
to Jerusalem for Passover and arriving late.

*Laid on him the cross:* To that point, Jesus alone had carried the cross.
By law, the Romans were permitted to conscript help for a prisoner in carrying the very heavy cross. Because of loss of vitality in having had no food
for hours and having endured the dreadful scourging, Jesus needed help with
the great burden. Likely they conscripted Simon, not because he was black,
but because he was a Jew whose travel situation indicated his importance.
What better way for the Romans to show their contempt for the Jews than
by compelling a prominent Jew to share the burden of the cross of one who
was being executed as King of the Jews?

*To carry it behind Jesus:* A condemned man was required to carry his
cross as a part of his punishment. Certainly the Roman soldiers would not

stoop to assist. Sometimes the two parts of the cross had already been fas-
tened together. Sometimes the cross beam was not affixed to the upright
beam until they reached the place of crucifixion. That factor and Luke's
expression that Simon carried the cross *behind Jesus* makes exact understanding impossible. It could mean that they carried the two parts together,
Jesus in front and Simon behind. It could mean that Jesus carried one part
in front and Simon followed carrying the other part. It could also mean
that Simon alone carried the cross—as Mark 15:21 and Matthew 27:32
seem to imply—and that he walked *behind Jesus,* Luke's detail. Truthfully,
Simon's taking over the cross, in whole or in part, is a detail which has no
theological importance, but it is a detail which seems to fascinate a multitude of readers and, hence, to demand this attention in the exposition.

*Verse 27:* A great company of people followed the shameful processional.
In the company were women who *bewailed and lamented him.* They are
not identified except as residents of Jerusalem (v. 28). Loud vocal demonstrations of distress and grief were customary in that day. One who has
witnessed a scene of public wailing over the dead or over other calamity in
Palestine today has a vivid mental image as a background for this—anguished wails, pulling out hair, clawing the face with fingernails. These
women were touched by the suffering which Jesus had already endured and
which they knew he faced in the dreadful crucifixion. Their grief for him
was genuine.

*Verse 28:* Jesus paused on the way to his own suffering to quiet their
anguish and to counsel them to save their grief for the tragic days which
would be experienced when Rome executed, not just one Jew, but the entire
city of Jerusalem.

*Daughters of Jerusalem* is a tender expression and at the same time in-
dicative of the women's pride in their history and their citizenship in Jerusalem. As a definite reference to women living in Jerusalem, it may exclude
the company of women who had traveled with and ministered to Jesus and
the Twelve in Galilee (8:13) although some of them were present to observe his crucifixion (v. 49). The reference does not necessarily exclude
them; every Jewish woman in Palestine shared, corporately, at least, in the
disaster of the destruction of Jerusalem.

*Do not weep for me:* This was a command to stop what was already in
progress—literally, "Stop your weeping over me." They were weeping over
him as if he were already dead. He did not say this out of lack of appreciation for their concern or lack of understanding of their distress. He knew
personally what it meant to weep in distress (19:41) and grief (John
11:35). He gave the command because he felt that it was no time for weeping for him. What he was facing was a necessary part of the redemptive
purpose of God; it had to be done. And he was sufficient for it.

*But weep for yourselves and for your children:* The word translated *but*
is a very strong adversative meaning "on the contrary," "rather than." The
word and tense of the positive imperative are the same as the negative one
regarding their weeping for him. The command was literally "on the contrary, keep on weeping over yourselves and over your children." The burden
to be borne by the residents of Jerusalem would be a continuous cause of
weeping in agony and despair until it reached its climax in the Roman de-

struction. Mothers and children would be especially victimized by its hardship.

*Verse 29: Behold, the days are coming* points again to those days of destruction which he had discussed upon his entry into the city on the previous Sunday (19:41–44) and upon his exit from the city on Tuesday (21:6, 20–24), all in relation to his own death. That was the key for the early church to interpret the destruction of Jerusalem as judgment on the Jewish nation for rejecting Jesus as the Messiah. They related both Jesus' prediction and the destruction itself to Jesus' teaching that last week about Israel's fruitless failure to carry out God's redemptive witness and God's purpose to give the responsibility of that redemptive witness to the Gentiles. At an early date the Christian community came to be predominantly Gentile.

When those days of destruction came, Jesus said, the hardships would be so bad that a woman incapable of bearing children would be regarded as blessed. That would be the very reverse of the historic view that a barren womb was a tragedy. Jesus' words are more effective when arranged in their literal meaning and position:

> Blessed: the sterile,
> the wombs that have never borne,
> the breasts that never gave milk.

*The barren* literally means sterile women—women incapable of conceiving a child. The other two phrases describe women who had never brought a child into the kind of world of turmoil and disaster which would be Jerusalem in that day. In every other situation in life, bearing children was the most exalted privilege of womanhood. But when Jerusalem's children were snatched from the nursing breast and slaughtered before the eyes of the mother, it would be more blessed to be childless.

*Verse 30:* In those days people would flee the stricken city and seek safety in the hills. *'Fall on us'* . . . *'Cover us'* may be poetic ways of saying, "Give us your valleys and caves as protection." A preferable meaning is, however, that the quick agony of being crushed to death by falling mountains would be preferred to the prolonged agony of those days in the hands of the Romans. The verse is an inverted quotation of Hosea 10:8—the cry of Samaria for the mountains and hills to crush them rather than let them fall into the hands of the cruel Assyrians. Jerusalem in the hands of Rome would be like Samaria in the hands of Assyria.

*Verse 31* is a figurative way of referring to Jerusalem's day of opportunity as green and living spring, but her day of no opportunity as dry and dead winter.

*If they do this* refers to what the Romans were doing to Jesus. *What will happen* refers to what would happen to Jerusalem. *When the wood is green* as a metaphor of spring refers to Jesus' presence and offer of God's deliverance from sin and judgment. They were days in which God's favor was extended. *When it is dry* refers to the absence of any offer of deliverance from judgment when those days of destruction came. Those would be days when God's favor was not extended. Jesus was in one sense the "green wood" of fruit bearing; he was, nevertheless, suffering death at the hands of the Romans. Israel was in that same sense the "dry wood" of fruitlessness; how much worse would be her fate at the hands of those same Romans. He spoke in view of all of that when he bade them to cease weeping for him, but to begin and continue their weeping for their own days of suffering and distress because they had rejected their day of opportunity.

Verses 32–43 account for the beginning of the crucifixion and the events which Luke records for the first three hours of Jesus on the cross. Mark 15:25 states that Jesus was crucified at the third hour, which was 9:00 A.M. by Roman time. Luke (v. 44) states that the darkness came on at the sixth hour—12:00 noon—and lasted until the ninth hour—3:00 P.M. Burial was mandatory before sunset—approximately 6:00 P.M. (John 19:31).

*Verse 32* contains the introduction of two other men who were crucified at the same time. They are identified as *criminals* (vv. 32 and 39), a word meaning doers of evil things. Mark 15:27 and Matthew 27:38 have the word *robbers,* a word meaning a bandit (highwayman) or a revolutionary, an insurrectionist. The word was more frequently used in the sense of a highway robber. Since, however, Jesus had been charged with treason as a potential insurrectionist, it would have been very appropriate for two such criminals to be crucified with him. The two may have been associates of the insurrectionist Barabbas, who had been set free instead of Jesus.

*Verse 33:* Jesus was crucified at a place called *The Skull.* The two criminals were crucified, one on either side of him. Jesus was in reality "reckoned with transgressors" (22:37). Mark, Matthew, and John all have the Hebrew word *Golgotha* with the indication that it means Skull. Luke has the Greek word *kranion* which is properly translated Skull. The commonly used English word, Calvary, is derived from the Latin text. The name most likely indicates a skull-shaped hill. Its location is disputed. Two traditional places are currently pointed out as the place, but evidence for positive identification of either one is lacking. One is in the Church of the Holy Sepulchre; the other is now a Moslem cemetery near an ancient burial cave once used as a place of Christian worship and now called the Garden Tomb.

There were three types of crosses used in crucifixions. One was the shape of the letter X; one was the shape of the letter T; and one was the upright beam and crossbeam commonly seen, ✝ . There is no positive indication as to which form was used for Jesus, but the placing of the inscription *over* Jesus' head (v. 38) most naturally suggests the one commonly seen in art and in church use today.

Sometimes criminals were tied to the cross and suspended there to die of starvation and exposure to the elements; crucifixion was in the nude, and exposure to heat in summer and cold in winter could be very severe. Sometimes the criminals were fixed to the cross by nails through the feet—superimposed one on top of the other—and hands, palms or wrists. If the nails were driven through the palms, the wrists would also be tied to the cross beam to prevent the hands from pulling away. From Jesus' demonstration of the reality of his resurrection by exhibiting the scars in his hands, it is positive that that was the form used in his execution. Death came from exposure, from loss of blood, and the consequent dehydration of the body which brought on a high fever and terrible thirst. Usually it took from thirty-six to forty-eight hours on the cross for death to occur. Jesus died in six hours.

*Verse 34:* Three of the much used "seven last words" or "seven last sayings" of Christ are only in Luke. Luke has only these three; the others are in Mark, Matthew, and John. The first recorded words of Jesus after his speaking to the wailing women (vv. 28–31) were words of intercession for sinners, *"Father, forgive them; for they know not what they do."* The saying is in Luke only and not in some of the best manuscripts of Luke. It is well attested, however, in some good texts. The address is the tender *Father* which he commonly used in his praying. Even on the cross he recognized the Father-Son relationship. His last words on the cross in Luke's account were also addressed to the Father (v. 46). Luke does not record his cry of being forsaken by God during the hours of darkness (Mark 15:34; Matt. 27:46).

*Forgive them:* The word *forgive* is the regular one for the dismissal or sending away of sins. His was an intercessory prayer for the forgiveness of men for whose sins he was dying. The object *them* is not identified as to persons. It may have been an all-inclusive prayer for the mass of sinful men. It may have been for the Roman soldiers who, even then at the foot of his cross, were gambling, with his clothes as the stakes.

*For they know not what they do:* One of the difficulties in interpreting this prayer of Jesus and in identifying the people for whom he prayed is the understanding of this reason—he asked for forgiveness because those for whom he prayed did not know what they were doing. If his prayer was for the Roman soldiers, this could mean that they were carrying out an execution order from a higher authority and, in doing their duty, were acting in ignorance of his innocence or of his person. Gambling was the popular diversion of soldiers; the executed person was regarded as dead already and having no need of clothes. They *cast lots* by the use of dice, or names placed in a helmet and drawn out by chance, or any other of several forms. If the criminals' clothes were of any value, the same thing was done for them. What they did was insensitive and totally lacking in concern, but it was not in hostility. Perhaps Jesus prayed for them, that out of all of that dreadful experience they would come to know the true identity of the one they had crucified, and would come to know redemptive truth. They were the most likely object of Jesus' prayer.

If his prayer was not for the soldiers, for whom was it? The Sanhedrin under the leadership of Caiaphas has been suggested. If so, then in what sense was it that they did not know what they were doing? If they did not know that he was the Son of God, it was because they had had plenty of evidence but hardened themselves in rejection. Was it for Pilate who had permitted Jesus to be executed even when he knew he was innocent? Or Herod, who had scorned him as nothing other than a stubborn magician? Or Judas, or Peter, or the nine who followed afar off? Only the beloved disciple went all the way to the cross (John 19:26–27). The likely prospects for identifying the object of Jesus' prayer grow remote the farther one moves from the soldiers. Whoever it was for whom he prayed, it is important that his love for sinful men was greater than the excruciating agony of the cross. That love overcame personal pain as he prayed for sinners.

*Verses 35–37* identify three groups of people in their actions at the cross. *The people* who stood nearby and watched it all are unidentified. Likely it was a mixed group including some of his friends and his mother who are named as witnesses in verse 49 and in John 19:25–27. Likely, too, it included the curious and the callous who are always attracted to the bizarre and the sensational. To them it was entertainment. Matthew 27:36 states that they sat down and watched him as moment by moment he died.

*The rulers* were the officers of the Sanhedrin—chief priests, scribes, elders. They had accomplished what they wanted. He was dying in humiliation. He would trouble them no more. They mocked him in his helplessness. *He saved others* was a part of their scoffing. They may have referred to his statements about forgiving the sins of people—such as the paralyzed man, or the sinful woman who anointed his feet in the home of a Pharisee in Galilee. They did not believe he could "save" sinners. They may even have referred to miracles which they had been unable to deny—the healing of the man born blind or the raising of Lazarus; both were recent acts there in Jerusalem and Bethany (John 9, 11). They granted that he had done these things, but now he could not save himself.

*If he is the Christ of God, his Chosen One:* In their thinking, God would never permit his Chosen One, his Christ, to suffer such humiliation and death at the hands of the heathen Romans. If he were really the Christ of God, let him convince them by saving himself from such shame and agony. There was theological truth in their words, but they were unaware of it. It was true—he could not save himself; that was the "cup" which the Father had given him. He had no choice and desired no choice but to drink it.

*The soldiers* were the third group. They finished their gambling to divide his clothes and joined in the game of mockery. They offered him a drink of *vinegar.* The word translated *vinegar* is the word for a cheap sour wine which was a part of the soldiers' food ration. It was the dregs of wine and was used only by the base, hardened soldier or the alcoholic. They did not actually give it to him; this does not seem to be the same as a later incident reported by Mark, Matthew, and John, as coming during the hours of darkness and near the end. The soldiers' offer at this point was a part of their mocking him. They held up some of their wine and invited him as the *King of the Jews* to come down from the cross and join them in a drink.

*Verse 38:* The charge by which Jesus was condemned was written, probably on a piece of board, and fixed on the cross above his head, *This is the King of the Jews.* Some manuscripts of Luke add that it was in Greek and Latin and Hebrew. The addition is not in the best manuscripts of Luke, but it is an unquestioned part of John 19:20. It was written in the three commonly used languages in the mixed population of Jerusalem and was a warning to others not to be guilty of the crime for which this man was executed. It was also a part of the mocking game of "King" which had been played with Jesus by the soldiers of Herod, the soldiers of Pilate, and the Sanhedrin. A striking commentary on the ancient way of reporting events is observable in the fact that there was only one inscribed board on the cross, but each Gospel has a different inscription:

Mark 15:26, The King of the Jews

Matt. 27:37, This is Jesus the King of the Jews

Luke 23:38, This is the King of the Jews

John 19:19, Jesus of Nazareth, the King of the Jews.

Theologically, they were all correct. Jesus was crucified on a charge of treason as a rival king to the Roman emperor.

*Verses 39–43:* The second of Jesus' words from the cross included by

Luke is a brief exchange between Jesus and one of the criminals crucified with him. As indicated above, this is only in Luke. Two of the three sayings in Luke's account are related to forgiveness and salvation.

*Verse 39:* Mark 15:32 and Matthew 27:44 state that the criminals who were crucified with Jesus joined the soldiers and the Sanhedrin rulers in mocking him. Luke reports the mocking by one, but a different reaction by the other. One of the criminals *railed at him.* The word translated *railed* is the word for blaspheming. He blasphemed, reviled, spoke evil things to Jesus. He asked, *"Are you not the Christ?"* The form of the question anticipates the answer, "Yes." Then *"Save yourself and us!"* The thrust of it was "If you are the Christ you claim to be, save yourself and us." Was he only scoffing? Or had he seen Jesus work and heard him teach, and now as he observed that Jesus prayed for his tormentors did he sense that there was some possibility of Jesus' extricating himself and his fellow sufferers from this dreadful fate? His only interest seems to have been in physical deliverance from the cross.

*Verse 40:* The other criminal understood only mockery in his companion's words. He did not share in that mockery or the evil words that had been heaped upon Jesus since their common fate had begun. Perhaps he had prior knowledge of Jesus; perhaps Jesus' conduct in those shameful and agonizing three hours had convinced him that this man was indeed God's redeemer. He rebuked the other criminal.

*Do you not fear God:* These words relate the criminal's conduct to God and to Jesus who was praying to God even in his death agony. Reverence for a God of judgment should have prevented a man in his own death agony from railing against one who was praying to God for the very men who had crucified him.

*Since you are under the same sentence of condemnation?* This may have been only a general reference to the fact that Jesus and the two criminals were sentenced to be crucified at the same time. Since, however, the word describing the men was frequently used for an insurrectionist and since Jesus was being crucified on a charge of potential insurrectionism, it is likely that what the man meant was that all three were condemned on the same charge—insurrection.

*Verse 41: And we indeed justly; for we are receiving the due reward of our deeds:* This was his confession that both criminals were guilty of the crime for which they had been charged and that their punishment was a matter of justice. He felt that they deserved what they were getting.

*But this man has done nothing wrong:* The criminal felt the very opposite about Jesus. He did not believe that Jesus was guilty of the charge of treason—of being a threat to the Roman government. He believed that Jesus was being crucified for crimes that he had not committed. He had watched him endure his mistreatment and suffering without resistance. He had heard him pray to his "Father" to forgive those who had crucified him.

*Verse 42: Jesus, remember me when you come in your kingly power:* As elsewhere in the RSV, *kingly power* is the translation of the word for kingdom. The only textual variant in the saying is that two of the best manuscripts of Luke have "when you come *into* your kingdom"; all the other good ones have "when you come *in* your kingdom." In Greek usage the preposi-

preters understand an unusually violent storm shutting out the light of the sun; Matthew includes earthquake as part of the disturbances in nature at the time of Jesus' death (27:51). No natural explanation conforms completely to the details.

The true situation is that the Gospel writers did not try to offer an explanation. They doubtless interpreted this as an act of God indicating judgment. In many Old Testament passages, judgment is associated with darkness and the failure of sun, moon, and stars (Isa. 5:30, 13:10; Joel 3:15; Amos 5:18, 8:9). That idea also occurs in Jesus' Olivet discourse (Luke 21:25; Mark 13:24; Matt. 24:29). Sin must be judged. God judged sin in the death of his incarnate Son on the cross. To know what sin means and what it cost God to forgive sin, one must look at the cross and see what sin did to his Son. Man is God's only creation who willed to rebel against him. When God judged man's sin, it was as if the remainder of his creation was in turmoil at what man's sin had brought to it.

*And the curtain of the temple was torn in two:* All three accounts include this phenomenon, and Matthew has the interesting addition "from top to bottom" (27:51), as if he meant that it was an act of God, rather than an act of men who would have had to tear it from bottom to top. Matthew also has this in immediate relation to his reference to the earthquake. That has caused some to understand that the trembling of the Temple caused the rupture. That raises many questions for which there are only conjectural answers and objections. Matthew's earthquake reference was more specifically to the manifestations of open tombs and the strange results which followed (27:51–52).

*The curtain* was the tremendous veil that separated the Holy Place (where sacrifices were made) from the Most Holy Place in the Tabernacle (Exod. 26:33) and later in the Temple (2 Chron. 3:14) into which only the high priest could go, and he only on the Day of Atonement. That Most Holy Place represented the very presence of God and the place where atonement was made for sin. Descriptions of the curtain in both biblical and nonbiblical accounts indicate its beautiful artistry with embroidery of scarlet, purple, and blue, including figures representing God's creation (plants, heavenly bodies in the varying formations of stars) and his servants (cherubim). It's size was proportionate to the size of the Temple. The Jewish historian Josephus reports that the curtain in Herod's Temple was approximately eighty feet high, twenty-four feet wide, and of a thickness proportionate to its size—several inches.

To the early church, there was great significance in this reported rending of the curtain, as if it were drawn back to reveal the Most Holy Place and make it available for men. A way was opened by which men could go freely into the presence of God without the mediation of a high priest. That is the greatest theme in the Epistle to the Hebrews. The author speaks of the rending of the flesh of Christ in his death as a rending of the veil which had separated man from God (Heb. 10:20). Man no longer needs an intermediary; the way to God has been opened; the veil in the Temple has been rent in twain and laid back for man's entrance. That concept is not developed in these Gospel references. It was developed in later Christian interpretation of the phenomenon.

*Verse 46* contains the last of Luke's three sayings of Jesus on the cross. Mark and Matthew report a loud cry of Jesus as he died but do not report any words spoken. John reports the words "It is finished" (19:30). Luke reports the words, *"Father, into thy hands I commit my spirit!"* The evidence suggests that the two sentences together are his last words; the exact order cannot be determined. It is a rather subjective theological reason which determines whether one places John's "It is finished" before or after Luke's words of commitment of the spirit.

*Father* continues the same attitude of confidence expressed in Jesus' first saying from the cross, "Father, forgive them . . ." (v. 34). He had no consciousness other than that he was completely in the center of the Father's redemptive will. That knowledge had sustained him through all the suffering of his public ministry. It sustained him in those last minutes when the reality of his incarnation was most excruciatingly painful. The beautiful early Christian hymn in Philippians 2:5–11 emphasizes that truth. Although he existed in the form of God, he did not regard that as something to be held on to by force. He gave up that form and took the form of a man. In that self-assumed limitation of his deity, he suffered as men suffer; he died as men die—and, yet, as no other man could die; he died even the humiliating and agonizing death of the cross. If anyone wants to affirm the heresy which denies the reality of the incarnation, let him look again at the cross.

*Into thy hands I commit my spirit:* The *spirit* is that deathless part of man which the Greeks thought of as living forever apart from the body— "the immortality of the soul"—but which Jesus and Paul taught will be embodied again in the resurrection. The Christian hope of survival after death is the hope of resurrection of the body, not just immortality of the soul. As Jesus had committed himself without reservation to the Father during the days of his flesh, so he committed himself without reservation to the Father as he ended those days of his flesh. The cry, "It is finished," was a cry of triumph at having brought to completion all the work of God in redemption history. The cry, "Into thy hands I commit my spirit," was the cry of faith in the Father's hands. Except for the plural form "hands" the saying is a quotation from one of the most loved of the Hebrew songs, "Into thy hand I commit my spirit" (Ps. 31:5). The song magnifies God as a refuge in time of storm or a fortress in time of attack.

*He breathed his last:* This is the rendering of a word meaning precisely "he breathed out"; a smooth English translation is "he expired." Mark has the same word (15:37). John has "he gave over his spirit" (19:30). Matthew has "yielded up his spirit" (27:50). In the KJV Matthew's expression is translated "yielded up the ghost." All of these indicate the same idea. As the breath (also the word for "spirit" in Greek) went out from the body of Jesus, he died. It is a plain and simple statement of the fact of death. There is no basis for the idea that Jesus, having held off death, willed deliberately to die at this point and relinquished his spirit. Death came as the natural result of the scourging and the crucifixion with the loss of blood and the resulting dehydration of the body and mounting fever.

*Verses 47–49* report the reaction of some of those who witnessed Jesus' death. The *centurion* was the Roman captain of a hundred soldiers. With a few of those soldiers, he had carried out the crucifixion. John 19:23 refers to four soldiers gambling for Jesus' clothes; whether the captain was included in the four or was an additional one is not indicated. The centurion had witnessed all the events, at least from the passing of the sentence by Pilate. Although it is not stated, it is practically certain that he had been present during all the trial of Jesus by Pilate, including the scourging and the Barabbas incident. He witnessed all that took place in the hours of Jesus' hanging on the cross. Mark 15:39 emphasizes his witnessing how Jesus died; Matthew 27:54 emphasizes the impression made on the centurion by the phenomena of the darkness and the earthquake. Luke has a general statement that the centurion's reaction came after he *saw what had taken place*.

*He praised God:* Matthew's expression is that he was "filled with awe." Awe-struck by all he had seen, and convinced that God was involved in all of it, *he praised*—gave glory to—*God*. He spoke of the greatness and power of the God who was involved in all of this. The expression was commonly used by the early Christians to refer to one who accepted the Christian faith. It may have that meaning here. It may also indicate that this was one of the ranking Roman officers who were interested in the religion of the Jews and were inquirers into that faith. Another example is the centurion Cornelius to whom Simon Peter preached and who professed his faith in Jesus Christ. That account, too, comes from Luke (Acts 10).

*Certainly this man was innocent:* Again, the centurion's words in Mark 15:39 and Matthew 27:54 are a bit different, "Truly this man was the Son of God"; the definite article, however, is not in the Greek text, which has "a Son of God." *Certainly* is a strong word of contrast, meaning that in spite of all the Jews' charges and rejection, Jesus "in reality" was innocent, or the Son of God. The RSV translation *innocent* is the rendering of a Greek expression meaning "righteous" or "upright." To render it *innocent* suggests that the centurion agreed with Pilate's conclusion that Jesus was not guilty and did not deserve to die; the centurion believed that Jesus' conduct in the trials and execution, along with the remarkable phenomena accompanying his death, vindicated Pilate's judgment—Jesus had not deserved to die.

To render the word "righteous" suggests a meaning closer to the Mark's and Matthew's "a Son of God." From that viewpoint, coupled with the expression of the centurion's awe and his praising God, it is commonly held that the centurion was converted to faith in Jesus as God's Son. That was the view registered in early Christian writings not in the New Testament. Those who doubt that interpretation emphasize that the Greek text does not have "the Son of God" but "a Son of God." That objection has to be considered with all the pieces of evidence. When all is evaluated, the strong impression remains that all three Gospel writers did understand the conversion of the centurion. Whatever the precise meaning of his words, it just does not fit the total accounts to understand him as saying no more than, "Too bad; we crucified an innocent man." The typical Roman officer would have had little concern about innocence or guilt; he left that to the judge and carried out the orders he received.

*The multitudes* were the people who had joined the processional or had stopped at the scene to watch three men executed. What they saw left them deeply distressed. And as they walked back into the city to their homes, they were *beating their breasts.* The action reflected their great distress over what had been done. They did not understand it all, but they knew a terrible act had been perpetrated on one who was obviously innocent. They feared its consequences upon themselves.

The *acquaintances* and *the women* constituted the third group whose reaction to Jesus' crucifixion is described by Luke. The Greek text has the adversative conjunction "but" (which the RSV translates as *and*), putting them and their action into strong contrast with the multitudes who were going back into the city indicating their distress as they went. "All" is used in the Greek text to indicate a large number of Jesus' *acquaintances*—"all those known to him." The suggestion is that of a large company. They are not identified further; probably all of the remaining eleven were there. There were likely other sympathizers and followers.

*The women* are identified in Luke only as the ones *who had followed him from Galilee.* Mark names Mary Magdalene, Mary the mother of James and Joses, and Salome. Matthew also names the first two but he has "the mother of the sons of Zebedee" where Mark has "Salome." The identity of the two is probable. John 19:25 lists either three or four women. He has three Marys: the mother of Jesus; Mary the wife of Clopas; Mary the Magdalene. The problem of identity is due to the expression "and his mother's sister." Some interpreters understand this, not as a fourth woman, but as an apposition with "Mary the wife of Clopas." In that case both Jesus' mother and his sister had the same name, Mary. Some interpreters understand that this "Mary, the wife of Clopas," is the same as Mark's and Matthew's "Mary the mother of James and Joses." Others understand that "his mother's sister" is a fourth woman in John, perhaps the Salome (Mark) who was "the mother of the sons of Zebedee" (Matthew). In which case, Jesus and the brothers James and John were cousins! Such a mixture of named and unnamed persons can never be identified with certainty. It remains one of the fascinating puzzles in the Gospels.

Luke's major interest was in the reaction of these *acquaintances* and *women.* They did not return to their homes when Jesus died but *stood at a distance,* watching all that went on. *At a distance* means only at whatever distance the soldiers had determined as the point beyond which the crowd could not go. Jesus had spoken to his mother and to the beloved disciple who were there with the other women in John's account (19:25). Whether this means that the soldiers had permitted them to come closer to the cross, or merely that the distance was not too great for recognition and speech is uncertain. They waited to see what would be done with the body of Jesus. Nothing would be done until the soldiers could dispose of all three, and the two criminals were still alive. If normal procedure were followed, the bodies would be thrown into the nearest pit where they could be easily covered, or more likely they would be thrown like the carcasses of animals onto the burning garbage heap in Gehenna. They watched, knowing that it would not be delayed. The sabbath would begin at sunset and the bodies could not be left on the cross on the sabbath.

Verses 50–54 contain the brief Lukan account of the burial of Jesus. The body of Jesus was not given the treatment customary for executed criminals.

That was forestalled, not by disciples or family, but by one who is entirely new to the Gospel accounts at this point.

*Verses 50-51:* The man was *Joseph;* he was distinguished from other men bearing that honored and common name by the indication that he was originally from *Arimathea.* This was the Ramah of Jeremiah 31:15 and Matthew 2:18. At the time of Jeremiah's lament, Ramah was a part of Samaria, the northern kingdom. Later it was reckoned in Judea and so Luke called it a town of the Jews. While Joseph was originally from Arimathea, the fact that he had provided for himself a burial place in Jerusalem indicates that he was at that time a resident of that city.

Luke described him as *a good and righteous man.* The reference is to genuine piety in contrast to the external self-righteousness of so many of his associates. He was probably a merchant. Matthew adds the fact that he was rich (27:57) and Mark uses a word indicating both wealth and respect (15:43). All three include that he was a member of the council—the Sanhedrin. Matthew and John state that he was a disciple of Jesus, and John adds that he was a secret disciple because he feared the remainder of the council (19:38). The parents of the man born blind feared the council because it had voted to exclude from the synagogue anyone who confessed Jesus as the Messiah (John 9:22). Luke adds that, while he was a council member, he *had not consented to their purpose and deed.* The word for *consented* means to cast one's vote; he had voted against the majority of the council members in the matter of Jesus' guilt and his deserving death. At that point he had been unable to remain silent and had declared his opposition. In so doing, he had likely ostracized himself from social and religious contact with the council.

*He was looking for the kingdom of God:* This recalls Luke's words about the righteous and devout Simeon who received the infant Jesus in the Temple and identified him as the deliverer whom God was to send (2:25). On that same occasion, the prophetess Anna had made a similar identification (2:38). She and Simeon were among those who were "looking for the consolation of Israel . . . the redemption of Jerusalem." Now at the end of the Gospel one appears who was of that same class of devout Jews who longed to see the messianic kingdom. Joseph anticipated the coming of the Messiah to bring peace to all the turmoil in Israel. He had found in the Teacher from Nazareth the one whom he believed would prove to be that Messiah.

*Verse 52:* Joseph was probably in the company of acquaintances who observed Jesus' death and waited to see what would be done with the body (v. 49). He did not wait long. He knew a proper place for burial which was near the place of the crucifixion (John 19:41). Speculation must supply details which are explicit in none of the Gospels but which appear to have been necessary. First, one may assume that Joseph requested the centurion's permission to bury the body of Jesus. Second, the centurion would not give that permission without authorization from Pilate. Third, the centurion accompanied Joseph to make the request of Pilate. This last has some basis in the Markan statement (15:45) that Pilate ascertained from the centurion that Jesus was really dead and then gave the permission. All of this is related to the fact that Jesus died in six hours, whereas a much longer time was usual—sometimes three or four days. The tremendous emotional burden on Jesus which had grown for months before the entry into Jerusalem, then every day of the week, and finally hour by hour on that last night—the ordeal of the scourging, the ordeal of the game of "King" (with its crown of thorns omitted by Luke), the loss of blood from the nails, dehydration from that loss and from exposure to the elements—all of this broke his physical constitution and mercifully brought an early death.

*Verse 53:* Having secured the needed permission, Joseph removed the body from the cross and prepared it for burial. From John 19:39–41 it is known that he was assisted by Nicodemus with whom Jesus had once discussed the way to be born of the Spirit (John 3:1–21), and who on another occasion had halted his fellow council members and incurred their wrath when they attempted to condemn Jesus without a trial (John 7:50–52). Two Sanhedrin members who were disciples of Jesus gave him honorable burial.

*Wrapped it in a linen shroud:* John's account adds details of the material used, the exact method in which the body was wrapped, and that it was the type of body preparation used by the Jews. The details of the linen cloth, the unusually large amount of perfumed oils and spices, and the description of the tomb indicate that only the very wealthy Jews could have been buried in that way. Christians have had no difficulty in associating the manner of his death with Isaiah 53:9, "And they made his grave . . . with a rich man in his death."

*A rock-hewn tomb* indicates a cave-like tomb carved out of a mass of rock. The sides of rocky hills were commonly excavated first to a vertical wall and then into caves for burial places. The comment that it was a burial cave that had not been used—*where no one had ever yet been laid*—may have some theological significance of its appropriateness for burial of such a person as Jesus. On the other hand it may be only another reference to the newness of the tomb (Matt. 27:60; John 19:41), and the fact that Joseph had prepared it for his own burial (Matt. 27:60). Its readiness for use and its nearness to the place of the crucifixion prompted Joseph to act while the others were only wondering what would be done with the body. Mark 15:46 and Matthew 27:60 add the final touch of the closing of the tomb by rolling a large flat wheel of rock over the opening of the cave. These convenient arrangements may still be observed in ancient burial places in Jerusalem. A groove a few inches deep to hold the wheel ran the full length of the face of the hill into which a cave was carved. The huge solid stone wheel fitted into that groove and could be rolled back and forth to open or to close the cave. Such was the nature of the place where Jesus was buried.

*Verse 54* indicates that the permission to bury, the preparation of the body, and the burial took the three hours from Jesus' death at three o'clock until sunset.

*It was the day of Preparation: Preparation* is a term used for the day before the sabbath. Mark 15:42 makes that clear for the Roman readers of the Gospel who would not know what the Jews meant by *Preparation*. It was the day when all preparations were made for the sabbath which followed—cleaning was done, food was cooked, supplies were bought, everything necessary would be done so there would be no work from sunset of Preparation until sunset of sabbath. John 19:31 makes it clear that this was not Preparation for Passover, but Preparation for sabbath of Passover week—a day of double meaning since it was sabbath of a holy week. John also explains the necessary removal of the bodies from the cross before the sabbath began.

*The sabbath was beginning:* literally, "was dawning." It seems a strange word to minds accustomed to associating "dawn" and the beginning of a new day with sunrise. The Jews began the new day at sunset; more specifically it began with the "dawning" or appearance of the first star. That was what Luke meant. It was nearing sunset when the cave was closed.

*Verses 55–56a:* The women from Galilee had watched as the burial preparations were made. They observed the tomb and its location, the stone wheel door, and how the body was laid in the tomb. On their way back to the homes where they were staying for the week, they secured materials for further anointing of the body. These they prepared in readiness for use at their first opportunity; that would be Sunday morning by our calendar. *Spices* were highly aromatic and in powder form. *Ointments* is the translation of the word for myrrh, a highly aromatic gum or oil product used in the preparation of bodies for burial. Some of these had already been used by Joseph and Nicodemus (John 19:39), but repeated anointing of a body in many cases went on for several days.

### 7. Saturday—a Day of Rest (23:56b)

*On the sabbath they rested:* From the days of the exodus, the seventh day of the week had been a day of rest as a memorial of God's finishing his work of creation and then resting on the seventh day (Exod. 20:8–11). Late in the exodus years, as they were preparing to go over into the land of their permanent residence, God's redeeming them from Egypt was added as a motivation for sabbath observance (Deut. 5:12–25). The *commandment* to which Luke refers is the commandment to keep the seventh day holy as a day for rest and worship, and abstention from work in any form. For the family and friends of Jesus, that was a sad sabbath.

### NOTE ON THE APPEARANCES OF THE RISEN CHRIST

Appearances of Christ after his resurrection are in all four Gospels, in Acts, and in 1 Corinthians 15:3–8. In point of time of writing, the oldest record is that of Paul in 1 Corinthians. It is impossible to make a definite identification of some of the 1 Corinthian appearances with those in the Gospels and Acts. Paul wrote of an appearance "to the Twelve," although Judas was a suicide before Jesus was crucified. Doubtless, "the Twelve," is a reference to the eleven remaining apostles, but identification with either Luke 24:26–43 (and the John 20:19–25 parallel), or John 20:26–29, is uncertain. Paul also wrote of an appearance to "more than five hundred brethren at one time" which some interpreters identify with Matthew 28:16–20, but there is not one shred of evidence for their identification. He wrote of an appearance to "all the apostles," which probably is a reference to the ascension appearance in Acts 1, but that is not certain. The main evidence for the identification is that the next statement is, "Last of all, . . . he appeared to me," which must be identified with the Damascus road experience (Acts 9:1–9). In addition to these uncertain ones, Paul includes an appearance "to James"; this is in no other account. The early church believed that the James involved was James the brother of Jesus.

In addition to these uncertainties of identifications, there are other details which make exposition of the total resurrection account difficult. Luke has only appearances in Judea. Matthew has one in Judea and one in Galilee. John has three in Judea and then an additional one in the "postscript" chapter 21. Mark's accounts are all in that part of his Gospel which appears to have been added later. The appearances reported are all in the other records but the details vary. For example, he has the Great Commission at the appearance to the apostles in the upper room on the evening of his resurrection, while Matthew 28:16–20 has it at some undetermined time later in Galilee.

The task of the interpreter is complicated by other matters. In the Gospel accounts, the details vary and may be placed in two categories: lines of agreement, and lines of difference. The Gospel accounts *agree* on these major details: (1) The time of the resurrection was early on the morning of the first day of the week (Sunday). (2) Women arrived first at the tomb. (3) The tomb was open and empty. (4) There were messengers at the tomb. (5) These messengers announced the resurrection of Jesus. (6) They also sent a message to the disciples. (7) Jesus subsequently appeared several times.

The Gospel accounts differ on these minor details: (1) The exact hour of the visit of the women to the tomb. (2) The names and the number of women. (3) The number and nature—"men" or "angels"—of the messengers at the tomb. (4) The exact time and wording of the message to the disciples. (5) The number and locations of the appearances. The agreements and differences relate to the particular theological interest of the individual writer. The appearances in Matthew both relate to the commission to the apostles to take the gospel to all nations. The appearances in Luke relate to Jesus' instruction regarding the significance of his death and resurrection and his preparing them to proclaim that message. Those in John include the reality of Jesus' resurrection and commission, but they feature the effect of Jesus' appearances on individuals: Mary Magdalene; Thomas; Simon Peter.

If one desires to study Jesus' appearances from some viewpoint of sequence from the day of his resurrection to the day of his ascension, the following hypothesis may be of some help.

*Appearances on the first day* (and perhaps in this order):

To Mary Magdalene (John 20:11–18)

To a group of women (Matt. 28:9–10)

To two on the road to Emmaus (Luke 24:13–32)

To Simon Peter (Luke 24:35; 1 Cor. 15:5)

To a gathered group on that evening (Luke 24:33–43; John 20:19–25)

*Appearance one week later:*

To the eleven (John 20:26–29)

*Appearances unidentified as to exact time:*

To James (no indication whatever; 1 Cor. 15:7)

To five hundred brethren (no indication whatever; 1 Cor. 15:6)

To eleven on a mountain in Galilee (some time after the first week;
    Matt. 28:16–20)
To seven by the Sea of Galilee (some time after the first week; John
    21:1–23)
*Appearance at the end of the forty-day period:*
To an uncertain number of disciples (Luke 24:50–51; Acts 1:9–12)
*Appearances which are of uncertain identification with the above:*
To the Twelve (1 Cor. 15:5)
To all the apostles (1 Cor. 15:7)

## 8. Sunday—a Day of Triumph (24:1–43)

As Jesus' last week began with Sunday as a day of triumph, it was
followed by Sunday as a day of triumph. It opened with Jesus' triumphal
entry as the Son of David king, offering himself one last time as the Messiah.
It was followed by days of tragedy as Sunday's cries of "Hosanna" changed
to Friday's cries of "Crucify." All the dark tragedy of Friday, however, could
not prevent his ultimate triumph over the powers of darkness by his resurrection on Sunday.

Jesus was buried as sunset approached on Friday afternoon. He was in
the tomb through the remainder of Friday and Friday night, all of Saturday
and Saturday night, and a part of Sunday. The first visitors to the tomb
about sunrise on Sunday found it open and empty. The implications are
that his resurrection had been but a short time before that (Matt. 28:1–6).

To some readers this creates a difficulty because of the statement about
Jesus' being in the heart of the earth three days and nights (Matt. 12:40)
and his being raised "after three days" (Mark 8:31; 9:30). It should be
noted that Mark's earlier reference was changed to "on the third day" by
the later writings (Matt. 16:21; 17:23; Luke 9:22) in conformity with the
time of his resurrection on the first day of the week. There is really no
discrepancy in the references. By all three methods of reckoning time—
Jewish, Greek, Roman—a part of a day was spoken of as the whole. There
are many statements in the writings of the rabbis that even a small part of an
hour was referred to as the whole. For Jesus to have been entombed part of
Friday, all of Saturday, and part of Sunday would have meant to people
in that day both "on the third day" and "three days and nights." They knew
no other way of making this reference. Besides that, if one insists on "three
days and three nights" (Matt. 12:40) as meaning three periods of twenty-
four hours each, and insists on Mark's "after three days" instead of Matthew's
and Luke's "on the third day," he has not settled his problem. He has only
put himself into the position of Jesus' resurrection coming on the *fourth* day
and that is ruled out by all the accounts.

### (1) The angelic announcement of his resurrection (24:1–12)

Verses 1–11 contain the return of the women to the tomb; their startling
discovery that the tomb was open and empty; the appearance of two men
who announced Jesus' resurrection and reminded them of his predictions
of it; their report to the skeptical eleven disciples and the others associated
with them. Verse 12 is disputed textually.

*Verse 1: On the first day of the week at early dawn:* All the Gospel accounts agree with this except for minor verbal differences: Luke, "at early dawn"; John, "while it was still dark"; Matthew, "after the sabbath, toward the dawn."

*They went to the tomb, taking the spices: They* means the group of Galilean women of 23:49, 55–56. (See discussion on 23:49.) They had secured the desired materials for the custom of continuing the application of additional perfumed ointments for several days. Only on rare occasions would this be done beyond the third day because evidences of decay would have started and, to their minds, that would have indicated that the spirit could not return to the body. If Jesus had been buried any day except the day before the sabbath, further anointing would have been done on the next day. The sabbath prevented that. The women went as early as possible and practical.

*Verse 2: They found the stone rolled away:* This is a simple statement that the tomb was open when they arrived about dawn. Mark 16:3 indicates that, as they were on the way, the women talked about how they would roll back the heavy stone door. Matthew 28:2 attributes the opening of the door to an angel who rolled it back and sat down on it as if to wait for the first visitors.

*Verse 3: When they went in they did not find his body:* The women entered the cave with its darkness greater than the dim light of dawn outside. They could see, however, that there was no body there. This is the first of the sequence of factors in any consideration of the Easter event. To the early Christians the empty tomb was a matter of tremendous importance. It receives primary emphasis in all the Gospel accounts (Mark 16:2–8; Matt. 28:5–8; Luke 24:2–7; John 20:1–10). Those who went first to the tomb did not go to seek a Risen Lord; they went to anoint the dead body of one whom they had loved. Even though Jesus had spoken often of his resurrection, they could not grasp the idea; they did not expect it; they were perplexed to find no body in the tomb (v. 4).

Verses 4–7 account for the absence of the body. Matthew 28:5 has one angel speaking to the women. Mark 16:5 has one young man who was sitting at the right as the women faced the tomb; although he has "young man," the reference recalls Matthew's angel who rolled back the stone door and sat down on it. John 20:12–13 has "two angels in white" seated inside the tomb and speaking to Mary Magdalene. Luke has two men. This is another instance in which the Gospels vary in the details of the event, but there is no question about the intent of all four to show that divine messengers were at the tomb and they spoke to the women about Jesus' resurrection.

*Verse 4: In dazzling apparel,* although verbally different, means the same as John's "in white" (20:12). John's word which is translated "white" means primarily "shining" or "glistening." In Acts 1:10, Luke's "two men . . . in white robes" has the same word for "white" which is used in John. The two Lukan reports—"two men . . . in dazzling apparel" at the tomb and "two men . . . in white robes" on the Mount of Olives at the ascension make it abundantly clear that in both passages he means angels.

*Verse 5: Why do you seek the living among the dead?* To the awe-struck women who *bowed their faces to the ground* rather than look on holy personages, the two angels announced Jesus' resurrection. Their question about seeking the living among the dead creates no problem in the previous emphasis on the tomb's never having been used. The tomb was a place for dead bodies and likely was sufficient for Joseph and his family. It was designed for "dead ones." One does not go to such a place to find "living ones." The word translated *the living* is one which came to be used by the Christians for the Risen Christ. He was "the Living One." *Among the dead* translates a term of association—"with those who are dead" or "in association with those who are dead." Jesus shared death with humanity whom he had come to save. His death was real; a burial place was necessary for his mortal body; he had no use for it, however, for his glorified body. In the other Gospels, a part of the message was "he is not here" (Mark 16:6; Matt. 28:6).

*Verses 6-7:* The sentence, "He is not here, but has risen" is omitted from the RSV text of verse 6 because it does not appear in *some* of the manuscripts of Luke. The omission is unfortunate and subject to challenge because the sentence is in *all of the best* manuscripts of Luke, and it is in all the manuscripts of Mark and Matthew. It belongs in the text as a part of the original Gospel record. For that reason it is being included in this exposition.

*He is not here:* There is no stated subject for the verb. The subject *he* has as its antecedent *the living* of the previous clause. Therefore, even this negative approach to the absence of the body is an affirmation of Jesus' resurrection—"The Living One is not here." That affirmation is extended in the next clause.

*But has risen:* This is the positive affirmation of his resurrection. The form of the verb more naturally requires the passive translation "he was raised" or "he has been raised." In the New Testament some references are to Jesus' arising from the dead as if by his own power; some are to his having been raised by God; and some have a simple passive with no subject expressed or implied; "he is risen." Of all these the one under consideration simply depicts an act which had taken place before the women arrived at the tomb. In later use the emphasis would come to be on the continuing state of life, as in Paul's literal "he is in a state of having been raised so he can never die again" (1 Cor. 15:4) which requires a different tense. Here the expression explains why the body was not there—Jesus was alive.

Verses 6-7 are a reminder of Jesus' prediction of his death and his resurrection *while he was still in Galilee*. On two occasions before they had started the journey to Jerusalem Jesus had spoken of his death and resurrection (9:21-22; 43-45). Actually the manner of his death—crucifixion—was not named in either of these sayings in Galilee. In the third saying, which was after they had reached Jerusalem, only Matthew's account indicates crucifixion as the means of death. The reference in verse 7 to crucifixion is doubtless a reference to the teaching of Jesus about his disciples' taking up their cross and following him. The synoptics place that teaching immediately after the first announcement of his death; many interpreters think, however, that it was actually spoken at a later time when bearing the cross as a symbol of submission to the will of God would have been more understandable. The meaning of these words to the women was that for months Jesus had been telling them that this was coming about, and now it had taken place. In Mark and Matthew, the announcement included a command that the women were to go and remind the disciples of those predictions and that he had promised that they would see him again in Galilee (Mark 14:28; Matt. 26:32).

Verses 8–11 include the report of the women to the other followers of Jesus and their unbelief.

*Verses 8–9: They remembered his words:* That has a strange sound for one who reads the Gospel with its build-up of interest in Jesus' death and resurrection from 9:22 to this point of its accomplishment. How could they forget? The only conjectural answer to that question is related to the un-willingness of Jesus' followers to accept the idea that he would die, their failure to understand his teachings about it, and their unwillingness even to talk with him about it or ask questions about it. All those matters are a part of the record in connection with the three occasions when he predicted it. By their unwillingness to hear and their desire to avoid the subject, they had built up such a mental block that the devastating experience of his death blotted out recall of his promise that he would arise from the dead. Now that they remembered, they went back with their carefully prepared but unneeded spices and ointments and reported *to the eleven and to all the rest* all they had experienced.

*The eleven,* of course, means the remaining disciples whom already Luke has started calling "apostles" (22:14; 24:10). *All the rest* means whatever other friends and relatives were present. As indicated in the exposition of verse 1, the number of women who went to the tomb is uncertain. Verse 9 leaves the impression that there was a rather large company of Jesus' followers and family. Although they would not all be staying in the same place in Jerusalem, they were in close touch with one another. They were bound together by their common grief and were reluctant to see the break-up of the association which would come when those from Galilee started their sad return journey without their leader who had brought them to Jerusalem for Passover.

*Verse 11* reports the reaction of the entire group. We are not to think of a calm assembly in which the women, through one chosen for the part, make their report. The two verbs used in verses 9 and 10 indicate a report by all and then reiterated reports by the many. We are likely closer to the situation if we think of the excited and half-hysterical women rushing into the pres-ence of the first group to which they came and all at the same time trying to report the event. That is the first verb, *they told all this;* the word means "to announce" (v. 9). The second verb for *told* (v. 10) is a different one meaning "to say," and the tense indicates repeated sayings. Questions were asked and answered by individuals or smaller groups of the women as the announcement was thoroughly discussed.

The conclusion of those who had not been to the tomb was that this was an *idle tale,* literally "nonsense." The tomb empty? Two men in white robes saying Jesus was alive? But no one saw him alive? *Nonsense!* It just did not make sense. An adjective form of this noun was commonly used in the sense of that which was frivolous, silly.

*They did not believe them:* This verb form is the same as that of the verb *told* in verse 10. It depicts repeated disbelief. Every time the story was repeated it met with disbelief. The more the women talked of their experience, the more the men doubted the reports. That which was being told was so stupendous that they had no equipment for understanding it or accepting it.

*Verse 12:* Again the RSV text omits a verse which is overwhelmingly supported by the ancient manuscripts of Luke—*But Peter rose and ran to the tomb; stooping and looking in, he saw the linen cloths by themselves; and he went home wondering at what had happened.* No early manuscript omits it until one in the sixth century. It is, however, one of the parts of Luke omitted by Marcion (about A.D. 140), and also by Tatian (about A.D. 180–190) in his arrangement of all four Gospels in one continuous account. Those who omitted it probably did so for one of two reasons. One, it could be thought of as an adaptation of John 20:3, 5, 6, 10 which was inserted to relate the visit of some men to the tomb as reported later in Luke's account (v. 24). Two, it could have been omitted because on the surface it seemed to contradict that part of the John 20 story which reflects belief in the resurrection as a result of the visit to the tomb by Peter and the beloved disciple. Because from the evidence of the manuscripts the verse belongs in the text, it is included in this exposition.

*Peter rose and ran to the tomb:* In John 20, Peter and the disciple whom Jesus loved (by tradition, John) ran to the tomb in response to a report by Mary Magdalene that unknown persons had moved the body of Jesus to some unknown place. It is of interest to note that Mary Magdalene was one of the women who visited the tomb and is listed first in the synoptic accounts. The impression in the Gospel accounts is that she was a leader in the group of women who followed Jesus, just as Simon Peter was in the group of men. An interesting side study is that in the literature of the Christians who, in the second century, became associated with the Gnostics, Simon Peter and Mary Magdalene are pictured as never getting along, and Simon ultimately tried to get her banned from the disciples' group (Gospel According to Thomas, Logion 114). There is no trace of that in the New Testament, unless her prominence in reporting the resurrection and Peter's prominence in checking the story and doubting it might furnish a seed from which hostility grew.

*Stooping and looking in, he saw:* This differs a bit from the John 20 account. According to John 20:4–8, John outran Peter but only stooped and looked in until Peter arrived and went on in. Then John went in and together they looked at the grave cloths.

*The linen cloths by themselves:* In Luke's account, the term *by themselves* (literally, "only") means that the linen cloths which had wrapped the spices and myrrh about the body of Jesus were there but the body was not in them. That is also true in John's account, but there is an added detail about the position of the separate cloth which had been wrapped turban-like about the head of Jesus. It was not connected with the other mummy-like cloths but had fallen over to one side when the head which supported it was withdrawn. What Peter and John saw was the linen cloths with their hundred pounds of spices and myrrh gum lying as they were when they had held the body—still in the form of the body but without the body in them.

*He went home wondering at what had happened:* To some readers this appears to be in conflict with John 20:8, and that may have been the reason for its having been omitted by some of the ancient students of the Gospels. It is the sort of conflict which comes half from statement and half from silence. John 20:8 has the statement that the sight of the grave cloths caused John to believe. What he believed is not clear. It may mean only that he believed the report which Mary had made that some unknown persons had moved the body of Jesus. John 20:9 states that as yet they did not know the Scripture that Jesus was to rise from the dead. Whatever the meaning that John "believed," there is no statement whatever about Peter's reaction—merely that the two went back home. Luke states that Peter went home *wondering at what had happened.* That must include: the secure burial of Jesus with the cave closed on Friday; the circumstance of the cave's being open and empty on Sunday; the presence of the grave cloths still in the cave and in a form as if holding a body, but without a body; the report of the women that divine messengers had told them that Jesus himself had predicted it. Peter could hardly have forgotten those predictions; he had opposed them vigorously. So he went home wondering. The term translated *home* is a prepositional phrase meaning "to himself"—"he went away to himself." He sought solitude to wonder over all the things he knew had happened and all the things others had reported as having happened. As yet, there was no indication of his believing that Jesus was alive, but he was working it all out in his mind. Likely that is what he was doing when Jesus appeared to him (v. 34).

### (2) The appearance on the road to Emmaus (24:13–33)

This is the first appearance of the Risen Christ in Luke's Gospel. It came on the afternoon of the day of his resurrection. It is the most beautiful of all the postresurrection accounts.

*Verse 13:* Two of Jesus' followers were walking from Jerusalem to Emmaus. *That very day* means the day of the visit of the women to the tomb and the perplexity which seized all the followers who heard the report. *Two of them* means two of that group who heard the report of the women but did not believe it. The two are unidentified except for the name of one of them, Cleopas (v. 18). The exact location of Emmaus is uncertain. Luke gives the distance because it was related to their return to Jerusalem later in the evening. *About seven miles* is the translation of "sixty stadia"; a Greek stadion was six hundred feet, so the distance was 6.8 miles.

*Verse 14:* The two were talking to one another about all those events of the last few days; probably the main topic was the events from the crucifixion to the reports that Jesus was alive. *Talking* translates a word for conversational talk; *with each other* translates a reciprocal pronoun—they were speaking back and forth to one another.

*Verse 15:* While they were engaged in the give and take of questions and suggested answers, Jesus drew near and was walking with them. The two words *talking* and *discussing* mean literally "conversing" and "questioning." *Jesus himself drew near* emphasizes that it was the very subject of their discussion who joined them—"and himself, Jesus." The verb form meaning literally "having drawn near" suggests that they were so engrossed in their discussion that they hardly noticed the traveler who came up to them; perhaps he overtook them; perhaps he came in from a side road. It was a natural action with no indication of the unusual or spectacular. *Went with them* is a progressive action tense, "he was going with them." For a while he walked and said nothing.

*Verse 16:* They did not recognize him. The reason which Luke gives was that *their eyes were kept from recognizing him.* Older versions translate the verb "were held." This was not a matter of dim light or tear-blurred eyes, as some suggest in Mary Magdalene's slowness to recognize him (John 20: 14–16). Certainly due to their grief and disappointment and even unbelief they were not mentally and spiritually disposed to encounter him here on the road. Luke, however, seems to intend more than that. The verb is in the passive voice—their eyes were kept from seeing his true identity. In these postresurrection stories, two themes appear: self-revelation on the part of Jesus; discernment on the part of the ones who saw him. Here it was as if he prevented their recognizing him until he had given them a long and understandable interpretation of the Messiah of prophecy as one who would suffer as a part of entering into his glory. They needed that understanding before they could be convinced of the reality of his resurrection.

*Verse 17:* Finally he entered the conversation by asking what it was that they were discussing. A clear statement on their part was necessary for what he intended to do in interpreting the events. The expression is plural—"what are these things making up your conversation which you are throwing back and forth at one another as you are walking?" "Throwing back and forth at one another"—a very literal translation—suggests some highly excited or even heated statements and questions making up their conversation. They stopped walking; in modern idiom "they stopped in their tracks." *Looking sad* is the rendering of a word meaning "dark-faced"—darkened by sorrow, by perplexity, or perhaps by impatience with the interruption by so uninformed a person. All of it was enough to cause them to be, in modern idiom, "long-faced."

*Verse 18:* The one named Cleopas answered. While attempts have been made to identify him with the Clopas in John 19:25, they have met with no encouraging degree of success. The wife of Clopas in John was with Mary the mother of Jesus at the cross. The two names Cleopas and Clopas are different ways of spelling the same name. Some have conjectured that the two with whom Jesus walked were Clopas and his wife. Others have thought of a father-son relationship. Whoever they were, they entered the same house in Emmaus which seems to have been their home (vv. 28–30).

Cleopas expressed surprise at Jesus' question. *"Are you the only visitor in Jerusalem?"* The word translated *only* means alone. The term *visitor in Jerusalem* is the equivalent of stranger, but technically it meant a Jew born outside Jerusalem but now a resident of the city. The entire expression suggested that Jesus must be a Jew who was so cut off from everyone else in Jerusalem that he had not heard of the things they were discussing. It was a way of saying that everyone in Jerusalem knew what had happened; how could Jesus not have heard?

*Verse 19:* Jesus' further question—*What things?*—may mean "what things exactly?" or it may mean "what kind of things?" The former is more likely.

He asked for an exact statement of the things which were troubling them. Later, he would use those very things in his interpretation of the prophet's concept of the Messiah.

*They said* means that both joined in supplying Jesus with the details of the last few days. Their conversation was about *Jesus of Nazareth.* Jesus was a common name. They identified him as the Jesus who was from Nazareth. From other passages it appears that in Jerusalem he had come to be known by that designation. The very meaning of his name was significant in his case—*Jesus* is the Greek for Joshua which means Deliverer or Savior. They described him as a *prophet,* one who spoke under the motivation of God and as his spokesman. The manner of Jesus' teaching had impressed his hearers of his authority. *Mighty in deed and word:* Both by his work and by his words Jesus had accomplished mighty things. *Before God and all the people:* He was approved by both God and the masses of the people.

*Verse 20:* He was not, however, approved by the leaders of the Hebrew religion. The *chief priests and rulers* refers, as always, to the ruling body, the Sanhedrin. The word used elsewhere for Judas's betrayal is here applied to the Sanhedrin—they *delivered him,* gave him over. This refers to their giving Jesus over to Pilate. To these men, that was the Sanhedrin's betrayal of a great and innocent Jewish teacher to the Romans. *To be condemned to death* means precisely "to a judgment of death." That was the goal which the Sanhedrin sought in turning Jesus over to Pilate; they succeeded in carrying it out. *They crucified him* indicates the Sanhedrin, not Pilate and his soldiers. The responsible ones ultimately were the chief priests and rulers who resented Jesus' influence with the people in upsetting and reversing many of their religious traditions.

*Verse 21:* The two turned from what had happened to what had been their hope. The tense of the verb translated *we had hoped* indicates continuous action in past time—"we were hoping." The pronoun subject *we* is emphatic. With the adversative conjunction *but,* it puts the followers of Jesus, including themselves, in strong contrast to the Sanhedrin. The Sanhedrin saw Jesus as a dangerous religious leader; his followers were hoping that he would prove to be *the one to redeem Israel*—that is, the Messiah, but in his role as a redeemer from sin. They seem not to have understood how he would redeem Israel from sin, but they kept on hoping that in some way he would pay the ransom price—the meaning of the word *redeem*—and free Israel from her spiritual bondage.

The force of their imperfect tense ("we were hoping") comes out clearly in their next statement that it had been three days since Jesus was crucified and nothing had happened except unconfirmed reports that Jesus was alive again. They were hoping right up to his death. When they saw him betrayed, condemned, crucified as a dangerous criminal, and buried in Joseph's cave, all their hopes ceased. That ended it. Then their hopes revived again when women reported that the tomb was empty and that angels had told them Jesus was alive and reminded them that he had predicted his death and resurrection. They remembered the predictions and they remembered his teaching about his death as a means of redemption for sins. Hope renewed; messengers were sent to check the story; hope died again.

*Verses 22–23* review the visit of the women to the tomb and their report of seeing some angels who announced that Jesus had risen from the dead. *Verse 24* reviews their response. Unable to believe the women (v. 11), some of the men went to the tomb. *Some of those who were with us* is masculine, indicating men. While no names are indicated here, John 20:2–10 identifies Peter and John as the two who went. The men found the tomb open and empty, just as the women had reported. They did not, however, see Jesus. The reports seemed to have been false. His body was not there, but they still had as evidence that he was alive only the report of women that angels had told them that he was alive. Cleopas and his traveling companion had apparently left Jerusalem without knowing about the appearance of Jesus to Mary Magdalene (John 20:11–18) and the group of women (Matt. 28:9–10) which took place that morning. They had turned their backs on the place where they had buried their hopes. They faced homeward, but they faced it without hopes for Israel's redemption. Their candidate for that role was dead.

In verses 25–27 Luke reports Jesus' answer to the sorrow, discouragement, and disappointment of the two disciples. Under his prompting questions they had set out their problem very clearly. Jesus desired that, because it gave him the opportunity he needed to interpret the events from a different viewpoint—the Messiah's way of achieving his goal as that way had been given through God's prophets. He addressed himself to their failure to believe what the prophets had spoken and had passed on to them in written form. The pronoun *he* is emphatic to contrast his approach from theirs. They had had their say; now *he* would have his.

*Verse 25: O foolish men, and slow of heart to believe:* The tone must have been one of tender chiding; it was the approach which would shame them into listening to his interpretation of the prophets, but would not rebuke them so severely that they would be repelled. The word rendered *foolish* means dull, a dullness resulting from not thinking or not considering. There was an explanation at hand for all the things which perplexed them. That explanation was in the Scriptures which they used constantly, which were read in every synagogue service on every sabbath. They were dull-witted not to consider them. *Slow of heart* means sluggish in heart. In Hebrew thought the heart was the seat of personality and intelligence was a part of personality. Dull-witted and sluggish intelligence had led to their state of grief unto despair.

*To believe all that the prophets have spoken:* Their dullness and sluggishness of heart was focused on one weakness—they did not *believe all* that which had come to them from God through his prophets. There was no question about their believing a part of the prophetic message. They believed the prophet's promise of a coming Redeemer for Israel. They believed the message that he would inaugurate the kingdom of God and that his presence with them would be the very presence of God. Where, then, were they falling short in believing? What part of the prophetic message had they failed to believe? In their dullness and sluggishness, where had they missed the way? It was that which Jesus proceeded to explain to them.

*Verse 26: Was it not necessary that the Christ should suffer these things:* The question is introduced by a negative particle indicating that the answer is "Yes, it was necessary." The term *was . . . necessary* is the impersonal verb treated previously meaning that which had to take place if a desired end should be met. The desired end in this case was the Christ's entering into his glorious triumph as the Redeemer. That which had to take place in order for that end to be met was his suffering. In order for him to enter into his glorious triumph of redemption, he had to suffer. That was clear all through Jesus' teachings and became climactically clear in his praying in Gethsemane—there was no other way. *These things* mean the very matters of rejection and crucifixion which had become a stumbling block in the path of their belief that Jesus of Nazareth was the Christ. They could not equate his humiliation and suffering with the anticipated Messiah who had been promised through the prophets.

*Verse 27:* Jesus began with the very foundation of their Scriptures—the first five books in their Scriptures—technically called *Moses.* Moses had been the one whom God had used in the birth of the nation of Israel through the exodus. Through him God had given the law. Through him God had led the Israelites for forty years in the wilderness, and then in the closing months had prepared them through the second giving of the law (Deuteronomy) for life on the other side of the Jordan. They were indeed his books. Jesus had called Moses a prophet. Moses had promised that God would raise up from among the people "a prophet like me" (Deut. 18:15). Jesus was that prophet (Acts 3:22–23; 7:37).

*And all the prophets:* The *prophets* constituted the second part of their Scriptures, consisting of the historical books related to the time of the prophets and the books of the prophets. In every synagogue service there was a reading of a section from the law (Moses) and a section from the prophets. In the singing of the psalms, they used the third part of their Scriptures called "the holy writings." On this occasion Jesus traced through the two major parts of their Scriptures—Moses and Prophets—the things concerning the Messiah, the Christ, and *interpreted to them.* The word translated *interpreted* is the word from which English derives "hermeneutics," the science of interpretation. The verb is a compound one meaning "interpreted thoroughly." *The things concerning himself* reflects the interesting situation. He was interpreting the Scriptures *concerning himself,* but they did not know that he was speaking of himself as that Christ.

There is no indication of the particular Scriptures which Jesus used. Two general areas are fairly certain. The writings concerning the suffering (death) of the Christ were doubtless of the same category which Jesus had used in his previous teachings. The major emphasis was on the Suffering Servant passages of Isaiah. His use particularly of Isaiah 53 has been noted in several places in Luke. The writings concerning his glory (resurrection) must be identified by the kind of Scriptures used later by the apostles in explaining the resurrection. One example is the use Peter made of Psalms 16:8–11 and 110:1 in his sermon at Pentecost (Acts 2:25–35). Paul also used Psalm 16:10 in his sermon at Antioch (Acts 13:35). These representative passages are from the third section of the Scriptures which is not mentioned in this verse, but it must be noted that in verse 44 Jesus did include all three sections—Moses, the prophets, the psalms. So Jesus linked his suffering (death) and his glory (resurrection) as a part of the prophet's message.

It was a brief course in Christology which any interpreter of the Gospels would like to have heard.

Verses 28-31 conclude this remarkable event. By the time Jesus completed his teaching, they had arrived at Emmaus. This was the destination of the two.

*Verse 28: He appeared to be going further* is the translation of a phrase meaning "he made as if he would go further." It was not simply a matter of pretending. Emmaus was not his home; it was only natural that he should go on.

*Verse 29: But they constrained him:* Their invitation was urgent. The word translated *constrained* means to press beyond one's ability to resist. Their pleading was so insistent that he could not resist. That is not to suggest that Jesus has to be begged. He never refuses the kind of invitation they extended. It is rather an indication of the desire of the two to continue an association which had already been of great comfort to them.

*Stay with us* is a simple invitation, "abide with" or "stop with" us. That they intended the invitation to mean "spend the night" is clear from their next words. All the details naturally suggest that this was an invitation to stay in their home rather than an inn.

*It is toward evening and the day is now far spent:* The two expressions really indicate the same thing—that it was late afternoon. The two terms are, however, different and rather poetic in quality. *Toward evening* means precisely "nearing darkness." The hours of darkness since their leader had been crucified had been hours of emptiness and grief. Here was one who, in talking to them of the Scriptures and purposes of God, had brought to them their only understanding and comfort. They longed for his presence as the darkness closed in. *The day is now far spent* is a poetic personification: "the day has already taken to its couch." The day had ended, the darkness was present, their invitation was urgent. So Jesus went in to stay with them. Their experiences, however, and their traveling for the day were not yet finished.

*Verse 30:* According to the Jewish custom of formal eating, they reclined on couches about the table. If others shared the meal, there is no indication of it. More like a host than a guest, Jesus spoke the customary blessing on the bread they would share. He broke the bread into pieces and gave a portion to each of them.

*Verse 31:* In that moment of the shared bread, *their eyes were opened and they recognized* Jesus. In the moment of their recognition, he became invisible to them. Previously, their eyes had been "kept from recognizing him" (v. 16). Now the very opposite was true. The verb translated "were opened" is a compound form meaning "fully opened." The other verb is also a compound form meaning "fully recognized." They knew without question that this one was Jesus and that he was undeniably alive.

Any attempt to determine the means of their recognition must be conjectural. Some have suggested that the familiar custom of Jesus in blessing and breaking the bread was the means. Some have suggested that the two observed the nail scars as he handed them the bread. There is absolutely no indication in the text other than the fact that whatever had veiled their eyes before no longer veiled them. As some degree of understanding had come to them in Jesus' interpretation of the necessity of the Christ's suffering, so some degree of comfort had eased their sorrow and perhaps some degree of hope had eased their despair. In the earlier presence of perplexity, sorrow, and despair, they could not recognize him. Now with these matters even partially dispelled, they recognized him fully. Their apprehension had sharpened. Perhaps, too, there was some element of that self-revelation on Jesus' part which marked some of the other appearances. He revealed; they perceived.

*He vanished out of their sight:* Precisely, the statement is "he became unseen to them." He was there at the table handing them bread. As they received the bread and the recognition of him, he disappeared. That was a phenomenon which would become increasingly common in other appearances. Those appearances give us two indications of the nature of his body following his resurrection: it was tangible; it was transcendent. It was a real, tangible body. He walked with them; he talked with them; they saw him with their physical eyes; they heard him speak; in later cases they touched him. On the other hand, his body was transcendent. It was not subject to the limitations of time, space, or material objects as it had been before his death and resurrection. He was there with them and suddenly he was not with them. Later experiences that very evening would make those two matters even more clearly evident.

*Verse 32:* The two did not register surprise at his suddenly becoming invisible to them. That was probably no more unusual in their mind than the fact that they had walked together for several miles and had shared a conversation on his death and resurrection without knowing who he was. They dwelt rather on their inner consciousness as he had walked with them on the road and talked to them of the prophets' message regarding the Christ. They spoke of the fact that as he walked with them and *opened . . . the scriptures* their hearts had burned. Their question opens with the negative particle indicating the answer, "Yes." The noun is singular, "our heart," as if one heart beat between them in the experience because both had shared the same sensation.

*Burn* translates a word meaning to glow with warmth. The warm glow was due to the gradual return of understanding, joy, and hope. That came, not simply by his being with them, because they had not even recognized him. Nor did it come simply by his speaking, because they did not recognize his voice; their ears were as closed as their eyes were veiled. The warm glow came in *what* he said as he opened the Scriptures. He made understandable that part of the prophets' message about the Anointed One's entering into glory through the door of suffering. Since that was true, all was not lost. Their Lord who had suffered and died could yet be God's Anointed One—the Christ. It was that which caused the warm glow in their hearts.

*Verse 33:* It was that same understanding, made more significant by their recognizing their companion of the road as the Living Christ, which sent them hurrying back to Jerusalem with news too good to keep even until the next day.

*They rose*—literally, having stood up—in *that same hour,* and *returned to Jerusalem.* Hurriedly, they started the return journey, but everything was different from the previous trip along that road. They had walked from Jerusalem to Emmaus. They may have walked back or they may have taken a faster method of travel. It does not matter how they went. They were under a compulsion to share their news.

It must have been well into the night when they arrived. They found an assembled group made up of the eleven and *those who were with them.* That refers to the group of assembled friends and family involved in those early morning reports that Jesus was alive. The events had bound them together as a group; as they had belonged together in their sorrow, they belonged together in their joy.

### (3) The appearance to Simon Peter (24:34)

Before the two could report their good news, they were greeted by news from the gathered group: *The Lord has risen indeed, and has appeared unto Simon!* The first clause has the sound of a confession of faith, *The Lord has risen.* It was, in fact, an early form of confession, and is still used as an Easter greeting. The form is the same as the words of the angels earlier that day. The only difference is the use of the noun subject, *The Lord has risen.* It has been noted frequently that *Lord* as a title for Christ is a characteristic of Luke even before Jesus' death and resurrection. It was the most natural one to use here.

*And has appeared to Simon.* This is the second appearance in Luke's account. The only other reference to it is Paul's brief "he appeared to Cephas" (1 Cor. 15:5). Several matters form the significant background for this appearance. Peter's boasting that he would die rather than forsake Jesus; his subsequent denial, and his bitter tears over his failure; the instruction of the young man at the empty tomb who charged the women to go and tell Jesus' disciples "and Peter" that Jesus had been raised (Mark 16:7); Peter's running to the tomb, finding it empty, and then going off to himself to wonder at all the events. He had all the background for experiencing an appearance of Jesus and a conversation too personal to be discussed with others. Perhaps that is the reason the Gospel accounts contain no detail of it. This personal apearance, with all the others, resulted in a changed Simon Peter when Pentecost came and a spokesman was needed to interpret the events.

### (4) The report by the two from Emmaus (24:35)

*Verse 35:* The two then reported what they had experienced. The emphatic pronoun is used for *they,* to put their experience and their report into strong contrast with that of the gathered group in Jerusalem. Of that group, Peter alone had seen the Risen Lord. (Luke never gives evidence of knowing the earlier appearances to Mary Magdalene and to the women.) Peter had seen him, but they had no information to impart about the nature of the appearance or of what had happened. In strong contrast, the two could relate their story of wonder and beauty. They explained carefully all the details. The word translated *told* is literally "they exegeted"—the word for the skilled interpreter's drawing out of a report or an event all the details with their meaning. They made a thorough report of his instructions in the message of the prophets concerning the Christ. They explained how they finally recognized him in the breaking and sharing of the bread and how he disappeared from their sight even as they received the bread from his hands. That disappearance had its opposite in the next moment.

### (5) The appearance to the group (24:36–43)

This is Luke's third postresurrection appearance of Jesus. The experience may include verses 44–49, but that is doubtful, and that section will be treated as a separate unit.

*Verse 36: As they were saying this:* The impression is that the two from Emmaus and the gathered group were completely absorbed in the report, unaware of anything else. Then suddenly they were aware of Jesus' presence with them—*Jesus himself stood among them.* The emphatic pronoun *himself* indicates the importance Luke attached to understanding that the Risen Lord was actually there and his presence was objectively experienced by the group. It was not an experience of mass hallucination. The details which follow indicate that. *Among them* refers to the entire assembly: the two, "the eleven," and "those who were with them"—an uncertain number. John's account stresses the absence of Thomas from the eleven on that occasion (20:19–25); Luke uses "the eleven" as a group designation to distinguish them from the others who were there—the women, etc.

The verb *stood* has no significance other than that when they became aware of his presence he was standing there in the group. In the parallel account in John 20:19–25 stress is laid on the fact that all the doors were securely shut because the disciples feared the Jews. They expected to be hunted down to share their leader's death. John's emphasis is another indication of the early Christians' interest in the nature of Jesus' body after his resurrection—it was not limited by time, space, or material. He needed no door to admit him to their presence. Nor did the group see him "walk through a wall" in some bizarre display. He simply made himself visible to them as if to indicate that he was with them all the time though not always visible to them.

The best texts of Luke include the part omitted by the RSV, *and said to them, "Peace to you."* In the important manuscripts, the earliest one to omit it is the sixth-century Bezae manuscript, which is the only one to omit several of the sayings in this section of Luke. (See exposition of 22:20; 24: 5, 12.) The RSV's omission was prompted by the view that the clause was inserted by a later copyist because of its unchallenged presence in John 20: 19. Manuscript evidence justifies its being an authentic part of Luke as well.

*Peace to you* was the traditional greeting of the Hebrew people. It is still very commonly used in the Hebrew form "Shalom!" It was Jesus' normal greeting to them, and his giving it in that circumstance was calculated to quiet all the turmoil which had disturbed their hearts in those recent days of stress.

*Verse 37:* At first his presence had the opposite effect. Three verbal forms describe their reaction to his presence. Two of the words describe their state of mind—*startled and frightened*—and the third gives the reason—they *supposed that they saw a spirit.*

*Startled* means terrified; *frightened* means full of fear. At the moment they sensed his presence, they were shocked with terror; the more they looked

at him, the more they were filled with awe-struck fear. It was man's fear of
that which he does not understand. They thought they were seeing *a spirit*.
This is one of the few times in which the Greek word for *spirit* was accurately
rendered "ghost" in older English translations. They knew it was Jesus, but
how could he suddenly be there with no evidence of arrival and entrance?
They believed in the life of the spirit after the death of the body. At least
the Pharisees and common people did, and there is no indication in the
Gospels of any Sadducees (who denied the life of the spirit after death)
among Jesus' disciples. So the group did not think "Risen Lord"; they
thought, "His ghost."

Verses 38–43: Jesus chided them for their failure to believe that he was
really alive even though they could see him and hear him. Then he demonstrated the reality of his body.

*Verse 38: Why are you troubled . . . why do questionings rise?* His
questions pointed to the evidences available for their believing that he was
alive. The tomb was empty; angels had announced that he had risen from
the dead; he had been seen by Peter; he had walked and talked with the two
on the road and had become invisible to them just as he had become visible
to this group. Why, then, should they react with fear and disbelief that he
was anything other than spirit? Let it be recalled to their credit that what
they were experiencing was absolutely unique. This was not a resuscitation
by which one returned to physical life and functions—as experienced by
the daughter of Jairus, or the son of the widow at Nain, or Lazarus. This
was a return of the body to life but in such transformed state that it was not
subject to physical limitations of time, space, and material. Even from his
earlier predictions that he would arise from the dead, they had no experience
for anticipating that it would be anything like this. They would have
anticipated no more than physical restoration to life. But this was far
beyond that.

*Verse 39: See my hands and feet:* Jesus pointed out the nail scars as
evidences that they were seeing a body and not a spirit. The John account
has "his hands and his side"—the nail scars in his hands and the sword scar
in his side. That is no denial of Luke's reference to the feet. John emphasized
hands and side because in the appearance one week later, Jesus invited
Thomas to examine his hands and side (20:26–29).

The same manuscripts cited previously omit *verse 40—And when he had
said this, he showed them his hands and his feet*—as a copyist's borrowing
from John 20:20. As in the other cases, the manuscript evidence favors its
belonging in the text of Luke. It adds only the detail that Jesus spoke of
his scars as evidence of his having a body and then exposed those scars for
them to see for themselves.

*Handle me, and see* was his invitation that they use not only the sense of
sight but the convincing sense of touch. A ghost they might see but not
touch; a body they could both see and touch. Interpreters inevitably discuss
the question of whether they did or did not touch his body. It is a detail
of minor importance. Without question, he would not have invited them to
if they could not have done so. There is actually no evidence that even
Thomas, in spite of his declaration that he would not believe without having
touched the scars, really touched Jesus in the subsequent appearance. He

was invited to do so; he confessed his recognition of Jesus; Jesus commented that Thomas had believed because he had seen, and then pronounced a blessing on all who would believe even though they had not seen (John 20:26–29). Centuries later, Thomas was the Gnostics' favorite apostle because they believed that he actually touched the Risen Lord with his right hand and that the hand never died. There was even a tomb with the inscription that it contained "The One Who Has the Ever Living Right Hand"!

*A spirit has not flesh and bones as you see that I have:* Some interpreters find particular significance in the absence of "blood" from Jesus' expression, which they interpret in different ways. Some of them understand that, since the life is in the blood, this meant that Jesus' life source was no longer in the blood; he was alive and he had a body but blood was not necessary to keep him alive. Some of them understand that his blood had been given up very literally as a sacrifice for sin. He no longer had it. Other interpreters understand the use of *flesh and bones* as evidences because they are the most readily observable. One can readily see flesh and bone structure, or even feel them. To see or feel the presence of blood is not so easy. This appears to be the meaning. He offered his body for sight or for touch as an evidence that he was really alive. All of it was to show the reality of his very emphatic words *it is I myself.* The very rare Greek expression can be very exactly rendered, "that I myself am myself."

*Verses 41–43:* Their reaction changed from fear to joy, but even in their joy that he was alive they still could not believe that his was a real body. It was one of those experiences which one accepts with great joy, realizes that it just might be true, and yet cannot believe it because "it is too good to be true." Jesus, as one last convincing demonstration, asked if there was any food in the place. They gave him *a piece of broiled fish*—fish cooked either by broiling or roasting. He ate it *before them*—literally "in front of them." The reading "and honeycomb" in older English translations is in none of the ancient manuscripts. It was known by some Christian writers as early as the middle of the second century, but no manuscript before the ninth century includes it. From the evidence, it does not belong in the text. Why it entered the early tradition is unknown.

Jesus' eating before them was no indication that he had to eat to sustain his body as before his death. Nor was it a trick of some kind to make them believe he had a body when he did not. He ate because he had a real body that could eat. Added to all the other evidences, it apparently convinced the group that they were seeing the Risen Lord and not a ghost. There again was that seeming paradoxical truth—it was a tangible body; it was a transcendent body.

# CONCLUSION (24:44-53)

Luke's account of the events of that first Easter Sunday apparently ends at this point. Verses 44–49 may be a continuation of the appearance to the group on that evening. If so, Luke's account of what Jesus said differs so radically from John's account (John 20:21–23) that the two cannot be recognized as the same event. The use of the English word *then* in verse 44 and again in verse 50 seems to establish a connected chain of events which ended with the ascension of Jesus on the night of his resurrection. That is a false impression. The opening of Luke's second volume (Acts) in which he links the ascension of Jesus and the continuing earthly witness of the apostles makes it clear that for Luke the ascension took place forty days after the resurrection.

## 1. A Summary of Jesus' Teachings Between His Resurrection and His Ascension (24:44-49)

The nature of the materials in verses 44–49 more naturally indicates a summary statement representing Jesus' teaching during that forty-day period when he was alternately with them and away from them. The paragraph opens with a link to the events of the day of his resurrection—his use of Moses and the prophets to explain his death (v. 44). It closes with a link to the events of the day of his ascension—the beginning of their witness in Jerusalem (v. 47 and Acts 1:8). In between these two days were the teachings represented in verses 45, 46, 48, 49, and in Acts 1:3–5. Both this section of Luke 24 and that section of Acts 1 are summary statements indicating the nature of Jesus' teaching during the forty days, in preparation of the disciples to continue the witness beginning in Jerusalem and reaching out to *all nations* (v. 47)—"the end of the earth" (Acts 1:8).

*Verses 44–45:* Jesus reminded them of his predictions of his death and resurrection and of his telling them that these things were a part of their Scriptures. This time he named all three sections of their Scriptures: Law (Moses); Prophets; Holy Writings. He understood that all the Hebrew Scriptures bore witness to his redemptive suffering and triumph. As he had opened the minds of the two on that first day, he opened the minds of others in subsequent appearances by interpreting for them passages of Scripture related to the full redemptive signficance of his death and resurrection (v. 45). All that God had been doing in the course of redemptive history was pointing to his own climactic work; the call of Abraham to build a

[333]

nation for God's redemptive purpose; the exodus under Moses in the giving of birth to that nation for his redemptive purpose; the establishing of a sacrificial religious system through the Tabernacle in the exodus years and the Temple in the years of their residence in the new home; the suffering and purging of the whole nation of Israel through the Babylonian exile; the focus on one tribe out of the entire nation after the exile—Judah; and, finally, the focus of the sin of the world on one person out of that tribe of Judah—Jesus of Nazareth. It was all one great whole.

*Verse 46* summarizes the history. It is all embraced in the word *thus.* Just as Israel had been a suffering people whose suffering was encompassed in the redemptive work of God, *thus it is written, that the Christ should suffer . . . .* The verb is in the tense for which English has no exact equivalent— "Thus it stands in a written state that the Christ should suffer." God had expressed his very character in the working out of that redemptive plan which had been written in every section of the Hebrew Scriptures. He is a redeeming God; he could not see man in need of redemption and not provide that redemption. It was a costly provision; it cost the humiliation, suffering, and death of his Anointed One. It was, however, of such greatness that it could not end in death, and, hence—*on the third day* the Christ should *rise from the dead.*

*Verses 47–48:* The suffering and triumph of Christ did not exhaust the redemptive message of the prophets. Properly understood, that redemption was not just for the nation of Israel; it was for *all nations.* Although Israel had missed that part of God's purpose in his choice of them, it had been plainly proclaimed by God's prophets. Their understanding was that God had chosen Israel to be a people for his redemptive witness. He would make himself in his redemptive nature known to them. They, in turn, were to make him in his redemptive nature known to the other nations. That was a major theme of Isaiah 40–53. Jerusalem, knowing God, was to make her high mountain into a pulpit from which she called out to all those around her, "Look! Here is your God." But Israel failed to do that. The Jewish people became exclusive in their possession of God. They took the position that they had the one true God; in that they were right. Then they took the position that other nations desiring to know God would have to become Jews in order to be acceptable to him; in that they were wrong. It was essentially that view which John the Baptizer had opposed—the view that· because the Jews were physically descended from Abraham they were automatically in the same covenant relationship to God as Abraham. Jesus had opposed it in the days of his flesh. Paul, later, would become the great leader in bringing the other nations to know God.

So Jesus' emphasis in this postresurrection teaching was that God's entire redemptive plan which had reached its fufillment in his death and resurrection was meant to be for Gentiles as well as Jews. In Luke's Gospel, Jesus started his public life as the Messiah with that announcement in his sermon at Nazareth (4:16–30); his fellow villagers tried to stone him to death for his heresy. Now at the very end of Luke's Gospel that same view is impressed upon those who would continue the witness after him—*repentance and forgiveness of sins should be preached in his name to all nations.* The word *repentance* means a complete change of outlook involving a new and very different life. *Forgiveness of sins* means the dismissal or sending away of sins. (See the discussion on repentance in 13:1–5 and on forgiveness in 5:20–24.)

The word for *preached (kērussō)* is the word for a herald's proclamation of a message. In one of its noun forms *(kērugma)* it came to be used in the New Testament for the content of the preaching of the early church. It has been made into the English word so freely used in biblical and theological writings today, the kerygma, meaning "the thing preached" or "the thing proclaimed." That which was proclaimed was redemption through the crucified and risen Christ through repentance of sin and faith in him as God's redeemer.

*To all nations* means to all people—Jew, Greek, Roman, and all others without exception—this is the logical conclusion. If there is *one* God, and he has provided *one* way of redemption, through *one* Savior, it follows that that salvation must be effective for and made known to the *one* mass of sinful mankind. In his death and resurrection—which in Paul's later interpretation stands for victory over sin and death—Christ has provided that one way. He commissioned his disciples to provide that necessary witness to all men. *Beginning from Jerusalem* sets their starting point as *all nations* sets their terminal point. In the overlapping account in Acts 1:8 the geographical extension is made explicit—"in Jerusalem . . . in all Judea and Samaria . . . to the end of the earth." Luke uses that threefold division for his account of the Christian movement going out from its Hebrew cradle, making its home in the Gentile world, and becoming a religion without racial barriers or identification. In the Gospel account, verse 48 stands for that part of Acts 1 which constitutes the disciples as the witnesses—*you are witnesses* (v. 48); "you shall be my witnesses" (Acts 1:8). The two are variant forms of the same commission.

*Verse 49* is a variant form of parts of Acts 1:4 and 8. The first part of the verse—*And behold, I send the promise of my Father upon you*—is recalled in Jesus' words in Acts 1:4, "wait for the promise of the Father." The second part of the verse—*stay in the city*—is recalled in Jesus' words in Acts 1:4, "he charged them not to depart from Jerusalem." The last part of the verse—*until you are clothed with power from on high*—is recalled in Jesus' words in Acts 1:8, "you shall receive power when the Holy Spirit has come upon you." This parallel alone is convincing evidence that verses 44–49 are a summary of the forty days of teaching culminating in the ascension in verses 50–53, just as Acts 1:1–5 is similar summary of the forty days leading up to the ascension in Acts 1:6–14.

*The promise of my Father:* This refers to the promise that the Holy Spirit would be sent to them after Jesus had gone away from them. It may go all the way back to the words of John the Baptizer that the one coming after him would baptize them with the Holy Spirit (3:16); that was definitely the reference behind the Acts 1:5 parallel. According to John's Gospel, a more recent promise of the coming of the Holy Spirit was in Jesus' teaching following the Thursday evening supper and preserved only in John 14–16. In that section a major theme is the coming of the Holy Spirit to be the continuing presence of the Father and the Son with them. Here in verse 49 the promise undoubtedly points to the coming of the Holy Spirit at Pentecost —ten days away.

*Stay in the city:* Those who interpret verses 44–49 as a part of the preceding appearance of Jesus to the group on the night of his resurrection find it necessary to explain that this imperative did not prevent the disciples' going to Galilee where Jesus appeared to them (Matthew 28; John 21) ·and then returning to Jerusalem. Such explanation is needless if the present approach is correct and these verses are a summary of the forty days. In that case, verse 49 represents a point at the end of that period—the point of the last appearance and ascension. Jesus was telling them that they should not begin that witness in Jerusalem (v. 47) and on to the ends of the earth (Acts 1:8) until they were empowered for the witnessing. Verses 52–53 and Acts 1:12–14 indicate their staying as he commanded.

*Until you are clothed with power from on high:* Compare again Acts 1:5 and 8. The witnessing which they were to do was very different from that which they had done when he sent them out in Galilee (9:1–6). Then they had restricted their travel to the villages of Galilee and to the Jews, many of whom were their own kin and friends. They proclaimed that the reign of God was breaking into history and called men to preparation and acceptance. Now they were to go beyond Jewish boundaries, both geographical and racial. They were to go to the ends of the earth and to all the peoples of the earth. They were to preach that redemption from sin was available through the death and resurrection of Jesus of Nazareth. For that, they would need power from beyond themselves. God would send that power but they were to wait for it.

The word *clothed* means to be wrapped up as in a robe. That was how the power which God would send would cover them. It is a similar figure to being "baptized with (or in) the Holy Spirit." To be immersed in the Holy Spirit means to be completely submerged in or enveloped in him. So to be clothed with power means to be enveloped in that power.

*Power* translates the Greek word *dunamis* which has come into English as "dynamite" or "dynamic." Always it means a mighty moving force. The word order in Luke is different from the English text. In the original text *from on high* is placed between *clothed* and *power;* hence, "until you are clothed from on high with respect to power." The source of their enveloping, their being clothed, was "the heights," that is, heaven—the abode of God. This being clothed from on high was what constituted their power for witnessing. They would move out and they would speak under the controlling motivation of the power given to them of God. In Acts that power would be realized in the coming of the Holy Spirit upon them (1:8); it took place ten days later at Pentecost (2:1–4).

## 2. The Final Apppearance and Ascension (cf. Acts 1:6–14) (24:50–53)

This is Luke's brief account of Jesus' ascension. A more detailed account of it Luke reserves for Acts 1:6–14, as a transition from the ministry of Jesus on earth before his ascension (1:1–2) to the ministry he continued to do through the apostles after his ascension (2:1–28:31).

The ascension took place from Bethany in the Gospel (v. 50) and from the Mount of Olives in Acts (1:12). The village of Bethany which Jesus had often visited was on the lower side of the Mount of Olives away from Jerusalem.

*Verse 50: Lifting up his hands he blessed them:* In Jewish religious ritual, when the high priest finished the sacrifice, he lifted his hands in blessing as he dismissed the people. Jesus had finished his sacrifice. The argument of the Epistle to the Hebrews, chapters 5–10, is that Jesus was a high priest who offered his own blood as a sacrifice which permanently removes sin. Here on the Mount of Olives as a high priest who had completed the sacrifice on the Day of Atonement, Jesus lifted his hands in blessing as he dismissed them. Neither account preserves the words of blessing. The Acts account preserves the words of dismissal; they were the words of the last commission—"You shall be my witnesses . . . to the end of the earth" (1:8).

*Verse 51: While he blessed them, he parted from them:* In those manuscripts previously cited as omitting some parts of Luke which appear to be genuine, the account closes with the words *he parted from them*. From these words alone, the impression is given that it was a disappearance, a becoming unseen to the disciples, as in the case of the two at the table with him in Emmaus (v. 31). As he was speaking he "stood away from them" and they saw him no more.

Luke's account in Acts 1:6–11 is given for the purpose of making clear how *he parted from them*—the ascension. The best manuscripts of the Gospel account, however, do include in verse 51 the phrase *and was carried up into heaven,* which appears to have been in the original text. *Carried up* is a passive form, but there is no indication of what agent did the carrying. In the Acts account, there is a similar passive construction but of a different verb—"while they were looking, he was lifted up"; there is no indication of the agent. There is, however, an added detail in Acts—"a cloud took him out of their sight" (1:11). The verb for "took" used here means literally "received under," and the impression is that he went up with no visible agent lifting him (both Luke and Acts) until at a height normal for clouds a cloud came under him and when the cloud had disappeared, he had disappeared (Acts account). The cloud recalls the Shekinah cloud of God's presence in the exodus. It also recalls the Son of Man riding on the clouds of heaven to be crowned with glory by the Ancient of Days (God) (Dan. 7:13). This is the more natural reference, since Jesus, during the last days in Jerusalem, had spoken of the Son of Man and the clouds of glory in relation to his triumph over sin and death.

To object to the eternal significance and validity of this passage because of the expression *up into heaven* is to quibble over words and miss the truth the accounts convey. The preposition *up* is used because men thought of God as dwelling "in the highest" or "on high." Modern man no longer thinks, as ancient man thought, of a three-storied world with heaven above, the earth in the middle, and hell below. What difference does a choice of prepositions make? What difference does it make whether one says he went "up" or "away" or "over" or "beyond"? Geographical or spatial direction from a given point is not of the remotest importance. The intent of the Gospel account is to show that as Jesus had in his incarnation come from the Father, so when he had completed his redemptive work in the world he returned to the Father.

*Verse 52:* Another omitted clause which belongs in the text—*they worshiped him*—gives the disciples' response to his words of blessing and benediction. *Worship* is used variously of bowing, kneeling, or prostrating one's self. Either of the first two fits this situation better than the third. As he spoke his blessing, they bowed or knelt (or both) to receive it. When it was finished and he had parted from them, they went back to Jerusalem *with great joy.* The many experiences of the forty days had taken from them their sense of perplexity, sorrow, and defeat. Jesus' teachings concerning the significance of his death and resurrection which they had so vigorously rejected at first, they finally understood. In their understanding, their perplexity had been changed to faith, their defeat had been changed to victory, their sorrow had been changed to joy.

*Verse 53:* They spent their time in the Temple worshiping God. They had not broken with the Temple. It furnished the best place for them to meet. In the porches where formerly they had gathered to hear Jesus' teachings, they now gathered to wait in prayer for the fulfillment of the promise that the Holy Spirit would come upon them and empower them to witness. Then they would go to take the good news to all men. Then they would learn the meaning of that imperative about taking up the cross and following him. They would also know the blessed reality of that promise,

AND LO! I—WITH YOU—EVEN UNTO THE END!